Writing and Publishing with Your PC

The ultimate reference for personal computer-based writing, illustrating, desktop publishing, printing, publisher relations, and book marketing and distribution

Russell A. Stultz

Wordware Publishing, Inc.

Library of Congress Cataloging-in-Publication Data
Writing and publishing with your PC / Russell A. Stultz.
    p. cm.
"The ultimate reference for personal computer-based writing, illustrating,
desktop publishing, printing, publisher relations, and book marketing."
Includes index.
ISBN 1-55622-582-2
1. Desktop publishing--United States.   2. Authorship.   I. Title.
Z253.53.S78   1998
686.2'2544536—dc21   98-5631
                                  CIP

Project Publisher—Jim Hill

Desktop Publishing—Russell A. Stultz and Martha McCuller

Copy Editing—Dianne Stultz and Beth Kohler

Cover Design—Alan McCuller

Printed in the United States of America

ISBN 1-55622-582-2
10 9 8 7 6 5 4 3 2 1
9804

Wordware Publishing, Inc.
2320 Los Rios Boulevard, Suite 200
Plano, Texas 75074
(972) 423-0090

Contents at a glance

Acknowledgements

The author and publisher wish to express their gratitude for the support and encouragement provided by the employees of Adobe Corporation, Corel Corporation, and Microsoft Corporation. Without their assistance, this book would not have been possible.

Contents

Part 1—Writing and Publishing Tools

Chapter 1 **About This Book** **3**

Chapter 2 **The Writing Project**. **11**

Part 2—Publishing Secrets

Foreword

Since the mid-1960s I've enjoyed a rewarding career in both the writing and book publishing fields. Early on I had the good fortune of working with many experienced professionals who eagerly taught me the special terms and processes associated with writing, copy editing, typography, illustrating, photography, and printing. The application of technology to these processes has been continuous in all areas. As an author of books distributed by a large international publisher, I knew that I needed a good set of tools—particularly a word-processing system and printer.

My first home PC and daisy wheel printer cost more than 7,000 1982 dollars; two years later I spent well over $100,000 of my own money for a two-station photo typesetter and a handful of fonts. The $7,000 system was replaced dozens of times as new, faster, more capable PCs became available. The typesetting system was recently given to a salvage company. In retrospect, I do not regret any of my investments in these machines, nor the time spent learning to use them. It's been fun.

Of course the early systems were extremely slow and difficult to use. Keystrokes were captured on PCs; the files were fed to the phototypesetter, which required extensive knowledge of typesetting control codes (not unlike today's popular HTML code set). The film output was slow and expensive. The number of available type fonts was limited. Line illustrations were hand drawn and manually pasted in place on the typeset page (or *galley*). And the responsible commercial printer had to tediously strip photos into place on the film negatives.

Today any of us can quickly produce a variety of high-quality, heavily illustrated documents at home using a PC, a laser or inkjet printer, and three or four good software packages. The entire investment to write and publish in either your office or at home is well under $4,000 if you're an informed shopper. And both the input and output processes are fast, highly automated, extremely versatile, and fun to use.

In this book I attempt to familiarize you with many facets of the writing and publishing process. It includes information about the use of your PC as a writing and publishing tool. Hundreds of hours were spent installing, using, and evaluating the software products described here. I also solicited both hard facts and the personal preferences of some of the most highly experienced graphics and desktop publishing people that I know. Not only are they intimately familiar with the software and systems described in this book, they use them every day to achieve commercial excellence. So, between us, we sincerely hope that this book supplies you with all the "writing, illustrating, and publishing secrets" that you need.

Part 2 of this book, entitled "publishing secrets," goes far beyond the mechanical processes involved in writing, illustrating, and desktop publishing. It examines the publishing business itself, by dissecting and exploring the key areas. You'll find information about pricing, sales and marketing, copyright, barcodes, and much more.

To demonstrate the application of the principles presented in this book, I wrote and illustrated this book using my PC, and the book was desktop published on a PC. Much of it was prepared on my WinBook FX notebook computer as I traveled to Europe and Australia on business. The final, desktop published pages were sent to the printer in digital format. As you can see, the quality is excellent.

Russell A. Stultz

Part 1

Writing and Publishing Tools

Included In This Part:

Chapter 1

About This Book

Introduction

Most historians still consider the printing press to be the single most important invention for communicating to the masses. The Gutenberg press is still revered as the machine that freed the souls of mankind by giving them the Word of God. Many avid computer users might argue with this view, as personal computers have set new standards in communications. PCs have revolutionized the way people write, illustrate, and use color in their communications. Although printing is still an important and dominant process, a number of other communication mediums are in use today. Consider the pervasiveness of television, the Internet, CD-ROMs, and videos.

What's in This Book

This book covers the many facets of written and graphic communications. It deals with your ability to communicate with written and published works. The fact that we can communicate our ideas on paper, computer and television displays, and overhead projection devices using the same basic tool set is a bonus. Regardless of the medium used, we can use our PC and any of a number of common application programs as the primary creation and development resource. Of course the way we maximize the impact of words and pictures varies with the constraints imposed by the final format, i.e., small type and grayscale pictures on paper or large type and colored pictures on a display screen. Major differences reside within the tools we choose to capture and deliver our words and pictures.

Today's technology gives us a vast number of choices. There are so many that the decision process has become nearly as complicated as the work itself. This book helps you identify and simplify the involved tools and processes. It helps you understand the software, peripheral devices (mice, graphic tablets, and scanners), procedures, and relationships commonly used in writing, editing, publishing, printing, and delivery. When you finish this book, you should be ready to tackle nearly any writing and publishing task, whether it is an organizational newsletter, flier, brochure, presentation, or an illustrated 500-page book.

Summary of Contents

This book provides you with an authoritative reference for a broad range of subjects that deal with the field of writing and publishing. In Part 1 you'll find advice about writing; software selection, operation, and feature comparisons; and tips on how to prepare a broad range of document types. Part 2, entitled Publishing Secrets, includes a wealth of information about the publishing business. There, you find background information about many of the processes and policies commonly practiced by trade publishers. For example, cover design and content tips and barcode preparation and application are presented. You'll also find a wealth of information about publisher and commercial printer relations, book proposals, author agreement terms, printing specifications, book pricing, marketing and sales techniques, discount structures, self-publishing, copyright law, ISBN assignment, and much more. Here's an overview of each of the chapters in this book. The diagram shows you the way the information is organized.

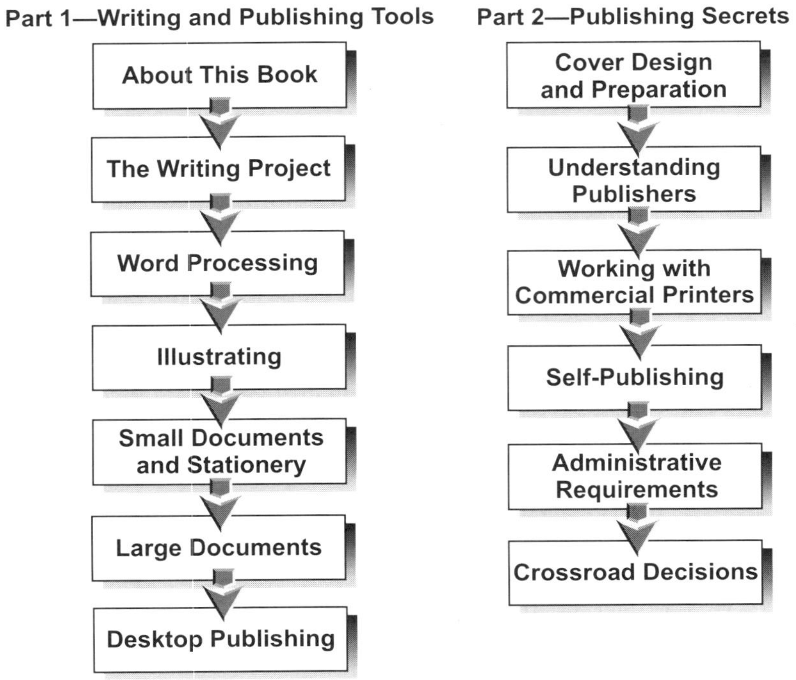

Part 1—Writing and Publishing Tools

- About This Book
- The Writing Project
- Word Processing
- Illustrating
- Small Documents and Stationery
- Large Documents
- Desktop Publishing

Part 2—Publishing Secrets

- Cover Design and Preparation
- Understanding Publishers
- Working with Commercial Printers
- Self-Publishing
- Administrative Requirements
- Crossroad Decisions

Part 1—Writing and Publishing Tools

1 **About This Book**—This chapter introduces you to the theme of this book and presents an overview of its contents. It also recommends the tools of the trade, i.e., a computer, printer, and a number of application programs that are ideal for writing and publishing.

2 **The Writing Project**—Here you are guided through the writing process, including tools on the PC you should master, tips on productivity, and do's and don'ts for preparing your manuscript.

3 **Word Processing**—A professional, feature-packed word processor is an essential tool for the serious writer and desktop publishing specialist. This chapter steps you through the selection process and highlights important word processing features. It also provides tips on how to use your word processor in the creation of professionally prepared documents.

4 **Illustrating**—Many books, particularly instruction manuals and illustrated references, contain a variety of illustrations. Here, you learn a bit about computer-generated and enhanced illustrations. You are also introduced to graphics software that is designed to produce both line art and bitmapped images.

5 **Small Documents and Stationery**—Read this chapter to learn how to produce small documents and stationery. You are introduced to Microsoft Publisher 97 and Adobe PageMaker, both of which are ideal for small document jobs. While Microsoft Publisher 97 is intended for stationery, fliers, newsletters, and brochures, PageMaker can be used for both small and large documents.

6 **Large Documents**—This chapter moves on to larger, multichapter publications. This includes books, reports, and product specifications. These documents typically include headers and footers, a table of contents, and appendixes.

7 **Desktop Publishing**—Full-featured desktop publishing software takes word processing to a new level in document control. In this chapter you examine the most popular high-end desktop publishing software for Windows 95. This includes Adobe FrameMaker, Corel Ventura 7, and QuarkXPress for Windows 95.

Part 2—Publishing Secrets

8 **Cover Design and Preparation**—This chapter provides a wealth of information about book covers. It examines cover elements, the use of copy, barcodes, and color. It also shows readers how to save hundreds of dollars in color separation charges by doing it themselves.

9   Understanding Publishers—Learn how to present your book ideas to legitimate publishers. Here you learn how to deal with publishers, what to expect from agents, and what is expected of you as an author. You will also learn about author agreements; how publishers price, market, sell, and distribute their books; and about the industry's book return policies.

10   Working with Commercial Printers—If you plan to have your documents printed by a commercial printer, it's important to know how to prepare a bid specification and shop for price. Here you also learn which decisions control the economies of your decisions regarding book size, color, bleeds, order quantities, and more.

11   Self-Publishing—The information presented in this chapter should help you make an informed decision whether to throw in the towel, or to take the leap forward into self-publishing. Before spending a small fortune on futility, see if you're up to the task of self-publishing, promotions, and order processing and fulfillment.

12   Administrative Requirements—There's more to book publishing than type, paper, and ink. This chapter presents information about the International Standard Book Number (ISBN) and Cataloging-in-Publication (CIP) data associated with most published books. This is particularly important information for those who intend to self-publish their work.

13   Crossroad Decisions—This chapter "ices the cake" by sharing some important insights, philosophies, and even a true story about success in the writing and publishing field. It also provides practical information about setting and achieving your goals.

Appendix A: Writing Product Documentation—This appendix is for those who plan and write product documentation for companies. It delves into the planning and estimating processes needed to complete a writing project on schedule.

Appendix B: Author Guidelines—Here, Wordware's author guidelines are included, which are typical of guidelines that can be obtained from other trade publishers.

Hardware and Software Requirements

This section describes, in general terms, a computer configuration that works nicely as a writing and publishing workstation. First, the hardware and operating system is presented. It is likely that your PC is either right for the job, or right with a few minor modifications.

Recommended Hardware

Most of the new computers sold today are quite adequate for writing and publishing. This book assumes you have an 80486- or Pentium-based PC running Windows 95, 98, or NT. It should have about a gigabyte or more of hard disk space, 16MB or more of random access memory (RAM), an SVGA display system, and a CD-ROM drive. If you have less than 16MB, you should increase your memory to at least 16MB. If you have to go to the trouble of a memory upgrade, go ahead and jump to at least 32MB. Both you and the software that you install on your computer will be much happier. Here is a recommended PC configuration.

Item	Recommended Minimum
CPU	Pentium 133 or faster
Cache	256K or more
Random Access Memory	32MB or more
Hard Disk Drive	2.1 gigabyte or larger, 10 millisecond access speed or faster
Floppy Drive	3.5 inch 1.44MB
CD-ROM Drive	4X or faster
Display Adapter	SVGA (256-color capable of 1024 x 768 pixels) with a minimum of 2MB video memory
Monitor	15-inch, .28 dot pitch (17-inch, .25 dot pitch is even better)
Printer	300 dpi laser or inkjet
Operating System	Windows 95, Windows 98, or Windows NT
Scanner	600 dpi, 256-color, flatbed (optional, but important)
External Storage	Iomega Zip drive with 100 MB or larger removable media

The computer described in the preceding table will perform well as both a writing and publishing resource. Although an i80486-100 DX based machine with 16MB of RAM may work for most applications, its performance will be marginal.

Recommended Software

If you are serious about writing, illustrating, or publishing, then you should acquire at least three categories of software. This includes full-featured word processing, illustrating, and desktop publishing software. Within the illustrating software category, two distinct subcategories of software are useful. First, you should have a bitmap-based drawing program, not unlike the Paint program supplied as a Windows 95, 98, and NT accessory. You should also have a program that produces vector graphics. This category of software produces smooth-line illustrations, which reduces jagged diagonal lines and circles often produced by the pixels that make up bitmapped illustrations. Some recommended software programs are mentioned in the paragraphs that follow.

Word Processing   In addition to the computer hardware and Windows operating system, you should also have full-featured word processing and illustrating software. For writing, the book deals with both Corel WordPerfect 7 and Microsoft Word for Windows, which is part of the Microsoft Office 97 suite.

Desktop Publishing   If you plan to produce camera-ready copy for printed books, then you should have a good laser or inkjet printer. Although many users rely on their word processor to produce final page output, professional publishing production departments prefer desktop publishing software. Therefore, you should consider obtaining a good desktop publishing program. Check out Corel Ventura 7, Adobe PageMaker or FrameMaker, and QuarkXPress. If you plan to produce small brochures, fliers, and business cards, then you should definitely consider Microsoft Publisher 97. All of these programs are examined in some detail in chapter 7.

Illustrating Software   If you plan to include illustrations in your books, reports, proposals, or brochures, or if you plan to create your own four-color cover and/or dust jacket artwork, then consider obtaining a good drawing program. Several useful illustrating programs are examined in chapter 3. These include Adobe Illustrator, CorelDRAW, Corel PHOTO-PAINT, Microsoft Photo Editor, and even Windows 95, 98, or NT Paint. Knowing a bit about each of these programs should help you decide on the one that is best suited to your work.

What About Macintosh Computers?

Today, most of us who have personal computers are using Microsoft Windows and Windows-compatible applications programs. Windows 95 and Windows NT dominate both the home and office markets. More than 90 percent of all personal computers in use today are Windows compatible. This book describes the processes associated with writing and publishing on one of these, which is probably what you have. If you have a Macintosh computer, several of the application programs described here are also available in a Macintosh version, such as Microsoft Word, Adobe's PageMaker and Illustrator products, and Quark's QuarkXPress desktop publishing software.

The Macintosh computer has a proud history as the graphic and desktop publishing workstation of choice and is still in use by many publishers and graphic design companies. However, with the introduction of 32-bit Windows PCs and major breakthroughs in processing speed and the Windows graphical user interface (GUI), things have changed. Today, a large number of excellent Windows 95, 98, and Windows NT-compatible application programs from such companies as Adobe, Corel, Microsoft, and Quark have made 80486- and Pentium-based PCs a good choice. This is particularly true in light of the price variance between PCs and Macs. Unfortunately, Macintosh computers, peripheral devices, i.e., disk and CD-ROM drives, memory modules, modems, and other peripheral devices, are much more expensive than the same items in the PC section. As a result, many corporate decision makers who make decisions based on economics rather than brand loyalty have abandoned Macintoshes.

Today's software publishers recognize that their primary market resides with Windows-compatible PCs. Practically every new innovation is developed first for the huge Windows-based PC market. Macintosh has become an afterthought by most software developers whose survival depends on sales volumes. Unfortunately, many purveyors of the personal computing market predict that Apple will continue to see a decline in its market share as the onslaught of new technology from such companies as Microsoft, Intel, AMD, and Cyrix continues.

What You Should Know

To be an effective writer and/or publisher, you should be familiar with your PC, how it works, and common Windows operations, including how to install and uninstall Windows applications. You should also be proficient in the use of menus, dialogs, your mouse (both buttons), and common key sequences for cutting, copying, pasting, linking, undoing, file operations, and more.

Common Names

In many instances, full program names are replaced by common names for brevity. For example, product names like Microsoft Word for Windows, Corel WordPerfect, and Adobe PageMaker are shortened to Word, WordPerfect, and PageMaker once they are introduced in this book.

Moving Ahead

The next chapter briefly describes the writing process and some important issues. In particular, it suggests which PC tools you should have and master, as well as providing tips about productivity, writer's block, and some key do's and don'ts that every professional writer should understand.

Chapter 2

The Writing Project

Introduction

This chapter provides a brief glimpse of some of the key issues involved in the writing process. Whether you are writing a report or an instruction manual for your company or preparing a manuscript for a trade publisher, the information found in this chapter and in the appendixes should supply you with an organized approach to either creative or commercial writing. Perhaps the tips and techniques found here will help you systematize your writing tasks to give you a higher level of confidence and ultimate success. These ingredients can contribute to making writing what it should be—an enjoyable and rewarding profession.

Important: Chapter 9 provides guidance for those writers who want to submit book ideas or formal book proposals to legitimate trade publishers. Be sure to examine the material and take it to heart, as it should give you realistic expectations, save you untold hours of futile effort, and perhaps help to reduce your level of frustration. Knowing exactly what your publisher needs and why can certainly contribute to landing a successful book deal.

The Writer

Many people think it's an easy step from reading to writing. If you're among this group, think again. Many who have tried their hand at writing more than a brief report often find themselves struggling. In fact, most simply give up. Writing is a demanding vocation that takes extensive research and organizational skills, long-term commitment, self-discipline, concentration, and the ability to communicate in a succinct and logical manner. And everything you write is on paper for others to judge.

It has been said that writers become "temporary experts." Therefore, a major benefit derived from writing is that of learning. Writers become immersed in the subject matter. They must learn enough to present information accurately and with authority. As a writer, you enjoy the benefits of learning new technologies, processes, and philosophies. The writing profession constantly expands your knowledge through research and communication—writing is a continuous education.

Deadlines

Successful writing professionals share an important trait—the ability to cope with and meet tough, inflexible deadlines. Writers who work for large corporations or news agencies, or who prepare manuscripts for book publishers will readily admit that difficult deadlines are often stressful. If handled properly, the stress can be channeled into challenge and appropriate actions. Good writers plan their daily output, measure their work, and allocate the required time to ensure timely project completion. They understand that if they put off their work for a single day, the whole house of cards may fall. Therefore, commitment and self-discipline are crucial. When you meet a difficult deadline, your self-esteem may soar. And you may even ratchet up the admiration of those who see the results of your work in the form of a clean, artfully crafted manuscript.

Those who write product documentation for a living also suffer the stress of deadlines, sometimes called "drop-dead dates." Company writers are often the last ones in the product development chain; the pressure is just as real, and is often exacerbated by their company's need to make billings on schedule by delivering a new product, including the user's manual, on or before a certain date. In addition to the company's need for timely revenue, a writer's employment status may also rely on timely project completion. Therefore, many experienced writers compare their job to taking the position at the end of a crack-the-whip line. They simply have to run faster than the rest of the people in the line.

The Temporary Expert

As mentioned earlier, writers are always learning. Their learning must take them well beyond simple knowledge. They must understand what they know well enough to teach others through their written words and drawings. This is a level of cognition that is beyond simple knowledge. It is beyond understanding and even beyond the ability to apply new knowledge. To teach others requires a rich level of cognitive thought. Therefore, in addition to being an effective researcher and communicator, a writer must be able to learn thoroughly—enough to teach others.

All good writers have the ability to become "temporary experts" within a short period of time. Fast learning drives writing efficiency. The research-to-writing-time ratio is discussed in a bit more detail in appendix A.

The Right Stuff

Any publisher will tell you that first-time writers are unpredictable and therefore considered a risk. Simply stated, they are unproven. Although most fledgling authors have the best of intentions, they rarely anticipate the effort, time, and discipline involved in writing a complete manuscript. Even when they complete a manuscript, it is often late. Therefore, before you waste the time of a publisher or potential client, be sure you have what it takes to deliver a complete, good-quality manuscript on schedule. When writing a book for a legitimate publisher, the delivery date can make or break the success of the book. Chapter 9 describes publisher relations and the legal and ethical obligations that writers and publishers have to one another.

Writer's Block

The writer must produce a set amount of material every day. If one or two days of work are missed, the writing time must be extended to evenings and weekends to get the project back on schedule. Distracting influences can place insurmountable roadblocks in the way. Illness, marital problems, equipment trouble, and similar issues can delay or even stop the project. In particular, marital conflicts or a death in the family often results in *writer's block*, which usually stops the writing effort dead in its tracks. Writer's block is an emotional malady that undermines one's ability to think coherently and to process and record information. It is a complete functional paralysis. The afflicted person is totally preoccupied with his or her personal problems and unable to concentrate on anything else. Those suffering writer's block may have a complete breakdown. Those of us who have seen writer's block in action can only sympathize with its victims.

The Writer's Tools

Every writer should examine the way he or she works. Your approach may be different than that of others. However it is done, be sure that you find what works best for you and stick with it until a better system is found. This section deals with the writing process and mechanics.

Organized Writing

Planning is the most important thing you will do in the preparation of a written manuscript. A good plan provides a basis for every action. It saves untold hours of rework or delay from unclear goals and missing resources. Although we all work differently, the basics should be similar. Look at the suggestions that follow and apply them where they fit.

Planning and Replanning

You should develop a comprehensive plan before you actually begin writing. Obviously, the starting point on your plan will vary with your circumstance. Are you beginning with a new book idea? Does your publisher want you to submit a new book proposal? Have you already written a preliminary manuscript? For discussion purposes, let's assume that a publisher or agent has given you the assignment to proceed with your book idea. However, they want an outline, a few sample chapters, and an author biography for the marketing and sales departments. If all check out, they have assured you that a contract is forthcoming. You should be prepared to deliver your manuscript at the earliest possible date.

Preliminary Outline

Write down a complete list of every topic that you plan to include in your book. Once the list is finished, sort it into logical blocks of information. Be sure that it flows smoothly from simple to complex, basic to advanced. Pick meaningful chapter names, a compelling title, and a list of features and benefits. Write a synopsis of each chapter followed by the list of topics. If possible, organize the topics into major and minor paragraph headings. Your publisher or agent will appreciate the thoroughness of your outline. So will you, as it comprises the skeleton of your book and will help you stay on target during the writing phase. With a well-organized outline in hand, you're well on your way—even euphoric, because you know exactly what you must do—you have a clear roadmap to your destination.

Initial Chapters

Pick two chapters about topics that you know well or that are easily researched. They should also be interesting. Use them to heighten the interest of your publisher or agent. Try to make them say, "I definitely want to see more." You can always write an introductory chapter, but know in advance that it may change once you begin fleshing out your book and encounter new, possibly more interesting forks in the road.

Time Estimates

Now you must make a major commitment in your time. How much time can you spend writing your manuscript? How many pages can you write and illustrate in an average week? What are some potential time conflicts that might arise during the course of the project? (Visiting relatives or friends, holidays, children's activities, illness, etc.) All of these factors should be considered in your time estimate.

Once you understand your output in measurable terms, such as pages per day or words per hour, and identify your available time, you can estimate a completion date with a fair degree of accuracy. Then add more time for polishing (or rework), the incorporation of your copy editor's marks, and indexing (if you are required to provide the index). Remember that once you provide your time estimate and a delivery date, you're stuck with it. It is a definite commitment. A lot of work and planning will be set in motion—all based on your delivery date. So be realistic.

The Gathering

Organizing your project also involves identifying and then collecting all necessary resource material. Needed resources vary with each book-writing project. First, be sure that you have an adequate PC system. This includes a good printer, scanner, and mass storage device. Acquire and learn to use the programs required to write and illustrate your book. Finally, gather all supporting reference materials including books, magazines, photos, drawings, and reports. Be sure to obtain background information for each so you can provide proper credits and/or produce a good bibliography.

Researching

Your research includes reviewing pertinent published material and artwork, and may also include scheduling and conducting interviews with subject matter experts. Use a memo pad, notebook computer, or tape recorder to record information. Be sure to organize it according to the chapters and sections of your book.

Writing

If you do not have all of the information required to write your entire book, you may have enough to complete several chapters. But you should be certain to have a firm plan for obtaining the balance of the information that you need.

You should also schedule large blocks of writing time. Allocate the days and times that you need to meet your deadline—and don't waver. If you know how much time it takes to achieve established milestones, your plan should work. If you get behind, increase your writing time commitment to catch up.

Your outline can be used as a measurement device for measuring your progress. Simply use it as a checklist. Put a checkmark and the date by each section as you complete it. This lets you see your progress; it also shows you what remains to be done. As you get into the project, this system lets you refine your estimates so you can calculate how much time is required to complete your manuscript. You can also use your checklist to provide feedback to your publisher. Both the percentage of work that is finished as well as the percentage remaining is easily calculated.

Polishing

Your first manuscript is called a "first draft." As the name implies, there's more to be done. It's time to polish your work. Before you submit the manuscript, check it for quality and completeness. Polish your wording, check references, revise the contents to match the final content. Collect everything that the publisher needs to continue the project. Take inventory. Check the contract for required items. Then send it.

Submitting

Be sure that your manuscript is securely wrapped and carefully addressed. Use a durable container. Pack all accompanying items with care. Include a table of contents and other front matter, back matter, artwork, sales and marketing information, and any required magnetic media. It's a good idea to include a list of the items included in the submission. Also, be sure to use a reliable delivery service. When you've done all of these things, you're still not finished. Be available to incorporate the copy editing marks.

Mechanics

In addition to being able to communicate clearly and concisely with the written word, there's still much more to consider. You must also be able to choose and to use the tools of your trade—your PC, your operating system and software, and the attached peripheral devices (scanners, mice, mass storage devices, etc.). You should also have professional reference materials, either on your bookshelf or online, to help you choose the right words, organizational structure, output formats, and style conventions. Most publishers offer their authors style guidelines. A sample of Wordware's style guide is included in appendix B. The same information can be downloaded from the "For Authors" link at http://www.wordware.com.

As a professional writer, you should be a competent typist. In today's PC-focused environment, not being able to touch type is a major barrier to writing. Even if you're overflowing with enthusiasm and creativity, the effectiveness at recording your ideas on paper will be stunted. Non-typists are often so consumed by the mechanics involved in navigating a keyboard that they can lose their train of thought before sentences are completed.

There are also those who learn how to "hunt and peck" with some proficiency. If you're one of these people, then you will always be a marginal typist and your output will be limited by your handicap. Unfortunately, your marginal skill may stunt you for life. If you don't touch type, obtain a good typing software package or enroll in a typing course. The few days it takes to learn to touch type will pay high dividends in productivity.

You should also be an advanced user of your word processing, illustrating, and file archiving software. And you should be able to use Windows like a pro. As a Windows PC user, you should be able to:

- Send and receive e-mail, faxes, and File Transfer Protocol (FTP) transactions
- Browse the World Wide Web and download software updates
- Install and use printers, scanners, mice, and modems
- Create archive files and extract compressed files with ease
- Back up your work for safekeeping
- Use the common shortcut keys for both Windows and your applications to save time. Some typical shortcut keys are listed here.

Where	*What*	*How*
Windows	Switch between applications	Alt+Tab
Windows	Display Start menu	Ctrl+Esc
Windows	Launch Windows Explorer	Right-click on Start button
Windows	Display shortcut menu	Right-click
Most applications	Display shortcut menu	Right-click
Most applications	Cut	Ctrl+X
Most applications	Copy	Ctrl+C
Most applications	Paste	Ctrl+V
Most applications	Select block of text	Shift+drag text
Most applications	Select multiple blocks or fields	Ctrl+Left-click
Most applications	Close window	Ctrl+W
Most applications	Close program	Alt+F4
Most applications	Select all	Ctrl+A
Most applications	Find	Ctrl+F
Most applications	Go to	Ctrl+G
Most applications	Undo last operation	Ctrl+Z

Once you know how to perform these tasks well, the only barrier between you and a successful book project is your ability to select a marketable topic, sell your idea to a publisher, carefully plan it, and then write it in an interesting way using a compelling style.

Some Do's

When you prepare a manuscript:

■ Set all page margins to at least one inch. This gives both you and your copy editor a place to write suggestions and other relevant annotations.

■ Print double-spaced pages to provide space for proofreading marks.

■ Set your text font size to 12-points to make reading easier for the copy editor.

■ Use a common, readable type style such as Times New Roman or Arial.

■ Avoid using more than four paragraph levels (Headings 1 through 4).

■ Set tab stops to correspond to columnar lists and tables (only one tab between each column entry).

■ Use one space between terminal punctuation (periods, question marks, exclamation marks) and the beginning of the next sentence. (The publisher's production department must remove double spaces.)

■ Remove extra spaces at the end of paragraphs.

■ Remove extra lines (carriage returns) at the end of documents (chapters).

■ Number every page. Use either sequentially 1 to n or use a chapter and sequential page numbering system, as in 3-1 to 3-n for the pages of chapter 3.

■ Always supply a two-paragraph-level table of contents. This is needed by the editor and is required to obtain Cataloging-in-Publication data well in advance of publication.

■ Always supply text and graphic files on diskettes or a Zip disk in an acceptable format (check with your publisher to determine acceptable formats).

■ Always maintain a backup copy of your work at least until the book is published (in case your files are lost or your computer is stolen or damaged). If you plan follow-on editions, you'll be glad you kept your files.

■ Supply a copy of each illustration either embedded in the manuscript or on a separate sheet following the callout.

- Always print a good black copy on either a laser or ink jet printer. If you must use a dot matrix printer (not recommended), make sure to install a new ribbon.
- Always respond to publisher inquiries in a prompt manner.
- If you plan to leave home for a while, tell your publisher when you are leaving, when you'll return, and above all—stay in touch.

Some Don'ts

When you prepare a manuscript:

- Don't use colored paper to print your manuscript.
- Don't use spaces in place of tabs for text alignment.
- Don't align columnar text using multiple tabs and spaces; set tabs (left, center, right, or decimal) and then align your columns to them.
- Don't use a small type size to save fifty-cent's worth of paper.
- Don't use an alien word processing or graphics package to prepare your files just because it's what you presently have. Check with your publisher and obtain and use approved software.
- Don't deliver your manuscript and diskettes using an unproven delivery service. Be sure that your package can be traced.
- Don't supply sketches of your artwork or insert hand-drawn labels and expect that your publisher will prepare the final illustrations for you.
- Don't copy your artwork or passages of text from other published sources without first obtaining written permission to use the material from the legal owner of the material.
- Don't use a photograph of one or more people in or on the cover of your book without obtaining a proper release from each person in the photo.

Moving Ahead

The next chapter discusses the most common tool used on PCs: the word processor. There, the most important word processing features are described. Be sure to learn how to use these, as they are vital to your writing productivity and the quality of manuscripts produced by every professional writer.

Chapter 3
Word Processing

Introduction

Your word processing skills rank right up there with your personal creativity and marketable publishing ideas. If you are skillful in the use of your word processor, you will be more productive and less encumbered by the mechanics of the project development phase, freeing you to express information clearly, quickly, and even elegantly. In this chapter some of the important word processing features with which you should be familiar are examined. When these features become second nature, both your writing and publishing efforts will be a breeze. You will also be able to produce manuscripts that can make a positive impression on your publisher. At the end of this chapter, you'll find information pertaining to the importance of using your spell checker, grammar checker, and thesaurus. Although covered in other chapters of this book, the importance of schedules is also discussed.

Important Features

The two most popular word processing software packages in use today on PCs are Microsoft Word and Corel WordPerfect. Although any Windows 3.1- or 95-compatible version of these two successful word processing packages will serve your writing and publishing needs nicely, this book is based on Microsoft Word 97 and Corel WordPerfect 7.0. Both of these are Windows 95 and Windows NT compliant—both 32-bit operating environments that provide many features not available under previous Windows or MS-DOS environments. The single biggest advantage is true *multitasking*, i.e., the ability to run several applications simultaneously. For example, you can receive e-mail or download shareware files over a dial-up adapter or network connection while performing a word processing task. You can also drag and drop or cut and paste information from one application to another, making it easy to combine the features of a robust word processing program with those of a full-featured illustrating program. For instance, you can combine Corel WordPerfect or MS Word with Corel-DRAW, Adobe Illustrator, or Windows Paint. Having said this, it's time to examine some of the important features found in Word and WordPerfect.

File Filters (Import/Export)

A file filter is nothing more than a file conversion utility that examines a file to determine its source and format. Once this is determined, the filter converts the file to a format that can be read and used by the importing program. Hence, the file filter converts and *imports* a file for use by the governing program. A clarifying example would be to import the text of an old WordStar file into either Word or WordPerfect. Another would be to import a CorelDRAW illustration into Word or WordPerfect. File filters are used to import spreadsheets, graphic files, database files, and other types of files into the body of a Word or WordPerfect document. In almost all cases files are imported using the File > Open, Insert > File, or Insert > Object dialogs. WordPerfect also includes an Insert > Spreadsheet/Database > Import selection for this purpose. Simply select the file type and open the file. If the filter you need is not present, it may be because it was not installed during the initial setup process. Check your

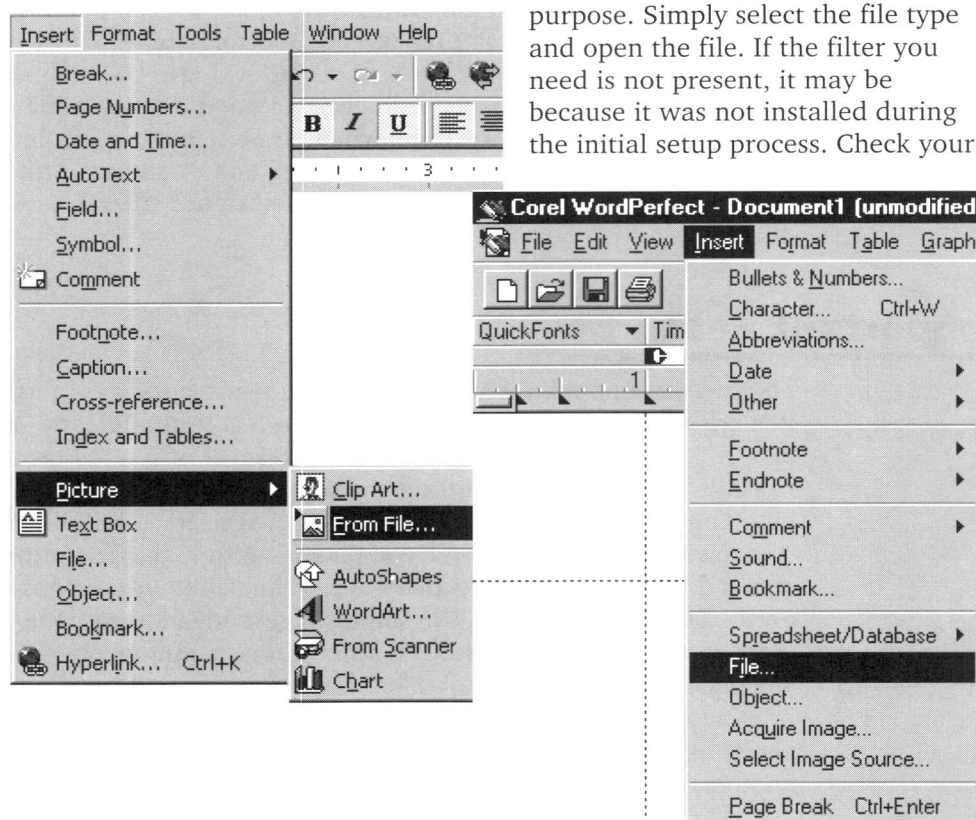

documentation. If the needed file filter is available on the CD-ROM that contains your program software, rerun setup to add the missing file filter.

Similarly, you may wish to save (or *export*) a file in a format that can be used by another program. For example, you may want to export your word-processed document as a rich text file. Once in this format, practically any other program can import the text, as this is a universally accepted format. You can use the File > Save As dialog to accomplish this task in both Word and WordPerfect. Within the dialog, select the desired file type and a useful filename. Then click Save to complete the job.

Once the file is saved in rich text format, practically any other program can import it. This technique is often used when a particular file filter is unavailable. Just export a file in a common file format and the need for an unavailable file filter is eliminated.

There is a drawback associated with the use of an intermediate format, such as the rich text and ASCII file formats. You often lose special text control attributes for font styles, font sizes, boldface, italic, and underline. When using a well-designed file filter, these attributes are maintained. Therefore, you can move from Word to WordPerfect and back and keep the special text effects intact. Of course, not all controls are maintained. Column widths in tables, special symbols, and a number of inserted objects are often lost in the conversion process. When this happens, you may have to manually touch up the converted document by reapplying the desired attributes including special fonts and symbols.

Styles (or Tags)

Tags originated in desktop publishing programs. They are normally an entry that defines the font, its size, alignment, and any attributes including boldface, italic, or underline. Hence, a tag applies a unique style to each kind of element within a document. Tags are created for chapter titles, different paragraph heading levels, different levels in a series of procedural steps, body text, table and illustration titles, and other commonly used text elements. They are given descriptive names, such as Heading 1, Heading 2, Body Text, Note, Step 1, Step a, etc. A collection of tags that have been created for a specific kind of document can be named and saved. Desktop publishing

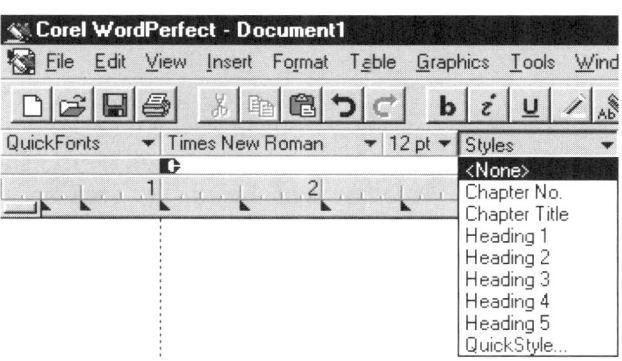

people call the saved tag file a *style sheet*, while others refer to it as a *style template*. When saved, the tags are available for use when a new document of the same type is ready for processing. Most good word processors also let you apply the style sheet of an existing document to a new one.

Advantages offered by tags and style sheets are numerous; productivity and consistency are both key benefits. First, you can type a text element and simply click the desired tag name to apply all established attributes. If a Heading 2 element is bold, underlined, and indented one tab stop, then every Heading 2 will be identical when you apply the tag. Otherwise, you have to remember and apply the attributes every time you create a second-level heading.

The tag goes beyond productivity and consistency. Good word processors, including WordPerfect and Word, provide the ability to automatically create a table of contents from tagged headings. Each tagged heading and its current page number are placed in the appropriate location within the table of contents. In addition to creating the list of headings, you can also select a desired layout for your table of contents from a series of choices. This is extremely beneficial. In addition to saving a lot of typing time, it lets you make massive changes to your document without having to go back and manually rework the corresponding heading and page number changes. Just rerun the table of contents feature. Within a few seconds, your new table of contents will collect the current version of your document. There is also a quality benefit; an automatically produced table of contents assures you that the heading names and page numbers are correct. Word's Insert menu, shown here, is used to access the Index and Tables dialog. If you are a WordPerfect user, use the Tools > Generate > Table of Contents menu to access this feature.

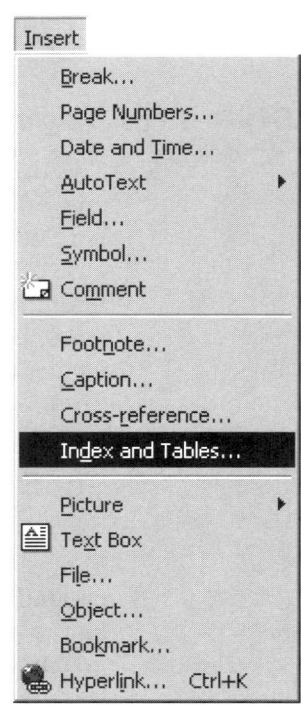

Headers and Footers

Headers and footers should be applied to your manuscripts as well as to your final publications. When preparing a manuscript, you should always number your pages sequentially using Arabic numbers, i.e., 1 through *n*. You should also put the name of the current section or chapter, whatever subdivision name you prefer, in the header at the top of the page. The information contained in headers and footers, as well as the way the elements are arranged (or the *layout*), vary.

A common practice is to put chapter titles at the top of each right-hand (odd numbered) page, set flush right to the outside margin. The publication title is often set at the top of each left-hand page and set flush left. The opening page of each chapter is most often an odd-numbered, right-hand page. Headers are typically omitted from a page that contains the chapter opening.

Both Word and WordPerfect have dialogs that let you control the layout of left- and right-hand pages. They also let you suppress the header and/or footer on the first page of a section. These are important when you print your document directly from a word processor. However, if you plan to use a desktop publishing program for your final output, then headers and footers are only used for the interim manuscript. Because page numbers will change when a desktop publishing program is used to produce the document in final form, the page numbers of the word-processed document, as well as the headers, footers, table of contents, and alphabetical index, will change. So don't waste an inordinate amount of time creating fancy headers, footers, tables of contents, and alphabetical indexes in a preliminary publication.

Contents and Indexes

Tables of contents were described in the preceding Styles (or Tags) paragraph. As mentioned in the previous paragraph, if you plan to desktop publish your final publication, there's no point in wasting a lot of time preparing fancy tables of contents and alphabetical indexes. However, if you tag each of your headings, including chapter titles, with established style names, then your word-processed table of contents is produced automatically by the table of contents utility included in your word processor.

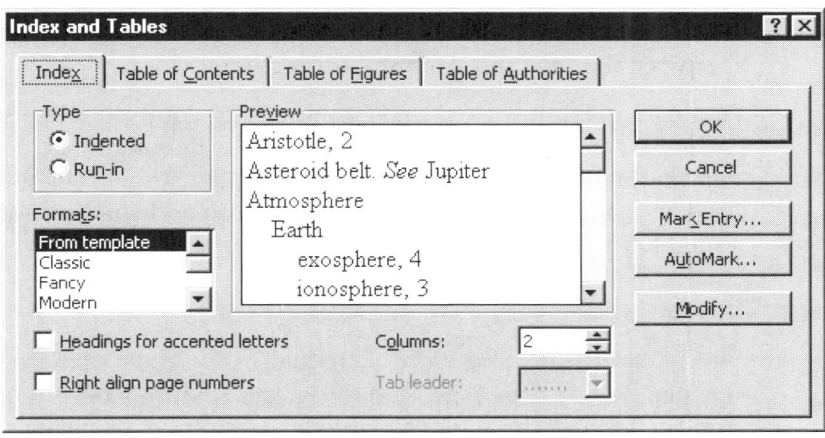

An alphabetical index is also created automatically by your word processor if you tag each word or phrase that you want to include in your alphabetical index. In reality, tagging words and phrases creates a *key word in context* index, rather than a complete alphabetical index. However, you can insert variations of the tagged word or phrase by adding them next to the original index entry. For example, you may want to tag the word "disk drive" to your index. Variations might include "drive, disk" and "magnetic media, disk drive." In Word, the Insert > Index and Tables selection displays the Index and Tables dialog. This is used to mark text entries for the alphabetical index. In WordPerfect, the Tools > Generate > Index selection is used to tag or create alphabetical index entries.

Table Controls

Anytime you want to organize and condense information, you should consider a table. Tables are of particular importance when writing and publishing technical manuals, reports, product specifications, and reference works. If you are word processing such a document, then it's important for you to have a complete understanding of the table controls.

Both Word and WordPerfect display a table button and pull-down grid that permits you to drag the number of rows and columns that you want to create. The columns are distributed evenly between the margins. A 3 x 6 table designates three columns by six rows. Word also has a Tables and Borders button that allows you to draw the rows and columns with a pencil cursor. This feature is exactly like sketching the lines that create the rows and columns. Both Word and WordPerfect insert gridlines between the row and column intersections.

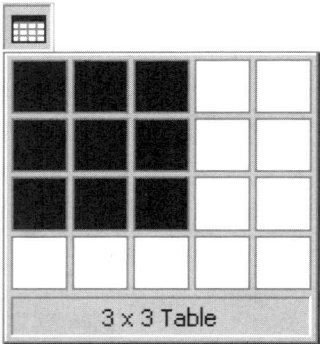

You can insert new rows and columns, cut, copy, or delete selected rows or columns, and paste the cut or copied rows or columns to a new location within a table. Be sure to learn how to merge table cells so you can bridge two or more columns or rows. You can also add shading and different line weights to your tables to enhance their appearance.

Graphic Tools

Both WordPerfect and Word include drawing tools that are ideal for creating simple line drawings. Both programs feature a button on their toolbar (or button bar) that launches the drawing utility. You can also import drawing objects such as clipart, pictures, and drawings created by other

illustrating programs. It's important to position, resize (or *scale*), and adjust text wrapping to create a pleasing page. All of these features are easily attained using either of the recommended word processors.

Illustration References

When inserting graphic objects into your documents, the size of the document files can get quite large. If this becomes a problem, keep your graphic objects as separate files. Be sure that each file has a descriptive name, such as CH03-05 for the fifth illustration of chapter 3. Then put references to each illustration at their insertion points. The reference might be CH03-05.CDR to designate a CorelDRAW illustration, which has the file extension CDR. Similarly, a drawing prepared with Microsoft Paint might be named CH03-05.BMP.

Obviously, if your word-processed document is the final rendition, then you must put the graphic objects into the document before printing it. However, if your document is simply a manuscript that will ultimately be desktop published, references to your illustration files will do nicely. If you plan to give the word processing and illustration files to another person for desktop publishing, the illustrations should be printed and labeled to ensure that each illustration is put in the correct location within your document.

Dynamic Linking and Embedding

Dynamic linking and embedding is summoned when you use the Paste link option. This is a powerful Windows feature that is common to most good Windows-compatible programs. In both Word and WordPerfect, the Paste Special selection is found in the Edit menu.

If you decide to embed your illustrations within the document, rather than using file references, you can use *Paste link* to establish a dynamic link to the source of the object, e.g., the original illustration, spreadsheet, or chart file. Applying this feature ensures that any changes made to the original illustration are automatically reflected in your document, thereby keeping your document updated. Similarly, if your document contains financial information or charts that reside in files created and saved using a spreadsheet or presentation graphic program, you should consider linking these objects as well, especially if the data is subject to change. If the illustrations are static, that is, if they will never change, linking the embedded objects is of no value.

All linked objects are automatically updated when changes made to the original file are saved. This eliminates the need to recapture the object (copy it to the clipboard), delete the obsolete version, and then manually paste and arrange the copied object back into your document.

In the illustrations shown here, notice the Paste Special menu selection within both Word and WordPerfect. These selections access the Paste Special dialog, where the Paste link option is found. As you can see, both word processors give you identical menu choices. The dialogs are also nearly identical.

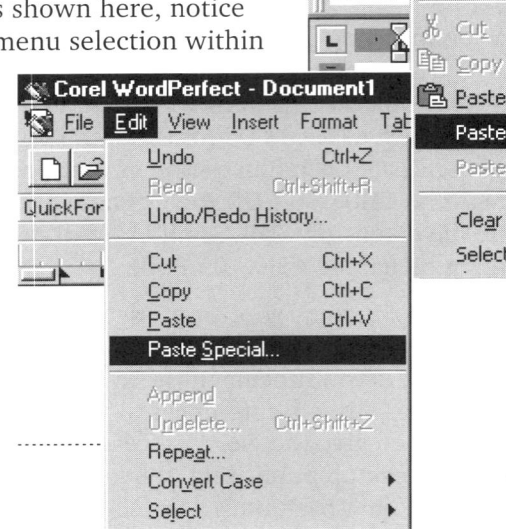

Spell Checkers

As a longtime author, I find the spelling checker to be one of the most important word processor add-ins in my arsenal of writing tools. Unfortunately, as a publisher, I find the spell checker to be one of the most underutilized word processing features by beginning authors. There is simply no excuse for any serious author to produce a manuscript without taking a few extra minutes to use the spell checker; believe me, editors spend hours correcting misspelled words. When this happens, the publisher is burdened with extra editorial cost as well as suffering a lost resource for other works in process. This experience may well discourage a prudent publisher from working on future projects with the offending author. So a simple oversight can lead to serious consequences.

Dynamic Spell Checks

Fortunately, today's spell checkers underline typographical errors and misspelled words as they are entered. By calling attention to the errors on screen, it's easy to fix the mistake on the spot. If you're one of those people who procrastinate, that is, "I'll come back and fix these later," your good intentions may never be realized. Fix the mistakes now, and you won't have to go through a rework cycle that takes more time in the long run.

Proper Nouns

Spell checkers challenge the names of many cities and people. You should probably add these words to your dictionary so they won't be continually challenged. Publishers frequently find the same proper nouns spelled in a variety of ways. In many cases, only the author knows the correct spelling. Publishers regularly encounter well-researched historical manuscripts that spell the same name or place two or three different ways. The copy editor can't just pick one, nor can he or she look up the name in a dictionary. It becomes necessary for the editor to contact the author for the proper spelling. Pay attention to detail; be consistent; be right! If you're not willing to do this, then you're not ready to tackle a serious manuscript.

Thesaurus

A good thesaurus is another handy tool supplied with most good word processors. WordPerfect includes an excellent thesaurus that provides both synonyms and antonyms for the selected word. Word's built-in thesaurus is also good, although it only displays synonyms for the selected word. However, the Microsoft Office 97 Bookshelf located on the Office 97 CD-ROM includes a number of reference books including a complete thesaurus. This reference provides a richer word list than Word's online thesaurus.

There are a few uses for a thesaurus that every writer should consider. First, if you're not sure that you've used a word correctly, check synonyms to make sure that you are saying what you mean to say. For example, writers often confuse the words "affect" and "effect." "Affect" is a verb while "effect" is a noun. You can check the word's application by looking at synonyms to ensure that you're saying what you mean.

Another frequently used application for your thesaurus is that of eliminating redundancy. How many times have you used the same word two or more times within a relatively short passage? This makes the passage awkward, if not ponderous, for the reader. You can use your thesaurus to find other words that have the same meaning, i.e., synonyms, to improve the readability of the passage.

Grammar Checker

Both Word and WordPerfect include excellent grammar checkers. In Word, the on-screen underlining (a green wavy line) shows you potential problems as they occur. WordPerfect requires you to run the grammar checker. You'll find that the suggestions are often valid and useful, particularly in the case of active versus passive voice, incomplete sentences, improper word formation, hyphenation, and punctuation. Many other problems in grammar are challenged by these utilities. You should always check to see what the grammar checker reports. This is true even when you think your sentence is properly constructed. For final authority, you should obtain and use the latest edition of *The Chicago Manual of Style*, which is the consummate style guide used by most publishers in the U.S.

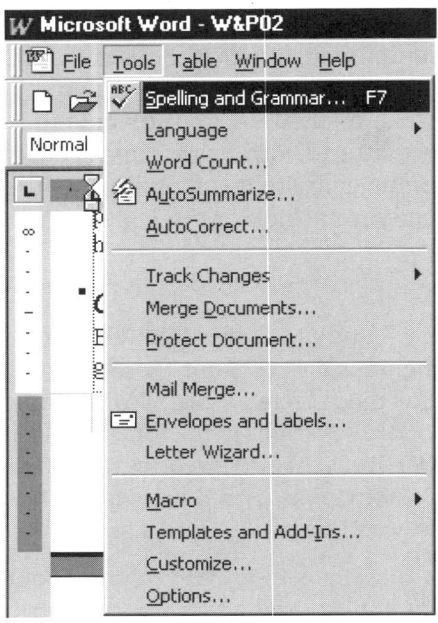
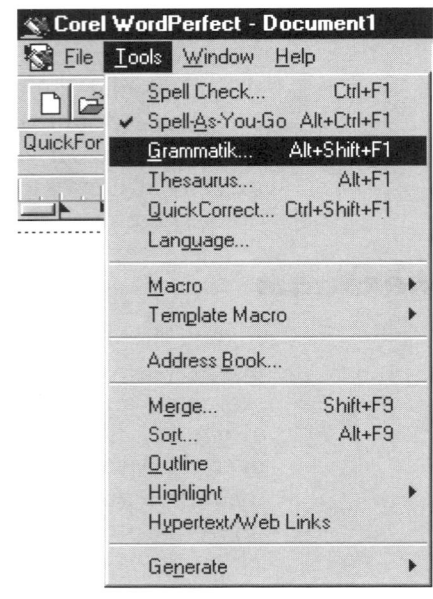

Respecting and using your writing tools is important to both you and your publisher. A well written, good quality manuscript goes a long way in making the right impression with your publisher's editorial department. And believe me, the word gets out. Your acquisition editor, your agent, should you choose to use one, and even some of the bookstore buyers get the word. Good work almost assures future business. Sloppy work severely limits your potential for future assignments. Good work ensures that your publication is processed in the minimum amount of time. It eliminates the aggravation, inconvenience, and schedule delays that result from extensive rework. It guarantees that the market exposure given to your book is maximized on bookstore shelves. Delays from rework (or late delivery) shorten the product life cycle and corresponding revenues.

Frames and Text Boxes

Frames and text boxes are nothing more than defined rectangular areas that contain text, table, graphic, or similar objects. These can be created within your word processor or by another program. Regardless of the source, frames and text boxes give you a number of powerful capabilities. First, you can move a frame or text box almost anywhere on the page by

simply clicking and dragging it. You can scale (or resize) frames and text boxes by clicking and dragging on one of the *handles*. Most frames and text boxes have eight handles. There is a handle in each corner of the frame or text box and one at the center of each side, making eight in all. Drag on a side to change the horizontal or vertical dimension; drag on a corner to resize the entire object. If you want to maintain the exact proportions, use a dialog to type a new scale value, such as 150 to enlarge the object to one and one-half times the original size (or 150%).

Borders

You can add borders to a frame or text box by selecting the frame or box and using the Format menu's Borders and Shading selection in Word. In WordPerfect, you can click on the icon located in the upper left-hand corner of the text box (or select the text box and right-click). A dialog is displayed that lets you pick border and fill attributes. In either program, you can select and set the font to white and set the fill to black for reverse type. You can also scale the text box and drag it to any desired location. You can even have text boxes inside text boxes. In any case, text boxes make excellent "sidebars" and "pull quotes." Both are used to draw a reader's eye to an important article or editorial feature.

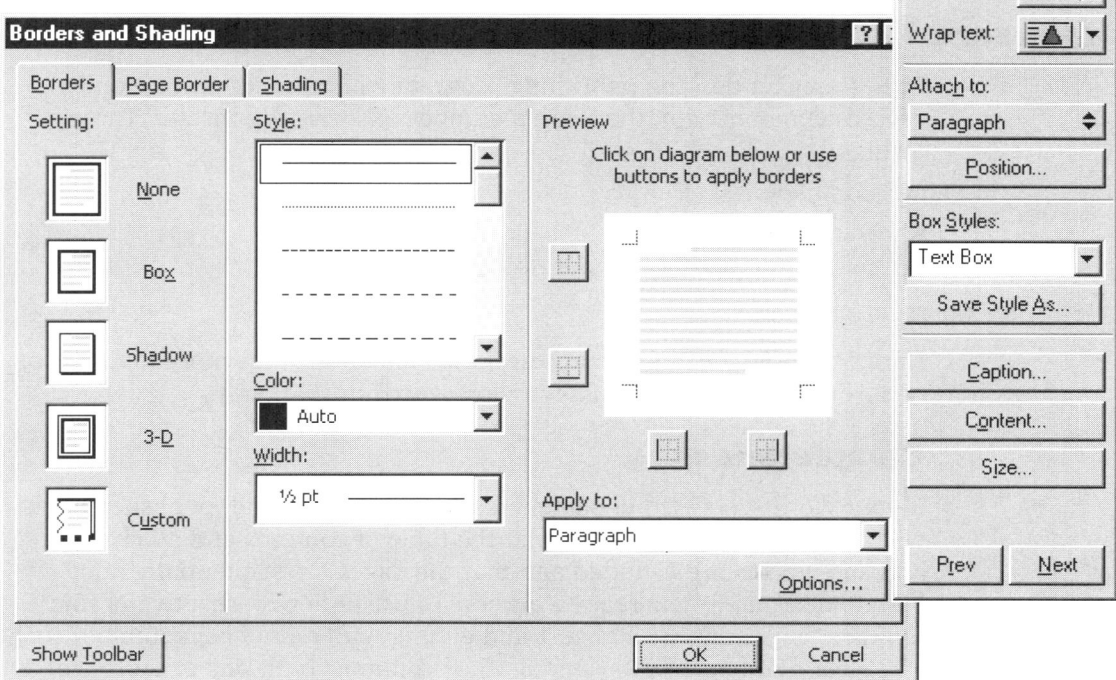

Shading

Use shading (or "Fill") to control the interior shade, texture, or color of your frames and text boxes. If you plan to print your document and then have it reproduced by a quick print company, your fill texture should be somewhere between 5 and 10 percent. Why? Because when it is printed on an offset press the dots will enlarge, which tends to "plug" the background fill. In other words, the dots get bigger and the fill becomes darker and frequently muddy looking. This in turn obscures superimposed text, making it difficult to read.

Manuscript and Final Copy

Today, a word processor is almost always used to prepare manuscript copy. In fact, many publishers insist on it. They also encourage authors to deliver final manuscript files as attachments to e-mail or as an FTP submission via the World Wide Web rather than by *snail mail* (post) or in printed form. Although desktop publishing programs are specifically designed to process final copy, many companies and individuals use word processors to produce their final output. Here, a few additional tips are covered regarding both manuscript and final copy preparation.

Manuscript

Even though a desktop publishing program will reprocess your word-processed manuscript, there are a number of issues to consider. These include:

■ Completeness

■ Quality

■ Treatment of graphics and tables

■ Timeliness

Here, you briefly examine each of these elements. Much more information regarding these and other issues is presented in chapter 4.

Completeness

If your word-processed document is complete, your final, published book will also be complete. Be sure that the table of contents and all chapters and appendixes are included and that the pages are sequentially numbered. Most publishers require authors to use either consecutive Arabic numbers beginning with page 1 and ending with a final page number such as 250 or numbers like 1-1 and 3-15. If you must omit one or more elements from your submission, include a list of missing items. Write down

the dates that you intend to send them, and be sure to honor your commitments.

You should also include all requested marketing information. This is often used as a resource for catalog, back cover, and promotional copy, which is important for introducing your book to the market. Sales representatives use this information to make purchase recommendations; bookstore buyers base their purchase decisions on the copy. Make sure that it's well written and compelling.

Quality

The quality of your work was briefly discussed in the paragraph dealing with spell checkers and grammar checkers. All successful authors are dedicated to a quality manuscript submission. Not only are professionally authored works well organized and easy to follow, editorial and production efforts are minimized. The text is extremely readable, pertinent, concise, carefully checked for technical accuracy, and well organized. All text and graphic files are in the proper format and useful right out of the box. Because professional authors frequently move on to their next assignment, they rarely have the time to spend reworking a previous manuscript. Professional authors are in business to make money; their productivity and financial future relies on quality work, an essential ingredient to their success.

Treatment of Graphics and Tables

Most publishing agreements require authors to provide camera-ready artwork. There was a time when this was a major burden. However, today's modern graphics programs and the abundance of royalty-free clipart have changed the rigor of supplying top-quality illustrations. Never send copyrighted artwork to your publisher for inclusion in your book without getting written permission to use the artwork from the copyright holder.

Tables are frequently used in tutorials and reference books. Today's word processing software makes the creation and editing of tables a breeze. A few clicks of the mouse have even entry-level word processing users preparing high-quality tables.

When including illustrations and tables in your book, be sure that they are properly and accurately referenced in your narrative. If you use table or figure numbers, check them carefully. Try to position graphics and tables as close to their callout as possible. Placing them immediately below the first callout or on the facing page (if the callout is at the bottom of the preceding page) is a common practice.

If your manuscript is heavily illustrated, be sure to compress your files using a file compression utility such as WinZip, PKZIP, LHARC, or ARJ. It is imperative that you check with your publisher to be sure that he has the necessary decompression tool to expand your compressed files. If you use PKZIP, be sure your publisher has the PKUNZIP program. You can also prepare a self-extracting archive, which is always a safe practice. This eliminates the need for your publisher to have the decompression tool. Be sure to include instructions with your files. Also, supply a list of what you have included in each of the compressed files.

A final tip is that you should make every effort to keep the file size of your compressed archives under 1.44 MB so that each file will fit on a single floppy diskette. This is particularly true of archive files that are submitted to your publisher as e-mail attachments. Large archives like those that bridge multiple diskettes are more vulnerable to data errors. There's nothing more frustrating for desktop publishing operators than to see a "broken archive" error message when they're ready to start a new book project. This means that they must contact the author for a new copy of the manuscript and graphic files. Therefore, small files offer better data integrity. Replacing one small archive is easier than replacing the entire book. Also, smaller file sizes make it easier for people to distribute files to coworkers in the office, rather than having to break up files and rearchive them or transfer them over a network. Although the network is the way to go, not all terminals are connected to the same network.

You can also deliver your files using Zip drive and a large Zip disk if you and your publisher are both equipped with them. The 100MB Iomega Zip disk is the most common. Higher capacity drives have also been introduced that store more than a gigabyte of information on small, removable media. The new devices and media are relatively expensive, so it will be awhile before they are common.

Timeliness

Professional authors meet their delivery schedules to ensure that their books enter the market at the earliest possible time. This maximizes the book's market exposure or time in the market, and guarantees the highest possible revenue potential. Therefore, conscientious authors deliver good quality manuscripts on time because they understand the dynamics of the market. Late delivery often equates to cancellation. The penalties associated with either a publication delay or cancellation cannot be taken lightly. When a book is cancelled, the investments in advance promotion and sales presentations are lost. In addition to lost time and money, the publisher suffers embarrassment and bookstores must cancel orders and reallocate their funds to other books. Needless to say, both late and cancelled books have disastrous implications. My advice to any aspiring author is do not

enter into a publishing agreement unless you are absolutely sure that you can deliver a useful manuscript on time.

Final Copy

If you intend to use your word processor to print final camera-ready reproducible copy (called *repro* in the trade), then make your printed output as clean as possible. Include professionally prepared headers and footers, illustrations, tables, appendixes, an alphabetical index, and any other elements that make your work rival those found on bookstore shelves. Once your final pages are printed, be sure to handle them carefully; store them in a clean protective folder, or wrap and tape them in clean paper and put them in a shipping box for safety. Be sure that you include all necessary special instructions relative to layout, your intentions with regard to page fronts and backs, and include a blank sheet to identify each blank page, such as those that back up the last right-hand page of a chapter. Your interface with commercial printers is presented in much greater detail in chapter 10.

Moving Ahead

If you plan to acquire and use illustrating software, the next chapter is important. There, you learn about color systems, the different types of graphics software, and the capabilities of each. Then specific graphic programs are examined in substantial detail.

Chapter 4

Illustrating

Introduction

Every document intended to persuade, educate, or inform people includes graphic elements. Even novels, which rarely include interior illustrations, incorporate compelling artwork on their covers to make them as attractive and appealing as possible to consumers. If you are writing and publishing documents, ranging from fliers to large publications, then you should know how to create, capture, or convert graphic objects, such as diagrams and pictures.

Today's graphic software for Windows 95, 98, and NT makes the creation, capture, and use of graphic elements a breeze. With the right software, inserting illustrations into your documents is typically accomplished with a few simple mouse clicks, drags, and key presses. This chapter defines types of illustrations. It examines the features found in several top-notch drawing packages and guides you through the general procedures used to create, acquire, edit, print, and export illustrations for use in your documents.

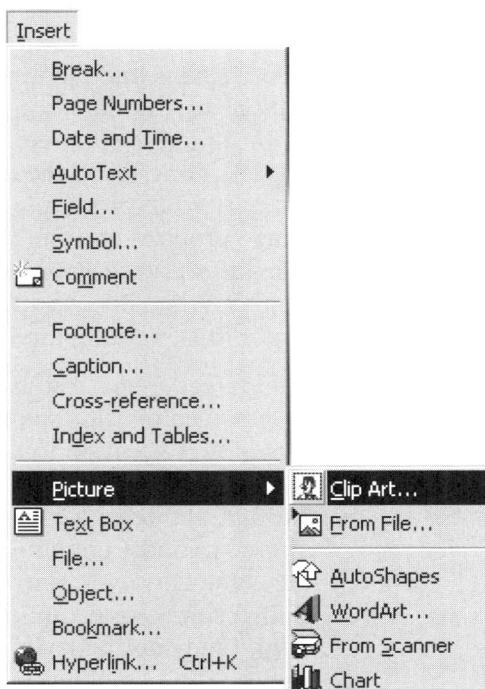

What You Should Know About Graphics

The old adage, "a picture is worth a thousand words," is as true today as it ever was. There are instances when an idea or description can only be conveyed with a clarifying line drawing, diagram, chart, photograph (or *tone art*), or a combination of two or more of these illustration types. Examples of line drawings are maps, architectural plans, and engineering sketches and design drawings. Tone art (sometimes called *halftones*) typically includes photographs or paintings; line drawings are created from pen, pencil, and brush strokes. All consist of different shades of color or shades of gray and black. The term halftone refers to black dots on a white background. The dots make up the images within an illustration. Small diameter dots produce light gray; large diameter dots produce dark gray. Large diameter dots that overlap produce solid black areas. The absence of dots results in white areas. Hence, a grayscale graphic is made up entirely of various sizes of black dots on a white background.

Your computer's display uses this same technique. A common 640 x 480 computer screen makes use of a matrix of horizontal and vertical dots. Individual dots, or picture elements (*pixels*), are turned on and off to create letters and pictures. The screen image is printed to a graphic printer in a similar way. Although the printer's dot resolution may be different than the computer display's, i.e., 300 or 600 dot-per-inch (*dpi*) printers are typical, the printer's driver software translates and scales the dot pattern to produce a high-quality output that maintains the correct image proportions. You should understand that even the old 300 dot per inch laser printer produces better quality output than a 1024 x 768-pixel display. Why? Because the 1024 x 768 resolution is distributed across a larger area, as compared to the dots *per inch* used by your printer.

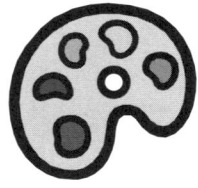

Computer screens also use the basic color palette, i.e., red, green, and blue to create colors. Today's display technology features more memory and graphic acceleration to achieve a 16.7-million true color display. These display devices, typically populated by 4MB of RAM, often sell for less than $150. If you have a color printer, such as one of the many inkjet printers offered by most popular printer manufacturers, you can take advantage of the color. However, since it is several times more expensive to commercially print color documents than it is black and white, your printed color output may not be a viable choice except for limited-run advertising or presentation handouts.

Line drawings can be either bitmapped or vector drawn. A bitmapped line is typically coarser than that of a vector-drawn line. Bitmapped (or *raster graphics*) lines are created from a pattern of relatively coarse rectangular "dots." Vector-drawn lines use the smallest pixels and are much smoother

in appearance. The description of a vector-drawn line is stored as a line between two endpoints, or coordinates. For example, a line may be described as extending from X1, Y1 to X2, Y2, where X1=100, Y1=100, X2=380, and Y2=540. Using a 640 x 480-pixel coordinate scale, this line begins at the upper left-hand corner of the screen at pixel row 100, column 100. The line moves down and to the right. Its endpoint is at pixel row 380, column 540. On the other hand, the stored description of a bit-mapped graphic includes the state of every pixel involved in the line. The description includes the on or off status as well as the color values required to produce the line. Therefore, files that store the information required to produce a bitmapped illustration are usually much larger than vector illustration files. In addition, the quality of a line produced by a bit-mapped graphic is inferior to that of the smoother vector graphic.

X1,Y1

X2,Y2

More About Vector Graphics

Vector graphics are comprised of lines and curves defined by mathematical expressions. These mathematical expressions are called *vectors*. The value X1,Y1 in the preceding paragraph is a vector object. Hence, coordinate points describe vector-drawn graphics on the screen. Recall your study of Cartesian coordinates in high school geometry; then think about the vector coordinates described above. A vector-drawn tire is produced from the mathematical definition of a circle. It is filled with a specific color and the coordinate values position it within the screen boundaries. If the size, location, or color of the tire changes, the program, such as Adobe Illustrator or CorelDRAW, redefines the mathematical definition of the shape, color, and location of the tire.

Vector graphics are resolution independent, i.e., not defined by a fixed number of pixels. Therefore, they are automatically scaled and retain a sharp appearance on your screen or printer, regardless of the resolution of the device. Therefore, when high quality is required, use vector graphics for both type and illustrations. Once the object is vector drawn, you can enlarge or reduce (*scale*) the drawn object and maintain clean, sharp lines.

You should know that your computer display uses a grid of pixels. Both vector- and pixel-drawn objects are displayed as pixels on your screen. Vector-based programs must render drawn objects into pixels for display. Vector-drawn objects display and print at the resolution available on your monitor or printer. Hence, vector-drawn graphics enlarge well and maintain sharp outlines and excellent definition. In contrast, scaling up a bitmap-drawn image enlarges the dots, making the lines that produce your type and drawing more jagged.

Bitmap Graphics

Windows Paintbrush is an example of a bitmap-based illustrating program. Adobe Photoshop, Corel PHOTO-PAINT, and Microsoft Photo Editor are pixel editors or *image editing* software. While Paintbrush is easy to use, it is restricted in its file conversion abilities. If you want to insert a quick map in a letter or fax to a friend, it's a good choice. However, if you want to retouch a digital photograph, use one of the other programs just mentioned. These programs produce bitmap images, also called *raster images*. The images use a grid, which is called a raster or bitmap. The grid is made up of small rectangles (you now know these as pixels) to represent the graphics. Every pixel in a bitmap drawing is assigned location and color value. A drawing of a bitmap-drawn tire uses a large number of pixels; each pixel is part of a mosaic that produces the appearance of a tire. Therefore, when you work with a bitmap-drawn image, you must define each pixel rather than an entire object, such as a line or circle.

Because pixels can represent subtle gradations in color or grayscale, bitmap images are ideal for continuous tone-generated images, such as photographs or paintings. Bitmap images are resolution dependent—that is, they represent a fixed number of pixels. Therefore, they often appear jagged and fuzzy, particularly if they are scaled for display or printing at a higher or lower resolution than that for which they were created.

Bitmap images are best at reproducing small changes in the different shades found in continuous-tone pictures. When enlarged or displayed or printed on higher resolution devices, their flaws are magnified and may appear quite jagged.

Bitmap images can be produced in different *resolutions*. The resolution is the number of dots or pixels per linear unit of measure used to reproduce displayed objects. Printers and display screens reproduce bitmap-drawn images in groups of pixels. Therefore, the resolution of bitmap images depends on both the display device and the resolution of the original bitmap image. In contrast, the resolution of vector-drawn images depends on the device used to print or display the picture.

Color Models

A number of color systems exist for displaying, printing, and storing graphics. These are based on established *color models* used to describe and reproduce color. The two most common color models are red, green, and blue (RGB) and cyan, magenta, yellow, and black (CMYK). Adobe

Illustrator uses an additional common model, hue, saturation, and brightness (HSB), to represent color values in palettes and dialog boxes.

Hue, Saturation, and Brightness (HSB)

The HSB model is based on the human perception of color. In the HSB model, all colors are described in terms of three fundamental characteristics:

- Hue is the wavelength of light reflected from or transmitted through an object. More commonly, hue is identified by the name of the color such as red, orange, or green. Hue is measured as a location on the standard color wheel and is expressed as a degree between 0 degrees and 360 degrees.

- Saturation, sometimes called *chroma*, is the strength or purity of the color. Saturation represents the amount of gray in proportion to the hue and is measured as a percentage from 0% (gray) to 100% (fully saturated). On the standard color wheel, saturation increases as you approach the edge of the wheel; saturation decreases as you approach the center.

- Brightness is the relative lightness or darkness of the color and is usually measured as a percentage from 0% (black) to 100% (white).

The Adobe Illustrator drawing program, presented later in this chapter, allows you to use the HSB model to define a color in the Color palette or in the Color Picker dialog box.

RGB

RGB color is the color model commonly used to create graphics that are displayed only on monitors, such as background wallpaper or web page illustrations. It's possible to represent a large percentage of the visible color spectrum by mixing red, green, and blue in different proportions and intensities. These colors are known as the *additive primary colors* because adding 100% of all these colors together creates white. When all are added together, all the light is reflected back to the eye, producing white. Additive colors have many applications including lighting, video, film recorders, and computer and television monitors. Your computer's monitor and your TV set create color by emitting light through red, green, and blue phosphors.

Cyan, Magenta, Yellow, and Black (CMYK)

The CMYK model is based on the light-absorbing quality of ink on paper, unlike the RGB model, which depends on a light source to create different colors. CMYK relies on the principle that part of the light spectrum is reflected by the ink to the human eye, while another part of the light spectrum is absorbed by the ink. The physical properties of pure cyan (C), magenta (M), and yellow (Y) ink pigments combine to absorb all color, which produces black. This phenomenon causes CMY to be *subtractive color*. However, the impurities found in all inks cause the CMY combination to produce a brown-gray color. Therefore, black (K) ink is added to produce black. Each pair of subtractive colors creates an additive color; additive and subtractive colors are called *complementary colors*. For those readers who are familiar with the term *four-color process printing*, you now know a bit more about what goes into the process.

Grayscale

Grayscale objects can be assigned brightness values ranging from 0 (black) to 255 (white). Therefore, grayscale can use 256 shades of gray. The values between 0 and 255 represent different shades of the grayscale spectrum. Grayscale values are represented by the percentages of black ink coverage, where 0% corresponds to white and 100% corresponds to black. You can use grayscale to convert color graphics to good quality black-and-white artwork. Programs like Adobe Illustrator discard all color information in the original artwork. The gray shades used to produce converted objects represent the luminosity of the original colors used in the graphic objects.

When grayscale objects are converted to RGB, the color values for each object are given the object's previous gray value. Grayscale objects can also be converted to CMYK to create four-color process *quadtones*. This eliminates the need to first convert using what is called the *duotone mode*.

Color Gamuts

The range of colors that can be displayed or printed is called the *gamut* of a color system. The miraculous human eye can view a much broader spectrum of colors than that of any gamut of any color system.

Among the color models used in Adobe Illustrator, RGB has the largest gamut. The RGB gamut contains the subset of colors that can be viewed on a computer or television monitor (which emits red, green, and blue light). Some colors, such as pure cyan or pure yellow, can't be displayed accurately on a monitor. The smallest gamut is that of the CMYK model, which consists of colors that can be printed using process-color inks. Colors that can be displayed on a screen but cannot be printed are referred to as *out-of-gamut colors*. This means that they are outside the CMYK gamut. Because you can view more colors on an RGB screen than can be printed using the CMYK gamut, it is clear that the RGB color gamut greatly exceeds that of the CMYK color gamut.

Acquiring Artwork

There are a number of ways to acquire and insert artwork into your documents. One of the ways is to obtain pictures or diagrams on paper. These can be scanned using one of the many popular scanners found in almost every computer store that specializes in computer hardware and software.

Scanners

You can acquire graphic images from paper using one of today's many flatbed or handheld scanners. If you're a serious writer, illustrator, or publisher, a flatbed scanner is mandatory. Scanners come in a wide variety of configurations. They come with driver software and almost all include image-editing software. Scanner prices range from around a hundred dollars to tens of thousands of dollars, depend-

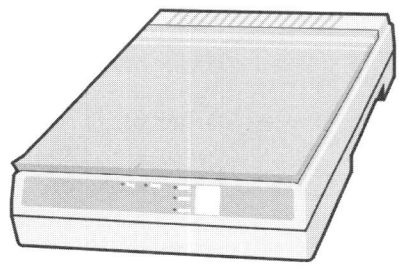

ing on the size and features. For home and small office use, you can purchase some excellent units for $99.95 to $149.95 at any computer superstore. For additional information about scanners, see the section entitled Scanners and Scanning later in this chapter.

Digital Cameras

Digital cameras are used to capture pictures in digital image format. Once captured, the image file can be transferred to a computer. There, it is imported into your pixel editor program, such as Adobe Photoshop, Corel PHOTO-PAINT, or Microsoft Photo Edit; touched up as necessary; and finally placed into your document. Digital cameras make an ideal tool for capturing and transferring almost any kind of object to a document such as a book. For example, if you are preparing a product catalog, you can snap a picture of each object and then paste it into the catalog adjacent to its description. Digital cameras are ideal for capturing three-dimensional objects, while scanners are better for capturing flat images from pictures, news clips, and books.

The prices of digital cameras range from around $500 to $5,000. Differences include lens systems and digital resolution. A high-end Minolta digital camera is equipped with the same lenses found in Minolta's professional quality 35-mm camera line. The Minolta RD-175 includes 131MB of memory for image storage. Most professional units permit variations in the resolution setting. Higher resolution settings use more memory. The Minolta unit, as well as several other brands from such manufacturers as Canon and Sony, use a PCMCIA card to transfer images to a computer so that they can be processed with your graphics software and then imported into your documents.

Clipart

Like scanners, you can also find a broad range of clipart on CDs in almost every full-line computer and office supply superstore. These include Micro Center, CompUSA, Fry's Electronics, Computer City, Egghead, Office Depot, and Best Buy. Other office supply stores, many full-line discount and appliance stores, technical bookshops, large bookstores, and software stores also carry a selection of clipart CDs. You'll also find advertisements for clipart CDs in many of today's trade magazines. The clipart you purchase on a 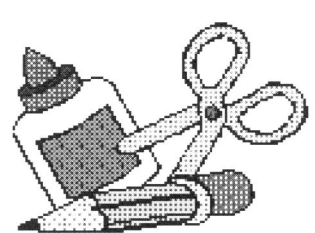 CD is distributed "royalty free." This means that the purchase price gives you permission to use and distribute the artwork in your documents. However, read the license carefully to ensure that the CD is free of any restrictions that may be a barrier to your intended use. Some only require that you include a credit line that names the photographer.

Clipart files are typically available in a common graphics format that can be read by most of today's popular graphic programs. Most programs come with conversion utilities (or *filters*) that read and write a number of common graphic formats. When you buy your clipart CD be sure that the format is compatible with the programs you plan to use. If you are using application programs from Adobe, Corel, and/or Microsoft, chances are good that you have the graphic file filter you need to read the clipart file.

You can modify the appearance of clipart, extract one or more features, or remove unwanted objects using your graphic software. For example, you can select one or more foreground objects by cropping out the background areas using a pixel editor. You can recolor objects, such as trees or meadows, to change the season from spring to winter. You can also change the size (or *scale*) of an object for emphasis. You can even combine elements from several different clipart files. Simply cut objects from two or more graphic files and paste them into another. Because graphic images are typically large, your computer will need plenty of memory to perform some of these tasks.

Computer Screen Captures

This book and many others that describe or teach computer applications require the capture, editing, and insertion of displayed elements such as computer menus, dialogs, and toolbars. A number of MS-DOS screen capture utilities, such as Hijack and Hot Shot Graphics, were used to capture and convert displayed screens. Today, Windows 95 and NT make screen captures possible without the use of special utilities. This process is described in detail near the end of this chapter in the Screen Captures section.

PC-Based Drawing Tools

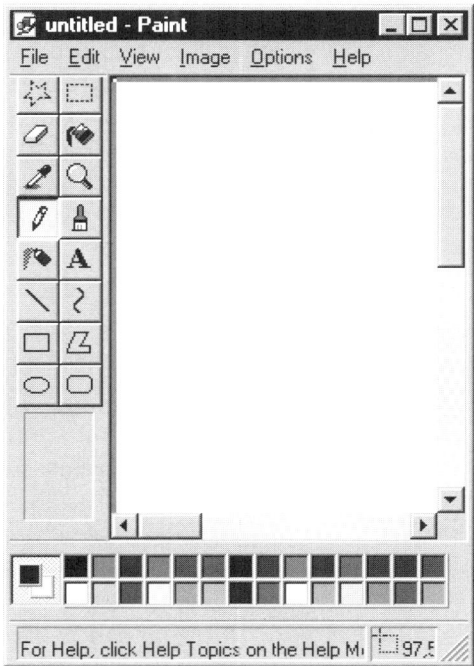

Every serious writer and publisher typically employs two or three different high-end drawing programs. They use one for bitmapped graphics, another for vector graphics, and sometimes a third for photo (or pixel) editing. In this section several popular programs used for creating and editing graphic files are described. Reading the feature descriptions is quite rigorous unless the package being discussed is installed on your PC. In that case, you can follow the procedures by displaying the menus and dialogs. They will definitely make much more sense.

Microsoft Paint

Microsoft Paint is a simple, easy-to-use bitmap-editing program that is ideal for creating and editing simple sketches that include lines, rectangles, circles, and text elements. For example, you can use Paint to draw and print a simple street map in a matter of minutes. When Paint files are saved, they are automatically assigned a bmp file extension. Paint lets you save an entire illustration or you can select and save one or more individual entities within a displayed illustration. Most of the screen illustrations in this book were clipped and saved using Microsoft Windows 95 Paint.

The bmp file format produced by Paint is also convenient to use. Every Windows-compatible word processing, desktop publishing, and illustrating program can import, display, and print Windows bmp graphic files. Therefore, if you are capturing screen images for a document, you should seriously consider using Paintbrush as your tool of choice. The Screen Captures section found later in this chapter shows you how to use Paint to edit and save screen objects.

Word Processing Drawing Utilities

Both Word and WordPerfect are delivered with built-in drawing utilities. Although simple to learn and operate, these utilities are often quite adequate for your drawing needs. It's easy to draw lines; open or filled rectangles, squares, ellipses, and circles; and text boxes. These utilities also permit you to modify line weights, styles, and colors. You can learn to use all of the features of these programs in a matter of an hour or so. Much can be said for simplicity, as it often translates directly into productivity.

If you plan to use the output of your word processor, rather than a desktop publisher, for your final document, you can print your text and graphics and deliver the printed output to your intended audience. However, if you intend to deliver your artwork to a publishing house, it is important that you determine their graphic file requirements. They may prefer a format other than that produced by the word processor's graphics utility. If they are using Macintoshes in their graphics department, you will probably have to convert your graphic files to TIF format. Fortunately, you can convert your drawings to an acceptable format prior to delivery. So be sure to determine which graphic file formats are acceptable by your publisher's production department before you waste your time and theirs sending the wrong file format.

Tip: If you wish to send a TIF graphic file from your PC to a publisher using Macintosh computers, follow these steps.

1. Obtain a copy of CompactPro for the Macintosh. (You can probably download it from the www.macworld.com web site.) You'll need a Mac to do this, so find a friend who owns an Internet-connected Macintosh.

2. Using your PC, convert your graphic file to TIF format using a built-in file conversion utility (or *filter*). Be sure that the file size will fit onto a 1.44 MB floppy diskette. (Note that the TIF bitmap format can be used by a Macintosh computer.)

3. Copy the TIF graphic file to an MS-DOS formatted floppy diskette.
4. Give the floppy diskette to a Macintosh user equipped with CompactPro. Macs can read files on PC-formatted floppies, either directly or by using a PC file exchange utility.
5. Use CompactPro to:
   ■ Convert the file to a self-extracting archive (file extension SEA).
   ■ Convert the compressed SEA file to BIN-HEX format.
   ■ Copy the file back to a DOS floppy diskette and attach it to an e-mail message to your publisher. In the e-mail message, instruct your publisher to use CompactPro to process the attached BIN-HEX file.

Of course you can also compress and send the SEA file directly from one Mac to another as an e-mail attachment. This eliminates the need to go back through your PC, but it will omit your e-mail reply address. If you intend to go Mac-to-Mac, put your reply e-mail address in the body text of the accompanying e-mail.

Adobe Illustrator

Many professional graphic artists will tell you that this is their vector illustrating program of choice. It has received outstanding reviews in many of today's personal computer magazines, such as *Windows Magazine*, as the best Windows-based illustrating program on the market. Unlike the simple drawing programs found in Word and WordPerfect, Adobe Illustrator takes longer to master, but the effort is well worth your investment in time. Illustrator is loaded with tools and advanced features for drawing, cropping, and color separation. A type font library and a number of useful add-ins accompany it.

Illustrator got its beginnings as the leading illustrating program for the Macintosh world, and won immediate acceptance from the graphic arts industry, which at one time was dominated by top-end Macintosh computers. All the technology has now been ported to the Windows platform, and the full set of Illustrator capabilities is now available to Windows users. Following is an overview of Adobe Illustrator.

Setting Preferences

Illustrator includes numerous program settings, which are stored in a preferences file. This file is located in the Prefs subdirectory inside the Illustrator directory. The settings stored in this file include general display options, separation setup information, display options, tool options, ruler units, and options for exporting information. Most of these options are set

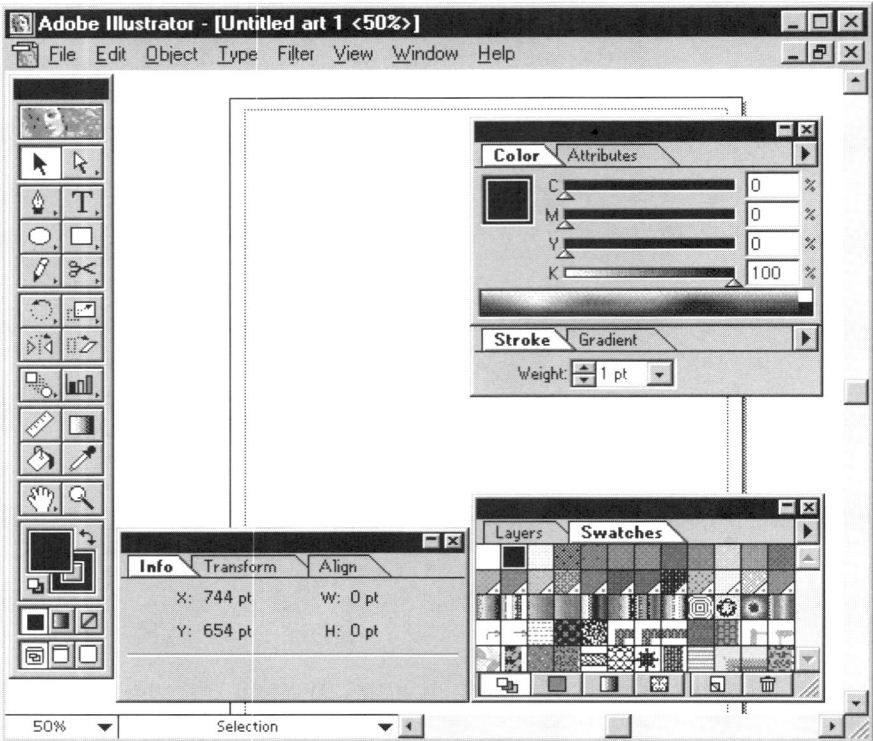

in dialog boxes that can be opened through the references submenus in the File menu:

■ The General Preferences dialog contains preferences for how various commands and tools work. To find an explanation of a particular General Preferences option, please see the index.

■ The Keyboard Increments dialog lets you set the increments in which baseline shift and kerning/tracking values increase or decrease when you use keyboard shortcuts.

■ The Units and Undo dialog box lets you set measurement units for the rulers, keyboard, and other distance units used in Illustrator, as well as the minimum level of Undo levels. For more information, see "Correcting mistakes" in the online help information.

■ The Guides and Grid dialog lets you change color, spacing, and subdivisions on the guides and background grids. For more information, see "Using guides and grids."

■ The Hyphenation Options dialog defines which language dictionary is used and lets you specify any words you don't want Illustrator to hyphenate.

■ The Plug-ins and Scratch Disk dialog lets you indicate where the plug-in modules are located and which disk to use as a scratch disk. (A scratch disk is hard disk space on your system that you use for working with large files.) See "Using plug-in modules" and "Using the scratch disk when working with bitmap images" in Adobe Illustrator's online help information.

To find an explanation of a particular preferences option or set of options, refer to Adobe Illustrator's online Help index. For general operating instructions, look in the Help Contents area.

Using the Toolbox

The first time you open a document, the toolbox appears on the left side of the screen. The toolbox contains the set of working tools with which you can create, select, and manipulate objects in Illustrator. flyout boxes are displayed by clicking the left-pointing triangles within the tool. This gives you access to the hidden tools. Use the built-in help for a description of each tool.

Drawing

Illustrator provides many ways to draw objects, ranging from simulated paintbrush artwork to detailed pen strokes. Used in conjunction with a mouse or a pressure-sensitive drawing tablet,

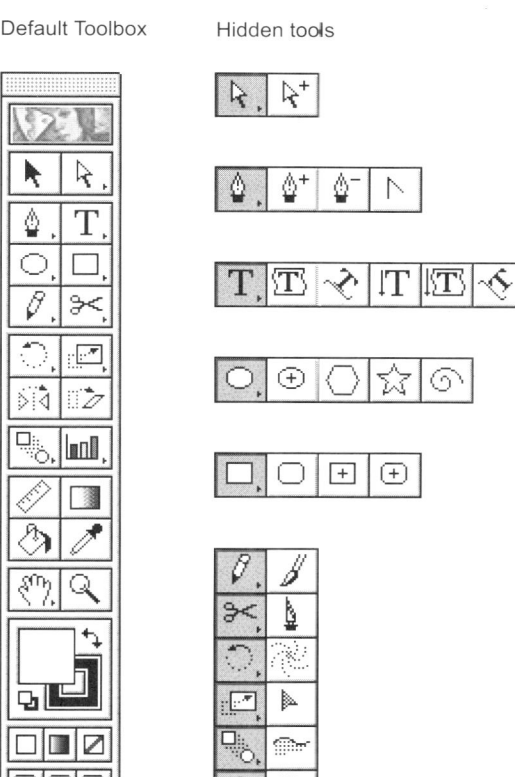

Default Toolbox   Hidden tools

Adobe Illustrator drawing tools give you a huge range of control and speed. Although some tools simulate the simplicity of pen and paper, drawing with a computer is definitely different from hand drawing.

Paths and Anchor Points

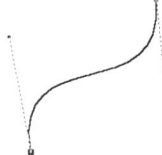

A path is any line or shape that you create using the Adobe Illustrator drawing tools, representing the outline of a graphic object. A single straight line, a rectangle, and the outline of a map are all examples of paths. A path consists of one or more segments. Anchor points, which define where each segment of a path starts and ends, "anchor" the path in place. By moving anchor points, you modify path segments and change the shape of a path.

A path is either open or closed. A closed path is a path that is continuous and has no beginning or end (and therefore, no endpoints); a circle is an example of a closed path. An open path has distinct endpoints; a wavy line, for example, is an open path. The first and last anchor points on an open path are called the endpoints. If you fill an open path, an imaginary line is drawn between the two endpoints and fills the path.

Drawing with the Pencil Tool

The pencil tool lets you draw paths as if you were drawing with a pencil on paper and is most useful for fast sketching or creating a more hand-drawn look than would result from using the pen tool. To draw with either the pencil or paintbrush tools, select the tool and move the cursor to the paper. Then left-click and hold down the mouse button to drag a line, much as you would press down and pull a pencil or paintbrush across a sheet of paper. Lift (release) the mouse button when finished. When you use the pencil tool, anchor points are set down for you as you draw; you do not control their position, although you can adjust their position once the path is complete. The number of anchor points used is determined by the length and complexity of the path and by the Curve Fitting Tolerance value set in the General Preferences dialog box.

Drawing with the Paintbrush Tool

The paintbrush tool lets you draw a closed path that varies in width, simulating a paintbrush stroke. You can constrain the paintbrush stroke to a single width. If you have a pressure-sensitive drawing tablet, you can vary the width of the paintbrush stroke by varying pressure on the pen tip. You can also select calligraphic brush strokes to draw script-like letters and lines. To draw with the paintbrush tool:

1. Select the paintbrush tool. The pointer changes to a paintbrush when you move it to the active window.

2. Position the tip of the paintbrush where you want the path to begin. Drag the paintbrush to draw the path.

3. Release the mouse button to display anchor points along the line's perimeter.

 ### Drawing with the Pen Tool

Unlike the pencil and brush tools, the pen tool draws a line by selecting the tool, clicking on the starting point of a line (that is, click and release), moving to the endpoint, and clicking again. Therefore, don't try to use the pen by dragging, as this produces unwanted results. Use the pen tool to create straight lines and smooth, flowing curves. This tool gives you greater precision than does the pencil tool. Most users find the pen tool to be the most important and powerful drawing tool in Illustrator, because it provides superior drawing control and accuracy.

Selecting Objects

Before you can modify a drawn object, you must isolate it from adjacent and overlapping objects. Clicking it with one of the selection tools does the trick. When selected, the anchors (or "handles") are displayed, and you can edit it by moving or copying it, deleting it, or adjusting paths. Select objects using the following selection tools:

 ■ The selection tool (solid arrow) lets you select entire objects or an entire path by selecting any spot on the path.

 ■ The direct-selection tool (hollow arrow) lets you select individual anchor points or segments on a path and displays all direction lines on a path for adjusting. This tool is common to many illustrating programs.

 ■ The group-selection tool (hollow arrow with +; accessed from flyout box) is used to select an object within a group, a single group within multiple groups, or a set of groups. Each succeeding click adds the next object in the grouping hierarchy to the selection. This is an extremely handy and powerful tool, as most illustrating programs force you to ungroup objects before individual entities can be edited.

Adjusting Path Segments

You can modify the shape of a path by moving one or more of its segments or by moving its anchor points.

■ Adjust curved segments by moving the segment between the points anchoring it or by moving one or more of its anchor or direction points.

■ You can also adjust a path by converting smooth points to corner points and vice versa. For more information, see "About direction lines and direction points" in the online help information.

■ To adjust a path globally, keeping each point along the path in scale, use the reshape tool. This tool lets you pick points along a path and adjust all of the segments along the path by dragging a single point.

■ To adjust quickly a path you are drawing, hold down Ctrl with the pen tool selected. Adjust the path and then release the key to resume drawing with the pen tool.

Drawing Rectangles and Ellipses

There are four rectangle tools and two ellipse tools to give you an easy way to create these common graphic objects:

■ The rectangle and ellipse tools let you draw rectangles and ellipses by dragging from one corner of the rectangle or edge of the ellipse to the opposite corner or edge.

■ The centered-rectangle and centered-ellipse tools let you draw rectangles and ellipses by dragging from the center of the rectangle or ellipse outward.

■ The rounded-rectangle tool lets you draw round-cornered rectangles by dragging from one corner of the rectangle to the opposite corner.

■ The centered-rounded rectangle tool lets you draw round-cornered rectangles by dragging from the center of the rectangle outward.

When you create an object with the rectangle or ellipse tools, a center point appears in the center of the object. You can use this point to drag the object or to align the object with other elements in your artwork. The center point can be made visible or invisible, but it cannot be deleted.

To toggle quickly between the rectangle and centered-rectangle tools, the ellipse and centered-ellipse tools, and the rounded-rectangle and centered-rounded-rectangle tools, press Alt when any of these tools are selected.

Drawing Polygons

The polygon tool draws an object with a specified number of sides of equal length, each side being the same distance from the center of the object.

Drawing Spirals

The spiral tool creates a spiral-shaped object of a given radius and number of winds, that is, the number of turns that the spiral will complete from start to finish.

Drawing Stars

The star tool creates a star-shaped object with a given number of points and size.

Tracing Artwork

If you want to create a drawing based on an existing hand-drawn illustration or one saved by another illustrating program, you can import the image into Illustrator and then trace it. This can save time and produce a closer copy than might otherwise be achieved. As of Adobe Illustrator version 6.0, you have the following ways of tracing artwork. Your approach depends on the source of the artwork you want to trace and how you want to trace it:

■ You can use the autotrace tool to automatically trace any image you bring into Illustrator.

■ You can place an EPS image into an Illustrator document, put it onto a layer, and dim the layer. This action dims any placed image on the layer without dimming any other artwork on that layer.

To trace over a placed image:

1. Create a new layer.

2. Perform the following steps:

   a. Choose File > Place to place an image onto the layer.

   b. Copy the image, and paste it onto the layer.

   c. Dim the layer by double-clicking the layer's name in the Layers palette, selecting the Dim Images option, and clicking OK. This dims any image on the layer.

   d. Trace over the image using the pen tool or pencil tool.

Moving and Aligning Objects

Editing your artwork is made easy in Adobe Illustrator by means of tools that allow you to move and arrange objects precisely. Adobe Illustrator provides tools that let you measure and align objects, group objects so that they are treated as a single unit, and selectively lock and hide objects. In addition, the Transform palette provides you with an interactive placement and transformation tool that enables you to specify the position and relative shape of an object.

Moving and Copying Objects

You can move objects in your artwork by cutting them from one spot and pasting them into another, by dragging them, and by using the arrow keys, the Move dialog box, the Transform Each dialog box, and the Transform palette. Dragging also enables you to copy objects between open Illustrator and Photoshop documents.

Deleting Objects

Deleting an object removes it permanently. To delete an object:

1. Select the object.
2. Press the Delete key, or choose Edit > Clear.

Rotating X and Y Axis

When you open a new document, the x and y axes are parallel to the horizontal and vertical sides of the window. You can rotate the axes by specifying an angle of constraint in the General Preferences dialog box. Rotating the axes is useful if your artwork contains elements that are rotated to the same angle, such as a logo and text displayed on a 20-degree angle. Instead of rotating each element you add to the logo, you can simply rotate the axes by 20 degrees. Everything you draw will be created along the new axes. You can then use the Shift key to constrain the movement of one or more objects so that they move in a precise horizontal, vertical, or diagonal direction relative to the current orientation of the x and y axes. Press Shift while dragging or drawing to limit movement to the nearest 45-degree angle. To rotate the axes:

1. Choose File > Preferences > General.
2. In the Constrain Angle text box, enter the angle at which you want the axes rotated. If you enter a positive number, the axes are rotated counterclockwise. If you enter a negative number, the axes are rotated clockwise.
3. Click OK.

Notes:

1. The rotation of the axes is saved in the Adobe Illustrator's Preferences file; it therefore affects new artwork in all documents until you change its value or delete the Preferences file.
2. The following objects and actions are aligned along the new axes:
   - Text objects, gradient angles you draw with the gradient tool, and objects you draw with the rectangle, ellipse, or graph tool
   - Scaling, reflecting, and shearing
   - Moving objects with the arrow keys
   - Any objects or operations to which you apply constraint (by holding down the Shift key while performing the action) limiting them to 45-degree multiples relative to the axes
   - The angle reported in the Info palette

3. The following objects and actions are not affected by the new axes:

- Objects that already exist
- Rotating and blending
- Drawing with the pencil or autotrace tool

Stacking Objects

You can stack two or more objects on top of each other. The order in which they are drawn determines how they display when they overlap. Stacking is used to make masks. You can change the stacking order, also called the painting order, of objects in your artwork at any time. This is done using the Object > Arrange menu. You can also create multiple layers to control the way overlapping objects are displayed. Grouping objects often affects the way the objects are stacked relative to nongrouped objects.

Using the Transform Palette

The Transform palette displays information about selected objects. You can use this palette to move, scale, rotate, and resize objects. To use the Transform palette:

1. Click Window > Show Transform.
2. Select the object.
3. Do one of the following:
   - To select the reference point from which you are modifying the object, click a handle on the square representing the object's bounding box on the palette.
   - To move an object horizontally, enter a value in the X text box.
   - To move an object vertically, enter a value in the Y text box.
   - To change the width of an object, enter a value in the W text box.
   - To change the height of an object, enter a value in the H text box.
   - To rotate an object, enter a new angle between 0 and 360 degrees in the Angle text box.
   - To shear an object, enter a value in the Shear text box.
4. Press Tab and Enter to apply the change.

Using the Measure Tool

Use the measure tool to determine the distance between any two points. Click the measure tool, click the first point, then the second. You can also click and drag to the second point. Hold down the Shift key to constrain the tool to multiples of 45 degrees. Check the Info palette to see the distance between the clicked points. The Info palette displays the horizontal and vertical distances based on the x and y axes, the absolute horizontal and vertical distances, the total distances, and the angle measured. Use the Units & Undo Preferences or Document Setup dialog to set the unit of measure.

Using Guides and Grids

Use background grids to help align text and graphic objects. You can also create and display alignment outlines, called *guides*. Grids are displayed as lines or dots over the image area. They do not print. If you want to place an alignment guide on the page, draw a line, rectangle, or circle and then define it as a guide. Like gridlines, objects that serve as guides do not print. Guides and grids provide similar controls:

- Selected artwork and tools snap to a guide or a grid when they are dragged within a distance that you define in the Grid and Guide Preferences dialog box.

- Grid spacing, along with guide and grid color and style, are the same for all images and are set in the Grid and Guide Preferences dialog box.

Grouping and Ungrouping Objects

Grouping several objects together causes them to be treated as a single unit. Once grouped, you can move or transform the objects within the group without affecting their relative positions, colors, line widths, etc. An example might be to group all objects in a map inset so it can be moved and scaled like a single object. You can also nest groups, i.e., combine a group with one or more other groups or individual objects. Illustrator "remembers" how group entities are created, so you can ungroup in reverse order. To group or ungroup objects:

1. Select the objects to be grouped or ungrouped. Selecting part of an object and grouping it will group the entire object.

2. Click Object > Group (Ctrl+G) or Object > Ungroup (Ctrl+Shift+G).

Locking and Hiding Objects

The Lock and Hide commands isolate parts of an illustration. This prevents them from being changed while you work on other nearby or overlapping objects. Therefore, when an object is locked or hidden, you can't select or modify it. The Hide command makes one or more selected objects invisible; this can improve performance when working on large, complex illustrations. Locked objects remain locked when files are closed and reopened. However, hidden objects reappear when files are reopened. You can only lock or hide entire objects. Selecting part of an object (anchor

points or segments) and locking or hiding it affects the entire object. To lock or hide artwork, choose from the following options:

■ To lock objects, first select the objects and then choose Object > Lock.

■ To lock all unselected objects, press Option (Macintosh) or Alt (Windows) and choose Object > Lock.

■ To hide a selected object, select the object and choose Object > Hide Selection.

■ To hide all unselected objects, press Option/Alt and choose Object > Hide Selection.

Modifying Shapes and Applying Special Effects

Illustrator provides a variety of tools and dialogs that permit modifications to your drawing entities. Here, several of these are explored.

Using the Transformation Tools

The transformation tools include rotate, reflect, scale, shear, and blend. Use these five tools to transform selected drawing objects. You can also use transform dialog boxes to supply numeric values, to preview the transformation before applying it, and to select other transformation options.

Tip: Transformation dialog boxes and commands can be opened by using context-sensitive menus. Hold down the right mouse button to display context-sensitive menus.

Rotating Objects
You can rotate an object around a fixed point that you select. The default point of origin is an object's center point. You can copy while rotating to create radial symmetry. A few applications of this technique include drawing one blade of a propeller and then rotating and copying it at 120-degree increments for a three-bladed prop. Use the same technique to draw the fronds of a palm tree or petals of a flower.

Reflecting
A selected object is reflected by flipping it around an invisible axis. You control the reflection point by specifying the axis line. You can create a mirror image of the selected object by copying while reflecting.

Scaling
You can enlarge or reduce a selected object by *scaling* it. You can scale horizontally or vertically, i.e., stretch or shrink in a single direction. You can scale both vertically and horizontally by selecting a corner and dragging diagonally. You can select the point of origin or use the default point of origin, which is the object's center point.

Shearing

Use the shear tool to slant or skew an object along an axis that you specify. Copying while shearing is ideal for creating an object's shadow. You can shear vertically, horizontally, or in both directions.

Distorting

Use the Free Distort filter to vary the size and shape of a selected object by dragging the corner points of a Distort box. The four outermost points of the selected object are represented in this box. The object's shape distorts as you drag the corner points of the box. To distort an object:

1. Select the object you want to distort.

2. Choose Filter > Distort > Free Distort. The object's image is shown in the Distort box. (If you don't want to see the object as you distort it, deselect the Show Me option.)

3. Drag any of the four corner points to distort the object. (To return the object to its original shape and try again, press Reset.)

4. Click OK.

Blending

Use the blend tool to create a series of intermediate objects and colors between two selected objects. You can blend between two open paths, such as two different lines, or between two closed paths, such as a circle and a square. The blend tool can produce airbrush effects such as complex shading, highlighting, and contouring depending on the way the blended objects are painted.

Tip: The blend tool is intended to create shaped blends made from a series of individual objects, each having a single stroke, fill color, or both. To create linear or radial blends between two or more colors, use the Gradient palette. For more information, see Creating and working with gradient fills in the online help.

About the Ink Pen Filter

The Ink Pen filter produces textured gradations, such as cross-hatching and irregular random textures. An example is the simulation of wood grain to achieve the look of a pen and ink drawing. The Ink Pen filter converts a selected object into a mask and then draws lines or shapes behind it. The shapes created by the Ink Pen filter are objects that can use a lot of program memory. To assure satisfactory performance during development of your illustration (to retain as much memory as possible during your

drawing tasks), apply your pen and ink effects as the final step in work. In other words, lay out the entire drawing, paint it, apply the ink pen effects, and save and print it.

The hatch style is the underlying design element of the ink pen effect. Use the hatch settings in the Ink Pen Effects dialog to adjust the hatch design. If you wish, you can create your own ink pen designs by drawing or selecting an object, naming it as a hatch in the Ink Pen Hatches dialog box, and then applying it to artwork using the Ink Pen Effects dialog box. Be sure to experiment with the application of different hatches before creating your own.

Special Effects

You can apply a variety of special effects to drawn objects using *filters* that change the shape and path direction of a selected object. Available filters include:

- Roughening
- Scribbling and tweaking
- Twirling
- Punking and bloating
- Rounding corners
- Adding drop shadows
- Changing gradients and patterns into objects
- Changing vector graphics into bitmap images

Using the Pathfinder Commands to Modify Shapes

The Pathfinder commands combine, isolate, and subdivide objects, in addition to building new objects formed by the intersections of objects, as shown in the Pathfinder Gallery. Most Pathfinder commands create *compound paths*, where a compound path is a group of two or more paths that are painted so that overlapping paths can appear transparent. Except where noted, the objects created by all Pathfinder commands are assigned the same paint style as the top object in the current layer's stack. To use the Pathfinder commands:

1. Select the objects you wish to modify.

2. Use Object > Pathfinder to locate and use one of the following Pathfinder commands.

Unite Command—Traces the outline of all selected objects as if they were a single, merged object. Any objects inside the selected objects are deleted.

Intersect Command—Traces the outline of all overlapping shapes in the selected objects, ignoring any nonoverlapping areas. This command works on two objects at a time.

Exclude Command—Traces all nonoverlapping areas of the selected objects, making overlapping areas transparent. In the areas where an even number of objects overlap, the overlap is made transparent; anywhere an odd number of objects overlap, the overlap is filled.

Minus Front Command—Subtracts the frontmost selected objects from the backmost object. You can use this command to delete areas of your illustration by adjusting the stacking order. For information about the stacking order, see Stacking objects.

Minus Back Command—Subtracts the backmost selected objects from the frontmost object. You can use this command to delete areas of your illustration by adjusting the stacking order. For information about the stacking order, see Stacking objects.

Divide Command—Divides a piece of artwork into its component filled faces (a face is an area undivided by a line segment). The resulting faces can then be ungrouped and manipulated independently.

Tip: If the Divide and the Outline Will Extract Unpainted Artwork option is on in the Pathfinder Options dialog box, any unfilled objects remaining in the selected artwork are deleted when you apply the Divide or the Outline command.

Outline Command—Divides an object into its component line segments, or edges. Each edge can be ungrouped and independently manipulated. This command is useful for preparing an image when you need to create a trap for overprinting objects.

Trim Command—Removes the part of a filled object that is hidden. It does not merge objects of the same color.

Merge Command—Removes the part of a filled object that is hidden. It merges any adjoining or overlapping objects filled with the same color.

Crop Command—Divides an image into its component filled faces and then deletes all the parts of the image that fall outside the boundary of the topmost object.

Repeat Pathfinder Command—Repeats the last Pathfinder command using the previous settings.

Note: Applying Pathfinder commands to complex selections, such as blends, may require large amounts of RAM.

Converting Strokes to Filled Objects

The Outline Path command traces the outline of all stroked paths within the selected artwork and substitutes a filled object having the same width as the original stroked path. This command modifies the outline of an object more than if it were only a stroke. You can also use the Outline Path command to create an overlay of your original artwork that strips out all stroked lines and replaces them with compound filled paths. The Outline Path command is particularly useful when you prepare artwork for trapping color separations. To create an outline of your artwork:

1. Select the artwork you want to outline. The image can contain both filled and stroked paths, but only stroked paths are outlined.

2. Choose Object > Path > Outline Path. The outline replaces the original artwork and becomes the selected object.

Cutting Objects

Use the Object menu's Slice command and the knife tool in the toolbox to cut objects into a desired shape. Cut objects must be ungrouped. The Slice command lets you use a selected object like a stencil to cut through other objects. The Slice command slices overlapping objects into discrete shapes according to the selected object's boundaries, and it discards the original selection. The knife tool slices an object along a freehand path that you draw.

Working with Compound Paths

A compound path is made up of two or more overlapping objects that are combined into a single compound object. The Compound Paths command is used to create paths that have transparent interior spaces where the original objects once overlapped (such as the interiors of the letters o and g). This method lets you create objects that are more complex than can be created using common drawing tools or Pathfinder commands. Use the direct selection tool to select part of a compound path, as compound paths act as grouped objects.

Tip: If you use complex shapes as compound paths, or if you use several compound paths in a file, you may have problems printing the file. If you experience printing problems, simplify or eliminate the compound paths.

Working with Masks

Masks crop part of an image so that only a portion of the image appears through a shape or shapes you create. In Adobe Illustrator, you mask objects by using the Make Mask command. You can select all masks in your artwork by using the Select Masks command.

Tip: If you use complex shapes as masks, or if you use several masks in a file, you may experience problems when printing the file. If this occurs, either simplify or eliminate the masks.

To see whether an object is a mask:

1. Select the object.
2. Choose File > Selection Info to see the status of the selected object in the Selection Info dialog.

Using Filters on Bitmap Images

Adobe Illustrator includes a number of filters that can be used to apply special effects to imported bitmap images. Examples of special effects include mosaic, special lighting, image distortion, and a variety of others. Some filter effects can be memory intensive, especially when applied to a high-resolution bitmap image. Use the following techniques to improve performance:

- Change the settings. Some filters are extremely memory intensive, such as the Glass filter. Try different settings to increase the speed of the filter.

- If you plan to print to a grayscale printer, convert a copy of the bitmap image to grayscale before applying filters. When you apply a filter to a color bitmap image and then convert it to grayscale, you may experience a different outcome compared to applying the same filter to a grayscale version of the image.

Plug-In Filters

Adobe Illustrator can use plug-in filters from other Adobe products such as Adobe Photoshop as well as plug-in filters supplied by third-party software

developers. Installed plug-in filter names are listed in the Filter menu and work the same as built-in filters.

Previewing and Applying Filters

Choosing the appropriate submenu command from the Filter menu accesses filters. You can check Illustrator's filter sample gallery to view filter examples. The last filter selected appears at the top of the menu. You can preview many Illustrator filters before they are applied. Applying a filter to large bitmap images can be time consuming. (Illustrator displays a progress dialog when applying a filter.) Therefore, it's a good idea to check the Preview box to determine a filter's effect before actually applying it. To preview and apply a filter:

1. Select the bitmap image that you want to filter.

2. Choose a filter from the submenus in the Filter menu. If a filter name includes ellipsis points, a dialog box appears.

3. If a dialog box appears, enter values or select options.

4. To preview the effect with the filter's preview box, use the following navigation methods:

   ■ Drag in the image window to center a specific area of the bitmap image in the preview box.

   ■ To see part of the image that is not visible, move the cursor inside the preview box to activate the hand tool. Drag to see the bitmap image.

   ■ Use the + or – button under the preview box to zoom in or zoom out on the preview. A flashing line beneath the preview size indicates that Illustrator is still rendering the preview.

5. Click OK to apply the filter.

Using the Color Halftone Filter

The Pixelate > Color Halftone filter simulates the effect of using an enlarged halftone screen on each channel of the bitmap image. For each channel, the filter divides the image into rectangles and replaces each rectangle with a circle. The circle size is proportional to the brightness of the rectangle. To use the Color Halftone filter, you specify a screen-angle value for each channel of the image. To use the Color Halftone filter:

1. Choose Filter > Pixelate > Color Halftone.

2. Enter a value in pixels for the maximum radius of a halftone dot, from 4 to 127.

3. Enter a screen-angle value (the angle of the dot from the true horizontal) for each channel, as follows:

   ■ Grayscale bitmap images use only channel 1.

- In RGB bitmap images, channels 1, 2, and 3 correspond to the red, green, and blue channels.
- In CMYK bitmap images, the four channels correspond to the cyan, magenta, yellow, and black channels, respectively.
- Click Defaults to return all the screen angles to their default values.

4. Click OK.

5. Click Open.

Using the Object Mosaic Filter

The Object Mosaic filter creates sharp definition in an image by clustering pixels of similar color values together into individual tiles. You can control the tile size, the spacing between tiles, and the total number of tiles, and you can preserve the proportions of the original image when creating the mosaic copy. The Object Mosaic filter works with any type of bitmap image format Illustrator can place, as well as with bitmap images created with the Rasterize command. When the Object Mosaic filter acts on a bitmap image, it creates a tiled copy, leaving the original bitmap image intact. To create a tiled effect on a copy of a bitmap image:

1. Select a bitmap image.

2. Choose Filter > Create > Object Mosaic. The dimensions of the bitmap image are displayed at the top left of the Object Mosaic dialog box.

3. Choose from the following options:

- Enter New Size values to determine the length and width of the mosaic in points.
- Enter Tile Spacing values to determine the distance in points between each tile in the mosaic.
- Enter Number of Tiles values to determine the number of tiles horizontally and vertically in the mosaic.
- Choose Height or Width in the Constrain Ratio option to lock the height dimensions or the width dimensions to those of the original bitmap image. Choosing Height calculates the appropriate number of tiles to use for the width of the mosaic, based on the original number of tiles for the height. Choosing Width calculates the appropriate number of tiles to use for the height of the mosaic, based on the original number of tiles for the width.
- Select the Color option or the Gray option to have the result appear as a color or grayscale image.

4. Click OK.

Painting

The current paint attributes are shown in the Fill and Stroke boxes in the toolbox when painting paths and objects. Filling an object paints the area enclosed by the path. Stroking an object outlines the path. Paths can be filled, stroked, or filled and stroked. Filling and stroking affect closed and open paths differently. Open paths fill as if a straight line connects the endpoints. By default, new artwork is drawn with a white fill color and a black stroke color. You can paint objects in your artwork with black, white, shades of gray, process and spot colors, gradients, and patterns. You can also use the eyedropper and paint bucket tools to copy paint attributes from one object to another.

Tip: Line attributes are available only when you stroke a path. The line attributes, which are available in the Stroke palette, control whether a line is solid or dashed, the dash style for a dashed line, the stroke weight, the miter limit, and the styles of line joins and line caps. You can also use the Stroke palette to make a line wavy or zigzag.

The Color and Swatches Palettes

When you create a new object or when you want to change the paint attributes of an existing object, use the toolbox, the Color palette, or the Swatches palette to change the object's paint attributes. Use the Fill and Stroke boxes in the toolbox to select an object's fill and stroke, to swap the fill color with the stroke color, and to return the fill and stroke to their default colors. Type "x" to switch between the fill and stroke selections. The Color, Gradient, and None buttons are located below the Fill and Stroke boxes. Click these buttons to change the selected fill or stroke to a color or gradient, or to remove the fill or stroke from the selected object.

Use the Color palette to edit and mix colors. This applies to colors that you create or colors that you have selected from the Swatches palette, from an object, or from a color library. To edit the fill or stroke color using the Color palette:

1. Choose Window > Show Color.

2. Do one of the following:

   ■ Position the pointer over the color bar (the pointer turns into the eyedropper), and click.

   ■ Choose a color model from the pop-up menu, and use the sliders to change the color values. You can also enter numeric values in the text boxes next to the color sliders.

The Swatches palette contains the colors, gradients, and patterns supplied with Illustrator as well as those that you create and save. You can add colors and gradients to the Swatches palette by dragging from the Color palette, from the Gradient palette, or from the toolbox Fill and Stroke boxes to the Swatches palette. When you create new colors, gradients, or patterns and store them in the Swatches palette, they are only associated with the current document. Each new document can have a different set of swatches stored in its Swatches palette. To choose a color, gradient, or pattern from the Swatches palette:

1. Choose Window > Show Swatches.

2. Click a color, gradient, or pattern swatch in the Swatches palette. The selected color, gradient, or pattern appears in the Color palette and in the Fill box or Stroke box in the toolbox.

The Swatch Libraries command is a Swatch-related command that allows you to import colors, patterns, and gradients from other Illustrator documents into a palette. This command also lets you import entire color libraries from other color systems, such as the PANTONE® Process Color System (PCS).

Painting by Dragging and Dropping

You can drag a color directly from the Fill or Stroke box, the Color palette, or the Gradient palette and drop it onto an object. Dragging and dropping provides the ability to paint objects without having to first select them. When you drag, the paint attribute is applied to either the object's fill or stroke, depending on whether the Fill or the Stroke box is currently selected.

Modifying Colors

A number of tools are available to select, modify, and edit colors in your document. You can use the Swatches palette to make global changes to spot colors throughout a document. Use selection filters to select objects with similar characteristics. Use the paint bucket and eyedropper tools to copy and place paint attributes from one object to another. Use Illustrator filters as shortcuts to changing color attributes, selecting objects by color, or blending colors between objects. Use the Color palette to specify the color you want applied to the black portion of 1-bit TIFF images. To colorize a 1-bit TIFF image:

1. Select the 1-bit TIFF image.

2. Use the Color palette to paint the image with black, white, a process color, or a spot color.

Creating Gradient Patterns

Gradient fills and patterns give you a variety of gradient patterns with which to work. A gradient fill is a graduated blend between two or more colors or tints of the same color. You use the Gradient palette to create your own gradients and, in combination with the Color palette and Swatches palette, to modify existing gradients. You can also add intermediate colors to a gradient to create a fill defined by multiple blends among colors. Gradient colors can be assigned as CMYK process color, RGB process color, or a spot color. When a gradient is printed or separated, mixed-mode gradient colors are all converted to CMYK process color.

Create a pattern by first drawing the artwork you want to use as a basis for the new pattern. Then drag the artwork to the Swatches palette or use the Define Pattern command. You can use any artwork for a pattern (with the exception of masks or gradients), or you can design a pattern from scratch with any of Illustrator's tools. Patterns are customized by resizing, moving, transforming, or coloring their objects.

Note: Libraries of patterns are included on the Illustrator CD-ROM. A smaller collection of patterns is available with the Startup file and program disks.

For best results, use fill patterns to fill objects and path patterns to outline objects, as patterns intended for filling objects (fill patterns) are different from those designed to outline paths (path patterns).

Outlining Paths with Patterns

The Path Pattern filter lets you outline objects with patterns and create borders, frames, and decorative and ornamental effects. Path patterns differ from fill patterns in their design, tiling, and names. A path pattern typically ends with a suffix indicating whether it applies to the side, outer corner, or inner corner of a path. You can choose path patterns from the Path Pattern library of almost 200 designs located on the Illustrator CD. The Illustrator Startup file and program disks contain a smaller collection of these designs. To outline a path with a pattern:

1. Create the artwork that you will outline with patterns. For best results, fill and stroke the artwork with None. (Work in Artwork view to see your artwork better.)

2. Select the object that you will outline with a pattern.

3. Open the file containing the path pattern that you want to use. Note that each Illustrator path pattern file contains up to six separate designs.

4. Choose Filter > Stylize > Path Pattern.

5. From the scrolling list, select a pattern. To select no pattern for part of a path, select None from the list. You can choose a different pattern for each part of the path.

Do one of the following:

■ Click the Sides box to select the option and apply the pattern to the sides of an object.

■ Click the Outer Corner box to apply the pattern to the corners of a rectangle or polygon.

■ Click the Inner Corner box to apply the pattern to the interior corners of an irregularly shaped object.

To adjust how the pattern fits the path, choose one of the following Tile Fitting options:

■ Stretch to Fit to lengthen or shorten the pattern tile to fit the object. This option can result in uneven tiling.

■ Add Space to Fit to add blank space between each pattern tile to apply the pattern proportionately to the selected object. You can let Adobe Illustrator determine the amount of space between tiles, or you can specify an amount in the Tile Size Spacing text box (for example, if you are using noncontinuous designs such as dots or discrete shapes).

■ Approximate Path if you are applying a pattern to a rectangle and want the pattern to tile evenly. This option applies the pattern slightly inside or outside the path, rather than centered on the path, to maintain even tiling.

To scale the pattern, in the Tile Size section, enter a new width or height for the pattern tile. If applying a pattern to a circle, use a width smaller than the circle's diameter for a donut effect, or match the tile's width to the circle's diameter for a solid effect.

Note: Illustrator path patterns use different file extensions to indicate the type of design:

■ Side for side
■ Outer for outer corners
■ Inner for the inner corners

Using Layers

All good drawing programs employ layers. You can organize your work into sections and place each section on a different layer. Once there, each

layer can be edited and viewed as an individual unit. Every Illustrator document contains at least one layer. Creating multiple layers gives you control over how illustrations are printed, displayed, and edited. The following rules affect how objects appear in layers:

■   Within each layer, objects are stacked according to the order in which they were painted.

■   Grouped objects are on the same layer; if you group objects from different layers, all objects are placed on the frontmost layer of the group, directly behind the frontmost object in the group.

■   When masking objects on different layers, objects on intermediate layers become part of the masked artwork.

Each layer is like an individual clear sheet that contains one or more objects. You can view objects down through layers as long as there are no filled objects to obstruct your view. You can create and modify objects on any layer without affecting the artwork on any other layer. You can also display, print, lock, and reorder layers as independent entities.

Selecting Layers

The Layers palette, accessed with Window > Show Layers, lets you create multiple levels of artwork that reside on separate, overlapping layers within the same document. You can also hide and lock layers and choose options for determining how layers are displayed and printed. All new objects are placed on the current layer. You can select a different layer by selecting a layer name in the Layers palette.

Duplicating and Merging Layers

Layers can be duplicated and merged. Duplicating a layer places a new layer above the currently selected layer, duplicates all the layer options from the original, and copies all objects from the original layer. Mask objects that affect multiple layers are released, i.e., the paths are copied onto the duplicate layer but are no longer masks. When you merge layers, the contents of all selected layers are merged into the top selected layer. Objects on merged layers retain their original painting order. Layers are easily duplicated or merged using the Duplicate Layers or Merge Layers command on the pop-up menu.

Moving Objects Between Layers

You can move objects from one layer to another by simply selecting and cutting from one layer, selecting another layer, and then pasting them. Use the Paste Remembers Layers option to paste objects back to the layer from which they originated.

Changing the Layer Order

You can change the order in which layers are arranged by dragging them from one location to another within the Layers palette.

Deleting, Locking, and Hiding

Layers are easily deleted, locked, and hidden. Use the Delete Layer command, click the Trash button, or drag the layer onto the Trash button within the Layers palette to remove a layer. Use the Lock command (or Ctrl+L) on the Object menu to lock a layer. When locked, entities on the locked layer cannot be edited. Hiding a layer has an effect similar to that of choosing Hide from the Object menu. Hidden layers cannot be viewed or edited. To hide or display a layer, click the eye icon to the left of the layer name. This turns off the Show option in the Layer Options dialog. Click again to turn the option back on and to redisplay the layer.

Displaying Layers in Artwork View

When you display a layer in the Artwork view, all objects on the layer are displayed as outlines. To display a layer in Artwork view, do one of the following:

■ Press Ctrl and click the eye icon to the left of the layer name.

■ Deselect the Preview option in the Layer Options dialog box.

To display all inactive layers in Artwork view:

1. Select the layer or layers you want to remain in Preview view.

2. Do one of the following:

   ■ Choose Artwork Others from the Layers palette pop-up menu.

   ■ Press Alt+Ctrl and click the eye icon.

Coloring Layers

You can apply different colors to your layers to make it easy to distinguish one layer from another. By default, the first layer uses light blue, the second red, the third green, and each subsequent layer uses a different color. Changing the layer color makes it easier to contrast the layer color with that of the drawn entities. If your artwork is primarily drawn in blue, set the layer color to black or red so that layer selection marks are easier to see as you work on the layer. Perform the following steps to specify a layer color:

1. Use the Layers palette to select a layer.

2. In the Layers palette pop-up menu, double-click a layer name or use Layer Options.

3. Pick a color for the drawn entities and click OK.

Dimming Images

The Layer Options dialog's Dim Images option is used to dim raster images on the selected layer. The option converts raster images back into dots, making it easier to edit objects on top of the image. The Dim Images option is ideal as a design tool. You can lay out artwork on top of raster images or use the raster image as a basis for tracing. To dim a raster image:

1. Use the Layers palette to choose a layer containing a raster image.
2. In the Layers palette, click Layer Options from the pop-up menu or double-click the layer's name.
3. Pick the Dim Images option and click OK.

Suppressing Layers from Printing

You can hide a layer to make it nonprintable by deselecting the eye icon. You can also use the Print option in the Layer Options dialog to make a visible layer nonprintable. Print suppression is ideal for outputting just those entities you want to examine, while omitting those that may interfere with clarity. When you put all typed elements on a single layer, you can hide other layers so that the type can be proofread by itself.

Using Type

Illustrator gives you a variety of tools to use with type. You can customize type for use as display type, manipulate type as a graphic object, align type vertically, flow type along and within a path, and wrap type in columns for body text. Illustrator gives you total control over type attributes, including font, type size, leading, kerning, tracking, baseline shift, horizontal and vertical scale, and letter orientation. You can set type attributes before entering your type or select and change the type later to fit a particular image or area. You can also set attributes for several type paths and type containers at once, if they are all selected.

Use the Character and Paragraph palettes to change type attributes. Some type attributes have separate submenus or palettes, eliminating the need to open the Character or Paragraph palette to change a single attribute. Also, you can use shortcut keys to change some common attributes.

Press Enter to apply a value in the Character or Type palette to the selected type object. Press Tab to apply a value and move to the next text box in the palette. Open the Character or Type palette using Type > Character or Type > Paragraph. Choose Show Options from the pop-up menu at the upper right of the Character palette. Choose Show Multinational from the pop-up menu of the Character palette for multilanguage and orientation options.

You can apply colors to type as with most other objects using the Color and Swatches palettes. You can transform type by rotating, scaling, or shearing it. Be sure the type baseline is selected when transforming a type object. Use the Type Orientation command of the Character palette to change the direction of selected type. Use the Create Outlines command to turn selected type into a set of compound paths. Once converted, you can edit and manipulate the type as you would any other graphic object. The Create Outlines command works only with Type 1 and TrueType font outlines.

Importing and Exporting Artwork

Illustrator can import and export a variety of graphic file types using the File > Open and File > Export commands. You can also import a graphic from the clipboard, or drag and drop a graphic from another application.

Printing Documents

As with all Windows applications, Illustrator uses the installed and selected Windows printer. You can limit your printing to one or more selected layers. During the development process, you can print intermediate copies of your illustration. Once the illustration is complete, you can print the finished product. In addition to being able to output to your printer, you can also print your illustration to a file.

Set up your document for printing by using the File > Document Setup selection. Click Print Setup and then click Properties. The dialog box varies slightly with the selected printer. Set the options you want, click OK to return the Properties dialog, and then click OK to finish the operation.

Printing Composites

If you are making color separations, you may want to print a color or grayscale composite proof to check your work or to send to a printer with each set of separations. A composite image helps you to design and proof your artwork and is ideal for checking your separation setup before printing final separations. When a composite is printed, all colors used in the file are printed. Overprinting specified in the illustration does not appear on the composite from most printers. Remember, printers, like color monitors, vary greatly in color reproduction quality. The composites from a color printer cannot be used in place of proofs made by your printer. To print a composite, pick File > Print, choose Composite from the Output pop-up menu, and set any other printing options required prior to clicking OK.

Crop Marks

Crop marks are used by commercial printers to define where the page is trimmed after your illustration is printed. Crop marks are positioned at the

outside corners of your illustration using the Make Cropmarks command. You can also select the Use Default Marks option in the Separation Setup dialog to automatically place crop marks and printer's marks into your separations. You can use the Japanese Crop marks option in the General Preferences dialog to create Japanese-style crop marks.

If you plan to separate a color illustration, be sure to set crop marks in the illustration prior to printing. If you forget to set crop marks, Illustrator sets them for you automatically when creating separations.

Trim Marks

Only one set of crop marks is printed on your illustration. If you need multiple marks, as when printing multiple business cards on a single page or several pages from the same illustration, use trim marks. Use the Trim Marks filter to create trim marks. The Trim Marks filter puts trim marks around an imaginary rectangle drawn around the image area of the object.

Producing Color Separations

The most common way to print color artwork is to produce a positive or negative image of the artwork on paper or film and then transfer the image to a printing plate to be run on a press. To prepare artwork for this process, called *color separation*, you first separate the composite art into the component colors used in the printing process. These are cyan, magenta, yellow, black, plus any spot colors needed to print the artwork. To produce high-quality separations, it helps to be familiar with the basics of printing, including line screens, resolution, process colors, and spot colors. All of these elements are discussed in the *Adobe Print Publishing Guide*, which is included with Adobe Illustrator.

You should make it a point to work closely with the commercial printer who will produce your separations to make sure you are supplying exactly what he or she needs to do a quality job. Following are the basic steps used to create a color separation.

1. Calibrate your RGB monitor to match the CMYK output more closely.

2. Check the colors in your illustration after you finish calibrating your monitor, as the colors may look different. Adjust the colors as necessary to achieve the appearance you want.

3. Set overprint options for colors that should appear transparent. By default, both fills and strokes in Illustrator appear opaque because the top color knocks out the underlying area. Knockouts can be prevented with the Overprint option in the Attributes palette. This option makes overlapping printing inks appear transparent.

4. Create a trap to compensate for on-press misregistration. Misregistration is caused when colors from different plates overlap or adjoin, causing gaps between colors on the final printed output. Commercial printers use a technique called *trapping* to create a small overlapping area between two adjoining colors. The overlapping area is called a *trap*, and helps compensate for gaps between colors in the illustration.

   Illustrator uses two methods for trapping artwork. The first method, the Trap filter, automatically creates a trap for artwork. It is designed for use on simple objects and on objects whose parts can be selected and trapped independently. The second trapping method changes the stroke of individual objects using the Stroke palette. Separate, dedicated trapping programs, such as TrapWise®, are available for trap creation. The *Adobe Print Publishing Guide* that comes with the program provides more information on trapping colors.

5. Place crop marks around the image to be separated. These points should be maintained when creating crop marks for color separations.

   ■ If you are setting crop marks in the original artwork and want the artwork to contain bleed (a margin added to the image so that it can be trimmed after printing), make sure that you extend the artwork past the crop marks to accommodate the bleed.

   ■ If you plan to separate several small pieces of artwork in the same file, you may want to create a set of crop marks or trim marks for each piece of artwork. You might want more than one set, for example, if the file contains several business cards that you plan to separate. To create more than one set of crop marks, draw or place the crop marks in Adobe Illustrator or use the Trim Marks filter.

6. Select the separation options and then print or save the file. Preparing a file for separation includes specifying which printer and halftone screen ruling to use and whether the separation should be a positive or negative image. You can also specify bleed around the illustration. The selected separation settings for the document are saved with the separated file. If a file that has never been separated is opened in Illustrator, the program returns to the default settings.

7. When you have completed setting up the separations, you are ready to print or save your separations.

Note: The output device (printer or imagesetter) you use to print separations must match the PPD file that was specified when setting up the separations. If the PPD file and output device do not match, an error message is displayed and the separations will not print.

Managing Color in Adobe Illustrator

Illustrator's Color Management System (CMS) helps you manage the colors displayed on your computer monitor and printer. The CMS uses industry-wide color-compatibility standards developed by the International Color Consortium (ICC) to ensure that colors appear as they should on your screen and your printer, and to ensure that Illustrator artwork colors appear correctly on other ICC-compliant software applications such as Adobe Photoshop and Adobe PageMaker.

The CMS automatically manages color issues among different color models—CMYK, RGB, and HSB—as well as color issues between your monitor and the final print image. Color management occurs only after you choose the color settings for your system in Illustrator's Color Settings dialog.

Tip: Illustrator color management is dependent on device settings that you set in the Color Settings dialog. To ensure proper color management operation on your system, change the color management settings each time you change monitors or printers.

Adobe Photoshop

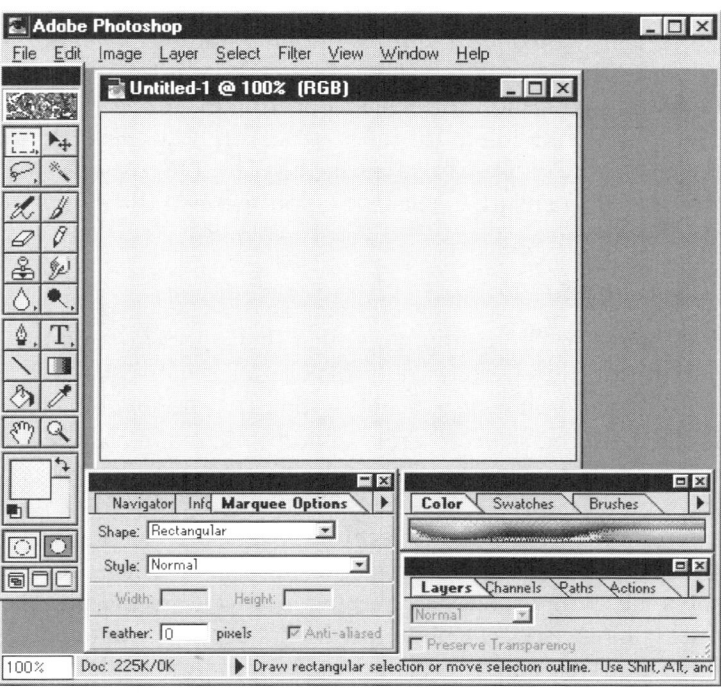

Photoshop is a bitmap image editor that is ideal for rendering photographic images. You can use Photoshop for scaling, cropping, and retouching bitmapped illustrations. These images can be acquired from clipart libraries, digital cameras, camcorder snapshot software, or scanners. Regardless of the method of acquisition, Photoshop gives you all the tools you need to enhance your bitmapped graphics.

A major strength offered by Photoshop is the program's exceptional color control. One professional graphic artist who regularly uses a variety of image editors prefers the color control offered by Photoshop to that of any other competing bitmap image editor.

As you can see from the illustration, Photoshop provides a number of convenient tools and palettes. Here, the program is examined in a fair amount of depth.

Overview

Photoshop's work area includes command menus along the top of the screen, a window containing the current image, and a number of tools and palettes used to edit images and to add new elements to your illustration. Palettes include such items as masks, layers, and channels. Commands and filters can be added to Photoshop menus by installing plug-in modules, which are software programs that add new features to Photoshop.

Images are brought into Photoshop by importing them. Photoshop can import a variety of graphic file formats. Another way to obtain an image is to draw one in Photoshop. Before starting work on an image, a color mode is selected, i.e., RGB, CMYK, HSB, etc. The artist must determine how to get the color displayed on a monitor to look like the color in the printed artwork. If the color isn't calibrated or if you haven't converted the image to CMYK, the printed colors and the displayed colors on the screen may vary. Reproducing color in Photoshop requires an understanding of calibration, image modes, and color correction. Hence, color separation artwork requires that you calibrate your monitor. See Calibrating in Adobe Photoshop: an overview in the online help for information on how this is done. If you are preparing artwork for online use, as in the web, Photoshop's calibration tools are useful to ensure consistent color between different web browsers and monitors.

Modifying Part of an Image

To modify part of an image in Photoshop, you must first select an area for editing. A border identifies the selected area; this border is called a *selection marquee*. Once selected, you can move, copy, paint, or apply any number of special effects to the selected area. In addition, *alpha channels* can be used to save selections as masks. Channels store color and mask information about an image. When a new image is opened, color information channels are automatically created. Therefore, every image contains information channels. Consider a CMYK image. It must have at least four information channels, i.e., one each for cyan, magenta, yellow, and black. Therefore, a channel is like a printing plate in which a separate plate is used to lay down a primary color. Extra channels are sometimes added to

an image to store and edit masks. These extra channels are sometimes referred to as alpha channels.

Duplicating

Use Image > Duplicate to duplicate a selected image. Type a name and click OK. To duplicate without naming, hold down Alt while clicking Image > Duplicate. Select Merged Layers Only to duplicate an image without layers.

Moving

The move tool is used to select and drag an image to a new location. The Info Palette tracks the coordinates of the moved object. When a selection is moved, it is put on a temporary *floating selection* layer, which is displayed in the Layers palette. Once you finish and deselect the move, the image returns to the original, underlying layer. You can press Ctrl and pick the move tool to activate it while another drawing tool is active. There are a few tools that cannot remain selected when the move tool is active: These are the pen, direct selection, and the add-, delete-, and convert-anchor point tools.

Note: Part of an image may be located outside the visible window when you drag or paste a selection onto a layer, apply a transformation, or add type or other drawn items. You can use the move tool to drag portions of the illustration that reside outside the viewable window back into view. You can modify or reposition the image using Free Transform or any of the Transform commands. You can also increase the window (or *canvas*) size to include hidden areas without losing them. When objects exist outside the visible canvas, they cannot be painted or modified.

Copying

Use Edit > Copy to copy a selected item. When a selection is moved within the same image or dragged from one image to another, it can also be copied. The valid drag and drop destination is outlined in boldface when you drag over it. There are times when you can drag and drop a selection between a Photoshop image and another application. You can also cut and paste selections between Photoshop and other applications.

Pasting

A wide range of pasting options are available to control how pasted selections appear in an image. Use the Paste command to paste a cut or copied selection into another part of the image or into another image as a new layer. Use the Layers palette to control the opacity and blending mode of the pasted selection. Use the Paste Into command to paste a selection inside another selection border, which acts as a mask for the pasted selection.

Deleting

Use Edit > Clear or press Backspace to delete a selection. Use Edit > Cut to cut a selection to the clipboard. Use the Preserve Transparency option when deleting a selection on a background or on a layer. This replaces the original location with the background color; when Preserve Transparency is deselected, deleting the original area replaces the area with the layer transparency.

Matting a Moved or Pasted Selection

When an anti-aliased selection is moved or pasted, some of the pixels surrounding the selection are included. This sometimes results in a fringe or halo around the edge of the moved or pasted selection. You can use the Matting command to edit out unwanted edge pixels.

Rotating Images

Use Image > Rotate Canvas and choose one of the following commands to move or rotate a selection:

To	Use
Rotate by a half-turn	180 degree
Rotate clockwise by a quarter-turn	90 degree CW
Rotate counterclockwise by a quarter-turn	90 degree CCW
Flip horizontally, along the vertical axis	Flip Horizontal
Flip vertically, along the horizontal axis	Flip Vertical

Transformations

To rotate, scale, flip, skew, or distort a selection or layer, use the Layer > Transform and Layer > Free Transform commands. The transformation affects all the layers in the linking group when you transform a linked layer. You can apply any combination of transformations in a single operation by using the Free Transform command. If you want to type numeric values for more precise control of your transformations, use the Transform > Numeric command.

Note: Although you can transform selections on the background, you cannot apply transformations to the background as a layer. Transformations can also be applied to an alpha channel by first selecting it in the Channels palette. To transform a layer mask, select its thumbnail in the Layers palette.

Rubber Stamp Tool

Use the rubber stamp tool to paint a copy, or an edited copy, of an image or color into either the same or another image. The Rubber Stamp Clone options are used to make a copy, or sample, of an image and paint a duplicate of the image. Other options are used to paint with a pattern or with an "impressionistic" copy of the image. Painted areas can be restored to their last-saved states.

Tips:

- To display the Rubber Stamp Options palette, double-click the rubber stamp tool; then choose the desired mode.
- To set the opacity, drag the slider.
- For Option, choose a Rubber Stamp option.
- When using one of the Clone options and a sample is wanted with data from all visible layers, select Sample Merged. When this option is deselected, the rubber stamp tool samples only from the data on the active layer.
- When using one of the Clone options, position the pointer on the part of the image you want to sample and use Alt+Click. The sample point is the location from which the image will begin to be duplicated as it is painted.
- To sample from any open Photoshop window without changing the active window, use Alt+Click with the rubber stamp tool.
- To paint with the rubber stamp tool, drag.

Smudge Tool

The smudge tool simulates dragging a finger through wet paint. The tool picks up color from where the stroke begins and pushes it in the direction of the drag.

Tip: Bitmap or indexed-color mode images can't be used with the smudge tool.

Perform the following steps to use the smudge tool:

1. Double-click the smudge tool to display the tool's Options palette.

2. Choose a mode and drag the slider to set the smudge "pressure."

3. Select Finger Painting to smudge the foreground color. If you choose not to use the Finger Painting option, the smudge tool uses the color at the pointer when you begin a stroke (or drag).

4. Click Sample Merged if Finger Painting is deselected and you want to smudge using colors from all visible layers. When the Sample Merged option is deselected, the smudge tool uses colors from the active layer.

5. To smudge an image, select the Finger Painting option and press Alt as you drag.

Focus Tools

The focus tools include:

- The blur tool—Use to blur hard edges or areas in an image to reduce detail.

- The sharpen tool—Use to sharpen soft edges to increase detail and clarity.

These tools cannot be used with bitmap or indexed-color mode images. Perform the following general steps to use the Focus tools:

1. Display the Focus Tools Options palette by double-clicking the blur or sharpen tool.

2. Choose either blur or sharpen as the Tool.

3. Select the mode, then drag the slider to set the tool's "pressure."

4. Drag that portion of the image you want to blur or sharpen.

Toning Tools

Toning tools are used to lighten or darken selected areas of an image. Toning tools include:

- Dodge tool—Use to lighten an area.

- Burn tool—Use to darken an area.

- Sponge tool—Use to change the color saturation or contrast of an area.

Dodging and burning are techniques used by photographers for lightening or darkening an area of a photographic print. To lighten an area of a print, photographers dodge the area by blocking the light that is applied to it during the exposure process. To darken an area, they burn the area by increasing the amount of applied light. Use the sponge tool to increase or reduce the color saturation in an area in small increments.

When using the Grayscale mode, the sponge tool is used to adjust contrast. Gray levels are moved away from or toward the middle gray. Note that the dodge, burn, and sponge tools cannot be used with bitmap or indexed-color mode images.

Type and Type Mask Tools

The type tool is used to add bitmap type to an image. Like most of today's good Windows programs, you can specify the type style, spacing, leading (space between lines), and alignment of the type. Normally, large bitmap characters appear jagged on the screen. However, if you use the Adobe Type Manager (ATM) program, which is installed with Photoshop, or if you use TrueType fonts, characters are almost as smooth and sharp as vector-drawn (or *outline*) type.

The construction of bitmap and vector images is presented in detail at the beginning of this chapter. Recall that bitmap type is created differently from the outline type; bitmap type is much coarser and requires more memory and disk space when saved. Bitmap applications render type at the resolution of the image. If the resolution of an image is 100 pixels per inch (ppi), the resolution of the type is also 100 ppi. Bitmap type cannot be edited once it is placed into the image. For best results, Adobe recommends that you import your Photoshop image into a page-layout program that supports PostScript language type and create the type using that program.

Painting

When painting with Photoshop, the current foreground color is used. The foreground color is displayed in the top color selection box of the toolbox. This color is used when you paint, fill, and stroke (paint the border of) selections. The background color is displayed in the lower color selection box. The background color is used to make gradient fills and to fill erased areas of an image. Black is the default foreground color, and white is the default background color. (If you are viewing an alpha channel, the default foreground and background colors are white and black, respectively.)

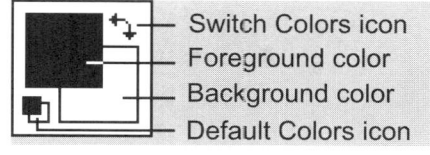

You can reverse the foreground and background colors by clicking the Switch Colors icon in the toolbox. Retrieve the default foreground and background colors by clicking the Default Colors icon in the toolbox. You can change the foreground or background color as follows:

1. Click the top color selection box to change the foreground color.

2. Click the lower color selection box to change the background color.

3. You can choose different colors by using the Color Picker and clicking OK.

 **Tip:** You can type X as a shortcut to quickly switch between the foreground and background colors.

Painting Tools

Painting tools include the paintbrush, airbrush, and pencil tools. Each of these paints with the selected brush and tool pointer. You can save time when working with painting tools by ensuring that the Brushes/Options palette group and the Color/Swatches palette group are open in your work area.

Eraser Tool

Use the eraser tool and the pencil tool's Auto Erase option to replace colors in an image either with the background color or with transparency.

Brushes Palette

Brushes are like pencil or eraser tips or paint brush widths; all can vary from narrow to wide. The Brushes palette contains the brushes you use for the painting and editing. Several round brush sizes are available for the painting and editing tools. Brush settings are retained for each painting and editing tool. This permits you to select a different default brush for each tool. The Brushes palette is also used to create and delete brushes, to define brush options, and to save and load different sets of brushes.

Painting and Editing Options

A number of painting options exist. These include:

- Opacity—Set the opacity used with the gradient fill, pencil, paintbrush, and rubber stamp tools.

- Pressure—Set the pressure applied by the airbrush, smudge, blur, sharpen, and sponge tools.

- Exposure—Set the amount of exposure used by the dodge and burn tools.

- Fade-out rate—Set the fade-out rate of brush strokes applied by the pencil, paintbrush, airbrush, and eraser tools to simulate actual brush strokes.

- Stylus pressure—Set the pressure applied by a digitizing tablet stylus when using the pencil, paintbrush, airbrush, eraser, rubber stamp, smudge, blur, sharpen, dodge, burn, and sponge tools.

- Blending mode—Set the number of pixels affected by a painting or editing tool by selecting a blending mode in a tool's Options palette. Blending encompasses three colors:
  - The base color (original image color)
  - The blend color (color applied by the selected painting or editing tool)
  - The result color (color resulting from the blend)

Filling

Use the Fill command to fill:

- A selection or a layer with a color
- A saved portion of an image
- A pattern

You can also use keyboard shortcuts to fill a selection quickly. To fill a selection or layer using shortcuts:

Select the area or layer you want to fill. Then:

- Press Alt+Backspace to fill with the foreground color.
- Press Alt+Shift+Backspace to apply a foreground color fill only to the areas that contain pixels. This operation retains the layer's transparency.
- Press Ctrl+Backspace to fill with the background color.
- Press Ctrl+Shift+Backspace to apply a background color fill to those areas containing pixels.

To fill a selection or a layer:

1. Select the area you want to fill. To fill an entire layer, select the layer in the Layers palette.

2. Choose Edit > Fill to fill the selection or layer.

3. Press Shift+Backspace to display the Fill dialog box. Then choose one of the following options:

   - Foreground Color, Background Color, Black, 50% Gray, or White—Use to fill the selection with the selected color.
   - Pattern—Use to fill the selection with a pattern.
   - Saved—Use to restore the selected area to its previously saved state.
   - Snapshot—Use to fill the selection with the contents of the snapshot buffer.

4. Choose a mode.

5. Set the opacity.

6. Select Preserve Transparency if you're working in a layer and want to fill only areas containing pixels.

7. Click OK to complete the fill operation.

Stroke Command

Use the Stroke command to apply the foreground color to paint a border around a selection or around the edge of a layer. Like the Fill command, you can select the opacity and blending modes of the fill. Stroke a selection or layer using the following procedure:

1. Select the area or layer you want to stroke.

2. Pick Edit > Stroke.

3. Set the width and location of the border. Width values range from 1 to 16 pixels.

4. Set the opacity.

5. Select a mode.

6. Select the Preserve Transparency option if working in a layer in which you want to stroke only areas that contain pixels.

7. Click OK to stroke the selection or layer.

Eyedropper

Use the eyedropper tool to pick the color from an area of an image as the foreground or background color. The image doesn't have to be active to be used by the eyedropper tool. (When using the eyedropper, clicking a background window doesn't select it as the active window.) You can also designate the size of the sample area read by the eyedropper tool. For example, you can sample the color values of a 3 x 3-pixel area at the pointer. When you change the size of the sample area, the color readouts displayed in the Info palette change accordingly.

Color Palette

The Color palette displays the current foreground and background color values. The sliders are used to adjust the foreground and background colors. To change the foreground or background color:

1. Select Window > Show Color.

2. Select the desired color model from the Color palette menu.

3. Before trying to edit the foreground or background color, check that the corresponding color selection box is selected (check the black outline). If it is not, click the box to select the foreground or background color.

Foreground color
Background color

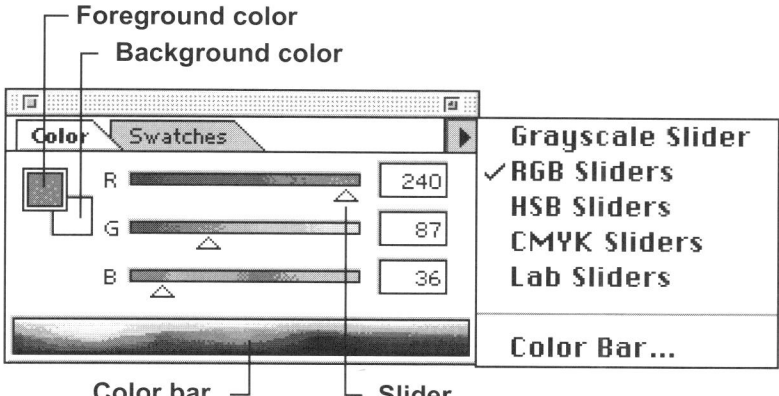

Color bar ─┘   └─ Slider

4. To change a color:

■ Drag the color sliders. Color changes as you drag.

Note: You can turn off the color preview using File > Preferences > General to deselect Dynamic Color Sliders. This may improve performance of computers with slow CPUs or disk access times.

■ Enter numeric values in the boxes to the right of the color sliders.
■ Click the color selection box, choose a color, and click OK.

Note: If an exclamation point inside a triangle is displayed in the Colors palette, an out-of-gamut color exists. This means that the selected color cannot be printed using CMYK inks. A close CMYK equivalent is shown next to the triangle. Click CMYK equivalent to use the equivalent color, which will replace the out-of-gamut color.

Swatches Palette

The current color palette is displayed in the Swatches palette. Use this palette to choose a foreground or background color from the swatches. You can also add or delete colors of your own to create a custom palette. A set of swatches can be saved and reloaded for use in other images. To display the Swatches palette, simply pick Window > Show Swatches. To choose a color:

■ Click a color in the Swatches palette to choose a foreground color.
■ Alt+click a color in the Swatches palette to choose a background color.

Color Picker

Use the Color Picker to select a foreground or background color from either a color spectrum or by typing a numeric value that corresponds to a color. The color picker lets you select colors based on the HSB, RGB, Lab, and CMYK color models. You can also choose from several custom color systems. To display the default Photoshop Color Picker:

■ Click the foreground or background color selection box in the toolbox.

■ Click the active color selection box in the Color palette.

If you've used a custom Color Picker, you can return to the Adobe Photoshop Color Picker by:

1. Choosing File > Preferences > General

2. Choosing Photoshop as the Color Picker name

Painting Modes

Adobe Photoshop features the following painting modes:

■ *Normal*—Each pixel is edited or painted to make it the resulting color. This is the default mode. The normal mode is also called the *threshold* mode when working with a bitmap-mode or indexed-color image.

■ *Screen*—Each channel's color information is examined and then the inverse of the blend and base colors are multiplied. This results in a lighter color. When screened with black, the color does not change. Screening with white produces white. The result is like painting an area with bleach.

■ *Overlay*—Depending on the base color, this mode either multiplies or screens the colors. Patterns or colors overlay existing pixels; highlights and shadows of the base color are kept. The base color is mixed with the blend color to reflect the lightness or darkness of the original color.

■ *Multiply*—This mode multiplies or screens colors. The actual application depends on the base color. Patterns or colors overlay existing pixels, preserving the highlights and shadows of the base color. The base color is mixed with the blend color, which reflects the lightness or darkness of the original color.

■ *Hard Light*—Use this mode to add shadows to an image. The mode multiplies or screens colors. If the blend color is lighter than 50% gray, the image is lightened. If darker than 50% gray, it is darkened. The resulting effect is like shining a bright light on the image area. Painting with either pure black or white results in black or white.

■ *Darken*—This mode selects the base or blend color based on the color information in each channel. Pixel values that are lighter than the

blend color are replaced, while pixels that are darker than the blend color remain unchanged.

■ *Soft Light*—Depending on the blend color, the image color either darkens or lightens. The resulting effect is like shining a diffused spotlight on the image area.

■ *Difference*—This mode determines the color information in each channel and subtracts either the blend color from the base color or the base color from the blend color. If the blend color has a greater brightness value, the base color is subtracted from it; conversely, if the base color has the greater brightness value, the blend color is subtracted.

■ *Exclusion*—This mode produces an effect similar to but softer than the Difference mode. When blending with white, the base color values are inverted. The image remains unchanged when blending with black.

■ *Lighten*—The color information in each channel is examined and the base or blend color, whichever is lighter, is selected as the result color. Pixels that are darker than the blend color are replaced, while pixels that are lighter than the blend color remain unchanged.

■ *Color*—Use this mode to create a result color with the luminance of the base color and the hue and saturation of the blend color. Gray levels within the image are preserved. The Color mode is typically used for tinting color images or for coloring monochrome images.

■ *Luminosity*—This mode creates a color having the hue and saturation of the base color and the luminance of the blend color. It creates an effect opposite from that of the Color mode.

■ *Hue*—This mode is used to produce a color having the luminance and saturation of the base color and the hue of the blend color.

■ *Dissolve*—This mode is used to edit pixels to make them the result color. The resulting color randomly replaces the pixels with either the base or blend color, depending on the opacity of area. This mode works best with the paintbrush and airbrush tools when a large brush is selected.

Channels and Masks

Channels are used to store color information about an image and to store selections. Opening a new image automatically produces color information channels. Additional channels (called *alpha channels*) are used to create and store masks, which permit you to isolate and protect parts of an image. In addition to image masks, there are also layer and "quick" masks.

Layers

Layers are like separate sheets of paper or canvas on which you can draw independently. Therefore, you can use layers to restrict the effects of drawing and editing to specific areas of an image without impacting other objects within your drawing. Like sheets of paper or canvas, each layer has its own foreground images and background. Operations that can be restricted to an individual layer include drawing, editing, pasting, applying masks, and moving entities. A special layer type, called an *adjustment layer*, exists to permit the application of tonal and color correction effects to all the layers of the drawing. Because layers remain independent until merged, you have the freedom to experiment with different graphic effects without worrying about losing valuable work.

Note: Images are created without a background when created using the New dialog's Transparent option. Images without a background or with layers can only be saved in Photoshop format. Images created prior to Photoshop version 3.0 only have one background layer. If you should open an old drawing in Photoshop 4.0 and then add a new layer, you can only save the drawing in Photoshop format.

Filters

Photoshop filters are used to apply special effects to images. This includes adding impressionistic or mosaic effects, adding or reducing noise (pixels with randomly distributed color values), applying lighting effects, distorting images, and producing many other fascinating effects. You can also create custom effects using the Custom filter or the Filter Factory, which is supplied on the Photoshop CD. You can save your own custom filters for use with other images.

Automating Your Work with Macros

Like most good programs, Photoshop includes the ability to store a series of frequently used operations (called a *macro*) and then recall the stored operations for later use with a single keystroke. The Actions palette is used to record, save, and recall your keystrokes and mouse clicks. Macros are ideal for automating common tasks to save time and to avoid the introduction of operator errors once you've perfected and saved them. For example, you may want to automate a File > Save As operation to automatically export drawings in another format to a specific file folder.

CorelDRAW

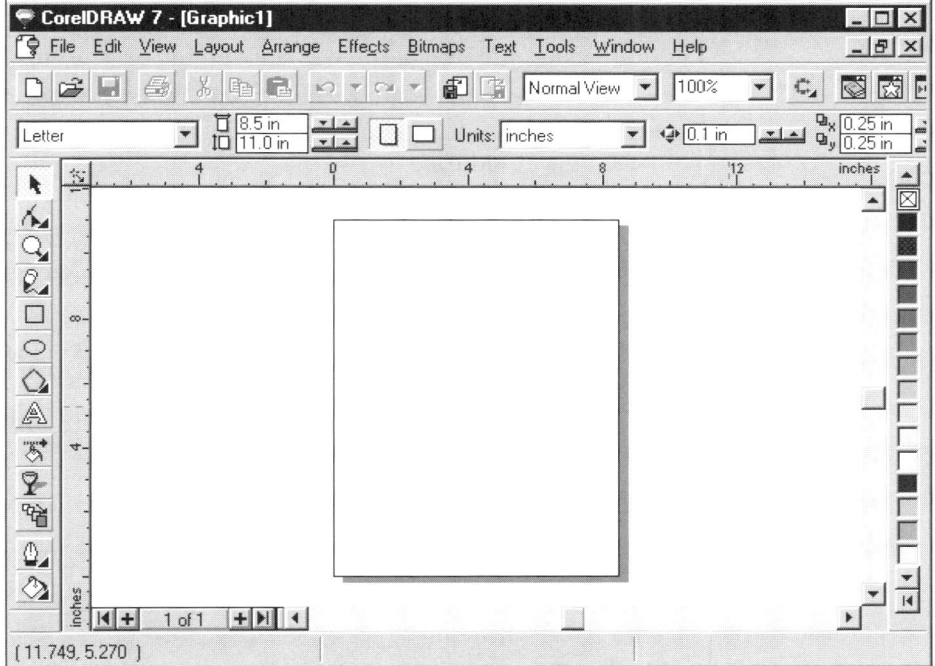

CorelDRAW is a top-end vector illustrating program that is used extensively by professional graphic artists. This program has an extensive tool set, and is perhaps the most sophisticated of today's excellent drawing packages. The CorelDRAW 7 and 8 Graphics Suites are supplied with a number of companion programs and tools. These include the Corel PHOTO-PAINT bitmap editor, a complete library of type fonts, and a companion CD that includes a large selection of clipart files. Also supplied with the Graphics Suite are:

■ Corel OCR-TRACE—Use to convert bitmap images to vector graphics and text. Once converted, objects can be edited independently.

■ CorelDEPTH—Use the supplied tools to create full-color 3D text and graphics; export them in formats compatible with CorelDRAW, Corel Ventura, and many other graphics and page layout applications. A set of wizards guides you through the steps of creating 3D text and graphics.

■ CorelTEXURE—Creates colorful, realistic textures used to enhance professional graphic productions such as charts, pictures, logos, and photo-collages.

- Corel MULTIMEDIA MANAGER—Use to help organize, manage, and manipulate multimedia files.

- Corel CAPTURE—Use to capture any item displayed on the screen; permits using the image in your documents or presentations.

- CorelSCAN—Use to create professional quality images acquired with scanners. Scan an image and correct imperfections without launching a separate photo-editor.

- CorelMEMO—Paste notes to yourself as you work.

- Corel SCRIPT and Corel SCRIPT DIALOG EDITOR—Write scripts (or automating *macros*) for many CorelDRAW tools; this is like creating your own add-ons.

- Corel Color Manager Wizard—Use this wizard to choose or create device profiles for scanners, monitors, and printers.

- Corel Print Wizard—Use to guide you through the steps required to make personal and professional printing choices.

Getting Started with CorelDRAW

When you start CorelDRAW for the first time, you must first select a starting point for your project. You can:

- Create a new drawing
- Create a new drawing using a template
- Open an existing drawing
- Import a file
- Paste a graphic from the clipboard
- Open a file that was recently open

After picking a starting point, begin creating shapes and defining object properties using the powerful repertoire of drawing and editing tools. Then save the file and exit CorelDRAW. The paragraphs that follow examine the CorelDRAW program and its primary features.

Setting Up the Drawing Page

It's important to set up your working environment before you start creating the objects that make up your drawing. The setup procedure includes five discrete tasks:

- Set up the Drawing Page properties using Layout > Page Setup.

- Set up a style template if you want to base your drawing on an existing template or style. Like word processors and desktop publishing software, CorelDRAW uses styles that can be created, saved, and recalled. A typical use would be to apply styles to frequently used text

tags. Templates are based on sets of styles that control the appearance of specific object types, including text, lines, and shapes. For example, you may wish to include a standard 0.02-inch line style, the color black, and 12-point Arial Narrow normal as your type style.

■ Set up measurement and alignment tools, including grids, rulers, and guidelines. These help you draw and position objects by establishing and using a precise coordinate system.

■ Set up the way you want to view your drawing using CorelDRAW's view controls (Zoom flyout and View Manager). Use these controls to change the magnification or reduction of drawing objects. You can also view your drawings as a simple wireframe (hides fills, contours, and extrusions), normal wireframe (hides fills), draft (shows low-resolution bitmaps), normal (shows all fills, objects, and high-resolution bitmaps), or enhanced (the best display quality).

■ Save your settings for the next drawing including the style, page, grid and rulers, file saving, snap, and zoom and view settings. The next time you start a new CorelDRAW drawing you can use the default template; a preset template for a specific drawing type; or a new, customized template that you create to fit a special need.

With this background, you should see how you can establish a convenient work environment every time you begin a new drawing.

Drawing and Shaping Objects

There are line and shape objects, text objects, and bitmap objects. Here, line and shape objects, such as circles, rectangles, and lines, are described. Each shape is an object, and each object is an independent entity that can be changed or moved relative to other objects. Each object has its own fill and outline. When you create a drawing, consider which basic shapes you can use. If you want to draw a building, you can start with rectangles and a triangle. Your shapes do not have to be drawn perfectly the first time, as you can edit each later. When the basic shapes are drawn and in position, begin refining them. Manipulate each relative to size and scale; you can use trial and error until your drawing achieves an acceptable state. Making mistakes isn't a problem, as they can be quickly undone. Before you edit an object's shape, you need to know something about its structure.

All shapes and lines are constructed from *paths*. A path defines the shape of an object. A path has no width or color, although you can apply a width and color by adding an *outline* to it. Paths are initially drawn as a thin black outline. This black outline makes paths visible when initially drawn. Paths can be changed from the default outline style to any outline style, including no outline. However, a path without an outline is only visible in wireframe view. A closed path, where the starting and ending point meet, can contain a *fill*, where a fill is a color or pattern that fills the area within the closed path.

A path is made up of *nodes* and *segments*. A path can change direction at a node point. The part of a path between two adjoining nodes is the segment. Every path must start and end with a node. To change the shape of an object, you drag the object's nodes and segments. Some objects, such as rectangles, can only be shaped in certain ways. If, however, you convert an object into a curve object (including text and rectangles) the curve shape can be changed in an unlimited number of ways.

Tools

CorelDRAW has a large number of tools used to draw shapes, lines, and much more. They are summarized in the lists that follow.

Shapes

Ellipse tool—circles and ellipses
Rectangle tool—squares and rectangles
Polygon tool—polygons and stars
Spiral tool—spiral shapes
Graph Paper tool—graph paper-like grids

Lines, Curves, and Irregular Shapes

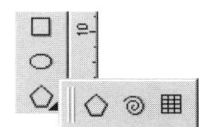

Freehand tool—Drags pencil-like lines across the image area or straight lines by clicking at each node point.

Bezier tool—Draws smooth, precise curves; each mouse-click places a node.

Natural Pen tool—Draws thick curve and variable thickness curve shapes. This tool works like the Freehand tool, except it creates a shape with a closed path rather than creating a simple path.

Dimension, Callout, and Connector Lines

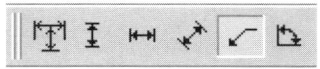

Vertical Dimension tool—Creates vertical dimension lines, which are always vertical regardless of the position of the objects being measured.

Horizontal Dimension tool—Creates horizontal dimension lines, which are always horizontal, regardless of the measured object.

Slanted Dimension tool—Creates slanted dimension lines; slanted dimension lines can be angled allowing them to change with the measured objects.

Angular Dimension tool—Creates dimension lines that measure angles rather than distances.

Callout tool—Draws a line that points to and labels an object. Once the line is drawn, a text cursor prompts you to enter the callout text.

Connector Line tool—Connects objects with a line. Connector lines move when an attached object is moved. Unattached connector lines become ordinary lines.

Note: There are a number of special features associated with dimensioning, Callout, and Connector Line tools. Be sure to check the CorelDRAW documentation to determine their behavior regarding linking dimension and connector lines, *snap points* (points at which connector lines attach to objects), and editing.

Shaping Lines, Curves, and Curve Objects with the Shape Tool

The shape of any curved object can be changed using the Shape tool. This is accomplished by selecting the object and then editing its nodes and segments. Curved objects are created with the Freehand, Bezier, Natural Pen, and Spiral tools. You can convert a rectangle, polygon, ellipse, or even text to a curve, which then permits use of the Shape tool for editing. In addition to nodes and segments, curved objects may also have what are called *subpaths*. You can check for the presence of subpaths by selecting a curved object with the Shape tool to see if nodes appear on more than one curve or shape.

Shaping Ellipses and Rectangles

Use the Shape tool to change the shape of ellipses into an arc or pie shape; use it to round the corners of a rectangle. Although shaping ellipses and rectangles is somewhat limited, shaping an ellipse and rectangle object is both easy and accurate. These objects retain their basic shape, even when shaped. The retention of the basic shape is helpful. For instance, after rounding the corners of a rectangle, you can easily return the corners to square.

If you want to change the shape of an ellipse or a rectangle without the constraints of the basic shape, convert the shape to a curve object. Once it is converted, you have the freedom to shape the object by adjusting the node and segment positions. After an ellipse or a rectangle is converted to a curve object, the absence of the original constraints are no longer available to help you to make a pie shape from an ellipse or simultaneously round all of the corners of a rectangle.

Shaping Polygons and Stars

Use the Shape tool to shape a polygon with *mirror editing*, which lets you shape a polygon or a star in various ways. Mirror editing, in contrast to other node editing, maintains the symmetry of a polygon as its nodes are manipulated. Each node of a polygon maintains symmetry because each node is associated with all other nodes within the object. When a node changes, the change is mirrored in all associated nodes.

If you want to change one node without mirror editing, convert the polygon to a curve object. Once it is converted, you can no longer use mirror editing. You can edit the object with fewer restrictions.

Splitting and Erasing Portions of Objects

Objects are split using the Knife tool and erased using the Eraser tool. Using the Eraser tool or the Knife tool on an object automatically converts that object to a curve object.

Knife tool—Use this tool to open closed paths or to separate objects into separate objects or subpaths. Unlike the Shape tool, the Knife tool permits you to  break any path without having to select the object or convert it to curves. The Knife tool performs its job automatically when clicking on a path.

Eraser tool—Use this tool to erase part of an object. This is much easier than separating one part of an object from another by editing individual nodes. Parts of the selected object are removed by passing over them; the affected paths are closed. When erasing connecting lines, the Eraser tool creates separate subpaths rather than creating new objects.

Transforming Objects

You can use the mouse or controls on the Property Bar or the Transformation Roll-Ups to change the appearance and orientation of objects. Transforming an object includes:

- Repositioning
- Rotating
- Scaling
- Stretching
- Mirroring
- Resizing
- Skewing

Although transformed, the objects retain their basic shapes. The quickest way to transform objects interactively is to manipulate them with the mouse. Although slightly slower, transform commands found in the Property Bar and Transform roll-up provide more control and precision. Note that multiple transformations can be applied to an object, multiple selected objects, or grouped objects. If you wish to reverse a transformation, use the Clear Transformations command. This removes any transformations made to the object, except for changes to its position. Clear Transformations applies to transformations made either with the mouse or the Transform roll-up.

You can see the effect of a transformation and keep the original intact by transforming a copy of the object. Then, you can keep both the original and the copies or delete either the original or the copies to achieve the desired effect.

Moving and Positioning Objects

Drag with the mouse or use the Position roll-up to move an object. You can also *nudge* selected objects in small increments with the cursor keys. Set the nudge distance in the Options dialog.

Rotating Objects

Drag an object's rotation handles for interactive (on-screen) control. Use the Property Bar or Rotation roll-up for more precision.

Skewing Objects

Drag an object's skewing handles to slant objects interactively. Use the Skew roll-up for precision.

Sizing and Stretching Objects

Drag an object's handles to resize or stretch it. Use the Property Bar and Transform Roll-Ups to transform objects with greater precision. Unlike scaling, which changes an object's size by percentage, sizing changes an object's dimensions by specific values. Objects are resized horizontally or vertically. You can also resize an object while retaining its aspect ratio. This changes its horizontal and vertical dimensions without changing the basic shape. When you stretch an object, you change its horizontal and/or vertical dimensions to alter the object's proportions. Just drag one of the object's side handles to stretch it either vertically or horizontally.

Scaling Objects

Drag on an object's handle to scale it vertically and/or horizontally. Use the Property Bar or the Scale roll-up for greater precision. Scaling does not alter the basic shape of an object. Unlike sizing, which changes one or more dimensions by a specified value, scaling changes the object's dimensions using percentage. To scale, change either the horizontal or vertical factor or retain the aspect ratio.

Mirroring Objects

Use the Mirror buttons to reflect any object or objects in your illustration. Mirroring horizontally flips an object from left to right or right to left; mirroring vertically flips an object from top to bottom or bottom to top. If the anchor point of a symmetrical object is located at its center, the object will not seem to move when mirrored.

Undoing, Redoing, and Clearing Transforms

Operations and commands are recorded in memory to permit use of the Undo command to remove an unwanted operation. This restores the drawing to a previous state. The Undo is recorded, which permits you to use the Redo command to redo one or more operations. Use the Clear Transformations command to remove all transformations performed on an object. This affects all transformations except for changes to an object's position.

Filling and Outlining Objects

Each object in your drawing is assigned a default outline and/or fill attribute, depending on the type of object you draw. The line that surrounds the object is its outline. The color or pattern contained within the object is its fill. These attributes vary with the type of object, and can be changed using the Outline and Fill flyout tools. Line and curve objects that have open paths have outline attributes, but cannot have fill attributes. Closed-path objects, such as circles, rectangles, and even text objects, have both outline and fill attributes. Text objects have additional attributes such as typeface, style, point size, line spacing, etc.

Fills

Use the Color Palette to control the fill attributes of your objects. A fill attribute produces a solid color, a fountain fill, a pattern fill, and others. The fill attribute can be turned off or on, depending on what you want to see. You can make an object's fill transparent to display objects behind it.

Outlines

All objects have outlines that can be manipulated in several ways. Outlines have an adjustable size, shape, and color. These attributes can be present in individual objects or to every object you create in a drawing.

Color Styles

The Color Styles roll-up is used to control the color style attribute of your objects. The color style attribute gives you the ability to modify your object's color in a single step. Color styles are also useful in the creation of a series of two or more similar solid colors that can be linked together to establish a "parent-child" relationship. Links between parent and child colors are based on a common hue. Adjusting levels of saturation and brightness creates different shades. This results in a style made up of related colors. The power of color styles becomes apparent when you decide to change a color or hue using the Color Styles roll-up. Making a change to the parent color automatically changes all child colors on all objects within the drawing. Therefore, if you define a color style based on a parent color and decide to change it to another, you don't have to redefine all shades. Instead, light and dark hues of one child color become light and dark hues of another.

Working with Color

CorelDRAW provides many powerful tools to control the colors used in your drawings. You can create and use new colors using these tools, as virtually millions of colors are available with the click of a mouse or stroke of a brush. It's possible to display more colors on your monitor using the RGB color system than you can print on paper using the CMYK color spectrum. Therefore, there is a definite need for tools that help users deal with color choices, since there should be a reasonable amount of consistency between what is displayed and what is printed.

Calibrating Your Color Devices

It is recommended that you use the Corel Color Manager to calibrate your display before you begin creating and editing a series of drawings. To avoid surprises when a commercial printer prints your document, the Color Manager can be used to control the way colors are selected, converted, and produced on your hardware devices. Corel Color Manager ensures that scanners, monitors, and printers are synchronized with your Corel software. Even if you don't have a scanner or color printer, it's still important to calibrate your system.

Color Models

Nine different color models are included with CorelDRAW 7, where a color model is contained on a chart of colored swatches. The color charts are used to select colors for your images. Color models use set mathematical values to provide a color measurement standard.

Color Palettes and Color-Matching Systems

Color palettes contain a collection of colors. The Color roll-up, on-screen Color Palette, and Uniform Fill dialog all display color palettes from which to pick. Other color palettes within CorelDRAW are from color-matching systems. Color-matching systems are color collections that are provided by companies that specialize in color reproduction. These permit color definition based on internationally accepted standards. To select a standard process color for your printed output, pick one using a swatch book from a universally accepted color-matching system. The most common example of an internationally accepted process color standard is the PANTONE Process Colors (i.e., PANTONE S184-6).

Arranging and Organizing Objects

Several tools are available to arrange and organize objects in drawings. Simple tools are used to do such things as copy, group, and combine objects. To access advanced tools, use the Object Manager, which performs global document operations. Advanced tools provide precise control of the vertical order, alignment, and distribution of objects.

As with most tools, you can set up preferences to control the way many of the tools described here operate. There are at least two ways to access these tools: a toolbar button or the equivalent menu command. When an operation requires further definition, corresponding dialogs and roll-ups provide access to the controls. Each feature also has controls that can be accessed from a Property Bar that is automatically displayed when the feature is active. Arranging and organizing operations include:

- Copying and deleting objects using Cut, Copy, Paste, Duplicate, Clone, and Delete.
- Ordering objects to place them in the desired position when objects overlap. Use the To Front, To Back, Back One, Forward One, Behind, and In Front Of commands to arrange the stacking order.
- Adding layers to contain discrete subsections of your drawing such as text, leaders and callouts, background patterns, etc. Layers are like transparent pages. Use the Layers roll-up to add, access, reorder, lock/unlock, remove, color, or print one or more selected layers.
- Grouping and ungrouping objects with the Group/Ungroup commands. Grouping combines selected objects so that editing operations are applied to the entire group. Ungrouping breaks the group back into the individual objects that comprise the group.
- Combining and breaking objects apart with the Combine and Break Apart commands, found in either the Arrange menu or the Property Bar. Use the Combine command to fuse multiple curves, lines, and/or

shapes to create a completely new shape with common fill and outline attributes. If original objects overlap, overlapped areas are removed to create clipping holes that show what's underneath. When objects don't overlap, they are still combined into a single object while retaining their separation. Combine converts rectangles, ellipses, polygons, stars, spirals, graphs, and text to curves before they become a single curve object.

Combined text objects are not converted to curves, but into larger blocks of text. To affect the shape of an Artistic text object with the Combine command, use the Convert to Curves command first to convert the text to a curve object. Note that you cannot convert Paragraph text to curves.

It's most common to combine objects to create complex shapes with or without clipping holes. However, you can also combine objects that have identical fill and outline attributes to conserve memory, reduce file sizes, and ultimately increase the redraw speed.

Use the Break Apart command to separate objects that were joined with the Combine command. This command is quite useful when you want to modify clipart that was created by combining several different objects. Once objects are returned to their independent (uncombined) state, you can edit any of the object's attributes or properties.

If you break apart a combined Artistic text object, the text breaks apart first into separate lines. Use the command a second time to further break the text into separate words. Paragraph text only breaks apart into separate paragraphs. You can recombine both Artistic and Paragraph text into their original state.

■ Welding, trimming, and intersecting objects is accomplished with the Weld, Trim, and Intersection commands found in the Arrange menu, the Roll-Ups toolbar, or the Property Bar. Welding combines two or more overlapping objects together to create a single object. Trimming reshapes an object by removing the area that overlaps another object. You can trim a circle out of a rectangle to create a new shape. The trimmed object retains its fill and outline attributes. Intersecting combines the area of two or more objects that overlap. You can use the shape and position of multiple objects to create an entirely new shape.

■ Aligning objects is accomplished with the controls in the Align and Distribute dialog. This dialog provides controls for precision alignment of any series of selected objects. The dialog gives you horizontal (flush left or flush right), vertical (flush top or flush bottom), and center alignment controls. You can also align with the edge or center of a page or the edge or center of the target object, which is controlled by the way you select the objects. For the best control, align selected objects to an adjacent grid line or use the Snap To commands. These commands snap objects to the grid, guidelines, or stationary target objects. When snapping is enabled, objects automatically "jump" to the grid, guidelines, or other objects for precise alignment.

■ Distributing objects is accomplished with the Align and Distribute dialog. Use this dialog to achieve even spacing of objects on either the page or the selected area, known as the *selection box*. Automatically placing objects at equal intervals saves the time it would otherwise take to measure and manually place each. You can arrange objects so that spacing is based on either the center points or specified edges. You can try one alignment control; if not satisfied, try another. In addition to controlling how objects are distributed, you can also choose the area over which they are distributed, i.e., the area of the selection box or the entire drawing.

Using the Object Manager

The Object Manager displays the hierarchical structure, or *stacking order*, of objects, layers, and pages in the drawing document. The Object Manager displays a small icon and a brief description of each object's basic fill and outline properties. The icons are interactive so that as you select and edit them you can see the changes in your drawing. Editing selected objects is accomplished using standard drawing tools, roll-ups, and dialogs or the controls within the Object Manager. The Object Manager provides the following features:

■ Drag and drop ordering of objects (within layers and between layers)

■ Drag and drop editing of objects' outline and fill colors

■ Drag and drop application of styles (color, graphics, and text)

■ Drag and drop grouping and ungrouping of objects

■ Drag and drop creation and editing of PowerClips

■ Layer property controls

■ Full compatibility with CorelDRAW's powerful object, page, and layer manipulation tools

■ Right-click menus offering quick access to frequently used commands

■ Object naming for easy identification

You can edit drawings using the Drawing Window, the Object Manager, or a combination of both. When an object is selected in either document view, it is automatically highlighted in the other view. Changes to objects are also shown in both views. You can perform drag and drop operations within the Object Manager, between the Object Manager and the Drawing Window, or between Object Managers for different drawings.

Creating an Object Database

CorelDRAW 7 features an Object Data roll-up that is used to create a database of information about all objects within a drawing. You can enter information about individual objects or groups of objects including times, dates, text, numbers, etc. Create a database by entering information for specific objects on the Object Data roll-up. The information is placed on a data sheet, called the *Object Data Manager*; categories of information are organized in columns. A technical drawing might contain part numbers, component names, cost data, and quantities in separate columns for each component within the drawing.

Once it is created, you can view the database information on any object in either list or data sheet format. The Object Data roll-up displays a list of all the information you've assigned; the Object Data Manager displays this information in a formatted data sheet. The basic features required to format or manipulate the database information are also available. For example, you can add or delete columns, indent rows to show subordination, and summarize data for selected objects. You can print a portion or all of the database.

You can copy data to different locations within the same or a different data sheet using cut and paste or copy and paste. Similarly, you can cut or copy data to another Windows-based database or spreadsheet document.

Working with Text

You can control your text through the application of both special graphical effects and sophisticated word-processing features. The Text tool lets you add graphical effects to short lines of text, and you can add and format Paragraph text to large text areas. You can also:

- Add drop caps
- Fit text to a path and edit the text
- Vertically align Paragraph text
- Wrap Paragraph text inside a selected object

Editing Text

Text can be edited in either the Drawing window or the Text Edit window. You can also exchange text with a word processing program, edit the text within the word processor, and merge text from a word processing document into your CorelDRAW document.

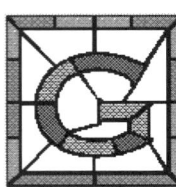

Creating Effects with Text

You can apply special effects to *Artistic text* to create 3D effects (extrusions), blending, perspective, and lenses. You can create Artistic text with the Text tool. Artistic text is typically used for single lines as in titles. For example, you can apply graphic effects, such as extrusions and blends, to Artistic text to achieve special effects. Artistic text objects can contain up to 32,000 characters. You can type Paragraph text directly inside objects. Just click the object and type directly in the Drawing window. Paragraph text can also be wrapped around objects. If you like to design your own fonts, you can even use CorelDRAW to create your own Adobe Type 1 and TrueType-compatible fonts and symbols.

Tips: The Text tool is both versatile and easy to use.

■ To apply formatting properties to text or to change individual characters, select the text with the Text tool.

■ To apply a change that affects the entire text object or multiple text objects, select the text with the Pick tool.

■ To move individual characters and reshape characters that have been converted to curves, select the text with the Shape tool.

Formatting Text

It's a simple matter to control the font type, weight, size, spacing, and other text properties using the Text tool, Text > Format Text dialog, or the Format Text button on the Property Bar where most formatting options are available for both Artistic text and Paragraph text. When using Paragraph text, you can add tabs, indents, bullets, and automatic hyphenation. There are several ways to format text:

■ Set up the Text tool options before you begin typing.

■ Change formatting characteristics to text already in your document.

■ Use established text styles and templates when working with a document that contains a large amount of text. This permits you to quickly format the text you are adding, and it adopts the text attributes that are already being used.

Paragraph Text Frames

Paragraph text frames, or simply "frames," are like resizable containers that hold Paragraph text. You can change the text by first selecting the frame and then applying the desired formatting controls. The changes are applied to all interior text. Applying transformations, such as rotating and

skewing, can also change the frame. As transformations are applied, you can choose to wrap lines of text to conform to the frame's shape and size.

Editing and Proofreading

When working with a large amount of text, you can use the Extract command to take text out of your drawing, while preserving its placement. Then edit it in a full-featured word processor. Use the Merge Back command to insert the edited text back into your CorelDRAW document. CorelDRAW 7 also includes several proofreading tools including a thesaurus, Grammar Checker, Spell Checker, and Type Assist. Type Assist automatically displays complete words in place of typed abbreviations, capitalizes certain words, and automatically corrects common spelling errors. All of these proofreading tools are designed to help you proofread your text to ensure both accuracy and efficiency.

Applying Graphical Effects to Paragraph Text

Several graphical effects can be applied to Paragraph text frames. These include:

- Applying envelopes—Create artistic shapes filled with text.
- Wrapping text around graphical objects—Place Paragraph text around objects, such as ellipses, rectangles, and wavy lines.
- Placing Paragraph text inside objects—Place Paragraph text inside an object to make the object's outline the Paragraph text frame.

Creating Graphical Effects with Artistic Text

As with most objects, you can apply special effects to Artistic text. Special effects that can be applied to Artistic text include extruding, blending, contouring, and applying envelopes, lenses, PowerClips, and perspective. You can also merge Artistic text and graphical objects with the Fit Text to Path command.

Creating and Modifying Typefaces

You can create typefaces and symbol fonts using the TrueType or Adobe Type 1 Export Filter. Instead of converting your image to a graphic file format, these filters export your graphic as an Adobe Type 1 (PFB) or TrueType (TTF) font. Once it is exported, you can use your new type character as a text character in CorelDRAW or other Windows applications. Your creation can be part of an existing typeface, or it can be used as a character in an entirely new typeface set.

You can customize characters in any of the typefaces included with Corel-DRAW or create totally different typefaces or sets of symbols. You can even use a scanner to create a typeface based on handwriting. However, the most common approach is to create or modify an existing typeface for a specific purpose, such as for an organizational logo.

When creating a type character, use a graphic created in CorelDRAW or a scanned or traced image. Convert scanned image files (PCX or TIF format) to a vector image using CorelTRACE. Scan a large original to achieve best results. To ensure that CorelDRAW can effectively handle the image, keep the traced image below 3000 x 3000 pixels.

You can choose to change only a few characters within an existing typeface, or to build an entirely new typeface. In either case, you must follow a step-by-step procedure to prepare your graphic object for conversion to a TrueType or Adobe Type 1 typeface character. The basic steps required to prepare and convert an object to a type character are:

1. Make a backup copy of the original font files if you plan to modify an existing typeface.

2. Set up guidelines to ensure precise alignment of the source object.

3. Convert the character to curves.

4. Modify the character to achieve a suitable design.

5. Create either a single or a combined object.

Once the typeface is created following the general steps, you should have a customized TrueType or Adobe Type Manager font file. Before it can be used, close CorelDRAW and then add the font to Windows. Use the Control Panel to add a TrueType font or the Adobe Type Manager to add a Type 1 font. If a character was exported to an existing typeface that wasn't renamed, remove the typeface from the list of installed fonts and then reinstall it. Corel highly recommends that you copy the original typeface and rename the copy. When you use your new typeface in a drawing, you will see your customized characters in the list of fonts.

Applying Special Effects

You can change the way objects look using the special effects tools. Special effects tools are described in the paragraphs that follow.

Blending Objects

Blending two objects produces a "progression" of objects that includes the two original objects and a series of intermediate objects between them. The intermediate objects create a smooth transition between the shapes and colors of the two original objects.

Contouring Objects

When an object is contoured, an effect like that created by contour lines on a topographical map is produced. A new dimension is added to a contoured object, because a series of concentric lines that radiate inside or outside the object's borders are added. The group of contour lines can contain as many as 999 lines separated by a distance varying from 0.00005 to 300 inches.

Applying Envelopes to Objects

Applying envelopes to objects provides an easy way to quickly reshape them. Add an envelope to the object and then use the mouse to move the nodes and control points. The envelope is displayed as a dotted red line with a series of squares along its path. The squares represent the envelope's nodes. Reshape the envelope by dragging the nodes in the desired direction. When the shape of the envelope is satisfactory, apply it to the object to reshape it according to the order and position of the envelope's nodes.

Extruding Objects

Extra surfaces are added to extruded objects to give them a three-dimensional appearance. An extruded square looks like a cube; an extruded ellipse looks like a cylinder. You can extrude any object including lines, shapes, and text.

Using Lenses

The Lens feature simulates the effect of viewing an object through different types of camera lenses. The type of lens selected controls the visual effect. You can apply lens effects to any closed shape that you have created using standard tools.

Working with PowerClips

Use the PowerClip command to put one object inside another. One object becomes contents of the PowerClip; the other becomes its container. You can create a container from any closed-path object such as shapes, lines, curves, Artistic text, and groups. A contents object can be any object you create within CorelDRAW or import from another program.

You can think of a container object as a window. The window's frame establishes the limits of what can be seen behind it. Parts of an object that extend outside the container are cropped. PowerClips are useful for placing bitmap images inside containers of different shapes.

Adding Perspective

Use the Add Perspective command to add perspective to your drawings. Perspective creates the illusion of distance and depth. You can use Add Perspective to create either one- or two-point perspective. One-point perspective makes an object look like it's receding from view in one direction. Two-point perspective makes an object look like it's receding from view in two directions. You can apply Add Perspective to any graphic or text object (or group of objects) created in CorelDRAW, to Paragraph text, and to bitmap images.

Using the Interactive Transparency Tool

You can distort objects, add new elements, or change an object's relationship to surrounding objects. Effects can be freely copied to or removed from objects. You can clone many special effects; cloned objects automatically update when the original is changed.

Working with Bitmaps

You should recall that bitmaps are graphics composed of dots (or *pixels*). Bitmap images have a fixed resolution and always look best in their original size. Scaling a bitmap image to enlarge or reduce it makes it coarse and jagged, because pixels are either added or lost. In contrast, vector graphics, which are represented by a series of lines and curves, resize nicely without losing quality.

You can import bitmap images and mix them with your vector images in the same drawing. You can also export your drawings in a variety of bitmap formats using the File > Export dialog. Exporting enables your drawing to be edited or combined in a bitmap editor. When bitmap objects are imported into CorelDRAW, they cannot be edited except for scaling and coloring. Use the Bitmap Color Mask roll-up to hide or show specific colors.

Bitmap images can be converted to vector objects by tracing them. You can use the OCR-TRACE utility supplied in the CorelDRAW 7 suite, which is probably the fastest way to make the conversion. You can also attempt automatic tracing using the built-in autotrace feature. Finally, you can manually trace a bitmap image with the Freehand and Bezier tools. The method you choose controls the quality of the outcome, so you may have to try each to find the best result.

Using the Scrapbook

The Scrapbook roll-up gives you drag and drop access to the folders that contain CorelDRAW's extensive collections of clipart, designs, and photos,

as well as a collection of preset fills and outlines. The Scrapbook is also used to organize, save, and retrieve custom designs, fills, and outlines that you produce. The Scrapbook contains four sections or "pages":

The Browse Page—Use to add items to your drawing from any available folder. You can also drag items to the Browse page from an open drawing.

The Clipart Page—Use to import clipart from the Clipart CD.

The Photos Page—Use to import photos from the Photos CD.

The Favorite Fills and Outlines Page—Use to save an object's fill and/or outline properties for use with other objects.

Printing

Before printing your drawings, make it a practice to preview them on screen to check their appearance. Just click File > Print Preview to see your drawing. Once you are satisfied with the appearance, you can print your document as you would when using virtually any Windows application. However, when you print your document for use by a commercial printer, you must consider adding crop and/or registration marks, a color scale or grayscale bar, and other items that help the printer achieve the results you need.

Output Methods

You can publish your final document in a number of ways. Before printing, consider your quality requirements and the number of copies needed. Following are some available options:

Print on a Laser or Inkjet Printer

You can use a laser or inkjet printer to print your document in black and white or color, depending on the mode being used. Obviously, if you plan to distribute more than a few copies of your document, desktop printing is slow and expensive. You can produce one good printed original and use an office copier if more copies are needed and high-quality output is not a factor, as with internally distributed reports, newsletters, and presentations. If you are incorporating color photos in your work, the office copier may be impractical. If your graphics are simple, the copier may be adequate. Be sure to use light, coarse screens to reproduce your master copy to achieve reasonably good reproduction on a photocopier. Set your printer's output to 300 dpi rather than 600 dpi when your document includes a number of grayscale images.

Create Camera-ready Images on a Laser Printer and Send Them Directly to a Print Shop

When black and white (grayscale) output is desired, your commercial printer can accept your laser printed output as *camera-ready reproducible copy* (called "repro" by many in the industry). Printing plates are made in a variety of ways; some small print shops have the ability to create photo direct paper or plastic plates that are suitable for several hundred printed impressions. Other commercial printers use high-contrast photolithographic negative film from which they burn metal printing plates. Metal plates can print tens of thousands of images without failure. In either case, your document is printed on an offset press to produce superior quality.

Send Your Graphic Files to a Service Bureau or Commercial Printer

This technique is becoming common in the industry. In fact, some publishers regularly communicate files from one computer to another using the commercial printer's BBS, FTP (File Transfer Protocol) site, or as an attachment to e-mail over the Internet. Publishers also submit their graphic files on magnetic media, including diskettes, Zip drive media, and CDs. Service bureaus and commercial printers that are equipped with imagesetters can produce either high-resolution film or plates used with offset presses.

Corel PHOTO-PAINT

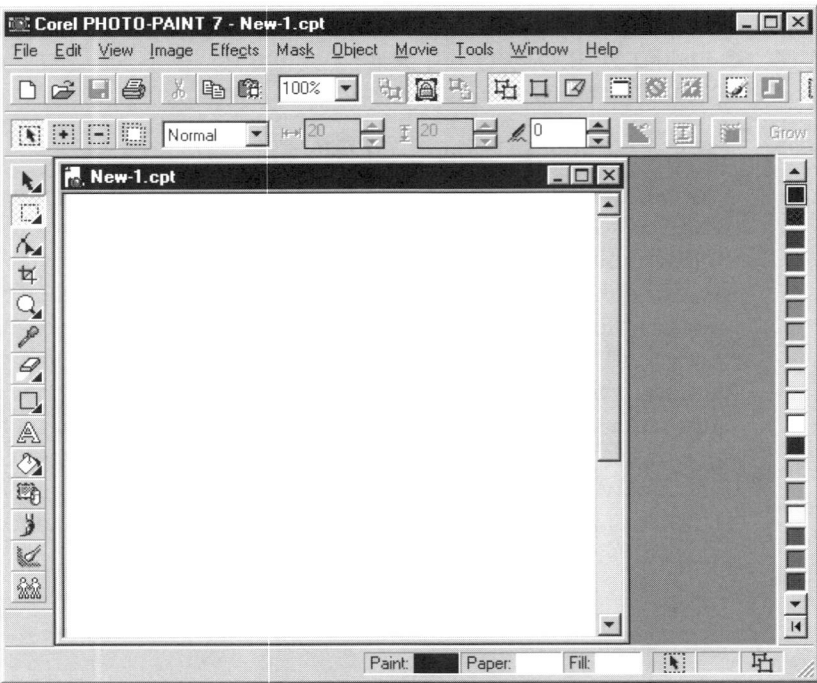

Corel PHOTO-PAINT is a heavyweight bitmap (or "pixel") editor that is used by many professional graphic artists, particularly those who favor CorelDRAW as their first choice in vector drawing programs. PHOTO-PAINT is supplied as part of the CorelDRAW suite of products, along with several other drawing tools, type fonts, and clipart images.

Editing an Image

With Corel PHOTO-PAINT you can create a new, blank document and add and paint objects that you draw from scratch, or create a montage created from bits and pieces of other images. The ability of the program to import a variety of file formats lets you work with many different images. You can also scan drawn, painted, and photographic images into Corel PHOTO-PAINT using scanner software. Once captured by Corel PHOTO-PAINT, the document can be saved as a standard image file.

Setting Up Your Image

Each time you create a new image, you are invited to select a color mode, paper color, image size, and resolution. The size of the image file as well as the quality of the printed output are both dependent on the color mode and resolution. When an image file is extremely large or uses high resolution, you should consider working on individual parts to reduce the amount of data being processed at a time. This can improve your system's performance.

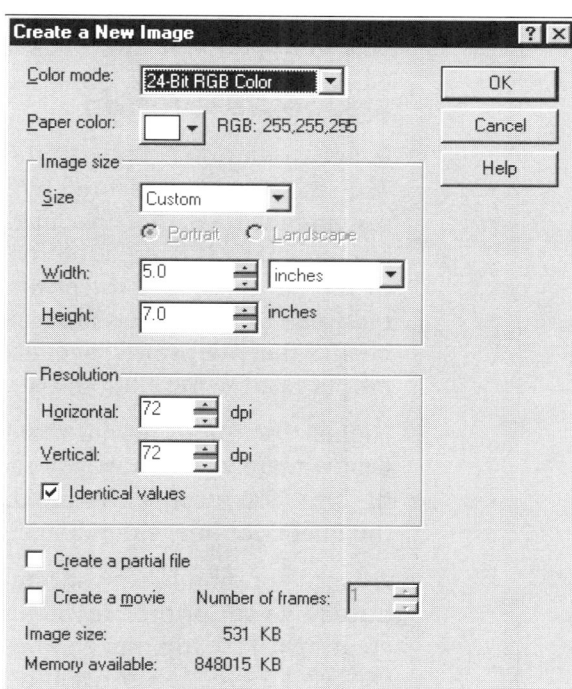

Color Mode

You can choose any of seven color modes. These include:

■ Black-and-white (1-bit)

■ Grayscale (8-bit)

■ Duotone (8-bit)

- Paletted (8-bit)
- RGB (24-bit)
- Lab (24-bit)
- CMYK (32-bit)

A color mode's bit count corresponds to the resources demanded from your computer and the number of colors or shades that can be produced. A single bit is either on or off; 1-bit color can only produce black (0 bit) or white (1 bit). A 32-bit color is capable of producing four billion possible colors (or *pixel depths*). Working with 32-bit colors requires a maximum amount of memory.

Image Size

The size of an image is the physical dimensions of the printed image. The image size is measured using inches, centimeters, or the pixel height and width. For printing purposes, you should know the size relative to inches or centimeters. If the image is intended for display, as on the World Wide Web or as part of a slide presentation, you should probably size it in pixels.

Image Resolution

Image resolution equates to the amount of detail contained by the image. The resolution is measured by the number of pixels (or dots) contained per running inch, i.e., dots per inch or *dpi*. The number of pixels contained in a bitmap image is fixed; therefore, the resolution of an image corresponds directly to the size of the printed image. When you print the image at a reduced size, the pixels are small and the resolution high. Conversely, images that are printed oversize cause the pixels to become enlarged. This produces a low resolution, coarse-looking output.

Higher resolutions permit more detail and smoother color transitions. Unfortunately, you must pay the price for better quality with a much larger file size. You must determine the most desirable resolution by balancing the quality of image detail against the size of the file.

As a rule of thumb, set your image resolution based on the dpi value produced by your printer. If you are printing at 600 dpi, there's no point in creating a 1200-dpi image. If the image will be displayed on screen, you can use an even lower resolution. Be sure to use a resolution setting that corresponds with that of the monitor.

Opening Existing Images

Existing images can include graphics found on clipart CDs, scanned photos, and graphic files downloaded from the Internet. You can import and edit digitized images if they have been converted into pixels, or *rasterized*.

You can also export your edited images in a wide range of graphic formats to make them usable by other programs. When a vector image is imported, a duplicate bitmap file is opened; the original vector file remains intact. This permits further editing using a vector graphic editor, such as Corel-DRAW or Adobe Illustrator. When an image either has high resolution or is exceptionally large, you can work on it in parts to reduce the amount of data your computer must handle. This approach speeds up the editing process.

You can open either an entire or partial image using the File > Open menu selection. Simply select the drive, folder, and filename to open an existing image. Click the Full Image box to open an entire image. Click the Partial Load box to open a partial image. Then choose a grid from the Grid Size list box and click the portion of the image you wish to open.

Scanning Images

When you scan images, be sure to use a good quality, high-contrast original. You can make minor adjustments to the image using Corel TWAIN. Major adjustments are made within PHOTO-PAINT, itself. Major adjustments include:

■ Resolution—72 to 96 dpi for display purposes, 300 to 600 dpi for printing purposes

■ Color depth—the number of displayed colors including black-and-white, grayscale (or *duotone*), and 16 million colors for high quality color photographs

Viewing Images

For convenient viewing, you can use the Zoom tool to magnify (zoom in) or decrease (zoom out) the size of your image. Zoom in for precision viewing and editing work. Zoom out to see more of your image. A Zoom Tool Settings roll-up lets you enable the right mouse button as a zoom out shortcut. When the button is disabled, just use Shift+Right Click to zoom out. Use the Hand tool or the Navigator pop-up to move the image around on the screen.

Aligning Objects

Use grids, rulers, and guidelines to align objects with precision. Although you can see these alignment tools on the screen, they do not print.

Maximizing the Work Area

For a full-screen view of your image, use the View > Full-Screen Preview menu selection. Press Esc to return to the normal view, where you can continue editing your image.

Dithering and Color Correction

Screen dithering is used when a 16-bit color monitor is in use, which prevents the display of a 256-color image. Dithering averages the depth of pixels, which mixes colors to produce the appearance of additional colors or gray shades. Most serious writers and publishers have super VGA (256-color resolution) monitors and are not bound by the need for dithering. Color correction is used to match displayed colors with those printed. Here, you use Corel PHOTO-PAINT's Color Manager to set up color profiles to match your printed output.

Photo Retouching

Photo retouching is required to either correct image problems or to enhance or emphasize features within an image. Correction and enhancement tools abound within PHOTO-PAINT. You can even repair damaged image areas to improve quality.

■ An *Intellihance* filter is available to correct tone, saturation, sharpness, and despeckle.

■ Masks restrict the effect of retouching to an isolated area.

■ The Clone tool is used to fill one or more damaged or missing areas of an image. The Clone tool duplicates pixels from a good area and lets you deposit them in another. This is ideal for repairing damaged or torn images. Since the Clone tool is a brush tool, the tool's brush size is adjustable. This feature lets you control the size of the cloned area.

■ The Dust and Scratch filter reduces unwanted, random pixels (or *noise*) from your image.

■ Copy your image if you are unsure about the outcome of your retouching work. If you goof, you can go back to the original image and try an alternate approach.

Focus and Grain

Three filters are available for controlling the focus and grain of an image.

■ The Noise Control dialog is used to adjust the noise in an image; just click on the sample thumbnail buttons to see how your image changes when you apply a particular effect.

- The Sharpen filter makes use of a Sharpen Control dialog to adjust the contrast of adjacent pixels. This gives the appearance of sharpness. Just click the thumbnail button to see samples of the image before you commit to a final filter setting.

- The Blur Control dialog is used to adjust the softness of an image. This has an effect of adjusting the focus of the selected image.

- The Sharpen tool is used to sharpen an area of your image by brushing it with the tool. This tool is found in the Effect Tools toolbar and Effect tool picker of the Property Bar and Tool Settings roll-up. Adjust the size and shape of the brush to control the effect.

- The Smear tool softens an area of your image by brushing it with the tool. Again, adjust control of the size and shape of the affected area by setting the brush shape and size (using the Brush Type box of the Property Bar and Tool Settings roll-up).

Tonal Corrections

You can use tonal correction tools to adjust brightness, contrast, intensity, saturation, shadows, midtones, and highlights. These controls help you restore detail lost in shadows or bright spots (highlights) and correct exposure and tonal quality.

- *Histogram Dialog*—
  The Image menu's
  Histogram selection
  analyzes the value of
  every pixel in the
  active image. It
  presents the value
  range and how many
  pixels are at each
  brightness level. All
  histograms have peak
  and valley values; it
  is the spikes that
  cause tonal problems
  within an image. The
  displayed bars should
  be evenly distributed
  for best tonal results.

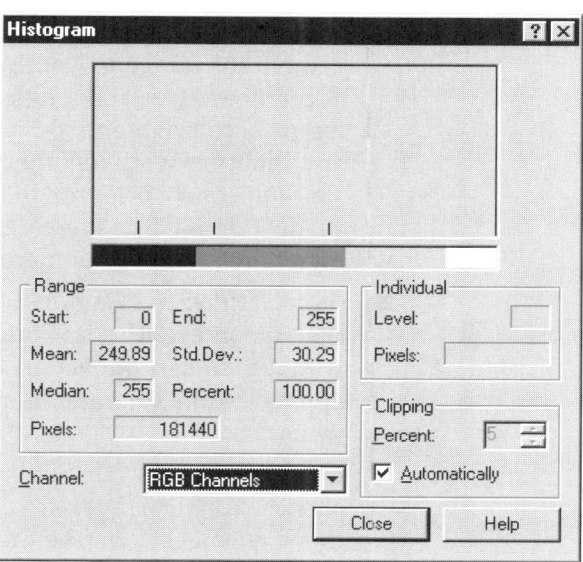

- *Level Equalization Filter*—Use the Level Equalization filter to improve the quality of an image. This filter is a precision tool used to adjust an image's shadow, midtone, and highlights areas. You can use it to retain shadow and highlight details; using the Brightness-Contrast-Intensity filter can cause shadows and highlights to fade, resulting in a loss of definition. Level equalization makes use of individual adjustment controls to automatically redistribute pixel values across the entire range of tonal values. Therefore, you can use Eyedropper sampling, equalization, or the histogram display options to simplify the brightness control of an image. By defining the beginning and end points of the tonal range, you can expand or reduce the pixel values that fall in between. Use the Level Equalization filter to redistribute shades that range from the darkest to the lightest. This filter can create colors to lighten or darken the shadows, midtones, and highlights by limiting brightness values to those that are suitable for printed output.

■ *Tone Curve Filter*—Like the Level Equalization filter, the Tone Curve filter also performs global tonal and color corrections. However, it provides more exact control over the value of an individual tone. When you encounter a color problem, use curve-based editing to isolate and change the color value of a limited area.

■ *Auto Equalize Command*—Use the Auto Equalize command to automatically redistribute pixel values across the entire tonal range. The result is the same as enabling the Auto-Adjust check box when applying the Level Equalization filter.

■ *Brightness-Contrast-Intensity Filter*—Use this filter to adjust the tones within the image by increasing or decreasing the tonal value of every pixel in the image. A Contrast slider is available to change the difference between the lightest and darkest pixel values. Increase the intensity to brighten light areas without lightening dark areas. Contrast and intensity work together; increasing contrast and intensity simultaneously prevents the increased contrast from washing out the shadow detail. The increase in intensity brightens the shadows and highlights, thereby counteracting a loss in detail.

■ *Gamma Filter*—A Gamma filter corrects for misperceptions common to the human eye. Use this filter to pick up detail in a low-contrast image without a major impact on shadow or highlight areas. Tonal changes applied by the Gamma filter are curve based, which targets midtone values.

■ *Color Tone Filter*—This filter offers thumbnail samples from which to choose. Tonal changes are either singular or cumulative depending on the way you click on the thumbnail samples. A Step slider is available to control the amount of change of each adjustment.

■ *Contrast Tool*—The Contrast tool is a brush tool that you can drag across the desired area to add more contrast. Recall that you can adjust the size, shape, and texture of the "brush tip" to achieve different effects.

Painting, Filling, and Editing

To paint, simply pick a color, click the Paint tool, and drag it across your image. For added control, select different nibs (or *brush/pen tips*), textures, transparency levels, brush bleed and fade-out rates, and the way the paint or ink combines with existing colors. The Paint, Sprayer, Mask Brush, Clone, Image, Effect, Undo, and Object Transparency tools are brush tools. Most brush tools have three tabs in the corresponding Tool Settings roll-up. You can access a particular tool's roll-up by selecting it and then right-clicking or pressing Ctrl+F8. The tabs access different tool attributes including the brush type. A Nibs roll-up lets you collect, view, and access your favorite nibs on a single palette, even when the Tool Settings roll-up is closed. You can also create custom brushes by changing the size, shape, flatness, transparency, and angle of your nib, the brush texture (second tab), and the artistic style (third tab). You can also change the paint

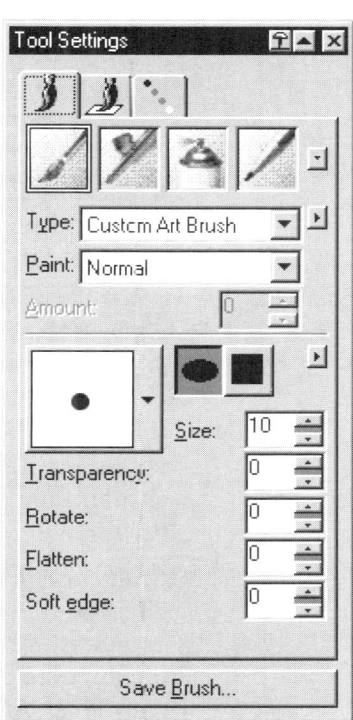

mode, which controls the way paint is applied to existing image colors. This ranges from replacing the base color with another or combining the existing color with the selected paint color in a blend. Blending methods include Normal, Add, Subtract, Difference, Multiply, Divide, If Lighter, If Darker, Texturize, Color, Hue, Saturation, Lightness, Invert, Logical AND, Logical OR, Logical XOR, Red, Green, Blue, Cyan, Yellow, Magenta, and Black. The blend methods can be reviewed in PHOTO-PAINT's online help information by selecting the Painting, Filling, and Editing tools entry in the Contents.

Filling

You can fill images using the Edit menu's Fill command. Four basic fill types can be applied to either the entire image or to a masked selection. These are:

■ *Uniform Fill*—This is the most basic type of fill; it applies a solid color to the fill area.

- *Fountain Fill*—This fill type produces a progressive fill that transitions from one color to another. It follows a regular pattern including concentric square, radial, linear, conical, or rectangular.

- *Bitmap Fill*—A bitmap fill is created from a loaded bitmap image; the best results are achieved using patterned images like bricks or stones that are easily tiled.

- *Texture Fill*—This is a fill that is produced using a mathematical algorithm that has customizable attributes. A texture fill places a single image in the specified image area. Dozens of preset textures, including water and clouds, are available for your use.

Fill Tool—You can use the Fill tool located on the toolbox to fill part of your image. First, define the fill area with a masked selection or by adjusting the Fill tool's color tolerance using the Tool Settings roll-up. Then fill the target area, which includes those portions of your image that fall within the defined color range. The Fill tool's Tool Settings roll-up includes anti-aliasing and transparency options. Anti-aliasing smoothes the edges of the filled area; transparency controls the transparency of the fill.

Gradient Fill Tool—The Gradient Fill tool is accessed from the Fill tool's fly-out. Use this to apply a graduated color to your image. The corresponding Tool Settings roll-up provides access to the type of gradient fill (circular, rectangular, etc.), the paint mode, gradient style, and maximum transparency level. After setting these options, edit the end-point positions and the direction that the gradient is applied using the object's adjustment handles.

Uniform Fill Dialog—Use the Uniform Fill dialog to select a color model and color picker for choosing a solid fill color. You can choose between a fixed palette, color blender, or mixing area instead of using a color model from which to select or create custom colors.

Fountain Fill Dialog—This dialog provides access to all controls required to customize, create, save, or delete preset gradients. Use this dialog to create a two-color gradient that transitions from the first color to the second, or create a custom gradient that transitions through three or more colors.

Bitmap Fill Dialog—This dialog provides access to all controls required to import, select, and customize bitmap fills. You can also scale the pattern to fit an area. This is like filling an image with a single, large tile. You can modify the size, number, and offset of the tiles depending on the desired outcome.

Texture Fill Dialog—This dialog provides access to all controls required to select and customize a textured fill. Use this dialog to select, unlock, and edit the properties of a texture. Preview your setup to see the results before you apply it.

Editing Your Artwork

Some tools are better suited for correcting mistakes while others are better for enhancing your images. Effect tools are examples of those that are well suited to enhance images; these tools are ideal for photo retouching and bitmap editing. For example, you can smear, smudge, and blend paint using the Smear, Smudge, and Blend tools found on the Effect Tools toolbar. Use the Sponge tool, also accessed from the Effect Tools toolbar, to add or remove paint.

If you want to reverse an edit or the application of an Effect tool, use the Undo tools. The Undo tools are best suited to correct mistakes or to remove the application of an undesirable effect. Other examples are the Eraser and Color Replacer tools. Both of these are used to apply the background color to an image. The Eraser tool applies the background color to any dragged object, while the Color Replacer tool only replaces the current paint color with the background color.

The Undo tools are available from a Toolbox flyout or as a separate toolbar. Use the Local Undo tool to reverse the last Paint, Clone, Image Sprayer, Shape, and Fill tool operation. Dragging with the Local Undo tool restores the pixels that were removed by the most recent brushstroke. You can use Edit > Undo List to selectively reverse a series of operations.

Text and Objects

Drawn objects, including lines, rectangles, ellipses (Shape tools), and text (Text tool) objects, are independent bitmaps that float on top of the main image. You can also create a transparent layer over your image and add drawn objects to that layer using nearly any tool in the toolbox. Use the Object Picker tool to select an object; when selected, handles are displayed. Drag the handles to resize the object. Double-click within the object's marquee to display arrows. These are used to rotate and skew the object. A circular icon is also displayed; move the icon to change the object's center of rotation. Triple-click to display distortion handles; click four times to display perspective handles. You can move, color, rotate, and reshape the object without affecting the pixels in the main image, until the object is merged into the background. When merged, it cannot be edited as an independent entity. If you want your images to remain separate and independently editable, you can save the image as a PHOTO-PAINT .CPT file.

Marquee

A marquee is the boundary around a selected object. When selected, a dashed outline is displayed. Use the Tools > Options menu and click the

Marquee tab to choose the marquee color and its position relative to the object. The object within the marquee overlays the main image until merged or cut to the clipboard.

Text

Text is an object and is treated like any other shape object. Object marquees are displayed around each character with eight sizing and scaling handles. You can move, apply transformations, and change font styles until the text is merged, at which time the marquee disappears.

Color

As a professional graphics tool, Corel PHOTO-PAINT provides the ability to work with literally millions of colors. The color spectrum is controlled by the color system you choose, i.e., RGB, CMYK, grayscale, etc. If you plan to give your artwork to a commercial printer, be sure to use the CMYK color spectrum. If printing to a black-and-white laser printer, use grayscale.

Corel Color Manager

The color balance is controlled by the Corel Color Manager, which is used to set the colors for your monitor, scanner, and printer. The Color Manager ensures that the colors displayed on your screen are as close as possible to those that are scanned and printed. It's important to calibrate your system even if you're not using a scanner or color printer. Once your colors are adjusted, you can use the View > Color Correction command to match the displayed colors on your other input and output devices. PHOTO-PAINT also includes a Gamut Alarm, which is turned on in the Corel Color Manager. The Gamut Alarm alerts you when a displayed color is beyond the range of your printer by displaying a single color in place of out-of-gamut colors.

Converting to a Different Color

Once your system is calibrated, you can use the Corel Color Manager to convert between color modes, i.e., RGB, CMYK, duotone, grayscale, etc. Whenever you convert from one mode to another, there is always some loss of information. To ensure the closest possible conversion, always calibrate your system before converting from one color to CMYK, because CMYK is based on the capabilities of your printer.

Color Correction Filters

You can adjust colors in your image with filters found in the Filter dialog. Before applying a color filter, you can use Preview to verify the filtered result. Following are descriptions of color filters.

- *Sample/Target Balance Filter*—Use this filter to correct colors by shifting color values from a color sampled directly from the image to a target color taken from a color model. You can adjust individual color ranges, i.e., shadows (low-point), midtones (mid-point), or highlights (high-point).

- *Color Balance Filter*—Use this filter to correct colorcasts in your illustration by shifting between CMY and RGB color values. Red flesh tones can be color corrected by shifting toward cyan. This filter can also be used to change the hue values of the overall image.

- *Hue/Saturation/Lightness (HLS) Filter*—Use this filter to adjust the colors using HLS values to change the intensity or hue of the colors within your image.

- *Replace Colors Filter*—Use this filter to replace one color with another. You can set the range value to replace an individual color or a range of colors.

- *Desaturate Filter*—Use this filter to remove the hue from all colors in an image to display them in their grayscale equivalents.

Creating Colors

You can create colors by selecting a sample from your image using the Eye-dropper tool. This color can be used as the current paper color, paint color, or fill color. You can also create colors using the Color roll-up, which is accessed with View > Roll-Ups > Color. Leave the roll-up displayed for instant access to the entire palette of available colors. The Color dialog is accessed using various names, i.e., Uniform Fill, Fountain Fill, Paint Color, Paper Color, and Select Color. Larger than the Color roll-up, this dialog offers more colors from which to choose and three selections: the color palette, color model, and numerical values for up to four color channels. Colors are taken from the right side of the dialog and blended in the Mixing Area. The lower part of the dialog is used to store your custom palette. You can add more custom color palettes using the Palette Options menu, accessed by clicking the right triangle button at the right of the palette near the bottom of the dialog. The Color dialog offers many other color editing features; every serious graphic artist should familiarize herself/himself with this powerful tool.

The Color Table

Whenever you convert an image to paletted color mode, the Color Table is displayed. A paletted color is an 8-bit color that stores and makes use of up to 256 colors. The Color Table is used to view, edit, and fine-tune the paletted colors of an image. The most common use for the Color Table is to prepare image files for use on the Internet. Therefore, the .GIF and .JPEG file types are commonly edited with the Color Table.

Color Channels

An 8-bit grayscale version of an image that contains color information is called a *channel*. Two kinds of channels are used by PHOTO-PAINT: color channels and mask (or alpha) channels. Masks are discussed in the next paragraph. Color channels are produced when an image file is either created or opened. RGB images have three separate color channels, i.e., red, green, and blue. Each of the three channels contains color information for each pixel that tells you how much red, green, and blue exists in each pixel. The color channels permit quick conversion from grayscale to color equivalents and vice versa. A Channel roll-up is available for editing an image's color channels. The roll-up is ideal for controlling both color and mask channels used by your image. Why would you use the Channel roll-up? If you have too much saturation in an RGB image, you can split it into HSB mode to brighten the Saturation (S) channel. Several other tools are available for controlling color channels. A Split Channels To command is available for reading color information from your image and then creating an 8-bit grayscale image file for each color channel that corresponds to the selected color model. A Combine Channels command is available to recombine channels that have been split. Combined channels do not have to be from the same image, and you don't have to merge the channels using the same mode from which they were split. The Channel Calculations dialog, which works with the open image, provides an additional way to merge channels. Instead of combining channels as with the Combine Channels command, you can use the Channel Calculations dialog to use different channel values, types, merge modes, and opacity levels.

Masks

Masks are used to isolate an area for editing while other areas remain intact. You can use a mask to select a specific area of your drawing. Looking through a mask is like looking at your image through a hole. The mask is black and the hole is white. Images that exist beneath the black areas, or "mask," are protected, while the images under the white hole are editable. You can change a mask's transparency value to control what part of a selection is editable. Once you select an area, you can apply special effects, adjust or copy the selection, change colors, or paint it without affecting the rest of the image.

Mask Types

Two types of masks exist. A regular mask defines a selection having a clear border. A color-sensitive mask defines a selection based on a pixel color. A

mask marquee outlines the selection and is displayed as a moving dashed line. The marquee isolates the unmasked area from the protected, masked area. Use the Tools > Options menu selection to change the position of your mask marquees.

You can also use a mask overlay to differentiate between the selection and the masked area. The overlay is a transparent, red-tinted "sheet" that over-lays the entire image. The transparent area is editable, while red areas are protected depending on the intensity of the red tint. Use the Mask > Mask Overlay command to access this masking method.

Saving Masks

Masks are only applied as a temporary tool; they can be moved, rotated, skewed, and stretched to accommodate your needs. Masks can be saved in a mask channel (temporary storage area for masks), to disk, or saved with the image file in a format that supports mask data. Otherwise, masks are discarded when the image file is closed or when you click outside the selection. If you have a complex mask that you want to retain, save it to a mask channel or to disk to avoid losing it. The following formats retain mask information: CPT, PSD, PP4, PP5, TIF (for grayscale, 256 color, 24-bit, and 32-bit images); TGA (for 24-bit images).

Mask Modes

Four mask modes exist.

■ Normal—The default mode used when first creating a mask on an image.

■ Additive—Add areas to an existing selection.

■ Subtractive—Subtract areas from an existing selection.

■ XOR—Used to define two or more selection areas. The XOR mode excludes overlapping areas from editing.

Shape Command

The Mask > Shape command is used to edit the shape of any mask selection by adding to or subtracting from the mask area. A Border command converts the marquee into two marquees. Both have the same shape and share the same center, but are separated by a specific number of pixels to create a frame-like selection. Use the Smooth command to smooth the edges of a mask. Use Remove Holes to select the protected areas that are completely enclosed by a selection. Use Expand and Reduce to add and remove a specified number of pixels at the edge of the selection.

Paint On Mask Mode

A mask is displayed in grayscale by working in the Paint On Mask mode to edit the mask as you would any other image. Add black to the mask to decrease the selection size (recall that black protects underlying pixels). Add white to increase the selection size (white exposes the editable area). Apply gray to increase the selection when it is painted on a black area. Painting gray on a white area of a mask changes the transparency level of those pixels included in the selection (editable area). You can also erase sections of a mask using the Eraser tool to add to the selection area. Use the Smear Effect tool around the edges of the selection area to make them more transparent, which increases the selection area.

Paths

A path is a line or curve that is terminated with square endpoints called nodes. A *closed path* completely encloses an area, such as a triangle, rectangle, or ellipse. An *open path* is one or more lines or curves whose endpoints (or nodes) simply terminate the object. Paths are placed on a layer above an image; they are independent of the image resolution and therefore unaffected by changes to image resolution. Paths provide the ability to edit shapes, because you can reposition the nodes with your mouse, which adjusts the position and length of the attached segment. Paths can be saved, copied, and exported as a bitmap image.

When you enclose a portion of an image in a path, it can be converted into a mask marquee. Then you can apply brush strokes or export the path's contents as a bitmap for use with CorelDRAW or Corel VENTURA. Therefore, paths provide another way to work with your illustrations. The power of a path is extensive, as it lets you edit any portion of an image that is enclosed with either a path or mask marquee. The Path Node Edit roll-up, accessed from the Tool Settings roll-up and the Property Bar, provides the controls needed to create, shape, save, remove, stroke, and convert your paths to masks. Just double-click the Path Node Edit tool.

Special Effects

Effects filters are used to change the look and feel of your images. A filter is essentially a program that executes a series of commands to produce the desired effect. For example, values are calculated to adjust selected pixel values based on the current values. The Motion Blur filter analyzes pixel values and then creates the illusion of motion by smearing the values along a preselected direction.

When you apply an effects filter to an image, you can see what is happening by viewing the image in Original and Result windows. Like all images, you can use the Zoom and Hand tools to adjust the views. You can also

Part
1

view the Original and Result windows full screen and switch between them for a better look. An Auto Preview button is also available to automatically update the Result window as adjustments are made.

In addition to effects filters, Corel PHOTO-PAINT also provides enhancement filters that are designed to improve image quality, i.e., contrast, intensity, sharpness, color correction, and more. Import and export filters are available to change the file format of images being opened or saved. Plug-in filters from third parties can also be used with Corel PHOTO-PAINT. These filters are added through the Effects > Options dialog.

Output Methods

All applications within the CorelDRAW Graphics suite use the same approach to printing. There are small differences for printing when using a specialized layout style or size, such as greeting cards. You can preview and rearrange your images before you print them using the Preview features. If you see a problem, correct it and preview the image again to verify that it is ready to print. Be sure to consider the need for crop marks, registration marks, and color bars before printing your final document.

Desktop Printing

A laser or color inkjet printer is typically used for desktop printing. If you plan to print more than one or two copies, desktop printing may be impractical. Consider using a photocopier to copy and distribute your reports and newsletters for internal consumption. However, if you want a good-quality result for customers, where "company image" is a concern, consider preparing camera-ready copy for use by a commercial printer.

Another alternative is to use one of the modern *lasersetters*, which is essentially a desktop laser printer that is capable of producing either paper or film output. Before considering this option, talk to your commercial printer, as they have some reservations about quality issues.

Camera-Ready Copy

Commercial printers can photographically reproduce your laser printer output to create printing plates. Then your document can be offset printed. This approach assures good quality reproduction and is used to faithfully reproduce hundreds or even thousands of printed copies. It is definitely the most cost-effective way to reproduce a large number of copies.

Service Bureaus

You can give a copy of your image files on diskette to a service bureau. However, the files must be in a useful format, such as PostScript or even Corel Ventura, depending on their internal systems. To date, most service bureaus accept PostScript file format, or *Encapsulated PostScript* (EPS). These formats are then processed by an imagesetter, such as a Linotronics. Some imagesetters can produce either camera-ready reproducible copy, film, and even printing plates, depending on the brand and model.

Microsoft Photo Editor

Microsoft Photo Editor is provided with Microsoft Office 97 Professional Edition. It is the simplest bitmap image editor of those described in this book. If for no other reason, it is presented because those readers who have Office 97 Professional will have it in their arsenal of programming tools. In addition, it serves the needs of many users who only require a minimum amount of image editing, file conversion, or photo retouch work.

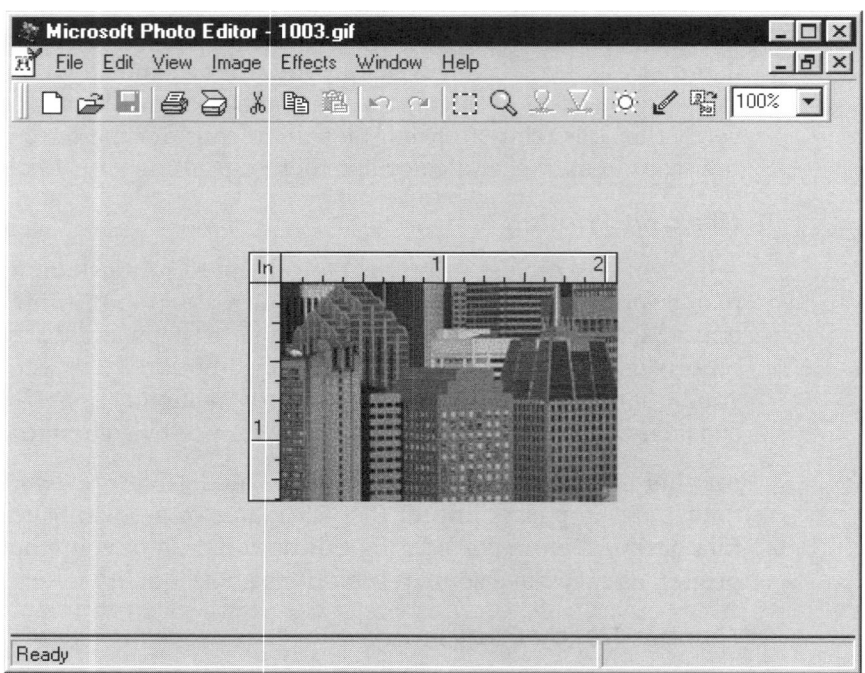

Getting Started

Like almost all Windows applications, you can create a new document or open an existing one. When opening a new document, Photo Editor lets you preview it before clicking the Open button. If you are opening a Kodak Photo CD image, you can adjust the resolution to comply with your file size and memory preferences. Like the other bitmap editors, you can also scan your image by clicking the Scan button on the standard toolbar. You

can save your images in the conventional way, or compress the image to save disk space. Use Save As to save a copy of the image or to change the file format. If you prepared the image for the World Wide Web, you can save it as a JPEG (*.jpg) file. A JPEG Quality Factor slider is available to adjust the image's quality level.

Photo Editor Toolbar

The Photo Editor toolbars give you access to a number of frequently used features including file, printing, and common editing operations. Other buttons include:

- *Select*—Selects part of the image for cutting, copying, or pasting. If you want part of an image, you can cut it, open a new blank image document, and then paste it.
- *Zoom*—Scales the editing view.
- *Smudge*—Reduces the contrast of an area; right-click for options.
- *Sharpen*—Sharpens the contrast of an area; right-click for options.
- *Image Balance*—Adjusts the image colors; select all colors or red, green, or blue individually.
- *Set Transparency Color*—Selects the transparency color; ideal for making the background transparent when an image is placed in a presentation or within a document.
- *Rotate 90°*—Rotates the image 90 degrees to the right.

Image Editing

The fastest and easiest way to adjust an image is to use Image > AutoBalance. This adjusts the brightness and contrast levels of the image. A number of other Image controls are available on the toolbar and in the Image and File menus.

- *Resize*—Use Image > Resize to change the size of a selected image. Enter the width and/or height or a percentage value.
- *Crop*—Select the Crop button and drag the desired area. Use Image > Crop to select the desired options, including mat (framing) margins, crop margins, and corner shapes. Then click OK to complete the job.
- *Rotate*—Use the Rotate 90° button on the Standard toolbar or Image > Rotate if you want to rotate by a specified number of degrees.
- *Set Transparent Color*—Click this button and then pick the color that you want to make transparent (invisible). This is ideal for creating a transparent background so that only the foreground image is printed.
- *Number of Colors*—Use File > Properties and select a type from the Type list. If you are using the Palette selection, click Custom, select the

number of colors, and click OK. When using Monochrome, click Custom, select the halftone options, and click OK.

■ *Resolution*—Use File > Properties, enter a number in the Resolution box, and click OK.

■ *Modify Color Palette*—Use File > Properties and select Palette or 256 color in the Type box. Then click Custom. Click Variable and enter a value in the Number of Colors box.

Applying Artistic and Special Effects

The Effects menu displays different options depending on the current selection. You can use either special effects or artistic effects to change the appearance of your image. You can try the various artistic effects and undo them if you are not satisfied with the result. Once you select an effect, adjust the controls in the corresponding dialog. Then drag the preview frame over part of the image you want to see and click Preview to determine the effect before it is applied. The special effects are applied in a similar manner. Click the desired effect, adjust the controls, and preview the image.

Printing

Printing with Microsoft Photo Editor provides a dialog that lets you adjust the size and position of the image on the page. You also see a preview of the image as it will be positioned on the page. A Center button is available to automatically center the image on the page. Once you are satisfied with the position and size, click Print to complete the task.

Screen Captures

If you are writing a book about software, you can capture menus, dialogs, toolbars, buttons, and even displayed documents; trim them; and save the trimmed image to a graphic file. You can also capture and save displayed images to graphic files. Once saved, your images are easily imported and placed in your word-processed or desktop-published documents. Follow the steps provided in this section to create and import your screen-captured graphics.

Color Schemes and Contrast

Before attempting to capture menus and dialogs, it is important to establish a screen display mode that provides good contrast. Use a white background, black text, and black or navy highlights. The Windows Standard Scheme found in the Appearance tab of the Control Panel's Display

Properties dialog works well. The accompanying graphic shows this dialog with the settings and a preview of the screen colors. Once your color scheme and contrast are acceptable, you're ready to continue the capture process.

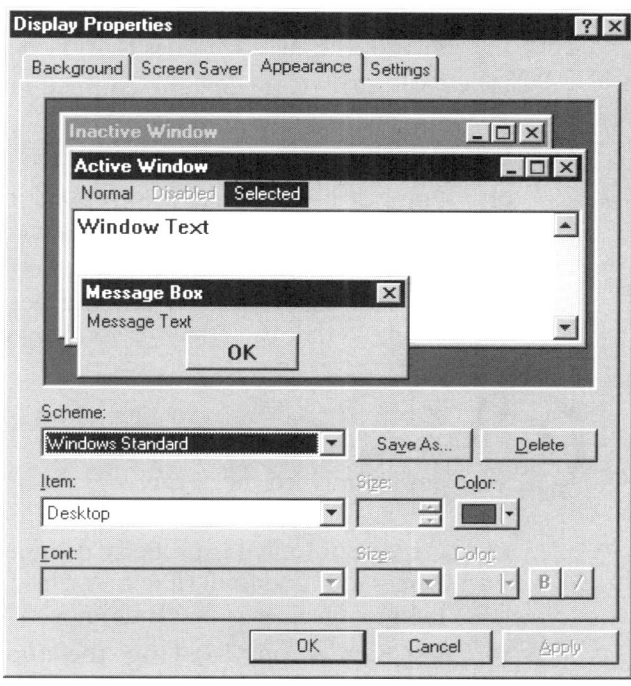

The Capture Process

Once you've established a readable display scheme, follow these simple steps to capture your image.

1. Display the target dialog, menu, toolbar, button, or graphic image.

2. Press the PrtScrn key to copy the screen to the Windows clipboard. (Use Alt+PrtScrn to capture a selected window.)

3. Start the Windows Paint program and display it full screen.

4. Use the View menu to suppress the display of unnecessary items like the Color Box and Status Bar. Leave Tool Box checked, as you'll need to access the Select tool located at the top right-hand column of the tool box.

5. Press Ctrl+V (or use Edit > Paste) to paste the screen from the clipboard into Paint.

6. Click and drag the displayed image, if necessary, to position it in the center of the screen so you can crop it with the Select tool.

7. Click the Select tool.

Tip:　You can also press Esc to activate the Select tool; knowing this shortcut allows you to hide the tool box so you can see even more of your image.

8. Carefully drag around the selection to crop it. Be sure to include the entire image with all edge lines that frame windows, dialog, and menus.

9. Press Ctrl+C to copy the cropped image to the clipboard. This replaces the screen image with the cropped image.

10. Press Ctrl+L to Select All and then press Del to clear the display.

11. Press Ctrl+V to paste the cropped image back onto your display; it is displayed at the upper left-hand corner of the work area.

12. Drag the image down and to the right so you can view all edges. If necessary, use the Select tool and the Del key to trim any unwanted background pixels so that the edges of your image are clean and sharp.

Tip: If you cut away part of an edge line or background area that you want to keep, press Ctrl+Z to undo the last action and cut again with more care.

13. Once your image is properly trimmed with clean, sharp edges, use the Select tool one final time to enclose the entire image. Include the entire image; unselected pixels are not saved.

14. Use Edit > Copy To to save the cropped image to a file. This displays the Copy To dialog.

15. Select a folder and give the file a memorable filename. Normally, you should save the image as a 256-color bitmap image. Windows Paint saves images in .bmp format.

16. If you are going to capture, edit, and save additional images, press Ctrl+N to open a new document for the next image. When prompted to save, type N or click the No button, as you've already saved the clipped image.

   Now that your images are captured, edited, and saved, you can import them into any number of word processing, desktop publishing, or graphic programs. This process is described in the following paragraph.

Importing and Scaling

A bmp image captured and saved using the preceding procedure is ready for use in a variety of documents. The graphic file can be imported into documents being word processed, desktop published, or illustrated. In some programs, such as Word, you simply use Insert > Picture and pick the From File option. WordPerfect is even easier, as you use Insert > File and WordPerfect determines the file type being inserted. In either case, filters are used to convert the image file to one that is compatible with the host application. Other programs include menu selections such as File > Open, File > Picture, or File > Import. Regardless of the menu and dialog

sequence, a format *filter* is used to convert the image file into one that is usable by the host program. If a suitable filter is not present, you'll be told by a dialog.

If you import the graphic into Adobe Illustrator or CorelDRAW, you can turn around and export the image into a different file format, such as JPEG, GIF, TIF, or PCX, depending on your ultimate needs. If you are using Adobe Photoshop or Corel PHOTO-PAINT, you can edit the image as described earlier in this chapter.

Once your image is acquired by one of your programs, you can normally resize it. This is called *scaling*. When it is resized, you probably want to maintain the proportion, or *aspect ratio*. Changing the size in one direction distorts the image. Most programs permit you to do this, but they also give you a percentage selection. If you want to reduce the image size by 25 percent, you can select the image and then use the appropriate Format > Object or Format > Picture selection to resize it to 75 percent of the original. You can usually drag a corner "handle" on a selected image to maintain the aspect ratio, as some programs constrain the vertical and horizontal dimensions to scale. Others let you drag vertically or horizontally, which stretches the image in one direction and results in distortion. For precision, use a dialog in which you can specify the scaling value as a percentage.

The original size of a bitmapped image displays and prints at the optimum quality. When you increase or decrease the scale of a bitmap image, recall that the pixels are modified to enlarge or reduce the size of the lines and shaped areas that comprise the image. This causes diagonal lines and image areas to become jagged and coarse, detracting from the image's appearance. Vector graphics, on the other hand, retain their quality as they are based on a mathematical formula for a shape, rather than a set of pixel values. Therefore, when using line drawings, consider using a vector-based drawing program like Adobe Illustrator or CorelDRAW. When capturing screen images, you have little choice. Since the captured image is bitmap based, try to capture areas that require little or no scaling to fit the document's page.

Scanners and Scanning

Most graphic artists and desktop publishing specialists prefer flatbed and sheet-fed scanners to the handheld wand style units. Flatbed scanners are easier to use than those that require you to drag them across the image area. Although handheld scanners can be used for business cards, small logos, and photos, professional graphic artists always choose flatbed units.

There are also drum and sheet-fed scanners that are designed specifically for professional prepress applications. These devices are priced between $20,000 and $40,000. These units are typically used for high-volume scanning jobs and are most often found at large printing firms, newspapers, and magazines. There are also slide scanners that are priced between $800 and $1,000. These are used to scan 35-mm slides.

A 600-dpi flatbed scanner that sells for $99.95 to $149.95 can fulfill your scanning needs. For example, I recently bought an excellent 600-dpi optical resolution scanner at a computer superstore for $149.95. It has an 8.5 x 14-inch scanning area. My graphics and DTP software use the supplied twain-compliant driver, making the acquisition of scanned images a breeze. When choosing a scanner, you should ensure that the unit you select has at least 24-bit color with a minimum resolution of 300 dpi.

Some flatbed scanner models are equipped with sheet feeders to permit multiple image capture. Small sheet-fed scanners employ rollers that pull a sheet of paper through the device, like the sheet-feeding mechanisms found in office copiers. One advantage of a handheld scanner is that you can scan pictures on large, unusually shaped, or heavy objects that could not otherwise be placed on the glass surface of a flatbed scanner. They are also small and lightweight, making them portable. Those of us who travel might opt for a handheld model so that we can acquire images in the field.

If you plan to scan an illustration or map in a published book or magazine, be sure to obtain permission from the copyright holder. This typically requires a telephone inquiry followed up by a letter and permission form that describes the purpose and use of the illustration. If you do not get permission for copyrighted material, you may find yourself in legal trouble. There have been instances in which the copyright holder required that all copies of those documents containing unauthorized use of material be recovered and destroyed. The alternative is typically an expensive lawsuit, financial remedies, and ultimate recovery and destruction of the offending material.

Some Concluding Opinions

After talking to daily users of these graphic programs and personally examining the features and ease of use, some conclusions about features, ease of use, and the demand for resources are reached. Among the bitmap editors, Corel PHOTO-PAINT offers the largest tool set, while Adobe Photoshop offers slightly better color controls. Other than that, they're probably a wash with the exception of the amount of disk space each requires (see the following table). Experienced users can perform

practically any bitmap editing or photo retouch task with either of these professional tools. Microsoft Photo Editor is adequate for many applications, but it has a small tool set and lacks the precise color controls available in either Corel PHOTO-PAINT or Adobe Photoshop. CorelDRAW and Adobe Illustrator are both excellent vector drawing programs, and either will suffice nicely for your line drawing and four-color cover rendering work. Both handle type and color admirably. CorelDRAW offers true layers and more pages than does Adobe Illustrator, although this advantage is rarely an issue unless you regularly prepare large catalogs.

Your final selection will depend on which interface you like best and the amount of computer resources you are willing to commit to the tools. This is rarely a constraint for fast professional workstations that are equipped with huge disk drives, lots of memory, and large graphic monitors. One thing professional users definitely need is the combination of a top-of-the-line bitmap editor and a vector drawing program. This permits them to combine bitmap images within their vector drawings for the best possible outcome. For example, photographic renderings are retouched and saved; the rendering is imported into a vector drawing program, where type, clean lines, shapes, and even barcodes can be added. The final result can be dazzling. Therefore, consider using both CorelDRAW and PHOTO-PAINT or Adobe Illustrator and Photoshop in combination. Like several professional graphic artists, you may even elect to have both of these powerful combinations on your computer.

If disk space is a factor (and it shouldn't be if you're in the business), here's a table of programs and disk space requirements based on the directories and files installed on the author's system. The values are rounded up to the nearest megabyte. Unfortunately, Quark was the only company that did not provide a full-featured version of their product in support of this project. Therefore, the demo version, which has printing and document size limitations, had to be used for evaluation.

Software	Disk Space (Approximate Values)
Adobe Illustrator	48MB
Adobe Photoshop	24MB
CorelDRAW	207MB (including PHOTO-PAINT and plug-ins)
Corel PHOTO-PAINT	15MB (plus shared files)
Microsoft Photo Editor	1.7MB (plus shared files)
Corel Ventura 7	139MB
Adobe FrameMaker	29.9MB
Adobe PageMaker	31.5MB
QuarkXPress	6.6MB (for demo version)

Just prior to the release of this book QuarkXPress 4.0 was released. A review in the February 1998 issue of *Windows Magazine* rated it as their favorite DTP application. It's a shame that Quark would not share this new release with us. It's probably worth considering, but for the time being, we can't really tell.

Moving Ahead

This chapter presented a fairly large amount of information about computer graphic programs. You learned about bitmap and vector graphics, color systems, and a good deal more. You should now have enough background to confidently choose your computer graphic tools. A bit more information about book covers and the steps involved in their design is in chapter 8.

The next chapter examines small documents and those resources that are typically used to produce them. Although this is not the primary focus of this book, it's important to know about the tools and processes used to produce small documents including product catalogs, brochures, and fliers. You may need to produce these document types in support of your marketing efforts.

Chapter 5

Small Documents and Stationery

Introduction

This chapter introduces you to small documents that are typically written and published for personal, organizational, and commercial purposes. Those of us whose homes are equipped with personal computers, printers, and the necessary software can easily produce party invitations, family newsletters, greeting cards, and other similar documents. Organizations such as schools, clubs, and churches make use of computers to prepare newsletters, bulletins, and educational materials. Businesses use their computers to prepare promotional materials such as sales fliers, catalogs, price lists, and postcards. Regardless of the document, its purpose, or the person producing it, the principles used to create and reproduce the document can be identical.

Fliers and Brochures

Fliers and brochures that represent products, services, or organizations often make an important first impression on those who read them. Therefore, it's important that your work be of reasonably good quality in both appearance and content. In particular, be sure that the message is clear, the graphics are attractive, and the text is carefully written and edited. Articulate the advantages associated with your product or service in a compelling way. If your budget permits the production of a four-color work, be sure to pick attractive, complementary colors. If you want to use colored stock and one color of ink, you can get some attractive effects by using screened illustrations and backgrounds.

Some people are extremely sensitive to certain color combinations, such as brown and chartreuse, or the selection of offensive or unrelated artwork.

133

Therefore, regardless of the quality of your message, shabby visual effects can defeat the purpose of your document.

Once you decide on a message and color scheme, if used, you must determine how you plan to produce your brochure. Since this book is for those who plan to write and publish their work, you will probably produce your own material using your computer. Assuming this is the case, some preparation choices are explored.

Word Processing

If you produce your fliers and brochures on a regular basis, such as *This Week's Special*, and have a good laser printer, consider using your word processor as a quick way to produce your handouts. Either Word or Word-Perfect will do nicely. Both provide all the tools you need to produce simple yet attractive fliers and small brochures. Your word processor gives you access to a wide range and size of text fonts, built-in graphic editors, table control, dot leaders, clipart, frames, borders, and background screens. These programs even let you perform runarounds, a feature that was once restricted to typesetters, and then with difficulty.

Weekly Lunch Specials
Bugle Boy's Restaurant
1212 Main Street
Downtown Lewistown, Montana

Monday...Pork Chops
Tuesday...Chicken & Dumplings
Wednesday..Corned Beef & Cabbage
Thursday ....Meatloaf, Mashed Potatoes & Gravy
Friday ....Catfish & Hushpuppies
Saturday ....Sauerbraten & Red Cabbage

Meals served with rolls, cornbread, and choice of two vegetables.

Served from 11 to 2:00—JUST **$4.75**

Saturday Night Dinner Coupon
$4.00 off any steak or prime rib dinner for two.
Good 5 to 9 pm through November 30, 1993

Consider using frames in your simple one- or two-page fliers or brochures to visually separate and outline different sections of your message. The Weekly Lunch Specials illustration contains an example of a word-processed flier. This flier was produced with Word. Here, three frames (or *text boxes*) are used. Three different borders, two typefaces, one clipart picture, and dot leaders are used. The entire flier took about ten minutes to produce including the time it took to conjure up the idea and to type the text.

A small flier, like the one shown here, can be duplicated and arranged on your printed page so that you can print four copies on each sheet of paper. Once printed, the copies can be cut and trimmed. Therefore, you realize a four-flier yield for every letter-size sheet printed. This is a good way to reduce the cost associated with printing. It takes fewer printed impressions and reduces the number of sheets required.

Desktop Publishing

You can also use a desktop publishing program to produce the flier like the one illustrated here. Microsoft Publisher 97 and 98, which is the simplest and easiest to use of the Windows-based DTP programs described in this book, is ideal for a simple flier like the example. The other DTP programs, such as Adobe PageMaker, Adobe FrameMaker, Corel Ventura 7, or QuarkXPress, can certainly be used. Competent users of one of these programs would probably opt to use one without hesitation. However, since these programs include all the features required to prepare large, complex, multichapter documents, their use is like choosing an aircraft carrier for a fishing trip.

Therefore, if you're an entry-level DTP user, then you should consider a program like Microsoft Publisher. It is a first cousin to word processing programs, fast to learn, and extremely easy to use. Like other DTP programs, Publisher uses frames to contain text, pictures, and other objects such as graphic shapes, tables, and imported spreadsheets and charts. Text can be flowed from one frame to the next. For example, a three-column text page requires three rectangular, linked frames. It's easy to create free-form documents by adding and sizing frames on the underlying page. The

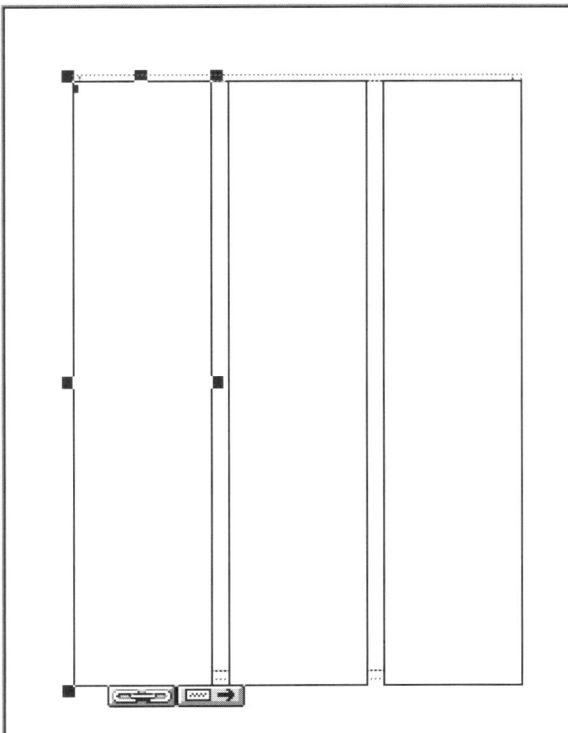

three-text frame example shows the text linking icons at the bottom of the left frame. This indicates that the text frame is linked to a following frame. Therefore, changes in one frame allow following text to adjust as necessary to maintain proper spacing.

Within your frames, you can easily insert the contents of your document by typing it. You can also cut and paste edited text from a word-processed document. Publisher is designed to operate interactively with Word, which gives you all of the editing power of a full-featured word processor and the graphic control of a DTP. Also like most DTP programs, you can put frames inside frames. This permits you to run text around small graphics. You can also group, ungroup, and control the arrangement of superimposed frames and other objects by selecting one or more and then using an Arrange menu.

One of the key advantages offered by Publisher is the large number of built-in, professionally designed document templates, or *wizards*. Clicking a wizard icon, which is labeled by document type, steps you through a

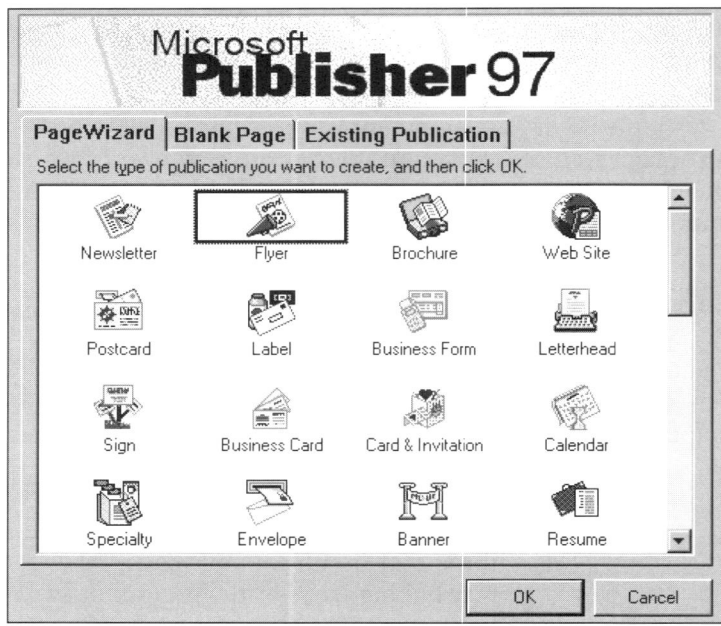

series of dialogs. You can pick from several designs, such as Modern, Classic, and Art Deco. You can also pick the number of pages and paper size and enter name, address, and date information, as appropriate. Publisher also provides a large repertoire of clipart images; a Design Gallery full of design element items like decorative borders, sidebars, fancy head-lines, and rules; and other impressive resources such as WordArt and a Web Site wizard. This wizard guides you through the creation and uploading of Internet- and intranet-compatible web pages. See *Learn Internet Pub-lishing with Microsoft Publisher 97* and the upcoming *Learn Internet Publishing with Microsoft Publisher 98* from Wordware Publishing, Inc.

Illustrating Program

You can also prepare high-quality fliers and brochures using a graphic pro-gram that is equipped with good text control. Examples of programs that are ideal for such use include Adobe Illustrator and CorelDRAW. A bitmap (raster) editor is only recommended for the preparation of interior bitmap images. A bitmap editor is really not suitable for the complete job, as the quality of text and graphic images is not maintained, particularly if you resize (or *scale*) the final product for printing. If bitmap images are required for your document, then you can import them, put them into position, and use vector graphics for the surrounding text and graphic objects. This provides the ability to mix vector and raster graphics within the same document. For example, photographs (bitmap images) can be combined with high quality line work and text elements (vector images) to achieve a dazzling flier or brochure.

Both Adobe Illustrator and CorelDraw offer an outstanding repertoire of drawing and text tools as well as advanced color control. If you plan to print your document in color, use the CMYK system. Be sure that you step

through the color correction procedures required to ensure the best possible color balance for your monitor, scanner, and printer.

If you are using a service bureau or a full-service printer that accepts files, you can save your document in encapsulated PostScript format from which film and/or printing plates are produced. If your document is full of color graphics, you may have to save it to a high-capacity storage device, such as an Iomega Zip disk, assuming that the service bureau or printer can accept this type of media. Today's read/write CD-ROM drives and media are also ideal for saving large, multi-megabyte documents. The CD format permits anyone having a modern CD-ROM drive equipped PC to read and process your files. If you do not have a high-capacity storage device, then you may have to use several floppy diskettes. You can use a compression program like PKZIP or WinZip to compress the files. Either of these programs have options that allow you to span multiple diskettes.

Catalogs

Catalogs can vary from a few pages to hundreds of pages, depending on the range of products being promoted. Catalogs are a good example of

documents that require both text and graphics to present and describe each listed items. Catalogs often include indexes to help readers locate the product of interest. Some are broken down into sections for different product categories, and therefore require headers and/or footers for section identification. A typical catalog page that was produced with CorelDraw 7 is shown here. Although CorelDraw includes 450 professionally designed wizards for many document types, including fliers, brochures, and business cards, a catalog wizard is not included. Even though CorelDraw and Adobe Illustrator are easy to use for preparing catalogs containing several hundred pages, you should probably consider using a desktop publishing program for the automation control offered for front matter, headers, footers, and indexes.

More information is presented about these features in the next chapter.

If your catalog is a simple one having four to eight pages, you can use a word processor or simple desktop publishing program. You can use the same approach as you would when preparing a simple brochure. However, if it is more than a few dozen pages, consider a high-end desktop publishing program. Most, including Adobe PageMaker, Adobe FrameMaker, Corel Ventura, and QuarkXPress, work nicely for producing catalogs and similar large documents.

As mentioned earlier, the sample book catalog page was prepared using CorelDraw 7. Text frames were used to position and compose the descriptive text, book cover title text, and header text. The covers are mock-ups; normally, you would import a bitmap image of a four-color cover rendering for this kind of artwork. The cover's front panel, or *lid*, can be imported from the original graphics file. You can also scan the cover if it is already printed. Of course, this is rarely the case during the design phase of a new product catalog. Finally, you can create cover mock-ups, as was done for the sample. This is sometimes necessary when the final product design is unavailable.

Stationery and Business Cards

Everyone who ventures into a business requires a supply of business cards and business stationery consisting of letterhead and envelopes. These items are easily created and printed using one of the desktop publishing programs or a good illustrating program. Professionally designed letterhead and business card wizards are available in both Microsoft Publisher and CorelDraw 7. It probably takes a lot more time to create a suitable logo design than to produce the final card and stationery using your PC. You definitely want to use a vector-based illustrating program, such as Adobe Illustrator or CorelDraw, to perform your design work. You may want to examine available clipart to see if there are any shapes or artistic letters that are well suited to your logo ideas.

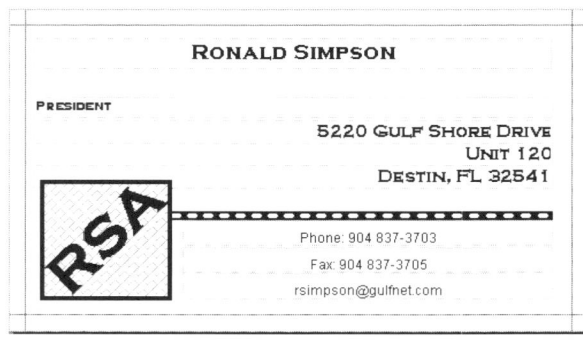

The adjacent example of a business card was produced using Microsoft Publisher 97's Business Card wizard. Publisher 97 also includes Letterhead and Envelope wizards. This card took less than five minutes to produce using the wizard dialogs. The series of wizard dialogs invite you to select one of twelve different design styles. It also prompts you to type

a variety of personal and business information. Two final prompts are included in the series. The first asks you if you want to continue your stationery design work by automatically moving to the Envelope and Letterhead wizards. The second and final dialog asks you if you want to print a single card or a sheet full of cards.

Newsletters and Bulletins

Newsletters and bulletins can easily be prepared using either a word processing or desktop publishing application. As with fliers and brochures, if the documents are simple, then use a simple application. If the newsletter grows to a tabloid format containing a few dozen pages with ad copy, lots of display type, and running headers, then you should probably move to an advanced desktop publishing program such as Adobe PageMaker or Corel Ventura 7. The simple variety of newsletters and bulletins addressed in this chapter are perfect candidates for your word processor or Microsoft Publisher 97 or 98.

The author's personal preference is Publisher 97 or 98, as it includes a Newsletter wizard that makes the creation and printing a breeze. The Weekly Blat example was created in a matter of minutes. Obviously, the text is *Greeked*, i.e., lines of random letters that show text size, spacing, and position. The wizard also supplies the artwork, and you are expected to replace it with your own appropriate pictures and illustrations. The beauty of a wizard is that it sets up your columns, headlines, and graphic elements for you, providing a starting place for your document. You can then replace or adjust any element to meet your personal needs. Once your template is set up, you can use a copy of it for following editions of your newsletter or bulletin.

Obviously, the most difficult task is that of researching and writing articles of interest to the intended audience. It's also important to use the appropriate graphic images, sidebars, and pull quotes to stimulate interest.

Formats

Small documents come in a variety of sizes and shapes. There are several keys to preparing an attractive, compelling, and economical document. Here are a few things to consider when planning your document.

Final Trim Size

The final *trim size*, i.e., the size of the paper stock, contributes heavily to the ultimate reproduction cost of your document. If your document is an odd size, that is, one that is not readily available, you will have to cut each printed sheet to the final size. This is particularly expensive if you are using a commercial printer, as it introduces another step in the reproduction process. Not only do you pay for the extra step, you pay for the paper wasted in the process. Therefore, consult your commercial printer to see what economical paper sizes are commonly stocked and available. Don't add unnecessary expenses that could be eliminated by placing a two-minute telephone call.

Most small offset duplicator shops are set up to handle standard letter-size and 11 x 17-inch paper. Most also have folders, which can turn an 11 x 17-inch sheet into a single-fold, four-page document. As a matter of fact, most offset print shops have duplicators that are designed to handle up to 12 x 18-inch stock. Exceeding this trim size will move you up to a full-grown printing plant and add the overhead costs associated with a larger payroll and the depreciation associated with more expensive photographic, film processing, and offset printing equipment.

Type Sizes, Typefaces, and Spacing (or leading)

Everyone quickly figures out that they can put more text on a page by reducing the type size. However, anything below 11-point may be difficult to read, depending on the typeface selected. Therefore, experiment with your typefaces and type sizes until you find the most readable combination for the allotted space. You may have to cut unnecessary words from your text, or rewrite a paragraph for economy, to get everything to fit. Text fitting is a common practice; however, don't change the meaning or impact of your message for the sake of space. Consider other alternatives, such as reducing the point size by a few tenths of a point or reducing the space between lines. The space between lines of text is measured from *baseline* to *baseline* and is called *leading*. (The baseline is an invisible line upon which the type rests. It touches the bottom of nondescending characters.) The term leading came from the days of hot metal type. Line spacing was achieved by inserting thin strips of lead between the type blocks of adjoining lines. Like type size, leading is also measured in points, where a point

Research indicates that typefaces with serifs, such as Times New Roman, are easier to read than gothic (*san serif*) letters.

Part
1

is approximately 1/72 of an inch. There are 12 points in a pica and 6 picas in an inch. The leading value is typically two points greater than the type size value. The notation 12/14 is used to describe 12-point type set on 14-point leading.

Type is measured from the top of an ascending character's stem to the bottom of a descending character's stem. The letters b, d, f, h, and k are examples of characters with *ascenders*, i.e., the part of the character that extends above a lower case character's body, or *x-height*. Descending stems extend below the baseline and are called descenders. The letters g, j, p and q are examples of letters with *descenders*. Letter

The baseline is an invisible line upon which the type rests.

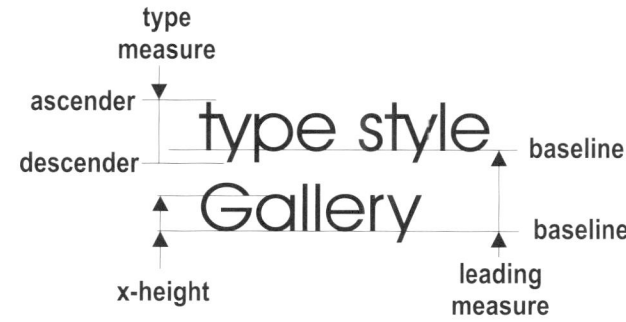

stem lengths often vary with the design of the typeface. With most typefaces, the leading should be greater than the type size to prevent having the descenders of one overlap the ascenders of the next line. Common combinations are 12/14 and 11/13. Using identical type size and leading values usually produces cluttered text that is difficult to read. However, if you choose a squat typeface, you may be able to specify the same type size and leading values, such as 11/11 or 12/12. In any case, experiment with the typefaces and interline spacing to determine what works best visually. The accompanying illustration shows measuring conventions used for type.

Screen Density

When printing a document that contains screened illustrations or filled text blocks, be sure to run and test print so you can check the dot patterns of screened areas. If the dots appear blurry or detract from the text, consider reducing the dots-per-inch (dpi) setting of your printed output. For example, if you experience plugging at 600 dpi, try printing at 300 dpi. Your Print dialog normally has provisions for changing the quality of the printed output. This is a case where lower is better.

When screened fills are used to create a text background, use an extremely light screen. Ten percent may be adequate to achieve the visual effect you want. Text set on a 20- to 25-percent screen will probably lose definition. Again, run test prints and carefully examine these areas for legibility and reproducibility. You can use an office copier to see how well the dot patterns are maintained when copied. This is an inexpensive way to test your screen settings before you send your document masters to a copy shop or commercial printer.

Layout

There are many things to consider when laying out any type of document. Small documents are usually easier to lay out than large ones, although brochures and newsletters can be challenging. First, be sure that you pick a suitable trim size as described in the Formats section found earlier in this chapter. Your layout should complement your message; never make the design more important than the message. This is a common mistake made by moviemakers in those instances when the cinematography supersedes the story line. Don't let this happen to your documents—you may lose your readers in the design or artwork.

Use meaningful titles, useful graphics, and other visual effects such as rules, sidebars, and pull quotes that make the article interesting. However, graphic elements, boxes, rules, and sidebars can be overdone. One reader observed, "There's so many italics and underlines that I feel like the writer is constantly shouting at me." Obviously, the overall impact was negative rather than appealing. Conservatism often equates to good taste. When using graphics, balance them on the page. Plan facing pages so that graphic elements are distributed in a balanced manner rather than clustering them in an unattractive knot. The sample two-page spread includes pictures and pull quotes that are reasonably balanced.

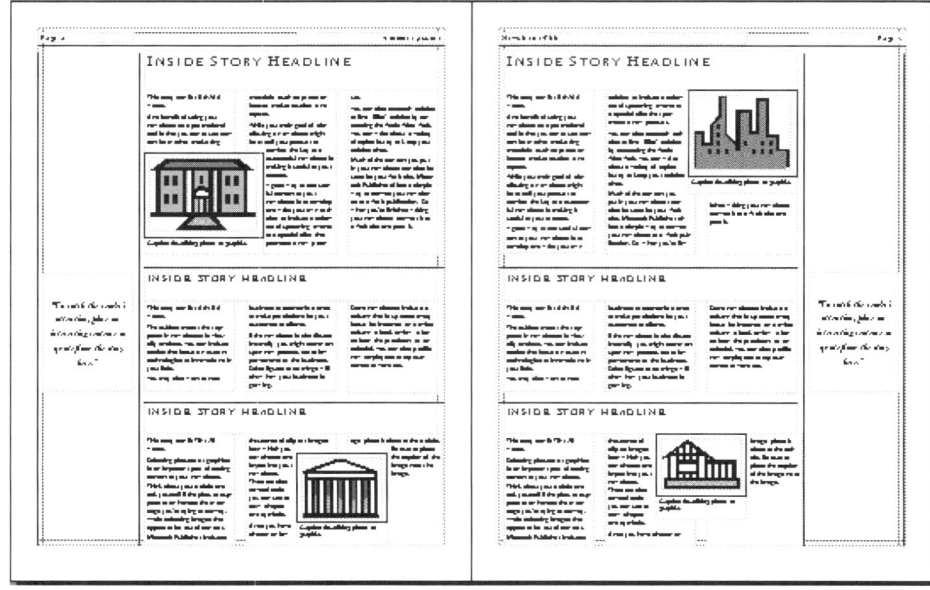

When articles span multiple pages, be sure to supply the appropriate "pointers." Use entries like "See Tournament on page 2" and "Tournament (Continued from Page 1)." Finally, print a proof of your document and compare it with a few professionally prepared examples. This is an excellent way to determine if your work measures up. Be as objective as possible, and don't be discouraged if your first attempt falls short. Remember that with a little practice, you can use your PC and the software described in this book to produce documents of any kind.

Postage

If you plan to mail your documents, you may want to check with your post office for the current regulations governing the use of third class mail, bulk mailings, reply postage, and postcard weight and dimension specifications. If you plan to print a direct mail piece, be sure that the revenue potential is greater than the underlying costs involved in preparation, printing, and postage. It is a good idea to experiment with a 100- to 200-piece sample mailing to determine the percentage of respondents. Once you have an estimate of the response rate and understand the corresponding revenue potential, you can make a more intelligent decision. Look at two examples.

Example 1:

Your product retails for $19.95 through a direct-mail campaign. The product costs you $10.00 to produce and package. The customer pays $3.00 shipping and handling, which is essentially your cost for packing material, labor, and shipping.

Your direct mail campaign costs $0.82 per piece, including the cost of the piece and postage. A 100-piece sampling yields three responses. Therefore, your 100-piece sample mailing costs $82.00. A three percent response yields $29.85 in revenue. Hence, the cost for a direct mail program exceeds the revenues. The decision must be to find another way to promote your product.

Example 2:

Your product retails for $119.95 through a direct-mail campaign. The product costs you $50.00 to produce and package. The customer pays $10.00 shipping and handling, which is your cost for packing material, labor, and shipping.

Your direct mail campaign costs $0.82 per piece, including the cost of the piece and postage. A 100-piece sampling yields three responses. Therefore, your 100-piece sample mailing costs $82.00. A three percent response yields $209.85 in revenue. Hence, the sample mailing indicates that the cost for a direct mail program will yield an excellent profit margin. The decision to promote your product through direct mail should be favorable.

Colors

If you have a generous budget, consider using color for a variety of elements within your document. However, your text should be predominantly black on a white or light pastel background to ensure good contrast and therefore readability. You can color sidebar text, rules, and graphic elements. Import color photographs, add color to headlines, and tint selected backgrounds. Choose your colors carefully. Don't overdo the use of color, as your document may cause sensual overload, which will definitely detract from your message. If you're in doubt about color choices, consider sticking with the colors provided by the built-in wizards. Check the color combination of similar pieces from successful, well-financed companies. They've probably paid a large fee to a top advertising agency for the layout and color recommendations of their promotional pieces. Finally, you can print samples and ask the opinion of several people to see which layouts and color combinations are most popular. This is certainly not a scientific poll, but it's better than receiving negative comments after you've produced the final document.

If you are working with a limited budget, the next notch down is a two-color treatment. Here, you can choose two complementary colors, such as black and navy. Use variable-density screens to provide different shades of gray and blue. You can even use a light-colored stock to achieve more color effects.

For the most conservative budget, stick with one color over either white or a light-colored stock. Be sure to consider combining variable-density screens with solids to maximize the impact of your document. Review the preceding Screen Density paragraph and adhere to the advice given there to ensure that your text-on-screen treatments are crisp and readable.

Schedule

If you must deal with a document that is produced on a regular basis, such as a weekly flier or newsletter, be sure that you establish deadlines for every element. This is particularly important if you must rely on others for contributions. When working with others, it's critical to provide a set of strong guidelines relative to text length, file types, image formats and sizes, and submission deadlines. Missing a submission from a single contributor can delay the entire document. The tighter the schedule, the more susceptible it is to failure. Therefore, it's necessary to manage the schedule of each contributor. Call them daily to check on their progress. You can

expect what you inspect. If you don't check, you may find yourself in an unrecoverable dilemma.

In addition to scheduling and managing submissions from contributors, you should also establish a reliable schedule for each step in the production and reproduction processes. Include a realistic amount of time for editing, word processing, desktop publishing, illustrating, proofreading and corrections, printing, and distribution.

Quality Control

The lack of an established quality control process can lead to serious and sometime costly problems. Documentation errors can require expensive revisions, recalls, extended customer support costs, product failure, false or misleading claims, legal problems, and a lot more. Therefore, establish a formal review procedure for your material. It is a good practice to have your document read by no fewer than three people before it is reproduced and distributed. Those who read it should include a professional grammatical editor, an experienced proofreader, and a person who is familiar with the subject matter. If you are involved in the preparation, your review will not have the objectivity and fresh look needed to catch obvious flaws. While writers tend to miss the same mistake over and over, experienced copy editors seem to find them in a brief glance.

Moving Ahead

With this treatment of small documents behind you, you're ready to examine both the conventions and tools used in the preparation of larger documents. Chapter 6 introduces you to multichapter documents and discusses the elements that are typically included in them. There, you'll also find tips on which software applications and specific features are well suited to creating and printing large documents.

Chapter 6

Large Documents

Introduction

This chapter describes the elements that are typically included in large, multichapter documents and books. It also presents common organizational structures, heading levels, and accepted practices. If you're an experienced writer, then you are probably familiar with much of the information presented here. However, if you are new to the diverse field of writing and publishing, then you should find this chapter extremely useful.

Books, Reports, and Product Specifications

Full-sized books and large, multichapter (or multisection) reports and specifications fall into the large document category. Because of their size, these documents often require "roadmaps" to the information and "mileposts" that mark your current position. To assist readers in their journey through the book, and to help them find specific information within, a number of navigation aids have been adopted over the years. These aids include such items as:

■ Title page—A page immediately following the outside cover with the document's title, author's name, and publisher's or company's name and address.

■ Copyright page—A page, usually on the back side of the title page, that contains the copyright line and additional information about the publisher, development team, etc. For trade publications (books sold in bookstores), *Cataloging-in-Publication* (CIP) *Data* and an *International Standard Book Number* (ISBN) are included here. (See chapter 12.)

■ Table of contents—A list of chapter/section titles, major paragraph headings, and corresponding page numbers.

■ List of illustrations—A list of illustrations and corresponding page numbers.

- List of tables—A list of tables and corresponding page numbers.

- Running headers and footers—Chapter, title, paragraph, subject, and/or page number information contained on each page (often omitted from the first page of a chapter/section).

- Chapter and/or section divisions—Divides a large document into topical subdivisions.

- Page numbers—A sequential Arabic number or a combination number that includes the chapter/section number and a sequential page number within the chapter/section.

- Paragraph numbers—A sequential paragraph reference number to help readers locate information.

- Footnotes and endnotes—Reference information found at the bottom of the page (footnote) or at the end of the chapter/section (endnote).

- Bibliographies—A list of referenced publications, reports, papers, etc. used in support of the information presented in the book.

- Glossaries—A list of special terms and definitions; usually located at the back of a book, but can be found near the beginning, depending on its importance and the author's personal preference.

- Appendixes—Additional information that is appended at the back of a book. Normally consists of reference information, bibliographies, tables, and charts that do not fit anywhere else in the book.

- Index—An alphabetical index is commonly placed as the last entry of a book. It serves as a roadmap to information within the book. It lists the topics and phrases and corresponding page numbers.

Elements Within the Document

The preceding list provides brief descriptions of the major components found in most large documents. In this section you find significantly more detail about many of the major elements that go into a book-sized document.

Cover

Cover types are usually determined by the purpose of the book and hence the *trim size* (outside dimensions) and the binding method used. A book's cover serves at least two purposes. First, it protects the interior pages. A book's cover also helps sell it. Appealing artwork combined with an engaging title attracts consumers. In its simplest form, the cover is simply another piece of paper. When the same stock is used for the cover as for the interior pages, it is said to be a *self-covering* book. Self-covered

documents are normally used as conference handouts, informal reports, or product specifications. These categories of documents are often three-hole punched and placed into three-ring binders or file folders for storage and protection.

Stitching

Self-covered documents are frequently bound with staples. Two staples along the binding edge is referred to as *side-stitched*. One staple in the upper left-hand corner is called *corner-stitched*. If the document is printed on folded 11 x 17-inch stock and stapled at the spine, the application is called *saddle-stitched*. Saddle stitching is normally limited to about 80-page documents.

SIDE STITCH   **CORNER STITCH**   **SADDLE STITCH**

You can also add a sheet of clear acetate (plastic) over the outside of a self-covered document for added protection. For improved protection, the cover stock is usually heavier than the interior stock. You can obtain heavy stock from any well-stocked office supply store.

Binding

In addition to "stitched" covers, there are dozens of other binding methods. These range from screw posts or metal clasps and *chipboard* (pressed paperboard found on the back of writing tablets) to cloth- or leather-wrapped chipboard. The most exotic cloth- and leather-bound books include end papers and cloth headbands, and the spines of the interior page signatures are Smythe sewn with durable thread and glued. The high-end books often include four-color dust jackets.

Other binding techniques use metal wire (spiral, etc.) and plastic combs (GBC Cerlox®). Spiral wire and plastic comb binding is often used for product service manuals and corporate procedure or policy manuals because they lay flat and are excellent for reference material. These binder types are sometimes found on cookbooks, but bookstore buyers often complain about these treatments. First, there are rarely readable spines on wire-bound books, so consumers will find it difficult to find a particular title when displayed spine out. Plastic comb binders sometimes have the title silk screened on the spine; this is a common practice and is done by commercial printers for an additional charge. Second, and just as important, both wire- and plastic-comb-bound books have a tendency to damage adjacent books. They nick and scratch other books when they are removed and returned to the shelf. Although they lay flat and are really better for reference purposes, they don't fit the accepted format found in retail bookstores.

Therefore, if your book is targeted to retail bookstores, you should use an adhesive-bound cover. Also called *perfect binding*, this is the most economical and structurally sound way to bind books when your print run approaches 1,000 units or more. Another treatment that is similar to the perfect binding process is used for some reference books that must lay relatively flat. Called Otabind® and Repkover®, these processes were developed in Germany to overcome the tendency that adhesive-bound books have of springing shut. The spine of the interior signatures (folded page sections) are not glued to the inside of the cover stock, as with perfect binding. Also, an elastic paper or fabric strip is glued against the spines of the signatures, separating them from the spine section of the cover. These processes allow a book to lay flatter, because the binding is looser and more elastic. Before you think you've found an alternative to plastic or wire, check the price. You may find the up-charge to be somewhere between 12 and 15 cents per copy. Unfortunately, the printers who are licensed to use these processes must pay a license fee for each bound book.

If your book is intended for the commercial book trade, be sure that the trim size is compatible with the bookstore shelves. The following three trim sizes (given in inches) are used most, although others within this range are quite acceptable: 5½ x 8½, 6 x 9, and 7½ x 9¼. Avoid unusual sizes, either large or small, that do not fit the general format found in bookstores. If you're unsure, go look.

Design and Preparation

The cover application often dictates possible design elements. Common reports and product specifications usually include large bold type on a plain paper or cover stock background. The title should be large and readable. Company reports that are used as a sales tool, such as the annual report of a large corporation, and *trade books*, i.e., books found on bookstore shelves that compete for the consumer's dollars, should include

attractive graphics. The spine of the book should include the title, author's last name(s), colors, and other graphic elements that make it appealing, as books are almost always stocked spine-out on bookstore and library shelves. Also, take advantage of the space on the back cover. Put sales copy, interesting graphics, promotional information, coupons, or other information of value. This is prime display space and should be used accordingly if your document is aimed at a commercial or trade market.

As a PC user, you can produce your own four-color separations using the illustrating programs described in this book. Four color no longer requires the use of expensive scanners and costly labor found in the lithography lab; you can combine and separate colored cover objects, i.e., type, graphics, and background colors, on your home or office PC. Once the files are ready, submit them to a film service bureau that is capable of outputting your files to film using a modern lasersetter. Almost every midsize city has a film service bureau that can accept your files and produce your cover film and a check print.

The major cost component of four-color work is for the preparation of your film and a color check proof. However, your charges for this process should not exceed $300 for a 10 x 16-inch or smaller 4/0 cover. The designation 4/0 stands for four colors over zero, or in plain English, the cover has four colors on one side and is blank on the other. If the local charges seem high, shop around. You may want to locate a service bureau in a large city, such as Los Angeles, Dallas, Minneapolis, Chicago, or New York. There, competition for your business is brisk, and your savings may outweigh the inconvenience of mail and telephone. Many service bureaus are connected to the Internet or have PC bulletin boards. This permits their customers to upload their files using standard data communications.

Front Matter

The front matter of a large document typically begins with the title page. It also includes a copyright page and table of contents. Optional elements include a list of illustrations, list of tables, foreword or preface, and any dedication materials.

Title Page

The title page of a bound book is the first sheet behind the cover. It is a *right-hand*, odd-numbered page and should include the document title in large type, any subtitle, plus the author's and/or company's name and the name and address of the publisher, as applicable. The title page is typically comprised of black text on white stock. With the exception of some publishing house or company logos and decorative rules or outlines, graphic elements are rarely included on a title page. The title page is normally counted as the first page of the book's *front matter* and is numbered as lowercase Roman numeral 1, i.e., page i. However, the number is not printed on the title page.

Copyright Page

The copyright page is located on the reverse side of the title page. The page number, which should be ii, is sometimes printed on the page. Because it is located on the reverse side of the title page, it is a *left-hand*, even-numbered page. The copyright page can contain several elements. Look at the copyright page of this book to see those elements. The most important entry on the page is the copyright notice. The proper form is either:

Copyright 1999 Rightclick Publishing, Inc.

or

© 1999 Rightclick Publishing, Inc.

The word Copyright and the symbol © are often used together in the form "Copyright ©" followed by the year and the name of the holder. However, this is improper, as indicated by international copyright rules. It is identical to saying copyright twice, and therefore redundant.

Other elements found on a copyright page include Cataloging-in-Publication (CIP) data and the book's International Standard Book Number (ISBN). Trademark acknowledgments are also included on the copyright page when they apply.

The CIP data is obtained from the Library of Congress for books that are commonly found in libraries. Libraries use CIP numbers to catalog books and for shelf placement. Some book categories, such as disposable workbooks and periodicals, are ineligible for CIP data.

The ISBN is obtained from the R.R. Bowker Company. You can request application forms to acquire both of these numbers. A large amount of information about copyrights, CIP data, and ISBNs is presented in chapter 12.

Table of Contents

The table of contents usually begins on page iii, and is numbered accordingly. Often entitled "Contents," it includes section and paragraph titles and opening page numbers. When paragraph numbers are used, these are also included with the paragraph titles. Dot leaders are often used to align the page numbers with the title entries. Tables of contents typically include chapter/section titles and two paragraph levels, i.e., the primary and secondary level paragraph titles. Depending on the structure of the book, you

may wish to include the third (*tertiary*) level paragraph entries, although this is an exception to the rule. Books that contain several layers of descriptive detail may have thousands of paragraph title entries, which could result in a huge content section. Therefore, be careful as to how many paragraph levels you decide to include.

A useful feature included with the word processors described in this book is the ability to create a table of contents automatically. However, this requires that you plan to use this feature in advance by tagging each of your headings with a style tag, i.e., Chapter Title, Heading 1, Heading 2, etc. Once the book is finished, you can use the automatic table of contents feature to collect the selected levels into an accurate contents matrix. You can even select a style to obtain the desired appearance. If you modify your book, delete the table of contents and rerun the feature to update any changes to titles and page numbers.

Lists of Illustrations and Tables

These entries are sometimes included in large technical reference books that include numerous charts, tables, and illustrations. Although rarely used in trade publications, technical specifications and reports often require them, depending on the governing preparation specification. When used, the tables and illustrations are usually numbered for reference purposes. These lists typically follow the table of contents. They often begin on the same page that contains the last entries of the tables of contents and should have the same appearance as the table of contents, i.e., use the same columns, spacing, and dot leaders, as applicable.

Foreword or Preface

These elements are located as the last element of the front matter. The author can pick either title, i.e., *foreword* or *preface*, as they both mean the same thing. The word *foreword* is a derivative of "before word." Remember this when you spell it, as many fledgling writers mistakenly spell it as "forward." You can think of *preface* as a face (or page) that precedes the body of your book. In either case, these elements contain introductory comments, either by the author or by someone who can lend credibility or interest to the book. In addition to introductory remarks, you often find credits and other acknowledgements. Sometimes a separate Acknowledgements page is included in books that have an extensive list of contributors. This page is usually placed between the table of contents and the foreword or preface.

Interior Elements

The main part of your book consists of the information presented in the chapters or sections. The following paragraphs describe the elements that typically make up chapters or sections. In the descriptions, the term *chapter* is used as the major subdivision, although many books use the term *section* in place of chapter. However, some books use sections to subdivide chapters. The following list itemizes the subordination scheme typically found in books and sets of books.

Volume or Book 1 of *n*—The first book in a set of two or more books.

Part 1 of *n*—Large books are sometimes divided in parts. Parts are subdivided by consecutively numbered chapters or sections.

Front Matter—Typically includes the title page, copyright page, table of contents, and preface.

Chapter—The major subdivision of a book when part subdivisions are not included.

Section—Sometimes used to subdivide books, parts, or even chapters.

Primary or First Order Heading—The first paragraph level used to subdivide a chapter or section.

Secondary or Second Order Heading—The second level paragraph used to subdivide primary headings.

 **Note:** There must always be two or more paragraph levels. For example, you must have at least two second order headings, two or more third order headings, and so on.

Tertiary or Third Order Heading—The third level paragraph used to subdivide secondary headings.

Fourth Order and Higher Headings—Further subdivisions of paragraphs.

Back Matter—Typically includes appendixes and an alphabetical index at the back of the book. May also include bibliography.

Headings

A wide range of headings is used within books. Chapter openings include the chapter number and a descriptive name. Paragraph headings consist of descriptive names. It's important to clarify subordination. For example, a primary paragraph heading may be all capital letters in a special boldface type font, and separated from the following text. Secondary headings may also be all uppercase boldface letters run in with following text. Third

order headings may be boldface upper- and lowercase letters run in or separated from following text, depending on your personal preferences. When more subordinate paragraph levels are required, you can use italics, underlines, and even special fonts to designate the level. See the following example.

Chapter 3

INSTALLATION INSTRUCTIONS

PRIMARY HEADING

This is an example of a primary level heading and following text. The next paragraph shows a secondary heading example.

SECONDARY HEADING   Notice that this secondary heading is run in with the first line of text. It is boldface and all capital letters.

Third Order Heading   This third order heading is upper- and lowercase run in with the first line of text. It is boldface.

Fourth Order Heading   This is a fourth order heading example. It is bold italic run in with following text.

<u>*Fifth Order Heading*</u>   This is a fifth order heading example. It uses underlined normal weight italic type.

You can also use indents and outdents to designate different heading levels. Note that these are only examples. You can create your own paragraph heading subordination scheme, as long as it is reasonably clear to the reader.

Tables

Whenever you have information that has two or more categories, you can choose to use either a list or a table. If the list can be organized into three or more columns, you should probably opt for a table. Tables are extremely efficient for presenting information that can be organized into rows and columns. In addition, tables are relatively easy to create and edit using the current versions of word processing and desktop publishing software.

Although table styles often vary from book to book, they should be fairly consistent within the same book. Both ruled and unruled tables are used. Some use rules above and below the column headings and after the last line. Others use exterior and interior rules to outline the table and separate both columns and rows. Still others use low density screened or colored fills within the column headings. You can experiment with rules, typefaces, and fills until you obtain a satisfactory effect.

Table 6-1. First Example

Date	Expense Item	Amount	Comments
11/26	Airfare	358.00	D/FW – SEATAC Round Trip (MasterCard)
11/26	Hotel	133.66	Seattle, WA Marriott (MasterCard)
11/26	Meals	48.50	Seattle and Redmond, WA (Cash)

Table 6-2. Second Example (bridged column headings)

Tool or Material			
Tool	Material	Part No.	Quantity
Screwdriver		FB126CS	1
	Adhesive	G123B	6 oz. tube
	Tape, Electrical	TE56C	100 ft.
Wrench, Allen		WHl66BT	1

Tables are either numbered or run in with text. When numbered, such as "Table 3-1 Tools and Materials," for the first table in chapter 3, it simplifies referencing. Numbered tables are usually titled. Run-in tables are usually referenced in text with a phrase like, "Tools and materials required for installation are presented in the following table." Therefore, the placement of run-in tables is much more important than that of numbered tables.

Illustrations

Like tables, illustrations may also be run in or numbered for reference purposes. Illustrations are assigned figure numbers. For example, "Figure 4-2 Packaging Material" would be the second illustration in chapter 4. Illustrations are typically line or screened drawings. The preparation of line art should use a vector illustrating program, while screened illustrations, such as screen shots or photographs, should be prepared using a pixel editor. Both applications are used for mixed illustrations that contain both screened and vector graphic elements. Again, today's word processing and desktop publishing software make it relatively easy to put one or more illustrations on a page. Automatic text runaround features make it easy to flow your text around inserted illustrations. Format dialogs are available to set the space between your artwork and the surrounding text.

Headers and Footers

Headers and footers are used to identify the chapter, book, or paragraph name. The specific information and placement often alternates between

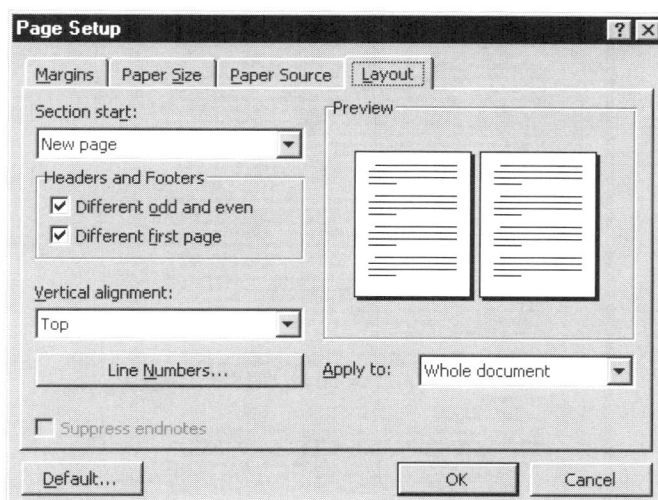

odd- and even-numbered pages. Footers may contain page and/or section numbers and names. Headers often contain the book's title on the left-hand (even-numbered) page and the chapter or section title on the right-hand (odd-numbered) page. The Page Setup or Headers and Footers dialog of most full-featured word processing and desktop publishing programs provides controls for setting the layout of both odd and even page numbers. Following are some examples of how headers and footers are sometimes used.

Example 1—Alternating Page Headers and Footers

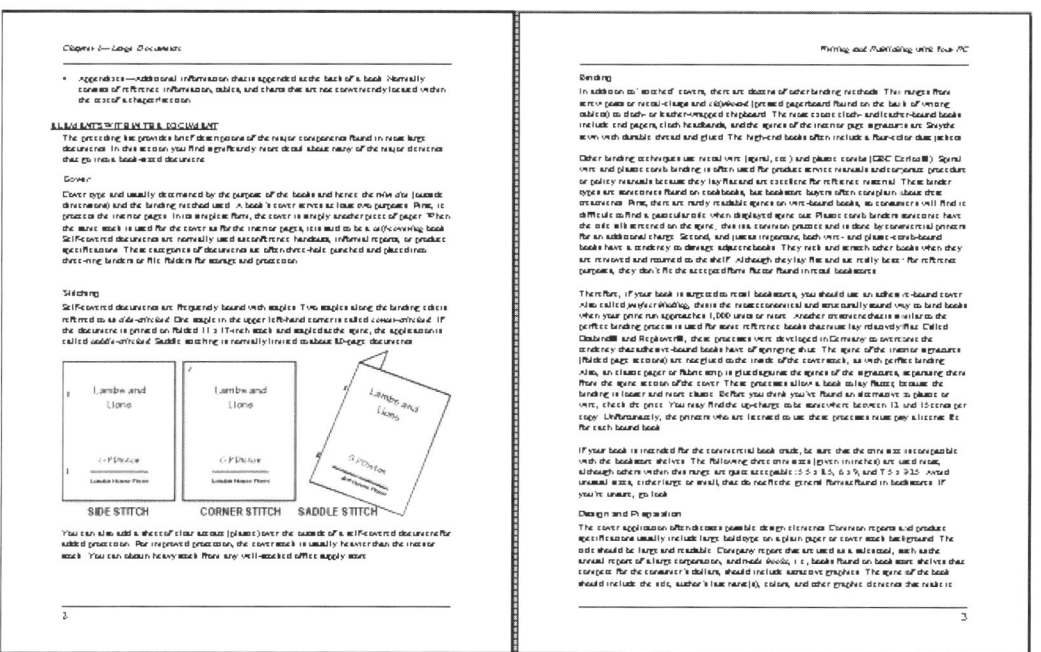

Example 2—Reversed Page Header and Footer with Centered Page Number

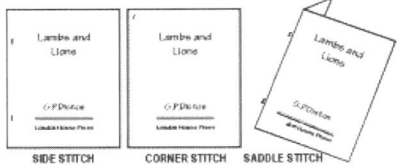

Example 3—Page Numbers Embedded in Alternating Header; No Footer

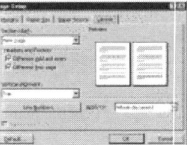

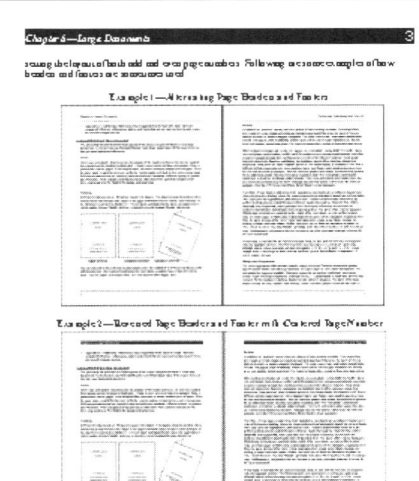

Footnotes and Endnotes

Like headers and footers, footnotes and endnotes also have controlling dialogs on full-featured word processing and desktop publishing software. Footnotes are located at the bottom of the page on which they are referenced, while endnotes are located at the end of the document, much like a bibliography. The references are typically superscript Arabic numbers that follow a word or phrase within the text. The text of each footnote, located at the bottom of the page on which the reference appears, typically cites the information source, such as a book, journal article, or quotation.

Example of Footnote

In Chapter 7 you begin your examination of Windows-based desktop publishing programs. There, you learn ways to prepare small documents that include both text and graphics elements. The tools introduced there include programs that are quickly learned and easy to use. In particular, Microsoft Publisher 97 is introduced, which is ideal for the preparation of small

[1] Footnotes and Endnotes, John C. Hughes, © 1995 Plantation Press

The illustration that follows shows Microsoft Word's Footnote and Endnote dialog and the Note Options dialog. Notice the available controls. You can choose either a footnote or an endnote; select the numbering sequence, the starting number, and the placement (bottom of page or beneath text); and choose special symbols within both the page text and the footnote or endnote citation.

Footnote and Endnote Dialogs and Controls

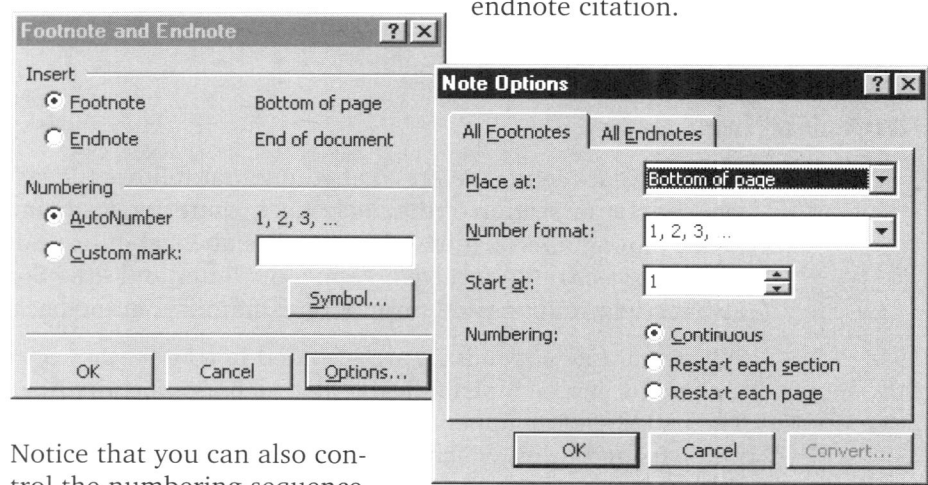

Notice that you can also control the numbering sequence between chapters (or sections) by using continuous numbers, restarting the numbers in each section of your document, or restarting the numbers on each page. The All Endnotes

tab, found in the Note Options dialog, omits the Restart each page option button.

References

Referencing information within the same book is done in numerous ways. The use of paragraph, figure, and table numbers makes referencing easy. You can use, "…as shown in figure 4-3" or "(See table 5-1.)." Notice that the parenthetical reference ends with a period because it is a complete sentence. When a numbering system is not used within a book, you can refer to a paragraph by its chapter number and paragraph title name, such as, "as described in the Tools and Materials paragraph of chapter 2." Note that the term *chapter* can use an initial capital letter or be all lowercase. The latest style guides seem to suggest lowercase, although the long-standing practice has been to use an initial capital letter when the word chapter or section is used in a reference.

When figures and tables are *run in* with text (inserted with the text of a document without the use of a number or title), the layout of the book is critical. References are usually in the form, "as shown in the following illustration," or "(See the table that follows.)." The words *follows* and *precedes* are used in preference to *below* and *above* as figures and tables often appear on a following or preceding page rather than below or above. Although this is a minor point, it is more accurate and certainly less ambiguous. Reference to page numbers, such as "(See the figure on page 123.)," is not recommended, as page numbers have a tendency to change during the production process. When this happens, your readers may never find the intended destination.

Back Matter

The term *back matter* refers to anything that follows the last page of the last chapter or section of the book. Back matter typically includes appendixes, bibliographies, glossaries, and alphabetical indexes. Bibliographies and glossaries often receive an appendix letter and title. Some publishers also include coupons and promotional materials in the back matter.

When multiple appendixes are included in a book, they are traditionally assigned a capital alphabetical letter, such as appendix A, appendix B, etc. The heading of an appendix carries the same style as chapter or section numbers and titles, which means that each appendix also has a descriptive title. You can reference an appendix using a phrase such as "listed in appendix B."

When your book includes sequential Arabic numbers, 1 through *n*, the page numbers in appendixes should continue the numbering sequence. If

your numbering scheme includes a chapter or section number prefix and a sequential Arabic number suffix, as in pages 3-1 and 3-2 for the first two pages in chapter 3, you should apply a parallel scheme to the pages in each of your appendixes. The first two pages of appendix A would be numbered A-1 and A-2. Similarly, the first two pages of appendix B would be B-1 and B-2.

The Alphabetical Index

Alphabetical indexes provide your readers with fast access to specific information within a book. Therefore, it's important to produce a complete, accurate index that points to the important topics within your document. Many educational institutions will not adopt books that do not include alphabetical indexes.

Good word processing and desktop publishing programs offer automatic indexing tools that let you mark titles, words, and phrases within your document for inclusion in the index. If you only mark the terms found in the text, you will produce what is sometimes referred to as a *key word in context* (KWIC) index. Although this type of index is certainly helpful, there are situations in which additional descriptive words or parallel terms can be extremely helpful, which improves the quality of the index. Some examples are shown in the following table.

Word/Phrase in Context	*Parallel Words/Phrases*
Disk drive	Hard drive Drive, disk Storage media Media, storage
Semiconductor	Integrated circuit Computer chip
Airliner	Passenger plane Airplane Commercial airliner

These are simple examples. The key is that you anticipate other terms or phrases that a reader may consider when searching for information within your document. Many index utilities allow you to insert words and phrases of your own, while others restrict your entries to what appears in your text. The major advantage to an automatic index utility is that when page numbers shift, the index entries are updated automatically. However, as a longtime author, I prefer to produce indexes manually. This process is only performed after a book's pages are typeset and all page numbers are set. Preparing an index from a manuscript copy is a waste of time, as all page numbers will change when the document is typeset in final form—the entire indexing process must be repeated.

The manual index is accomplished by turning each page in the final document and typing a list of the words and phrases followed by the page number on which they appear. When a topic spans several pages, enter the page number on which the topic begins. Sometimes authors enter multiple page numbers, such as:

> Software, applications, 16-23

Rather than:

> Software, applications, 16

Giving a range of pages often requires much more effort than it is worth in terms of value to your readers.

Once a list of words, phrases, and page numbers is typed, use an alphabetical sort routine to arrange the list in ascending alphabetical order. All modern word processors include such a routine. For example, Word's sort utility is found in the Table menu, while WordPerfect's Sort dialog is accessed from the Tools menu.

Once the list is sorted, you must collect identical entries and gather the page numbers. The following list shows several identical entries. Notice how several entries are combined on a single line.

Entries beginning with "Internet."

> Icons, 59
> Internet, 11
> Internet, HTML, 55
> Internet, 43
> Internet, JavaScript, 78
> Internet, JavaScript, 124
> Internet, web browsers, 18
> Itinerary, travel, 4

Combining and subordinating the Internet entries.

> Icons, 59
> Internet, 11, 43
>   HTML, 55
>   JavaScript, 78, 124
>   Web browsers, 18
> Itinerary, travel, 4

Notice how combining entries condenses the size of the index. Also, notice how entries are subordinated with indentation. Subordination requires that a term exist alone as well as with modifiers.

Once the list is typed, sorted, and combined, you can apply any number of styles to your index. The fist word of each new alphabetical entry can be set in boldface, the letter can be centered above the index column, and so on. Indexes are normally set in two or three columns. Wrapped lines should use *hanging indents* to make it easy to identify each index entry. The following illustration presents an example of an index.

Example of 3-Column Alphabetical Index with Letter Headings

Index

A

Ability, 333
Accessibility, 267
Acquisition editors, 251, 270
Adhesive binding, 150
Administrative requirements, 303
Adobe FrameMaker, 168, 199-209
    dtp checklist, 234
Adobe Illustrator, 47-75
Adobe PageMaker, 166, 190-199
    dtp checklist, 233
Adobe Photoshop, 75-88
Advance marketing, books, 278
Advance sales, books, 279
Agent URLs, 272-273
Agents, 251, 271-273
Agreement, author, 254-267
    alternate formats, 264
    author copies, 265
    author needs, 261
    author qualifications, 260
Agreements, with agents, 271
Alphabetical index, 148, 161, 174
Appendixes, 148
Application forms, copyright, 320
Application tools, 185
ARJ, 34
Artwork,
    acquiring, 43
    submission, 269
Ascender, 141
ASCII text (TXT) files, 178
Author agreement, 254-267
Average labor multipliers, 344

B

Back cover, 246
Back matter, 154, 160
Barcode, 243, 246
Barcode scanners, 243
Baseline, 141
Basis weight, paper, 290
Beneficiaries, author agreement, 267
Bibliographies, 148
Bid specifications, 288
Binding methods, printing cost, 292
Binding, 149, 291
BIN-HEX format, 47
Bitmap graphics, 38-40
Bleeds, 180
Book clubs, author agreement, 265
Book covers, 148
Book potential, author agreement, 260
Book proposal, 14, 253
BOOKLAND EAN (EAN 13) barcode, 243, 246
Books, reports, and product specifications, 147
Bookstores, 281
Borders, word processing, 31
Bulk, paper, 290

C

Caliper, paper, 290
Camera-ready copy, 187
Cataloging-in-Publication (CIP) Data, 152, 327
Catalogs, 137
    book, 278
CD-ROM drives, 137

Chain bookstores, 279
Channels of distribution, 241, 243
Chapter and/or section divisions, 148
Chapter, book subdivision, 154
Chapters, page numbers, and blank backs, 184
Chroma, 41
CIP Data Sheet for Books, elements and example, 328-329
Clipart, 44
Clipboard, 185
CMYK, 40, 41, 244, 291
Color gamuts, 42
Color models, 40
Color schemes and contrast, screen captures, 126
Colors, 144
Common names, 9
CompactPro, 47
Competing works, author agreement, 266
Completeness, 274
    manuscript, 32
Compression, file, 34
Computer screen captures, 45
Computer screens, 38
Computer-To-Plate (CTP), 289
Consignment, 282
Consistency, writing style, 274
Contents and indexes, 25
Contact proof, 289
Co-op advertising, 281
Copy editors, 273
Copyright
    and national origin of the work, 305

367

You can condense the type in your indexes and reduce the space between columns to fit more text on each line. This reduces unnecessary line breaks and the overall size of your index. Using small type in seldom-used references is not as offensive as using small type within the narrative of your document. Therefore, when your index is extremely large, consider using type as small as 8-point on 9-point leading. Obviously, your selection depends entirely on the body size and corresponding legibility of the selected typeface. Therefore, experiment with several typeface and size values until you achieve a suitable result.

Page Makeup

The page makeup process, sometimes called *pagination*, as applied to large documents is more efficient when you take advantage of the publication management features provided by your word processing or desktop publishing program. Although you can manually enter page numbers, chapter titles, and front and back matter, it's significantly easier and much more reliable to use the multichapter control features. Therefore, it is well worth your investment in time to learn how to use these features. In both word processors and desktop publishers, you must establish and use style names, or *tags*, to take full advantage of the available features.

Word Processing

Both Word and WordPerfect make use of *master documents* and *subdocuments*. The master document is a control document in which front matter, chapters or sections (called subdocuments), and back matter are inserted. The subdocuments themselves are independent document files that can be opened and edited independently. You can also open and edit them within the master document. They are referenced from within the master document. When the master document is printed, much of the pagination, content compilation, and indexing work is performed on the entire document quickly and accurately.

For example, when you print the master document, consecutive page numbers are automatically assigned and printed without the need to intervene. If the last page number of chapter 3 is 24, then the first page number of chapter 4 is 25. You probably want each new section to begin on a right-hand, odd-numbered page, which is the common practice. When some of the preceding sections end on right-hand, odd-numbered pages, blank pages are automatically inserted for you. If you want to omit a header from the first page of each section opening—no problem. The master document can automatically take care of this detail for you.

You can look at different views of a master document to check paragraph subordination. You can display a simple list of section names, a specified number of paragraph levels in outline form, or the complete text. When displayed in outline format, you can quickly see if you only have a single paragraph-level entry, or if one is out of place. A toolbar is available to let you quickly promote or demote paragraph headings to a different level to maintain proper subordination. This feature gives you a fast way to view and organize your document. The accompanying master document view shows three paragraph levels.

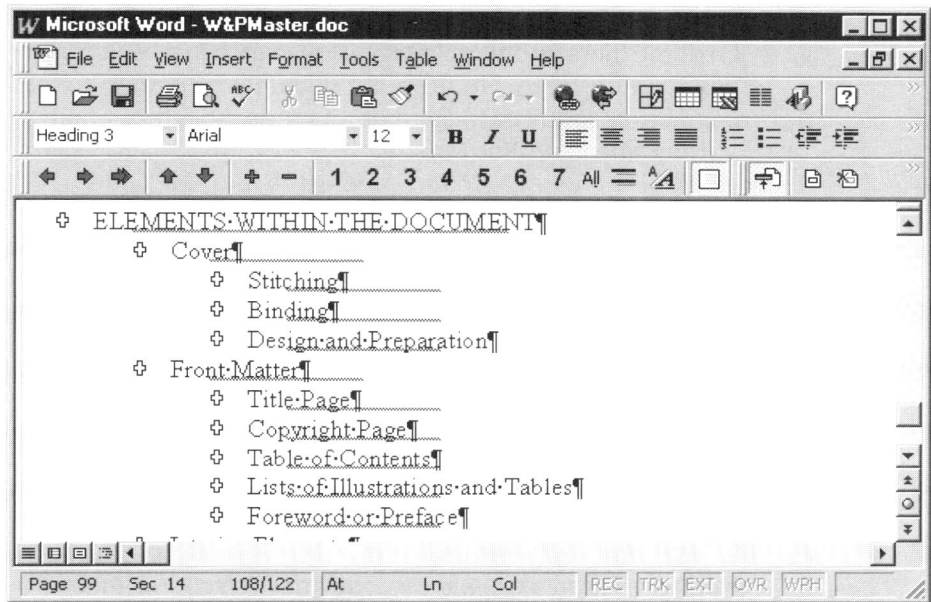

Part

1

It is necessary to use paragraph heading and body text styles if you want to use your word processor's master document feature. You should recall that you also have to use heading style tags, such as heading 1 or heading 2, to compile a table of contents. The master document uses these style tags to create a table of contents that includes every subdocument (section) within the book.

Desktop Publishing

The high-end desktop publishing programs, such as Adobe PageMaker, Adobe FrameMaker, Corel Ventura 7, and QuarkXPress, all automate the pagination process to one degree or another. Each achieves pagination, i.e., header and footer control, page numbering, and the generation of contents, in different ways. Corel Ventura 7 provides the most controls for pagination, and is the richest in typography controls (tool buttons, menus, and dialogs). Once you become a skilled user, you can accomplish similar results with practically any full-featured desktop publishing program. However, once you become competent in the use of a high-end desktop publishing program, you may find that the others are neither similar nor intuitive. It's difficult to make a direct knowledge transfer from one program to another, with the possible exception of typography terminology and basic file management tasks.

This is not as true with a program like Microsoft Publisher 97, which is ideal for fliers and newsletters. However, because Publisher 97 is not intended for large, multichapter documents, it does not offer sophisticated pagination controls. In spite of this shortfall, you should seriously consider putting Microsoft Publisher 97 in your toolkit, as it is perfect for creating quick fliers and newsletters, and it is by far the simplest desktop publishing program to use. In spite of its simplicity and ease of use, professional desktop publishing operators will almost always use their high-end programs to create even the simplest documents. Why? Because they know that they can create any type of document using their high-end programs. So, like most of us, they avoid taking the time required to install and learn yet another program, particularly if it doesn't add any new capabilities.

Because the pagination control features are so varied among the different desktop publishing programs, a brief overview of the way each handles multichapter documents is provided. Perhaps these descriptions will help you decide upon one of the programs mentioned here. Before getting into the detailed descriptions, you should know that some of the desktop publishing programs use a master document/subdocument approach much like word processors. A master document contains a list of the publications; subdocuments are individual chapter files that are inserted (or listed) in the master document. You can work with individual chapters by opening the chapter file to perform normal editing tasks. You can reorganize the position of each of the chapters by moving their position within the master document. Apply identical styles to headings, notes, and common elements within each of the subordinate documents to produce accurate front matter. If you plan to produce an automatically generated alphabetical index, be sure to mark each of the index entries within the text of each subdocument. You will certainly be glad you took the time to be consistent throughout the document, as the alternative to automated front and back matter is extensive manual labor and a high potential for errors and omissions.

Adobe PageMaker 6.5

The term *multiple publication document* is used by PageMaker to identify large documents that are created from multiple files. When you first open a new document, a Document Setup dialog invites you to select the page size, margins, and page number settings. Once your individual documents are created and saved, you can create a master template that includes common book elements. Common elements include margins, columns, text styles, headers and footers, colors, and other design elements used on each of the pages of the document. It is necessary to set up page number markers in the master template. If you use page number prefixes, add them or change the numbering format for each section template or publication.

When you plan to use the automatic table of contents feature, be sure to use consistent paragraph styles throughout all subdocuments. If you are using color, specify the color in the master template. This guarantees that the colors are the same throughout all publications that are based on the master template.

When you assemble multiple publications into a book, you can work with each publication as part of one large book. This permits you to create an index and a table of contents and print the book; however, you still have the ability to work with each publication independently. Individual publication file sizes are smaller than that of the entire book. Therefore, when working on your document, the memory and disk resources are relatively small and your computer's performance is better.

You can assemble a book by creating a book list in one of the publications included in your book. The Book Publication List dialog, shown here, is

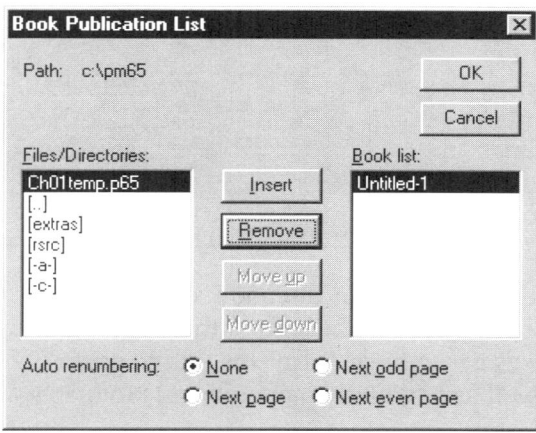

used for this purpose. Consider using the table of contents or the index publication. The book list identifies which publications you plan to assemble into your book. When the index is produced or the book is printed, PageMaker uses the book list in the active publication. The list is used to repaginate the book and compile index or table of content information. When the book list is not contained in the open publication, these tasks are only performed on the publication that is currently open.

Be sure that the book list is arranged in the proper order, as the order controls the order in which PageMaker repaginates and prints each publication. If a publication is out of order, the page numbers, index, and table of contents will also be out of order.

Although a publication can only contain a single book list, individual publications can belong to any number of books. This is a convenient document assembly feature, particularly if you tend to use "boilerplate" documents that fit in several different publications. To create a book list:

1. Open the publication that will contain the book list.

2. Use Utilities > Book and double-click the name of each publication file you want to add. The files can be located in different folders on your hard drive or network.

3. Click Move Up or Move Down to change the position of a selected publication.

4. Click Remove to delete a selected publication from the list and click OK to complete the task.

Adobe FrameMaker 5 and 5.5

Adobe FrameMaker has been in use on Sun Microsystems workstations and PCs for several years. It was originally designed with large documents in mind, and includes many features that lend themselves to the creation and maintenance of large, multichapter books. Several companies produce books containing a thousand pages or more using FrameMaker. To create a multichapter book, use the File > New menu to open a dialog from which you can choose a document type. Click Book and then the page orientation. If you are not using 8.5 x 11-inch paper in either the portrait or landscape orientation, click Custom. This dialog permits you to input the *trim size* (page dimensions) of the final, trimmed book page. Once the dimensions, margins, columns, and the pagination fields are set, click Create to display the first page of the chapter.

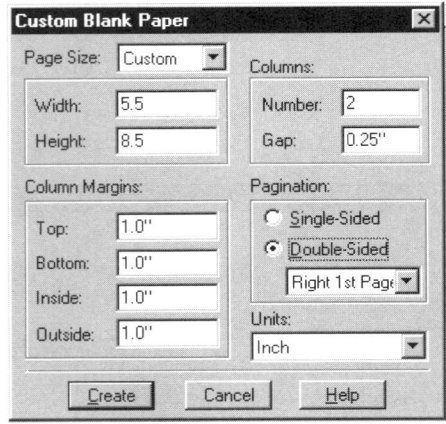

A master page contains standard text frames for the body text as well as for headers and footers. In addition, page numbers and other repetitive elements are added to the master page. You can also control the page number style and sequence, as well as beginning page numbers for each file.

Once a series of chapter documents are created and saved, you can open a new document and then save it using a publication name of your choice. Then use File > Generate/Book to open a Book window. Here, you can generate books and files used to produce a final paginated book.

Unlike a document file, a book file lists each of the filenames that comprise a book. Each of the files must be opened, edited, and resaved individually. When the Book window is open, book management menus are available from which document files are added, removed, and rearranged. You can also generate a table of contents, index, list of figures, and list of tables using the Book window menus and dialogs. Like all desktop publishing programs, each of the individual chapter (or subdocument) files should use an identical set of styles and master page layouts.

Although FrameMaker is an excellent page makeup and book assembly program, it is not as intuitive as some of the other desktop publishing programs that make use of familiar toolbar buttons and shortcut keys. For example, to center align text on a line, the key sequence Esc j c (for justify center) is used rather than the familiar Ctrl+E or the Center button. However, like any other program, using the program familiarizes you with both its operation and shortcut keys. If you're willing to invest some time learning Adobe FrameMaker, you'll be able to produce practically any kind of document, regardless of the size.

Corel Ventura 7

Large publications are created with Corel Ventura 7 by assembling all of the chapter files into a publication. Corel Ventura features a Ventura Navigator that lists each of the chapters as well as the master pages and illustrations that comprise a publication. Selecting a chapter file and then right-clicking displays a shortcut menu. This menu provides access to a number of chapter- and master-page-related operations, including saving, closing, go to, and properties. You can also use the Navigator to drag either master pages or chapters from one publication to another. This trick requires that you simultaneously open both the source and target publications. Once you've copied the desired items to the target document, you can close the source document.

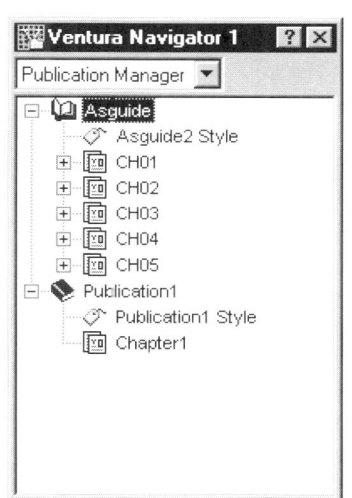

The general procedure for preparing a multi-chapter document follows. It assumes that you use your word processor to create your copy, although you can type your text directly into a Ventura text frame.

1. Create and save the text of each chapter using your word processor.

2. Open a new publication page.

3. Use Page > Master Page Properties to set up the page dimensions and orientation, i.e., portrait or landscape.

4. Use View > Master Page to display the Master Page view.

5. Use Format > Frame to set up margins, columns, and default typography (baseline, justification, widows and orphans, headers and footers, page numbers, etc.).

6. Return to the Page Layout view and use File > Import Text to add the word-processed text to the open Ventura document. You can import more than a single text file into a chapter.

7. Save and name the chapter; the default extension vp is automatically assigned.

Note: Saved Ventura 7 files include all elements of the document including style sheets. Prior versions saved multiple file types for chapters, text, style sheets, etc.

8. Use the Tools > Navigator menu to display the Ventura Navigator dialog. This dialog displays the name of the open publication.

9. Right-click on the publication name within the Navigator. Then click New Chapter to open a new, blank chapter file having the same page layout and text styles as the first chapter.

10. Add or type the appropriate text file for the new chapter.

11. Continue this process for as many chapters as required.

The Ventura Navigator is also used to display the contents of the table of contents and index. These are produced using the Format > Table of Contents/Index menu selection and corresponding dialogs. The dialog prompts you for the locations of these elements. Normally, you would create a new, blank chapter into which the index or contents is compiled. Once there, you can block copy the index or contents to the appropriate location in another chapter. For example, you would want to insert the contents into the first chapter immediately following the copyright page.

QuarkXPress 3.3.2

QuarkXPress was originally developed for the Macintosh computer and is among the leading desktop publishing programs used by commercial type houses and service bureaus that use Macs. It was rewritten for the Windows environment and has not had sufficient time to capture a significant market share. However, those who are making the move from Mac to Windows will certainly want to take a serious look at QuarkXPress for Windows as a potential desktop publishing tool, particularly if they are familiar with the operation of the Macintosh version.

Quark did not provide a full-featured program in support of this book, so a demonstration version of version 3.2.2 was used for feature evaluation. The demo program disables saving and some printing features. This limitation prevents the ability to fairly evaluate multichapter document preparation, and therefore only a cursory examination could be performed. After a careful review of the help topics and all menus and dialogs,

QuarkXPress 3.2.2 for Windows did not appear to include a suitable set of pagination features. The closest thing to a pagination feature was the Page > Section dialog, which is used to control page number sequences. Headers and footers can be created manually. QuarkXPress's Help information indicates that page numbers are placed in text boxes. Unfortunately, these must be created and placed manually. Perhaps version 4.0 automates this feature.

Legal Issues

When you publish a book, there are a number of legal considerations that come to the forefront. These include:

Copyrights—Be sure to properly copyright your own work in addition to obtaining the proper rights to use copyrighted work from other resources. (See chapter 12.)

Liability—You must pay particular attention to any potentially inflammatory language that might result in a libel lawsuit.

Damages—Certain instruction manuals and user guides should include disclaimers in order to limit liability resulting from incidental damage caused by product use or the misapplication of information contained in the book.

Permissions and Release Forms—If you use photographs, artwork, text excerpts, or even software or web site excerpts from other resources, be sure to obtain the proper releases from the legal owner of the adopted material. Develop a collection of release forms for artwork, photographs, text excerpts, and electronic media.

Liabilities

Not long ago a publisher printed and began distribution of an expensive four-color coffee table book that included hundreds of pictures of copyrighted artwork. The owner of the artwork threatened the offending publisher with a lawsuit and required that the distributed books be immediately recalled and destroyed. The publisher quickly complied to avoid the expense of what would certainly have been losing litigation. The situation was well known to most people associated with the market in which the incident occurred. The book's publisher probably lost close to $100,000 on the project, and their action was viewed as stupid by many who are familiar with the event.

In some instances aggrieved copyright holders are less aggressive and will often settle for a firm commitment from the violating publisher to discontinue production of the work in the current form. In these cases, the offending publisher must often agree to exclude the copyrighted material from subsequent editions of the publication. Even the mildest of violations can be costly in time and product loss.

Serious cases can cost the offending publisher tens of thousands of dollars in legal fees and product loss. Therefore, be sure that your material does not infringe on the rights of others. If it does, you may find yourself talking to lawyers. You should also know that in most author agreements used by publishers the author agrees to indemnify and hold the publisher harmless for any material that violates the property rights of any third party. As a practical matter, both the publisher and author are named as defendants in a lawsuit, in spite of the agreement between the author and the publisher. In other words, the plaintiff "follows the money," in the belief that the publisher more likely has the ability to fund either an out-of-court settlement or a financial judgment. However, the author agreement, which indemnifies the publisher against author plagiarism or the use of inflammatory or libelous material, gives the publisher recourse against the violating author. When this happens, the author will definitely regret his offense, as he could well wind up in financial and emotional ruin.

The object lesson here is for authors to be extremely sensitive to the use of other people's work, and to refrain from damaging or libelous language. Similarly, publishers must be vigilant; their editorial staff should look for potential pitfalls, particularly in books that address controversial topics.

Obtaining Permissions: Release Forms

As a practical matter, most authors and publishers like to be quoted, particularly if the book in which they are quoted provides a descriptive credit line. This is usually viewed as free advertising for the cited work, and can potentially result in a sale of the book or software from which the material was taken.

Even with this benefit and the absence of malice, it is still advisable to prepare and store release forms for use by those who are willing to give you permission to include their text, graphic images, computer programs and files, or music in your publication.

Your release form can be a word-processed page and should include the following information:

■ Name, address, telephone number, fax number, and e-mail address of the requesting publisher

■ Name and address of the granting publisher

■ Title of the work in which the excerpted material will be used

■ A brief description of the work and its intended audience

- Purpose (or reason) for use of the excerpted material
- The territory (usually worldwide rights in all languages)
- Request from the granting publisher for the language to be used in the credit line
- A statement that certifies that the granting publisher is the legal owner of the cited work, has the right to give permission for use of the excerpted material, and holds the requesting publisher harmless for its use
- Signature and date blocks for both the requesting and granting parties

In addition to these elements, you can send a copy of the final book to the granting publisher to demonstrate your compliance with their request for an appropriate credit.

Quality Issues

Everything a writer or publisher does is on paper for everyone to see. Every typo, misspelling, inaccurate reference, and misleading or incorrect statement becomes a glaring error. Quality control for writers and publishers must be a proactive and pervasive program, rather than a last-minute review.

It's both interesting and universally accepted that most errors are caught either in final page proofs or after a book is printed. Just ask anyone who has been in the writing and publishing business awhile, and they will agree. A little common sense tells us that this doesn't have to be the case—but it almost always is! The rework of final pages and the need for errata are expensive, embarrassing, and almost always unnecessary. An appropriate quality control program can eliminate most of the cost associated with rework and errata. The quality program cost is always cheaper than the eleventh-hour costs associated with rework. Although the cost in consumer dissatisfaction can't be quantified, it certainly exists.

There's nothing like a good checklist to remind every contributor of the things they need to inspect. Checklists typically include entries such as:

- Title
- Author name (as it will appear on the book) and contact information
- ISBN
- Price
- Key task completion dates (schedule)
- Credit lines
- Trim size

- Number of copies
- Page makeup specifications (margins, headers and footers, type styles, etc.)
- Barcode requirements
- Names of key project contributors (project editor, desktop publishing specialist, etc.)
- Contact information (phone, fax, and e-mail)

Writer Responsibilities

Every writer is responsible for the accuracy of his or her manuscript. With the advent of computer-based spell checking, thesaurus, and grammar checking utilities, there is little reason for extensive mechanical errors. The writer should also ensure that proper names are correctly spelled, as the editor may not have access to authoritative sources of information. In addition, the writer should comply with accepted writing practices relative to grammar, parallelism, subordination, and reference conventions. Consistency is key to clarity; don't vary the names or spelling of people, places, or things without a good reason. Finally, the writer should use the outline view to ensure proper paragraph subordination. Never submit printed material and document files without ensuring that every chapter and appendix has been carefully checked using these tools. The small amount of extra time required to run a spelling check on the manuscript can save the publisher's editorial and production staff hours of unnecessary work and unnecessary delays.

Alphabetical Index

Because the writer is a content expert, he usually participates in the preparation of an alphabetical index. The writer should compile a comprehensive list of words and phrases found in the book. All index entries should be meaningful; never include incidental references that send readers on fruitless searches. The index entries should direct readers to hard information about the corresponding word or phrase. Also, each entry's page number should be carefully checked as it is typed. Sending a reader to the wrong place is frustrating and reflects badly on the work. Once the list is compiled and sorted, combine identical entries. Verify that the sort routine has put each entry in the proper place. Finally, spell check the index, print it, and save the result to disk. Read the printed index carefully and make any necessary corrections. Then send the final work to the publisher.

Technical Books

When writing a technical book, particularly one that is tutorial in nature, the writer must ensure that the procedural steps and program code are as accurate as possible. If you include source code, either in the book or on a companion diskette or CD, be sure that it is compiled and executed to verify its accuracy. Appendix A describes a two-step quality control program that is often required by governmental agencies.

Publisher Responsibilities

The type of publication being produced dictates the duties of the publisher or company publications department. In the case of a legitimate trade publisher, the publisher is responsible for grammatical editing, page and cover design, proper pagination, the final title, delivery to the printer, marketing, and distribution. The publisher ensures that the front matter, i.e., table of contents, list of tables and/or figures (if used), copyright, Cataloging-in-Publication (CIP), and acknowledgements and credits are properly executed. The publisher also writes and applies back cover copy and the necessary barcode. Books intended for exclusive distribution to bookstores must have an EAN barcode; books that are distributed by mass merchandisers require UPC barcodes. Books that go to both markets place the EAN barcode on the inside front cover and the UPC barcode on the back cover. Detailed coverage of these topics is provided in chapter 8.

The publisher should use the most recent edition of the prevailing style guides and dictionaries. Good editors catch hyphenation, punctuation, and consistency mistakes. However, even the best copy editors cannot assume responsibility for the quality of your writing or illustrations. If they find themselves involved in extensive rewrites or must have the artwork redrawn, they will probably send the manuscript back to the author with a general note explaining the problem. This, too, is the responsibility of a good copy editor—knowing when a manuscript is unsuitable for publication.

Printer Responsibilities

If your book is being produced for the retail trade, it must compete in quality with other books found on the bookstore shelves. The printer should be experienced in printing, binding, and shipping books of this quality. The printer must know that the final product must be no less than excellent—no exceptions. Supply a sample of a good quality book to show your printer what you expect. Look at samples of work he has produced to be sure he can meet your requirements.

The printer must do the job right the first time. If he doesn't, you can expect him to print the book again the right way for no added charge. In fact, you can expect a reduction in price, as you will suffer a loss in sales and customer dissatisfaction from late delivery. Delays due to rework at the printer's facility cause you to miss shipment dates, delay billings, and even lose orders. Unfortunately, when a printer's quality is poor, it's normally because their personnel are not well trained or supervised, their equipment is substandard, or both.

Finally, the printer is expected to pack and ship your books to you in durable cartons of the proper size. The packing should be tight to keep the books from shifting inside the box during transit. The boxes should be properly marked with the title of the book, ISBN, and the quantity of books contained in each carton. Labels should be securely attached to each carton to show the destination address.

As you can see, quality must be designed into the process from beginning to end. When the proper tools are in place and every contributor is sensitive to quality issues, you can rely on a positive outcome. You will optimize the book's utility, appearance, and profitability.

Moving Ahead

In chapter 7 you begin your examination of Windows-based desktop publishing programs. There you examine the features of these programs for preparing large, multichapter books. There, the programs are examined in more depth to help you decide which one best fits your needs. Of course, this will depend on the type and size of published documents that you regularly produce. If you produce both small and large documents, you may wish to consider installing two desktop publishing programs on your computer. If you resist learning more than one program, you may only want one. In any event, if you are new to the field, you will know much more about desktop publishing programs when you complete chapter 7.

Chapter 7
Desktop Publishing

Introduction

This chapter provides overview information for several popular Windows 95/NT-based desktop publishing programs. Its goal is to familiarize you with the key features and some of the differences among the top-selling desktop publishing programs that are in use on Windows PCs. The PageMaker and QuarkXPress programs have their roots in Macintosh graphic workstations. FrameMaker's origins are in Unix-based workstations, while Ventura Publisher was incubated and grew in Intel-based PCs. For example, FrameMaker was first used on Sun Microsystems workstations; the early Ventura program was introduced for PCs using the MS-DOS operating system. The first release of Microsoft Publisher was designed for use with Windows 3.1.

All of these programs have come a long way. Corel Ventura 7 is richer, faster, and easier to use than it was a few years ago. Adobe PageMaker has also evolved from a Macintosh-like program to a full-fledged Windows product; experienced Windows users can get up and running quickly with familiar shortcut keys, menus, and toolbars. Needless to say, Microsoft Publisher 97 and 98 use familiar Windows metaphors throughout, making them the most intuitive for Windows applications users. But, because Microsoft Publisher is specifically aimed at small documents, such as fliers, brochures, newsletters, stationery, and web site pages, it is not the best choice if you plan to process large, multichapter books. However, it is an outstanding choice if you produce material in the small document category.

As you peruse the information in this chapter, you may want to jot down a few notes about each of the products being described. In particular, pay close attention to ease of use, the repertoire of features, the difficulty of learning, versatility, and the resources required by each of the programs. A good starting point is to determine what features are important to you, personally. Are you doing small documents such as brochures, booklets, or newsletters? Are you specializing in large, multichapter books? Do you have to produce a variety of documents that encompass both small and large documents? Your answers will point you to one or perhaps even two of the desktop publishing programs described in this chapter.

Desktop Publishing Programs

The different desktop publishing programs that are reviewed in this chapter include:

■ Adobe FrameMaker 5 and 5.5

■ Adobe PageMaker 6.5

■ Corel Ventura 7

■ Microsoft Publisher 97 (with a few words about Publisher 98)

■ QuarkXPress 3.3.2

General operating procedures and a look at some of the key screens, menus, and dialogs are presented in the Desktop Publishing Software Reviews section of this chapter. Before examining each of the desktop publishing programs, some important background information is presented. This information is intended for those readers who may be unfamiliar with the category of desktop publishing or typography.

Software Compatibility Issues

Most modern software programs include a variety of file filters that permit you to import files created by other programs of either the same or similar category. Some open other file formats directly, while others use import and export selections. For example, Word can read and write WordPerfect, rich text format (RTF), ASCII text (TXT), Microsoft Works, and Write files. Similarly, some desktop publishing programs can import files from popular word processing, database, and spreadsheet programs. However, not all desktop publishing programs read the files produced by other desktop publishing programs. The data structures and format control schemes used by each desktop publishing program are quite unique.

There are a few ways to exchange information between two different desktop publishing programs. One would be to export your file in a common file format, such as rich text format (RTF), WordPerfect, or some other format that is common to all of the programs that you use. Once saved, the file can be imported by another program. If the target desktop publishing programs cannot open or import one of the listed file formats, you should consider cutting and pasting text between programs.

For example, you can simultaneously open two desktop publishing programs. Next, highlight and copy the contents of one file to the Windows clipboard. Finally, switch to the target program, display a blank page, and paste the text from the clipboard to the cursor position of the destination document. The amount of information that can be transferred depends on the capacity of your computer: specifically, the amount of memory used by each desktop publishing program in addition to the total amount of memory available to the clipboard. Another approach might be to copy text from a desktop publishing program into your favorite word processor. Copying files from one Windows program to another is easy once you understand the rudiments of cut-and-paste and drag-and-drop.

Measures

Both type size and line leading are diagramed and described in the Type Sizes, Typefaces, and Spacing (or *leading*) section of chapter 5. Here, some additional information about type measure is provided. Desktop publishing programs typically give you a choice relative to the units of measure you can use. Your personal preference dictates your choice. You can work with inches, centimeters, or picas and points. Commercial type houses around the world use picas and points as their preferred unit of measure. This is the measure used by both professional typographers and commercial printers, although local measurement conventions, such as inches and metric measures, are still in heavy use. Most of us tend to mix measures; we measure page and margin sizes in inches or centimeters and type in points and picas. The key is to use familiar measures so you can control the outcome—use measures that you can easily visualize.

Picas and points are typically used to measure line lengths and column widths; points are used to measure type size and line spacing (*leading*). For a scale of relative size, there are 12 points in a pica and 6 picas per inch. Therefore, there are 72 points in an inch, give or take a few ten thousandths of an inch. You can obtain a scale measured in picas and points, called a *line gauge*, from most graphics art supply stores. Line gauges have picas and points along one side and inches (or centimeters if you work in a metric-oriented country) along the other edge. Most printers keep a line gauge in the pocket of their aprons. In fact, they are so common, many printer aprons have a deep, narrow pocket specifically designed to accommodate one. Although you can convert points and picas into inches or centimeters using a calculator, it's a good idea to familiarize yourself with pica and point measures and then begin using a line gauge to check your dimensions.

Layout Tips

Information relative to the layout symmetry of facing pages is discussed briefly and illustrated in the Layout section of chapter 5. In addition to accomplishing visual symmetry, or balance, through the careful placement of the graphic, text, and tabular elements of a document, there are other issues to consider. These include:

■ Trim (Page) size

■ Margin settings and line lengths

■ Font selection and line spacing

■ Crop marks

■ Chapter openings and blanks

■ The use and placement of graphic objects and *runarounds*

Trim (Page) Size

The first decision that you must make when laying out a document is to determine the page size and orientation. If the page layout is not dictated by a customer specification, then you must select a trim (page size) yourself. Your selection should be based on convention, i.e., what's typically accepted in your target market, and economy. If you intend to have your book displayed on trade bookstore shelves, then you should consider a standard trim. Small books often use a 5½ x 8½ or 6 x 9-inch trim. Larger books commonly use 7½ x 9¼ to 7 x 10-inch page dimensions.

Paper

Paper represents approximately 35 percent of the manufacturing cost of a book. This percentage varies with the current cost of paper, which fluctuates with energy costs, plant capacities, and market demand. Whatever the current cost, the most economical trim size is the size that minimizes the amount of paper wasted when the final book is cut to size. The size you use should be determined well in advance of your desktop publishing work. Discuss economical page sizes with your commercial printer to determine which size best fits his presses. This varies with the equipment used by different printers, so you may want to obtain some bid estimates early in the process.

Bleeds

A bleed is any printed object, such as a *bleed tab*, that exists at the outside edge of a trimmed page. Bleed tabs, which are typically reverse (white on black) letters located at the outside edge of the page, are common to alphabetized directories. When bleeds are used, extra paper is used to

accommodate the cut edge. This allows the black background of a printed tab to "bleed" off the edge of the page.

Margin Settings and Line Lengths

After you've determined a trim size, you must next determine the outside dimensions of your text and graphic objects. This includes both body text and marginal text, such as headers, footers, and footnotes. If your book is adhesive bound, the inside (binding-edge) margin should be slightly wider than the outside margin, as adhesive-bound books often obscure the bound edge of the page. A wider inside margin minimizes this problem; consider using at least ¾ of an inch (4.5 picas) for your interior margins. A ½-inch (3-pica) outside margin is quite adequate.

Obviously, the trim size of the printed page and the inside and outside margin widths dictate the typeset line length. The line length also contributes to the readability of your copy. Excessively long lines are more difficult to read than short ones. You can shorten the line lengths of a wide format book by using two or more columns or by using hanging indents for your body text. Although this complicates the typesetting process, it definitely improves the readability. When two or more columns are used, you must also set the space between columns, called the *gutter width*. The sum of inside, outside, and gutter margins subtracted from the trim width leaves the total space available for text and graphic objects. Hence, the line lengths of each column are easily calculated: For example, if you are using two equal columns on a 7½-inch page width with the margins shown in the following table, the line length of each column is 18 picas.

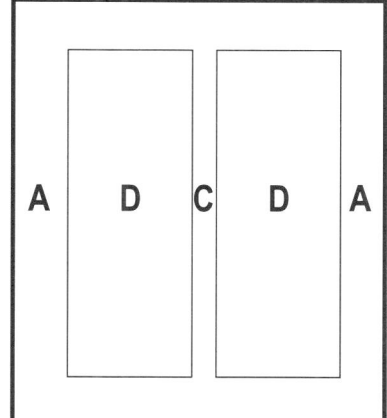

Key	Item	Dimension
A	Inside margin	4½ picas (54 points, ¾-inch)
B	Outside margin	3 picas (36 points, ½-inch)
C	Gutter margin	1½ picas (18 points, ¼-inch)
D	Column widths	18 picas (3 inches)
	Total line length	36 picas (6 inches)

In addition to the inside and outside margins, the top and bottom margins must also be established to make room for the headers and footers. Several dimensions must be determined. First, the distance from the edge of the page to the top of the header text or the baseline of the footer text must be established. In addition, the distances between the body text and the header and footer text must be established. The type size of the header and footer text added to these dimensions control the overall depth (top-to-bottom measure) of the body text. Continuing the example with a 9¼-inch page height, consider the following dimensions:

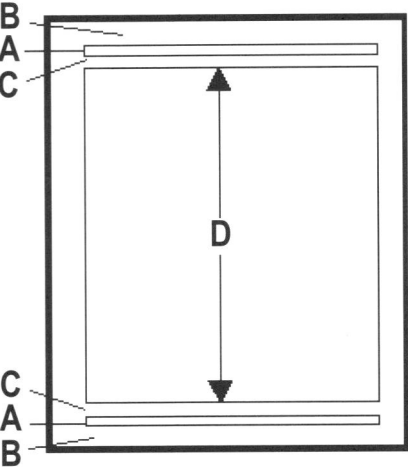

Key	Item	Dimension
A	Header/Footer	10-point type (ascender to descender)
B	Top/bottom margin	4½ picas (54 points, ¾ inch)
C	Header/footer space	2½ picas (30 points)
D	Column depth	47 picas, 8 points (572 points)
	Total 11/13 text lines per page	44 (11-point type on 13-point leading)

As you can see, there are a number of dimensions that must be known to establish a coordinated page design. Be sure you understand these dimensions and how they interact before you begin your desktop publishing tasks.

Font Selection and Line Spacing

The preceding example required 11-point type on 13-point leading to fit 44 lines of text in the allotted column depth. In addition to understanding how many lines of text fit within a column, you should also consider the impact on the book's page count. Large type and leading expands the size of a book. If you're looking for economy, then you must tighten up your text by selecting a smaller type size, a condensed type style, tighter leading, or all. Text fitting is only one consideration. A primary consideration involves the readability of the selected font and size. Extremely small type makes a book difficult to read. Selecting excessively large type can explode the book's page count, making it more expensive to print, ship, and warehouse. Of course, if you have a small manuscript, you may want to employ strategies to bulk up your book. To achieve a spine width that is large

enough to be seen on a bookstore shelf, it may be necessary to resort to some of the following measures. Use:

- Large, expanded type
- Additional white space (more leading above and below headings and paragraphs)
- Wider inside and outside margins
- Wider indents (use for subordination of paragraphs; use more hanging indents)
- Deeper top and bottom margins
- Large header and footer type (consider adding graphic elements to your headers)
- More graphic elements (use for chapter openings and within body text)
- More illustrations, pull quotes, and sidebars
- Bulkier paper

All of these strategies are employed for bulking books. Conversely, you can reduce the size of a book by taking opposite measures. Use smaller, condensed type; fewer illustrations and sidebars, and specify paper that has a high pages-per-inch (PPI) rating. (See Text Stock in chapter 10).

Crop Marks

Crop marks should be included on your printed pages. They mark the edges of your trim area, and are used by printers to register the pages during film and plate making operations. The crop marks are also used as guides when the final bound pages are trimmed. All professional desktop publishing programs give you the option to print crop and registration marks within the program's Print or Preview dialog. Therefore, if you plan to print camera-ready reproducible copy (called *repro*), be sure to include crop marks on the printed page.

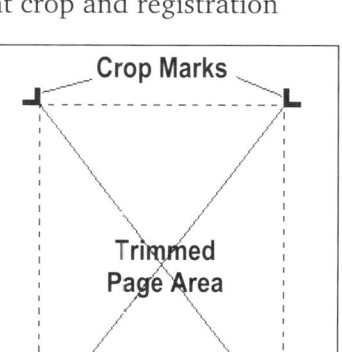

If, for some reason, a crop mark cannot be provided, then put one or more repeating elements on each page. Then a uniform dimension can be established from the elements to the trimmed edges. If rules are used in your headers and footers, you can use the edge of the rules as a reference point. Although this approach is crude and definitely more difficult for the printer to use, it can be done when absolutely necessary. The accompanying illustration shows how crop marks are placed at the outside edges of the trimmed page.

Chapters, Page Numbers, and Blank Backs

The first page of each chapter or section within a book normally begins on a right-hand, odd-numbered page. Page 1, therefore, is typical of a chapter opening. When a chapter ends on a right-hand, odd-numbered page, the back side of that page will have a blank (unprinted) back. This convention is used so that the following chapter can open on a right-hand page. There are exceptions to this practice in books that contain a large number of small chapters or sections. The exception minimizes an excessive number of blank backs to reduce the overall page count of the book. Therefore, if you find yourself faced with a reference-style book that contains fifty or more small chapters, you should definitely consider opening your chapters as they fall, i.e., on either right- or left-hand pages.

When you submit a book to a printer, you should provide a printed proof copy of the book and a "reproduction assembly sheet" to show the page numbers included in each chapters as well as those pages that are blank. This eliminates any guesswork relative to the layout of your book. Following is a brief example of a repro assembly sheet.

Reproduction Assembly Sheet

Description	Pages	Blank Pages	Description	Pages	Blank Pages
Front Matter	i-viii	iv, viii	Chapter 6	101-124	124
Chapter 1	1-10	None	Chapter 7	125-152	None
Chapter 2	11-24	24	Appendix A	153-166	166
Chapter 3	25-40	40	Appendix B	167-184	None
Chapter 4	41-72	72	Bibliography	185-186	None
Chapter 5	73-100	None	Index	187-192	190, 191, 192

As you can see, the preceding example of a reproduction assembly sheet accounts for every page in a book. It tells the printer exactly how each page is placed in the book. The assignment of an odd or even page number also tells the printing personnel exactly how each page is arranged in the book relative to right- and left-hand orientation. Most preformatted sheets also provide a space for the total number of pages, total blank pages, and contact information including names, addresses, telephone and fax numbers, and e-mail addresses. If you supply your document in digital (PostScript) format to your commercial printer, you must supply additional information with your reproduction assembly sheet. For more information,

see the Digital Data (Files) paragraph of the Output Options paragraph a little later in this chapter.

When submitting a four-color cover with a blank back (the most common case), you use the term (4/0) to tell the printer that the cover is four-color process on one side and blank on the other. The "4" designates four color; the "0" designates blank. If 4/1 is used, it tells the printer that the cover is 4-color on one side and 1-color on the other. The expression 4/4 specifies that four-color printing is applied to both sides of the cover stock.

Tools of the Trade

In addition to presenting information about the writing and publishing processes, this book describes the "tools of the trade." This includes Windows-based word processing, illustrating, and desktop publishing programs. A few additional tools include such devices as high-capacity removable drives (see sidebar) and scanners.

Selecting the right programs to use and knowing how they work is an important start. However, understanding how they can be used interactively to achieve a smooth, coordinated work environment extends the utility of each. Here are a few examples of how you can use these programs together. Once you are familiar with each and try these techniques, you will likely find even more ways to use these programs as a unified resource.

The Clipboard

The Windows clipboard is a marvelous tool, as it lets you move text and pictures from one application to another. Simply cut or copy a selection from one application, move to the target application, select an insertion point in the open document, and paste the contents of the clipboard. If you want to create a link between the pasted object and its source, use Edit > Paste Special in place of Edit > Paste. When linked, changes to the source object automatically update the pasted object in the target application. This powerful Windows feature provides an excellent way to place spreadsheets, charts, illustrations, and tables into your published documents.

Application Tools

Most of us would much rather create copy using a good word processing program than typing our text directly onto the blank page of a desktop publishing program. Why? Because we are more comfortable using the familiar word processing program that is designed especially for text creation and editing. The tools offered by today's word processing programs, including the spelling, grammar, and thesaurus utilities, are extremely useful. In contrast, the desktop publishing program provides infinitely better text and pagination control. Similarly, you should usually avoid the use of a simple drawing aid found in your word processor when you have access to a full-featured illustrating program. Therefore, maximize the quality of your work by picking the right tool for the job.

Fortunately, the desktop publishing programs take advantage of the power of most of the other program tools. They do this by importing both text and graphic files created by other popular programs. Therefore, be sure to create and spell check your text using a compatible word processor. Similarly, use a good illustrating program to produce your drawings. Once created and saved, use your desktop publishing program to integrate the output of your other programs. If files are not directly compatible, you can usually export the document or illustration from the originating program to a mutually compatible format. A few minutes of experimentation usually reveals the preferred processes.

Format Control

When you use your word processor to create your source text, use the text attributes, i.e., boldface, italic, and underline, that you plan to use in the final document. You should also use table controls, as most high-end desktop publishing programs properly interpret and display word-processed tables. Text attributes and tables are usually transferred when imported into the desktop publishing program. You may also want to use the font styles and sizes that you plan to use in the final document, although these settings are lost when the text is transferred and tagged. You can even set up your page size and margins to approximate that of the final book. This will give you a reasonable idea as to the size of your final document.

To do this, you can create paragraph and heading styles in your word processor that correspond to those used by your desktop publishing program. This helps you produce a manuscript that resembles the final book. Regardless of how your manuscript looks when displayed in your word processing program, remember that these paragraph styles are lost once the document is imported into your desktop publishing program. The style settings of your desktop publishing program must be applied to reestablish the desired formats.

Once a large, multichapter document is ready to be desktop published, you'll find that it is easier to *preprocess* each chapter of the document before importing it into the respective chapter of the desktop published document. Preprocessing includes typing the style (or *tag*) controls using your word processor before importing the document into your desktop publishing program. Although top-end desktop publishing programs also

feature macros, the macro features supplied by programs like Microsoft Word and Corel WordPerfect are usually easier to use. Of course you must know how the heading and paragraph tags work and are applied before you can preprocess the document. Using Corel Ventura as an example, here's what a few sample tags look like.

Part

1

Note:
Body text tag codes are not needed as anything not specifically tagged defaults to body text.

Tag Description	Example Tag Codes and Document Content
Heading	@head 1 = Introduction
Body text	This document is designed for use with the Tritium Industries Cyclatron Accelerator. This unit features the following capabilities:
Bullet	@bullet = Multiply the processing speed of the primary central processing units.
Bullet	@bullet = Increase the size and efficiency of cache memory.
Bullet	@bullet = Monitor the performance of the entire system.
Heading	@head 2 = Installation Tips
Body text	To install your Cyclatron Accelerator, proceed as follows:

Note that each code must correspond to one identified by the desktop publishing program.

When you first create a list of styles in your desktop publishing program, be sure to create a style entry for every heading and paragraph type that is needed. Although you can create new styles as you need them, it's usually more efficient to develop them ahead of time. Most commercial shops have several basic style sets that correspond to the different types of documents they prepare. These lists are easily modified as new requirements occur.

Output Options

When you prepare your document for the printer, you have a number of options. You can provide printed camera-ready copy, film, or even printing plates, depending on the kind of equipment you have. Documents are also supplied to printers in digital format as PostScript PRN files. They can be printed to a file that is either placed on a collection of diskettes, a high-capacity removable media drive, or even on a CD. All of these options depend on the kind of equipment that you have. Following are descriptions of these options.

Camera-Ready Copy

The oldest and most common way to submit a document to a printer is to provide camera-ready reproducible copy (often called *repro*). This is most often black type set on white paper. The technology used to produce repro has come a long way in the last few years. This is particularly true with the availability of high-resolution laser printers, sometimes called *lasersetters*.

Lasersetters

A lasersetter is nothing more than a high-resolution laser printer. Common laser printers achieve 600 dots per inch (dpi), while those designed for use in typesetting typically achieve 1,000 to 1,200 dpi. There was a time when the price for these units ranged in the thousands of dollars. Today, they can be acquired for around $1,200. Some lasersetters can process 11 x 17-inch paper, film, and even printing plate material. These units cost more. However, for many applications, the high-end units are not essential, as a plain 300-dpi office laser printer can be used to prepare repro.

Phototypesetters

Laser printers in the home and office and lasersetters in many typographic service bureaus have largely displaced phototypesetters, such as the Compugraphics and Linotronics systems. However, many of these devices are still used by the graphics departments of large companies, commercial printers, and graphic service bureaus. Phototypesetters produce extremely high quality output (2450 dpi) on photographic paper, negative film, and even plate material. Fully equipped printers and service bureaus frequently use these to process PC- and Macintosh-generated PostScript files. These files are raster image processed (RIPed) and then used by the phototypesetter to produce film for book pages, brochures, and the CMYK negatives used to produce four-color separation work.

Film

Today, photolithographic negatives (or high-contrast film) are often supplied to printers instead of camera-ready repro. This can save the cost of having the commercial printer produce the film. However, this can be false economy, because the film must be prepared somewhere unless the book is supplied in plate or digital format. In either case, a cost analysis should be conducted to determine the real cost of film submission.

When film is supplied, it can save the time required to process the film by the printer, as well as the time used to prepare and review a blueline proof copy. Bluelines are typically supplied to the customers of commercial printers to ensure that the film is clear, and that the book is assembled in the proper order. It is essentially an approval copy that gives the printer authorization to proceed with the printing process. The bluelines are also used to make last-minute changes, which require the affected pages be reprinted and sent to the printer for new film. Therefore, supplying final

film can eliminate these steps, but it also eliminates what can be some important checkpoints.

Plates

Some devices that are used to output film are also used to output printing plates. Unless the printing plates are supplied to a printer having a small sheet-fed duplicator, there is really no practical advantage in supplying single-page printing plates to a commercial printer that has a large-format press. These printers are generally equipped with large sheet-fed or web-fed presses. They use film that is stripped up, page positioned, and mounted in 16-page signatures. Once the pages are stripped in place, a 16-page plate is produced. The resulting plates are mounted on the master cylinder of the printing press, from which 16-page signatures are printed. Signature sizes vary with the size of the press, i.e., 8-, 12-, or 32-page signatures can be used, but the 16-page format is common.

Digital Data (Files)

If you wish to submit your document in digital format, i.e., PostScript PRN files produced by the Linotronics 330 print driver supplied with Windows 95/98, the reproduction assembly sheet should include additional information. The filename for each chapter (such as Chapter1.PRN) must also be included. If your PRN files are compressed into Zip files, then an inventory of the Zip files and their contents must also be included. Some printers can even use the desktop published source files along with the supporting document and graphic files (RTF or DOC, BMP, TIF, WMF, etc.). This permits them to make necessary corrections on site, without the need to shuttle pages back and forth by delivery service for last-minute cosmetic fixes.

You can add the Linotronics 330 printer driver to your system using the Add Printer utility found in the Printers folder of the Control Panel. The Windows 95/98 system disk or CD includes the necessary drivers. Once drivers are added, you must select and set up the Print Properties to produce usable output. Most printers can provide setup details; the dialogs that correspond to setup are provided later in this book.

High-Capacity Drives: Note that the submission of PRN and supporting files are often accomplished using a high-capacity removable drive from Iomega or SyQuest. The Iomega Zip drives are the most common and are available from most stores that sell computers. Iomega includes both parallel port and SCSI models.

The 100-MB Zip disk is the most common format, and the removable disks cost about $10 each (not bad for the equivalent of 70 1.44MB floppies). Iomega recently introduced an Iomega Jaz 2GB removable drive which sells for U.S. $649. A 3-pack of Iomega 2GB Jaz disks goes for $447.

The SyQuest SparQ removable cartridge has a 1-GB capacity. The SparQ drive retails for $199 and a 3-pack of cartridges is priced at $99. The SparQ drives are also offered in both parallel and SCSI port configurations. At $33 per disk, this is only 3 cents per megabyte—not bad.

If your printer uses a high-capacity removable drive, find out which model he has. This will guide your selection when you acquire a high-capacity removable drive.

Desktop Publishing Software Reviews

The remainder of this chapter examines five desktop publishing programs. The reviews include a narrative overview, some general operating procedures, and a list of features. All desktop publishing programs are frame based. Text, pictures, and other objects are placed within frames that are created and positioned on an underlying page. Some desktop publishing programs create default frames for body text, headers, and footers when you set up the page format (sometimes called *master page*). Other programs require you to click on a frame tool and drag a frame onto the page. Guidelines and snap grids can be turned on as an aid to precision frame alignment.

Adobe PageMaker

Adobe PageMaker is an intermediate level desktop publishing program that has been in use for many years. As mentioned earlier, PageMaker has its roots in the Macintosh world, and therefore has a strong following in the Mac camp. Windows users also find the recent releases of PageMaker to be a capable desktop publishing program, and the 32-bit version of PageMaker is feature-laden and easy to use. It comes with good on-line help and useful "plug-ins," and uses familiar Windows metaphors for file handling and editing.

When using Adobe PageMaker 6.5, handy dialogs and "palettes" provide shortcuts to frequently used tools and formatting controls. An overview of the PageMaker menus follows.

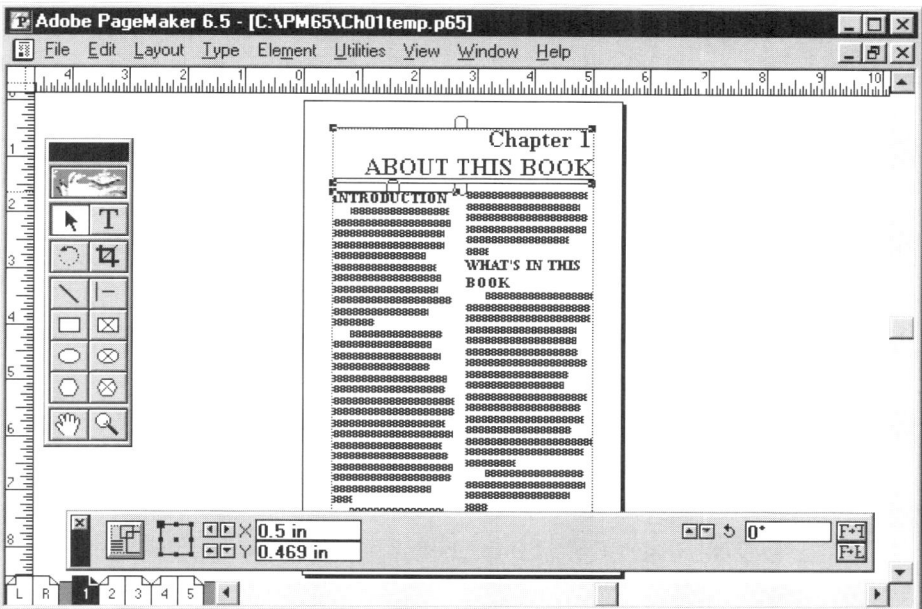

File—In addition to beginning, opening, saving, and closing files, printing, and exiting the program, this menu provides access to several other helpful features.

■ *Revert* removes all changes since the last save.

■ *Place* imports text, spreadsheet, graphics, and database files into the current document.

■ *Acquire* imports TIF images into the current document.

■ *Export* saves the contents of your publication in a variety of document or text formats.

■ *Links Manager* displays all active links between your publication and linked files. It is also used to update or edit the links.

■ *Document Setup* is used to change the publication's page layout settings that were first established when File > New was used. Margin changes are applied to the document master page.

■ *Printer Styles* saves, retrieves, and applies the print settings for a selected publication. This eliminates the need to reset your print dialog options for each print job.

■ *Preferences* is used to control settings that apply to publication-wide behavior.

Edit—Like most Windows applications, Edit selections include Undo, Cut, Copy, Paste, Clear, Select All, and Deselect All. Other editing selections are:

■ *Paste Multiple* duplicates a specified number of selected objects. They are displaced (or "offset") from the original object by a supplied value. This selection works when the clipboard contains an object and a publication is open.

■ *Paste Special* makes use of the Windows OLE server by letting you link a pasted object to its source program. It is identical to the Edit > Paste Special selection found in other Windows applications.

■ *Insert Object* launches the OLE server application so you can paste an OLE-embedded object into your current publication.

■ *Edit Story* displays the selected story in PageMaker's built-in word processor. It opens a new story window if no text is currently selected. Use Edit > Edit Layout (or the Ctrl+E shortcut) to toggle between the Edit Story and Edit Layout views.

■ *Edit Original* opens a linked object in its source application.

Layout—In addition to navigating between pages (Go to Page, Go Back, Go Forward) and inserting and removing pages (Insert Pages and Remove Pages), a few other useful selections are found here.

■ *Sort Pages* provides the ability to move pages using a thumbnail view of the publication. Once moved, PageMaker reorders and renumbers them.

■ *Go Back/Go Forward* returns you to the previous or advances you to the next page in the series of pages that have been viewed since the publication was opened.

■ *Column Guides* is used to set the number of columns on a page and the space between them.

■ *Copy Master Guides* displays the guides set on the master page that is presently being used. The master guides serve as an alignment reference and do not print. Use Layout > Column Guides to add or change columns on master pages and publications.

■ *Autoflow* causes text to automatically flow into following columns until all text has been placed. Pages are added as necessary to accommodate inserted text. When the text is flowing, press Ctrl to switch between manual and automatic flow.

Type—This menu is used to control the text and paragraph elements of your publication in addition to a number of other type-related controls. The selections are summarized in the list that follows.

■ *Font* is used to select and apply a type font to a selected range of text, to the next text that you enter, or to the entire publication.

■ *Size* is used to select and apply a type size, from 4 to 650 points in 0.1-point increments, to a selected range of text or to the entire publication.

■ *Leading* is used to set and apply the space between lines for a selected range of text or to the entire publication. Leading is the measure between consecutive lines measured in points. Leading values can range from 0 to 1300 points.

■ *Type Style* is used to set the style for a selected range of text or to the next text that you enter. You can apply the type style to individual characters, as is the case with other text formatting commands.

■ *Expert Kerning* provides fine control over letter spacing for areas containing large type such as headline and poster-size type. Every character pair is automatically evaluated within the selected range. Manual kerning is automatically replaced by kern-pair values.

■ *Expert Tracking* applies size-dependent letter spacing to a selected range of text rather than adjusting the space between individual letter pairs, as is done with manual kerning. Expert Tracking plots tracking values as lines on a grid. Each line represents one track; you can customize tracking for different type fonts and sizes.

■ *Horizontal Scale* controls the proportional width of characters within a selected range or for the entire publication as a default setting. Use the Other command to set a custom character width that ranges from 5 to 250 percent.

■ *Character* is used to set the type font, size, and other attributes of a selected range of text. You can use this selection to override the applied style setting, without changing the style itself.

■ *Paragraph* is used to apply type attributes (size, font, indent, tabs, etc.) to an individual paragraph. It can also be used to change the attributes of an established style. This changes all paragraphs that use the changed style.

■ *Indents/Tabs* is used to set the left and right paragraph indent levels, the first-line indent, and tab stops. Use Indents/Tabs for a selection, the next text entered, or as a default setting for the entire publication.

■ *Hyphenation* is used to turn automatic hyphenation on or off using the Hyphenation dialog. Hyphenation can also be turned on or off for a specific style using the Define Styles dialog.

■ *Alignment* is used to change the alignment of a paragraph to center, right, justify, or force justify. It is applied to one or more selected paragraphs.

■ *Style* applies a defined style (one that exists in the Styles palette) to one or more selected paragraphs. An entire paragraph need not be selected to apply the selected style to it.

■ *Define Styles* is used to create a new paragraph style or edit an existing paragraph style. Each style contains character and paragraph formatting attributes (typeface, size, leading, alignment, indents, tabs, etc.).

Element—Element performs operations on a variety of publication elements. Each selection is briefly described below.

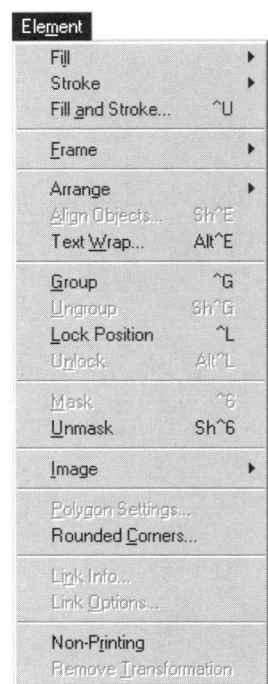

■ *Fill* specifies a fill pattern for a selected rectangle, ellipse, polygon, box, or oval. Patterns are opaque and hide whatever is behind them. Use Arrange to move them behind other objects or text.

■ *Stroke* is used to set the line weight and pattern used by the rectangle, ellipse, and polygon tools. Line weights can be specified up to 800 points in 0.1-point increments.

■ *Fill and Stroke* sets fill and stroke attributes for a selected object. Use this selection to either overprint or knock out background objects.

■ *Frame* permits you to attach text and graphics to a frame. This selection is also used to set the attributes of either the frame or its contents. Attributes include such items as border settings, alignment, the offset from adjacent text or objects, etc. The selection is also used to move between frames, to change a rectangle to a frame, or to change a frame to a graphic. A frame must be selected before you can use Frame.

- *Arrange* is used to move a selected object to the front, to the back, forward, or backward. For example, you may want to move a filled rectangle behind text.

- *Align Objects* is used to align two or more selected objects relative to their current positions. It also distributes the selected objects evenly.

- *Text Wrap* is used to set the way text flows around a graphic object. For example, text can wrap around a rectangular shape (called *runaround*), wrap around the sides of an irregular shape within a frame, or cover the graphic object as a background or foreground.

- *Group* and *Ungroup* selections are used to combine two or more objects into a *group* so that the grouped objects act as a single unit. Ungroup separates the selected group into its component parts.

- *Lock Position* freezes the position and size of an object. Those attributes that do not affect an object's size or position can change.

- *Unlock* reverses the effect of the Lock Position command to permit movement and resizing of the selected object.

- *Mask* is used to cover part of an object so that only part of it shows through a graphic object, such as a rectangle or ellipse. Mask objects by positioning a mask object on the object that you want to mask, select both objects, and click Element > Mask.

- *Unmask* removes the mask effect from the selected objects.

- *Image* provides options that are used to adjust the contrast, brightness, or screen pattern applied to bitmapped images. Image does not operate with EPS, draw-type graphics, or color images unless they have been saved in Paint or TIF format.

- *Polygon Settings* is used to change the shape (Number of sides and Star inset) of a selected polygon. As many as 100 sides can be used. Increasing the inset forms a star-like shape. Five sides and a 55% Star inset produces a good five-pointed star.

- *Rounded Corners* is used to apply a round corner to a rectangle object. The companion dialog offers six different corner settings.

- *Link Info* displays link information about a selected OLE object that is linked to external text and graphic files or applications. You can use the Links Manager to reestablish links when a file is moved from the original folder to another. You can temporarily unlink files from the current publication to minimize its file size and then relink the files when you are ready to print it.

- *Link Options* controls the way PageMaker processes linked files. Linked files can be stored in your publication file and be updated when the original is edited. You can also set an alert that tells you when a linked file has been changed.

■ *Non-Printing* is used to suppress the printing of one or more selected objects. You can hide or display nonprinting objects using the Layout > Display Non-Printing menu selection.

■ *Remove Transformation* is used to cancel rotation, reflection, and/or skewing that has been applied to an object. Be sure to select the object before using this menu item.

Utilities—This menu provides access to a number of companion utilities and plug-ins provided with Page-Maker. Each menu selection is described in the following list.

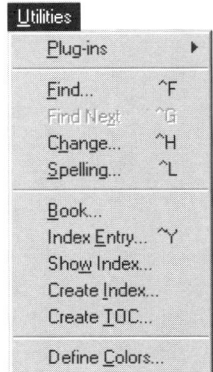

■ *Plug-ins* displays a list of installed PageMaker plug-in utilities. A *plug-in* is the same as an *add-in* that is used by many other common applications.

■ *Find/Find Next* locates a supplied text, character, or formatting value in either a selected passage, the entire publication, or all open publications. Find Next continues the search from one found item to the next.

■ *Change* both locates and replaces the supplied text, character, or formatting value.

■ *Spelling* checks for misspelled words and typographical errors. The check is performed on a selected passage, the active publication, or all open publications. Spell checks are only run in the Story view.

■ *Book* assembles two or more publications into a book. Double-click the name of each file you want to add to create a book list that contains the names of all publications that comprise the book. Use Move Up or Move Down to change the position of a book in the list. Use Remove to delete an unwanted publication from the list. Each publication usually contains a single chapter or section of the book. The publications must be listed in the proper order to achieve proper pagination. You can create an index and a table of contents from all of the publications contained within a book. You can also print the entire book. The book list can be placed in one of the publications within the book, such as the table of contents or index.

■ *Index Entry* opens a dialog in which your index entries are defined. Be sure that you have selected a word or phrase or that your cursor is properly positioned before using this command. You can also press Ctrl+Y to pop up the Index Entry dialog.

■ *Show Index* displays your index entries alphabetically. Select a letter to see all entries.

■ *Create Index* assembles and formats the index into a single "story." The index is inserted at the cursor position. It can apply to either the current publication or to an entire book comprised of those publications contained in the book list. Be sure you have a text frame prepared and ready to receive the content of your index.

■ *Create TOC* produces a table of contents that includes all paragraphs in the book or individual publication. The TOC entries are based on the status of the Include in TOC attribute found in the Paragraph Specifications dialog. Therefore, mark each heading style that you want to include in the table of contents.

■ *Define Colors* displays a dialog that lets you edit custom colors that can be applied to text or graphics. You can also import colors from a library of industry standard or custom colors.

View—This menu provides access to different publication views as well as how different guides are displayed or hidden.

■ *Display Master Items* displays or hides all master page objects that correspond to the current publication.

■ *Display Non-Printing Items* displays those items that have been designated as a non-printing object using the Element > Non-Printing menu item.

■ *Zoom In/Zoom Out* are used to magnify/reduce the page view to the next higher/lower magnification.

■ *Actual Size* displays either an entire page or a two-page spread at actual size.

■ *Fit in Window* displays either an entire page or a two-page spread within your publication window.

■ *Entire Pasteboard* displays the entire underlying "pasteboard" so you can locate and view an object on the current page. Note that the pasteboard metaphor is a derivative of manual paste-up when typeset galley was cut into page-size swatches and pasted on underlying pasteboard.

■ *Zoom To* lets you zoom directly to one of six magnification settings (25%, 50%, 75%, 100%, 200%, and 400%).

■ *Show/Hide Rulers* turns on or off the vertical and horizontal ruler display. Use Ctrl+R to toggle the rulers on and off.

■ *Snap to Rulers* provides for accurate placement of text and graphics by snapping them to the increments displayed on the ruler. The rulers must be shown to use this feature.

■ *Zero Lock* prevents you from changing the zero point of the rulers by removing the adjustable cross hairs from the upper left corner of the screen. The rulers must be shown to use this feature. If you move the ruler setting, you can double-click in the cross hair box to restore them to zero.

■ *Show/Hide Guides* turns the column ruler and margin guides on and off. The guides must be shown before you can use Snap to Guides or Lock Guides.

■ *Snap to Guides* accurately snaps text or graphics to the established column and ruler guides.

■ *Lock Guides* keeps you from accidentally moving your column guides when you reposition text or graphics on a page. It is definitely annoying to grab and move your guide rather than an intended object.

■ *Clear Ruler Guides* is used to hide ruler guides that are shown on the current page or two-page spread. Lock Guides must not be active for this command to work. Ruler guides are placed on your page by dragging them from either the vertical or horizontal ruler. Remove ruler guides by dragging them off the page and back to the ruler from which they came.

■ *Send Guides to Back/Bring Guides to Front* is used to put guides either behind or on top of page objects. Bring them forward to select a guide; send them back to select an object on the page.

■ *Show/Hide Scroll Bars* is used to show or hide the scroll bars. This command only works when a publication is open.

Window—The Window menu includes the Tile and Cascade selections common to many Windows applications. It also lets you show or hide the tools and palettes for type control and colors. Other selections follow.

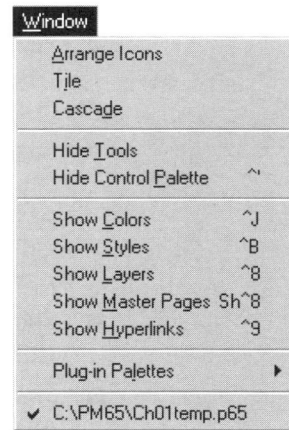

■ *Show/Hide Styles* is used to display or hide the Styles palette, which lists paragraph styles. Styles are applied by placing the cursor within a paragraph or selecting a range of text and then clicking the desired style name from the Styles palette.

■ *Show/Hide Master Pages* opens the Master Pages palette. Here, you can create, edit, or apply master pages to the current publication.

Part
1

- *Show/Hide Hyperlinks* opens the Hyperlinks palette. This palette is used to create, edit, and apply hyperlinks to a selected text passage or graphic object. A hyperlink lets the viewer of a web (PDF or HTML) document jump to another location within the document or to another web site on the Internet. A hyperlink can also be configured to send an e-mail message to a specified e-mail address.

- *Plug-in Palettes* is used to display or hide the palettes supplied with PageMaker plug-ins. A Show/Hide Library option displays or hides a palette that is used to store, catalog, and retrieve text and graphics for placement into your publication. A Show/Hide Scripts option displays or hides scripts and folders that contain scripts. Scripts automate frequently used PageMaker operations.

Help—PageMaker provides useful online help information about most of the features found in the program. You can access context-sensitive help about a command by pressing Ctrl+?.

Adobe PageMaker is a full-featured Windows desktop publishing program that can be used to produce a variety of document types that range from small brochures and fliers to multichapter publications. It should definitely be included on your list of prospective desktop publishing programs. The online help provides an extensive set of operating procedures that can have you up and running within a few short sessions. Your familiarity with the way Windows programs work and, more specifically, typesetting conventions, will accelerate your learning time.

Adobe FrameMaker

This program is ideal for large, multichapter applications. It has all the necessary controls for front and back matter, running headers and footers, equations, and all other tools considered useful for large, multichapter publications with complex pagination requirements. The graphics departments of many corporations have used FrameMaker for several years in its various incarnations. The versions of FrameMaker evaluated for this book are versions 5 and 5.5, which were installed and run under Windows 95. A few basic features that are displayed on FrameMaker's desktop are briefly examined. Then an overview of the purpose and/or use of each of Frame-Maker's menu commands is presented.

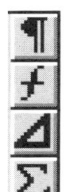

Control Buttons

There are four buttons located above the vertical scroll bar at the right side of the screen. These are used to display toolboxes and dialogs.

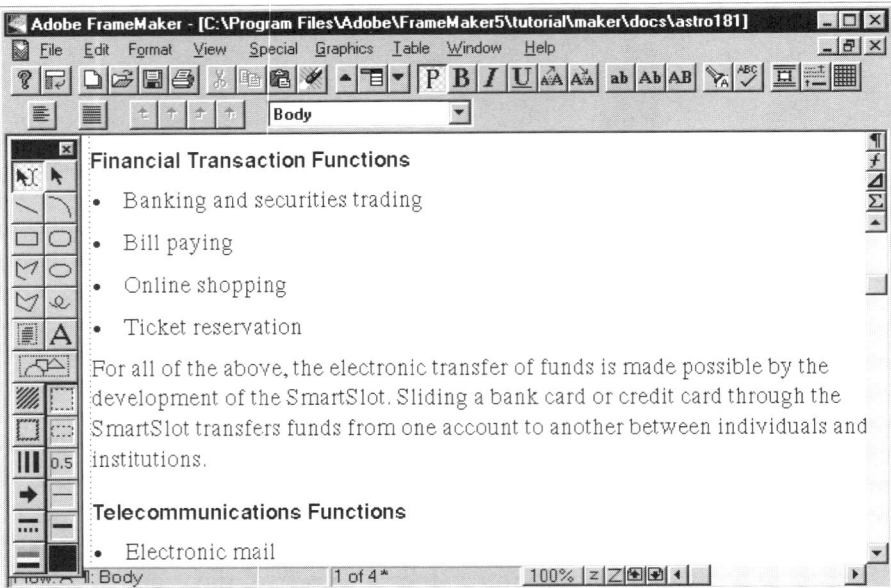

Paragraph Catalog—The top button displays the Paragraph Catalog, where paragraph formats are stored. The same dialog is displayed using Format > Paragraph > Catalogs. Here, all stored paragraph formats are maintained. You can apply a format to a selected paragraph or to all paragraphs by clicking a format in the list. An alternate is to choose a format from the Paragraph Format pop-up menu, which is accessed using the Format > Paragraphs submenu.

Character Catalog—The second button displays the Character Catalog where character formats are stored. You can also display this dialog using Format > Characters > Catalog. The current document's character formats are stored here; you can apply a catalog format to selected text.

Tools Palette—The third button displays a toolbox containing drawing tools and drawing properties. You can also use Graphics > Tools to display this tool palette.

Equations Palette—The bottom button displays the Equations palette. As you can guess, this palette is used to create mathematical equations. You can use it to insert math symbols, align equation elements, and position expressions within equations.

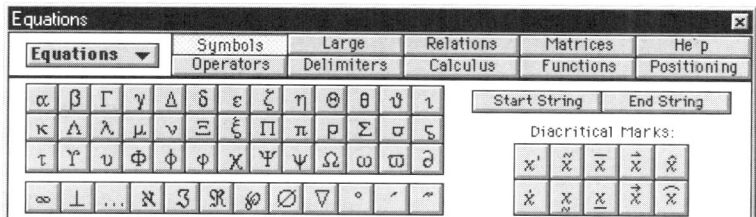

FrameMaker calls its toolbars QuickAccess menus. You can rotate through the different menus by clicking the Next/Previous button, which is located next to the Plain text button. FrameMaker offers a Quick Menu and a Complete Menu setting, which is selected using View > Menus. A survey of FrameMaker's Complete menu selections is presented next.

File—The File menu is not unlike other Windows applications, as it is used to create a new document, open existing ones, save, save as, import, print, set up printing, and exit. Other entries that may need some clarification are listed below.

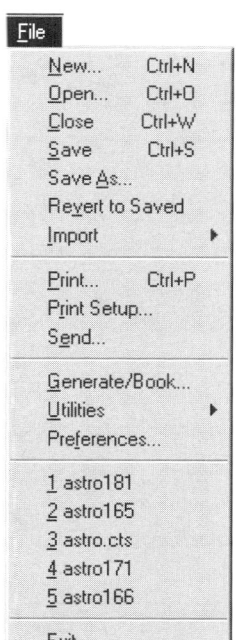

- *Revert to Saved* cancels your changes and restores the document as it existed when it was last saved.

- *Send* is used to transfer your publication file to a specified address using a Windows messaging profile, such as Internet Mail.

- *Generate/Book* displays a dialog that is used to produce a multichapter book that includes the current publication, to generate a table of contents, and to generate an index. Once you create a Book window using this selection, you can add additional publications to the list of books, rearrange their order, and delete them from the list. Once all publication names are arranged in the proper order in a Book window, you can generate an automatic table of contents and index using this selection. Note that when the Book window is displayed, additional menu items appear in the File menu. The File > Add is used to add more publication names (chapters) to the book. File > Rearrange is used to change the order or to delete book names from the list.

- *Utilities* is used to perform several tasks. You can compare two versions of a document for differences in content and cross-references. You can use Reports to obtain a word count. Finally, the HTML mappings, convert, and info selections are used to map headings to corresponding HTML formats, convert the document to HTML, and finally to display information about the converted document. The FrameMaker 5.0 HTML utilities make use of *WebWorks Publisher* and *WebWorks HTML Lite*. These HTML utilities can convert entire books and groups of files

to HTML files, which can then be displayed by a common Internet web browser. Graphics, tables, and equations are automatically converted; the utility also produces and saves complex style mappings that can be used again with other documents. FrameMaker 5.5 also offers the same capabilities without the use of the WebWorks add-in.

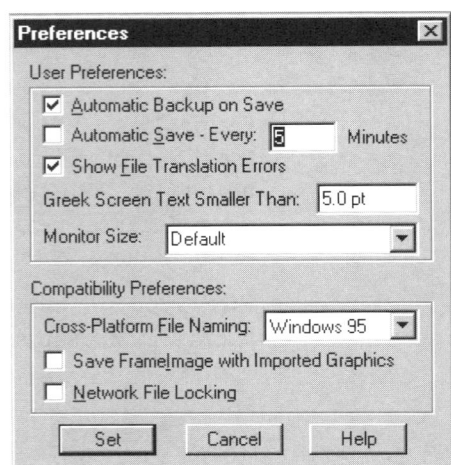

■ *Preferences* is used to set user and compatibility preferences. The Preferences dialog is shown in the adjacent illustration.

Edit—The Edit menu is not unlike many other edit menus found in common Windows applications. You'll find the Undo, Cut, Copy, Paste, Paste Special, Clear (Delete), Select All (in Flow), Find, and Find/Change selections here. The Spelling Checker and Thesaurus are also found here, as FrameMaker doesn't include a separate Tools menu. Some of the unique menu entries are described in the list that follows.

■ *Copy Special* is used to copy text and paragraph formats, conditional text *tags*, and table column widths. Conditional text is marked with a conditional tag that sets it apart from unconditional text. Conditional text or graphic objects are used if you want to maintain different versions of the same document. They are created by using Special > Conditional Text. Conditional text can be hidden or displayed at your discretion to produce the desired document version.

■ *Text Inset Properties* displays a Text Inset Properties dialog. A text inset is a block of text that has been inserted from another source document. Normally, the inset text is linked and can be updated when the text is

modified in the source application. Use the Text Inset Properties dialog to view and change the properties of a selected inset.

■ *Update References* displays the Update References dialog. Here, you can update cross-references, text insets, and linked OLE objects. This operation is typically performed following updates to the source documents. Cross-references are typically paragraph headings or figure titles that are marked as such. You can also cross-reference words or phrases, which is called a *spot cross-reference*. These references require that you place a "Cross-Ref" marker in the source text using the Special > Marker window. Once you mark it, you can insert the spot cross-reference.

■ *Links* displays the Links dialog, where you can examine and update all linked objects.

■ *Object* is used to edit or open a selected object. This menu item is only available when an imported object is selected.

Format—The Format menu controls the attributes of your text. Here, you can select and apply fonts, sizes, styles, character, and paragraph settings. You can also change the layout of a document and work with headers and footers. The menu selections are described in the following list.

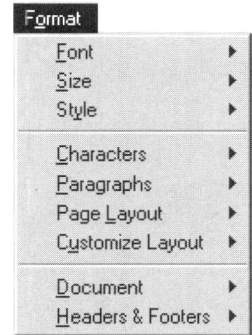

■ *Font* displays a list of available type fonts from which to choose. Select the text and then pick a font. If you are not pleased with the effect, pick another font until you like the result.

■ *Size* displays a list of type sizes. The current size is checked. Pick another size to apply it to the selected text.

■ *Style* displays a list of type attributes, i.e., normal, boldface, italic, underline, subscript, etc., from which to choose. Most style selections are available as buttons on the first QuickAccess menu. Clicking a style applies it to the selected text.

■ *Characters* presents a list of special characters and symbols. The list varies with the type of document being processed. This menu also provides access to the Character Designer dialog (used to set symbols, such as bullets) and the Catalog, which lists all current characters and lets you select and delete.

■ *Paragraphs* displays a list of paragraph tags in addition to providing access to the Paragraph Designer dialog (used to change tag settings) and the Catalog, which lists all current style tags, and is used to apply them to selected paragraphs.

■ *Page Layout* provides access to a number of dialogs used to design the basic page layout of the document. Here, you can adjust such design elements as column size and placement, lines, and page size.

■ *Customize Layout* lets you create a custom text frame or change the way an existing text frame reacts with adjoining frames. You can also split, rotate, and unrotate a selected text frame.

■ *Document* performs operations on numbering, footnote properties, change bars, "smart quotes," and "smart spaces." Smart quotes insert curved quotation marks when a single or double quote is typed; smart spaces eliminate the need to type more than one space in a row.

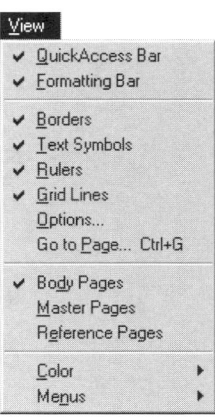

■ *Headers & Footers* operates with a master page. This selection displays the Variable dialog shown here. Here, you insert page numbers, dates, filenames, and a variety of other variables at the cursor position within a header or footer.

View—The View menu controls which of FrameMaker's controls and menus are displayed in addition to how the current publication is displayed.

■ *QuickAccess Bar* turns the display of the Quick-Access bar on and off. You can display any of four different bars using the Next/Previous button located next to the **P** (plain text) button. You can rotate the QuickAccess bar's orientation to the left side of the screen using the second button of the QuickAccess bar.

■ *Formatting Bar* turns the formatting bar, located below the QuickAccess bar, on and off. The formatting bar contains paragraph style names, tab buttons, and text alignment buttons.

■ *Borders* turns the frame borders on and off in the Body Pages view.

■ *Text Symbols* turns the display of unprintable text symbols, such as paragraph returns and tabs, on and off.

- *Rulers* turns the vertical and horizontal page rulers off and on.

- *Grid Lines* turns an alignment grid on and off. The grid measure is set with the View > Options dialog.

- *Options* displays the View Options dialog, where view selections are set.

- *Go to Page* jumps to a selected page number.

- *Body Pages* displays the text of your publication, where it is edited.

- *Master Pages* displays the underlying page, where column frames, headers, and footers are edited.

- *Reference Pages* displays special style attributes, such as rules attached to headings. Use this display to select and edit these attributes.

- *Color* displays the Define Color Views dialog. Up to six different views are established by setting which colors are displayed normally, cutout, and invisible. A Color Definitions dialog is also available to select the color system, i.e., CMYK, RGB, HLS, etc. (See chapter 4). Colors can be adjusted and deleted using the dialog's slider controls. A "Common Color Picker" is also accessed from this dialog for color adjustments.

- *Menus* is used to choose between the Quick and Complete menus. Custom menu configurations are retrieved using the Modify selection. You can develop and use custom menus of your own. See Menu Customization in FrameMaker's online manual.

Special—The Special menu contains a variety of commands, many totally unrelated to each other, that are used in the preparation of your publications. Page Break, Footnote, and Cross-Reference are typical of the commands found here. A summary of each is contained in the following list.

- *Page Break* inserts a page break at the current text cursor position.

- *Anchored Frame* displays the Anchored Frame dialog. This dialog shows the position and size of the selected anchored frame. (Anchored frames, which can contain graphics, text, or both, flow with an "anchor" and eliminate the need to reposition the frame each time a document's layout changes.)

- *Footnote* is used to insert a footnote callout at the current text cursor position and to enter the text of the footnote text at the bottom of the page.

- *Cross-Reference* displays the Cross Reference dialog. Here, you can create, edit, or delete cross-reference formats. In addition, you can display the cross-reference source and even convert the cross-reference information to editable text.

■ *Variable* displays the Variable dialog. Here, variable fields, called text placeholders or *variables*, are defined and edited. An example of a variable is a date or name. Variables can be used repeatedly throughout a publication. When the variable's definition is changed, it is updated throughout the document.

■ *Marker* displays the Markers dialog, which is used to insert a marker into your text. A variety of marker types are available for controlling the content of running headers and footers, index entries, and cross references. For example, you can mark a passage as the source for the page's running header text.

■ *Equations* displays the Equations dialog from which you can construct mathematical equation objects.

■ *Conditional Text* displays the Conditional Text dialog. Here, you specify the use of conditional text, which can be included or excluded from a document to accommodate different versions of the same basic publication.

■ *Add Disconnected Pages* permits you to insert a page to the current document that is not connected to the text flow of the adjoining pages.

■ *Delete Pages* is used to delete one or more pages from the current document.

Graphics—The Graphics menu contains a number of graphic-related selections for grouping, ungrouping, aligning, stacking, rotating, and more. One or more graphic objects must be selected for most of the menu items to be active. Each is summarized in the following list.

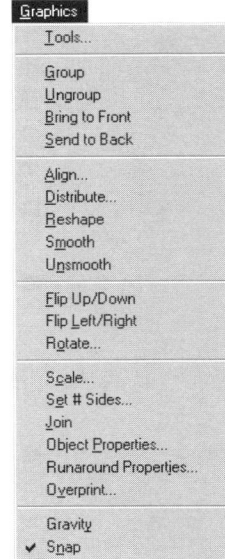

■ *Tools* displays the Tools dialog, which includes buttons for creating and editing frames and graphic objects.

■ *Group/Ungroup* are used to combine selected objects into a single group and to break them apart as necessary.

■ *Bring to Front/Send to Back* are used to adjust the position of one or more selected objects when they are overlaid (or stacked on top of each other).

■ *Align* is used to adjust two or more selected objects horizontally, vertically, or centered.

- *Distribute* spaces a series of selected objects equal distance across or down the page.

- *Reshape* is used to change the shape of polygons, arcs, and freehand curves.

- *Smooth/Unsmooth* are used to round the corners of rectangles and to increase the corner radius of rounded rectangles. Polylines are converted into a series of Bezier curves. The Unsmooth command reverses the process by decreasing the corner radius. After smoothing a polygon or polyline, you can reshape the curve using the reshape handles and control points.

- *Flip Up/Down* rotates the selected object 180 degrees vertically.

- *Flip Left/Right* rotates the selected object 180 degrees horizontally.

- *Rotate* displays the Rotate Selected Objects dialog. Here, you can perform clockwise or counterclockwise rotation by a specified number of degrees.

- *Scale* is used to change the size of the selected object by a percentage factor or by specifying new width and height dimensions.

- *Set # Sides* is used to change the number of sides on a polygon or circle object.

- *Join* combines ungrouped lines, polylines, open arcs, and freehand curves.

- *Object Properties* displays the Object Properties dialog. Here, you can see and modify the size, offset, color, angle, border width, and scaling of the selected object. The dialog also shows the file type and directory location of an imported object.

- *Runaround Properties* is used to set the way text flows around a selected object. This includes Don't Run Around, Run around Bonding Box, Run around Contour, and As Is. The Runaround Properties dialog is also used to display and change the gap between the object and surrounding text.

- *Overprint* is used to control the way one object is printed over another background object. Overlapping objects can overprint or be cut out. This is useful when making color separations.

- *Gravity* causes objects to attract the pointer when drawn, resized, or reshaped. The gravity snap is useful when connecting objects to the center of the borders of another object.

- *Snap* causes selected objects to snap to the underlying grid. This helps you maintain the alignment of frames and objects.

Table—This menu contains the commands that are used to create, edit, and format tables. Each command is briefly introduced in the following list.

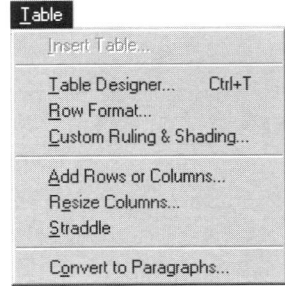

- *Insert Table* displays the Insert Table dialog where you can specify the table format and then insert it.

- *Table Designer* is used to control basic table formatting properties, such as indents, spacing, and alignment, in addition to ruling and shading.

- *Row Format* displays the Row Format dialog where row heights and starting points are defined.

- *Custom Ruling & Shading* controls ruling styles and placements in addition to fill and color control.

- *Add Rows or Columns* is used to add a new row or column. You can also select the placement of the row or column relative to the current position of the text cursor.

- *Resize Columns* is used to change the width of one or more columns. A variety of controls are available including measures, scaling, and distribution.

- *Straddle* is used to connect two or more adjoining cells into a single cell. This is typically used when headings span two or more columns or rows.

- *Convert to Paragraphs* converts the selected table contents into paragraph text by row or by column.

Window—This menu is typical of many Window menus found in popular Windows applications. Two of the Window commands are described for clarification.

- *Arrange Icons* evenly spaces all displayed document icons when they are minimized on the desktop.

- *Refresh* redraws the active document on the screen. This removes residual pixels that may obscure certain elements within the displayed document.

Help—The Help menu contains a broad range of information that describes FrameMaker commands and publishing procedures.

■ *Context-Sensitive Help* is used to describe the command in use.

■ *Contents* lets you select a subject from a displayed list. An Index button provides access to topics by clicking an alphabetical letter at the top of the Index window. Hyperlinks are contained within descriptions for expanded definitions.

■ *Keyboard Shortcuts* displays a list of useful key sequences designed to save time. This includes access to a number of menu commands in addition to special symbols and spaces such as em dashes, em spaces, nonbreaking spaces, and many other special characters and symbols.

■ *Samples & Clip Art* includes a list of document types that you can open and examine. These documents are ideal as models for your own documents. Open them, examine them, or even replace the text and graphic objects with your own and save the document under a new filename. The Clip Art selection displays a number of clipart elements and symbols for the following categories: arrows, balloons, dingbats (special symbols), electronic, flowchart, hardware, icons, maps, office, people, symbols, and transportation.

■ *FrameMaker Overview* introduces new users to FrameMaker. It is essentially a 10-minute FrameMaker presentation.

■ *Tutorial* presents an introductory online training session that steps you through the creation and editing of a publication using supplied document files.

■ *About FrameMaker* displays the version, registered user, and copyright information.

Corel Ventura 7

Corel Ventura 7 is a full-featured desktop publishing system. It was completely overhauled by Corel Corporation, and the 32-bit Windows rendition is both impressive and easier to use than previous versions. *Windows Magazine* listed Corel Ventura 7 as the best desktop publishing program in its list of recommended software applications. Ventura 7 is used by many PC-based graphic arts and publications departments because of its repertoire of features and versatility. Ventura 7 comes with a number of companion programs including those shown in the following illustration.

Most of the accompanying programs and utilities, such as Corel CAPTURE 6, Corel Database Publisher, Corel Color Manager Wizard, Corel SCRIPT Editor 7, and, of course, Corel PHOTO-PAINT 6, are useful to many, but not necessarily all, users. Therefore, you may wish to examine each to determine how it applies to your work. For example, the Database Publisher would be extremely useful to those users who prepare directories.

Getting Started

The general approach to getting started is to pick your page dimensions and margins. Then you can begin entering your text or import it from an existing word-processed document. Similarly, graphics as well as other object types, such as tables, charts, and spreadsheets, can also be imported into frames. You can add additional text frames for such things as sidebars and pull quotes. Next, you can begin formatting your chapter titles, headings, body text, bulleted and numbered lists, notes, and tables.

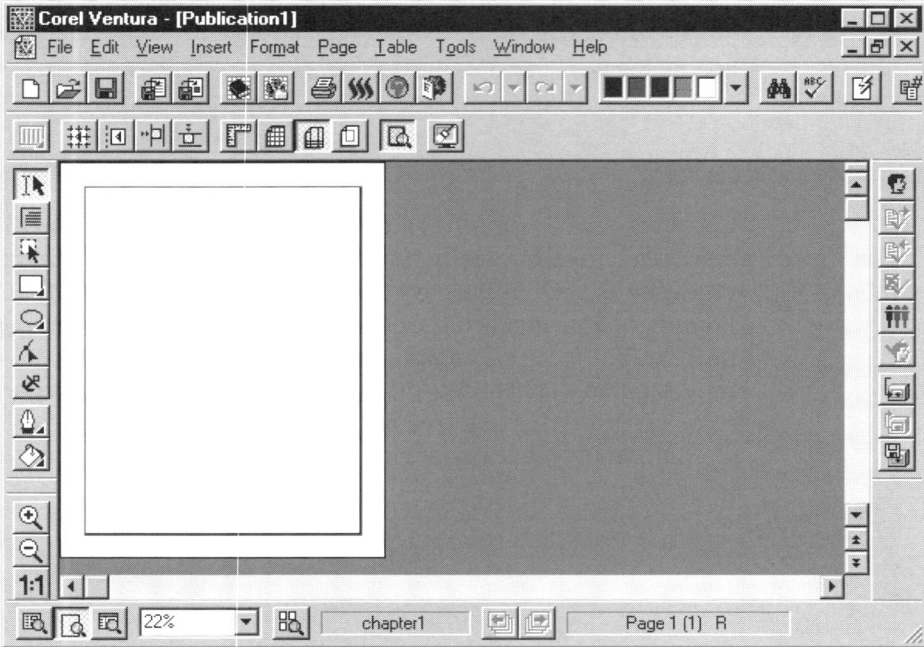

Styles (or "paragraph tags") are easily added and edited. Following are the general steps used to begin a new document.

1. Start Ventura Publisher and display a new, blank document.

2. Use Page > Master Page Properties to set the page (trim) dimensions.

3. Click View > Master Page; then use Format > Frame > Margins and display the Advanced dialog to set the top, bottom, left, and right margin dimensions. Click Apply and OK.

4. Right-click on the page just formatted and pick Mirror Properties to Facing Page if you want your inside and outside margins to alternate between left- and right-hand pages. Otherwise, pick Copy Properties to Facing Page.

5. Click View > Page Layout to display the first page. Now you can import text by clicking on the text frame and then using File > Import Text (or pressing F9) and selecting an appropriate file from the File > Import dialog. You can also type text directly into a text frame, although this is a rigorous way to create a new document. You can use View > Copy Editor if you want to display your text and tag codes in text editor format.

6. Insert pictures by first creating an empty frame. With the frame handles displayed, use File > Import Picture (or press F8) and select the picture file from the Import Picture dialog.

7. Use the Pick Tool on the Toolbox to edit text; use the Paragraph Tool and either right-click to display a shortcut menu or use the Format > Manage Tag List (you can also right-click to display the shortcut menu) to add and edit your tags.

8. The tabs on the Tag Properties dialog are used to adjust different tag attributes. Be sure to familiarize yourself with the use of each. You can check Ventura's online help information to determine the purpose of each dialog.

9. Once your tags are established, simply select a paragraph within your document and select the desired tag name from the tag list (left-hand end of the Property bar).

10. Use the Ventura Navigator (Tools > Navigator) and right-click on the document name to add new chapters to your document.

Command Overview

The preceding general procedure is enough to get you started. However, because Ventura 7 is a sophisticated program with hundreds of features, it usually takes several sessions to become comfortable with its use. As with the other programs in this chapter, a summary of Ventura's menus is presented to help you better understand the program's features and where to find them.

File—The File menu includes most of the same commands as most common Windows applications, such as New, Open, Save, Save As, Print, Print Setup, and Exit. Some of the unique commands are described in the list that follows.

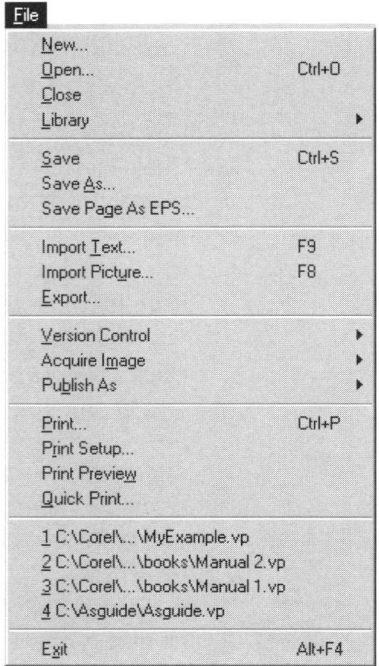

■ *Save Page As EPS* saves the current page as an Encapsulated PostScript picture. The resulting picture file can be imported and positioned using the File > Import > Picture command.

■ *Import Text* is used to import a text file into a selected frame. Ventura includes file filters that allow you to import text from a wide variety of word processors and spreadsheet programs.

■ *Import Picture* is used to import a picture into a selected frame. Ventura includes several graphic file filters that load most graphic file formats.

■ *Export* is used to export the current document in RTF, ASCII, or ANSI standard format. The Export dialog gives you the option of saving formatting codes and other controls inserted by Ventura.

■ *Version Control* provides three options: Archive Current, Retrieve Current, and Retrieve Publication. Archive Current saves a copy of the current document as an archive file. Retrieve Current opens an archive version of the current document. Retrieve Publication retrieves the previously saved archive version of the document.

■ *Acquire Image* provides access to three subcommands: Acquire, Acquire From File, and Select Source. Acquire is used to obtain images from input devices such as scanners and video capture boards. Acquire From File opens a scanned image file so that you can color correct it. Select Source opens the TWAIN image input source; the specific source varies with the available scanner drivers installed on your system.

■ *Publish As* provides access to four publish subcommands. Adobe Acrobat and Envoy convert the document into a portable electronic format for use with Adobe Acrobat and Envoy. Users having the Acrobat or Envoy-compatible viewers can view the document including text, graphics, and photos. Corel Barista is used to save the document in Java format for viewing by an Internet web browser. The Java format is generally superior to standard HTML format and preserves

the look of the original Ventura document. HTML converts the document into HTML format, which also permits your document to be viewed on Internet web browsers.

■ *Print Preview* displays the active document on the screen to simulate its appearance before you print it.

■ *Quick Print* reduces the printing time required to print your document by eliminating complex fills and EPS pictures. This command is typically used to produce a check print of the current document.

Edit—As with the File menu, the Edit menu also contains many familiar commands such as Undo, Cut, Paste, Paste Special, Copy, Delete, and Find and Replace. Additional commands are described in the following list.

■ *Repeat Edit Text* is used to repeat the last command issued whenever applicable.

■ *Duplicate* makes a duplicate of the selected frame or graphic object. You can use Tools > Options to set the offset value, i.e., the distance that the duplicate is offset from the original.

■ *Edit Item* is used to edit those items that were inserted using the Insert > Marker, Insert > Variable, and Insert > Index Entry commands.

Edit	
Undo Attach OLE Object	Ctrl+Z
Redo Load Text	Ctrl+Y
Repeat Attach OLE Object	Ctrl+Alt+Y
Cut	Shift+Delete
Copy	Ctrl+C
Paste	Ctrl+V
Paste Special...	
Delete	Delete
Duplicate	
Select All	Ctrl+A
Find & Replace...	Ctrl+F
Edit Item...	Ctrl+D
Order	▶
Group	Alt+G
Ungroup	Alt+U
Convert To Curves	Ctrl+Shift+V
Manage Overrides...	Ctrl+F10
Object	
Links...	

■ *Order* arranges the selected frame or graphic in front or in back of other superimposed objects. Two or more objects must be selected to access this command.

■ *Group/Ungroup* is used to group or ungroup two or more objects. When two or more objects are grouped, they act like a single object. Therefore, a group can be selected and moved as a single object.

■ *Convert to Curves* converts a selected graphic object or frame into a series of curves or lines. Once it is converted, you can use the Node Edit tool to edit the curves or lines. CAUTION: Once it is converted, you can't return the converted object to its original object type unless you use Edit > Undo, which cancels your editing work.

■ *Manage Overrides* cancels the formatting that was applied with the Format > Paragraph Overrides command. It can also add the selection's attributes to the paragraph tag.

Part

1

- *Object* displays a dialog that is used to edit an embedded object. This command is also used to convert the selected object into another object type.

- *Links* is used to display a list of all linked objects in the current document. You can use this command to update, break, or change links. The command is also used to open a selected object in its source application.

View—Ventura's View menu contains several familiar commands such as Zoom, Go To, and Toolbars. The more unique commands are summarized here.

- *Copy Editor* opens a word processor window that is used to edit text. Paragraph tag names are shown in a frame to the left of the text. Typesetting control codes are displayed in red. Both tags and typesetting control codes can be edited in this view.

- *Page Layout* displays the document in WYSIWYG (what you see is what you get) format. You can also edit your text and tags in this view.

- *Master Page* displays the underlying pages and frames. Use this view to change the basic format of your document, including the trim size and margins.

- *Snap* controls the position of graphic objects and frames on the current page. When Snap is on, the objects snap to the underlying grid. You can modify the dimensions of the grid by changing the Tools > Options > Selection dialog's Frame and Graphic Snap values.

- *Frame Borders* displays or hides the lines around a frame. Hiding the lines is more representative of the page's appearance. You may decide to add a rule around your frame if it provides visual separation from surrounding objects or text.

- *Hide All Pictures* hides or displays imported pictures. When they are hidden, an X is displayed inside the frame. When pictures are hidden, the screen redraws more rapidly.

- *Hide This Picture* hides or displays the picture in a selected frame.

- *Rulers* displays or hides the vertical and horizontal rulers.

- *Color Correction* offers six different subcommands. *Accurate* attempts to adjust colors within the document to match colors in a white-balanced photograph. *Apply to Text* determines whether color correction applies to all elements within the document or only to text. *Fast* adjusts the

display of the colors within the document to approximately match colors in a white-balanced photograph. *Gamut Alarm* shows colors that cannot be reproduced by the selected printer. *None* turns off color correction; use the Fast or Accurate commands to turn color correction back on. Finally, *Simulate Printer* attempts to display the colors within the document to match the output of the selected printer.

Note: If you prepare documents in color, it is imperative that your scanner, monitor, and printer exchange colors in a predictable manner. Therefore, be sure to use the Corel Color Manager Wizard to calibrate each color device attached to your system. You can run the Color Manager Wizard directly or select a color profile using the Tools > Color Manager command.

■ *Refresh Window* redraws the screen, which removes unwanted latent pixels produced by earlier operations.

Insert—The Insert menu is used to access and place a variety of things within your document. This includes such items as symbols, cross-references, equations, footnotes and endnotes, index entries, markers, variables, and a number of object types. Each Insert menu command is summarized in the entries that follow.

Insert
Symbol...
Cross-Reference...
Date and Time...
Equation...
Footnote
Endnote
Index Entry...
Marker...
Variable...
URL...
CorelMEMO...
Object...

■ *Symbol* accesses a symbol dialog from which you can locate and insert special characters like trademark and copyright symbols. A number of special font sets are available that include a variety of symbols and shapes. The Wingdings and Dingbats font sets are typical of fonts that provide collections of special symbols.

■ *Cross-Reference* places a cross-reference to an item, such as a figure or table. Item locations are marked using the Insert > Marker command described below.

■ *Date and Time* inserts the current date and/or time into your document. The date or time is placed at the present text cursor position; the format is controlled by the current paragraph tag.

■ *Equation* starts the built-in equation editor. The equation editor provides the tools required to prepare complex mathematical expressions and equations.

- *Footnote* inserts a reference to a footnote at the insertion point; the footnote text is displayed when the Page > Enable Footnotes command is active.

- *Endnote* inserts an endnote reference at the current insertion point.

- *Index Entry* displays the Insert Index Entry dialog. You can mark a word or phrase as the index text or type the entry directly into the dialog. The default entry is the word in the document that is selected by the text cursor.

- *Marker* inserts a cross-reference "marker" at the current insertion point within your document. Markers are used to designate the target location of a cross-reference callout, such as a figure or table title.

- *Variable* inserts a variable marker at the insertion point within your document. This command lets you mark words and passages in your document that are subject to change. Names, dates, and specification values are typical of variables. The Format > Publication command displays a dialog in which you can specify the text that you want to insert at variable markers.

- *URL* inserts a Uniform Resource Locator (Internet web site address) at the text insertion point. The URL is displayed as hyperlink text if and when your document is converted to an HTML or Barista document and then viewed with a web browser.

- *CorelMEMO* displays the CorelMEMO dialog where you can type a reminder to yourself for later viewing. Memos do not print; they are strictly for your own information.

- *Object* is used to link or embed an object created by another application into the current document.

Format—The formatting menu includes a number of special commands for setting and adjusting the formats of frames, paragraphs, and characters. It also is used to manage automatically generated items such as the table of contents and alphabetical index of a large document. The Format commands are summarized in the following list.

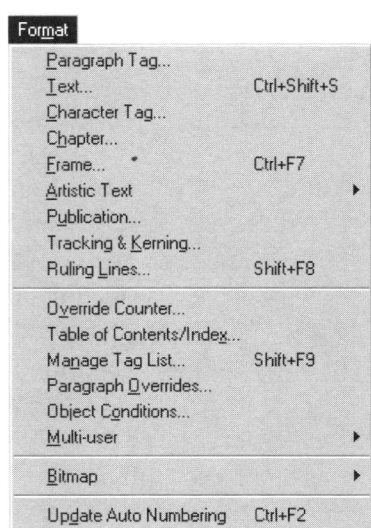

- *Paragraph Tag* displays the Tag Properties dialog, which is used to set the attributes of the current paragraph tag.

- *Text* displays the Text Properties dialog, which is used to select the font, size, color, kerning, style, shift up, and various font attributes.

- *Character Tag* changes the format properties definition of the selected character tag. Character tags can be applied to characters within a paragraph without affecting the paragraph tag.

- *Chapter* displays the Chapter Properties dialog, which is used to set the layout of the current chapter.

- *Frame* changes the margins, dimensions, position, columns, angle, and the way text flows around the selected frame. You can also add, move, or remove captions, and control orphans, widows, and vertical justification. Use this command to change the size and position of a picture within frames that contain pictures.

- *Artistic Text* gives you two choices: Edit and Fit Text to Path. Both apply to artistic text added with the Ellipse text tool. Use Edit to modify selected text. Use Fit Text to Path to conform artistic text to the shape of a frame or graphic object. This causes the text and the object to become linked as a group. Changing the shape of the object causes the linked text to dynamically change.

- *Publication* displays the Publication Properties dialog. This dialog is used to establish access rights to the current document, conditional tags for creating multiple versions of the same document (like variable fields in a form letter), and defines which text is active when Variable Text, Text Before, and Text After are used.

- *Tracking & Kerning* adjusts the letter spacing (called *tracking*) or the space between two letters (called *kerning*) for the fonts available in your system. This command is also used to export established kerned pairs and to import tracking information established in other documents.

- *Ruling Lines* creates, edits, and applies ruling line styles. Ruling lines are applied to rectangular frames and paragraphs as borders.

- *Override Counter* changes the starting number and format of a selected page, table, or figure number.

- *Table of Contents/Index* is used to create a table of contents or index for the current document.

- *Manage Tag List* is used to display the properties of a selected paragraph tag. Here, you can change and apply new properties to your paragraph tags. You can also create new paragraph tags.

- *Paragraph Overrides* displays the Paragraph Properties dialog. Here, you can make changes to a paragraph without affecting all paragraphs that use the same tag. A paragraph override is removed using Edit > Manage Overrides, which reapplies the original tag properties.

Overrides are also copied by selecting the desired paragraph, then picking Edit > Manage Overrides, Transfer Overrides to, and a tag from the list. Finally, select the Overrides that you want to transfer.

■ *Object Conditions* marks a selection as one or more versions for use in a conditional document. You can define the conditions and set which version to display or print with the Format > Publication command.

■ *Multi-user* is used on networks. Use it to assign a document's read-write privileges to selected users. Only those users having write privileges can make changes to the document.

■ *Bitmap* is used to set a number of attributes for a bitmap object including brightness, contrast, color, orientation, and more.

■ *Update Auto Numbering* updates the numbers used by automatically numbered paragraphs after numbered paragraphs are added, deleted, or moved.

Page—The Page menu deals with those commands that apply to the current page. This includes commands that display or hide footers and headers, set and apply master page properties, and set snap grids and alignment guidelines. You can also insert and delete pages using this menu.

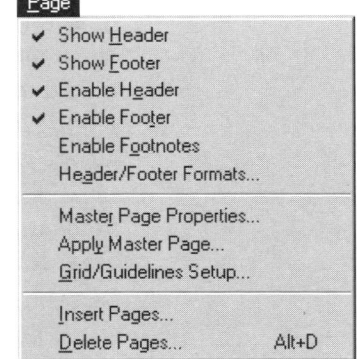

■ *Show Header* shows or hides a page header.

■ *Show Footer* shows or hides a page footer.

■ *Enable Header* enables or disables headers for all pages that use the current master page.

■ *Enable Footer* enables or disables footers for all pages that use the current master page.

■ *Enable Footnotes* enables or disables footnotes and footnote reference markers within the body text. When disabled, the text is automatically rearranged to fill the space vacated by reference markers.

■ *Header/Footer Formats* displays a dialog in which you can pick header and footer contents and positioning. Once they are applied, you can edit header/footer formats in the Master Page View. You can also select header or footer text in the Page Layout View and then edit it directly.

■ *Master Page Properties* lets you establish the page dimensions using the Master Page Properties dialog.

■ *Apply Master Page* displays the Apply Master Page dialog from which page settings can be applied to selected pages.

- *Grid/Guidelines Setup* is used to set snap grid dimensions or the initial position of a horizontal or vertical guideline. The grid or guideline is turned on using the View > Snap menu.

- *Insert/Delete Pages* display dialogs from which you can insert or delete one or more pages.

Table—The Table menu is used to create and format tables. Once they are created, you can add rows and columns to perform calculations, sort interior data, and more.

- *Create Table* displays the Table Properties dialog. The General tab lets you specify the number of rows and columns, the number of header (column heading) rows, grid lines, and column properties. A Position tab lets you set the space above and below the table, cell spacing, vertical justification, and the alignment and indentation of interior text. A Skew tab is used to slant either the column or row headings.

- *Format Table* displays the same Table Properties dialog as Create Table. The cursor must be within the table to access the selections on the Table Properties dialog.

- *Auto Formats* is used to select and apply one of fifteen different preset formats.

- *Sort* displays a Sort dialog in which you can sort one or more selected columns in either ascending or descending order.

- *Function* displays the Function Wizard where you can insert or edit a function. There are several function categories from which to choose including date and time, engineering, financial, and mathematical. Functions are used to perform calculations or to convert data found within the cells of the table. For example, you can sum a series of cells using the Function Wizard. Cell references are similar to those used in spreadsheets. R2C3 is the cell located at row 2, column 3.

- *Autofill* is used to enter values within a series of cells. You can fill up, down, left, or right. A Fill Series dialog permits you to control the direction, type, and date unit (if used) of the fill series.

- *Recalculate* is used to reevaluate the result of a function when a value changes within one of the cells included in the calculation.

- *Insert Row* is used to insert one or more rows before or after the current row.

■ *Insert Column* is used to insert one or more columns before or after the current column.

■ *Insert/Delete* is used to insert or delete a selected row or column.

■ *Merge Cells* is used to combine two or more selected cells into a single, larger cell.

■ *Split Cells* restores merged cells to their original cell entities.

■ *Cell Borders* provides access to a series of dialogs used to set border line widths, styles, and colors.

Tools—The Tools menu offers a variety of special tools including a spelling checker and thesaurus. Other special tools unique to Ventura are described in the list that follows.

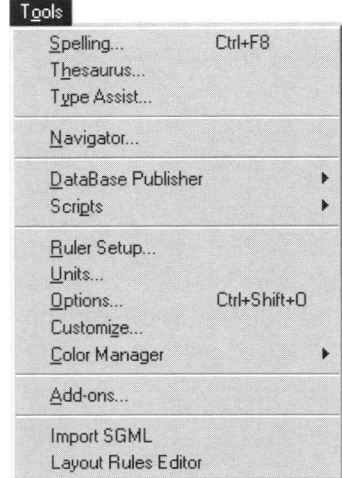

■ *Spelling* is used to check spelling and typographical errors within the open publication.

■ *Thesaurus* provides word definitions and a list of available synonyms that can be used in place of the selected word.

■ *Type Assist* is used to automate the typed entries. Examples include the automatic capitalization of the first letter of sentences and the names of days and automatically changing straight quotes to typographic quotes.

■ *Navigator* displays the Ventura Navigator. This dialog is used to add new chapters, remove graphics from text frames, and much more. All serious users of Ventura Publisher make extensive use of the Ventura Navigator, especially in the creation and placement of tables of contents and indexes.

■ *DataBase Publisher* is used to create documents based on information contained in a database. Catalogs and directories are ideal candidates for this feature. Formatting and layout instructions are stored in a file called a recipe. You can use recipes more than once to automate complex publishing tasks. You can edit recipes and apply them to new documents.

■ *Scripts* is used to create, edit, and play macros, i.e., a series of frequently used keystrokes and mouse clicks.

■ *Ruler Setup* displays the Ruler Properties dialog. This dialog is used to change the unit of measure used by the horizontal and vertical rulers in addition to setting the origin, size, zero point, and tab style.

- *Units* displays the Set Global Units dialog. This dialog sets the units of measure used by Ventura. Dimension choices include inches, points, picas and points, millimeters, ciceros and didots, and didots.

- *Options* displays the Options dialog. As in most Windows programs, this dialog is used to set up the way Ventura operates and looks. Ventura's Options dialog contains six tabs. These are the View, General, Copy Editor, Save, Selection, and Page tabs. Use this dialog to set the way you want Ventura to look and work.

- *Customize* displays the Customize dialog. Here, you can modify toolbars, menus, and keyboard shortcuts to your liking. For example, you may want to set a toolbar button or shortcut key to open frequently used dialogs. The Format > Manage Tag List and Format > Paragraph Overrides are good examples of frequently used dialogs that you might want to access using either a shortcut key sequence or toolbar button.

- *Color Manager* creates a System Color Profile, which is based on your monitor, scanner, and printer. Once the profile is established, Corel Ventura captures, displays, and prints color more accurately.

- *Add-ons* accesses a list of Corel Ventura add-on programs. These are supplemental software that extend the capabilities of Ventura by adding custom commands and features. You can obtain add-ons from independent software developers, or you can create your own.

- *Import SGML* is used to import a document prepared using the Standard Generalized Markup Language (SGML). SGML tags are used to define document elements such as headings, subheadings, and body text. SGML documents are platform and application independent. The popular HTML (Hypertext Markup Language) is a subset of SGML and is the major code set used to format documents contained in web sites on the Internet.

- *Layout Rules Editor* is used to create one or more layouts for a logic file (.LGC). Layouts let you display and print SGML documents in Corel Ventura. Ventura includes several sample layout files, with the extension VLR, to use as examples for creating your own layouts. The sample layouts are normally found in the \Corel\Ventura7\Sgml directory. Before you begin using the Layout Rules editor, you should review the Help information that describes Import SGML and the Layout Rules Editor.

Window—The Corel Ventura 7 Window menu is similar to many found in popular Windows programs. In addition to the common commands such as New, Cascade, and Tile, a few special items are worthy of clarification.

■ *Navigator* is used to display the Ventura Navigator. Navigator is used to move to different chapters, the current publication's table of contents or index, master pages, cross-references, and scripts. You can drag and drop elements from the Navigator to chapters (frames) within the open publication.

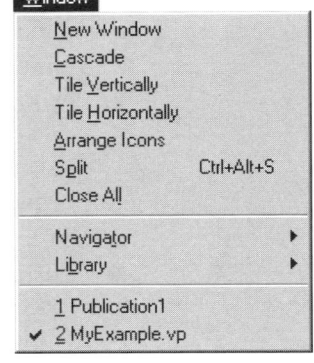

■ *Library* displays available Ventura libraries that contain such items as text, pictures, tags, or entire chapters. When a library is open you can move text, tags, and graphic objects from pages into the library or from the open library onto pages. You can also move objects between open libraries.

Help—The Help information supplied with Corel Ventura 7 is excellent. Consider using it to find out how to perform formatting operations. A brief explanation of each menu item follows.

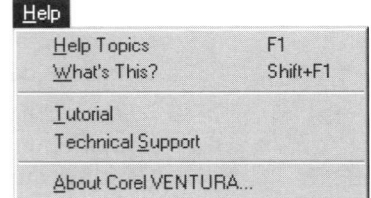

■ *Help Topics* displays the Help Topics dialog. Here, you can examine general topics; view an index of terms including commands, menus, and functions; and use the Find feature, which locates key words within the help information.

■ *What's This?* provides a description of a selected item.

■ *Tutorial* guides you through the basic operations of Corel Ventura 7 and common add-ons.

■ *Technical Support* provides information about Corel's technical support and customer service resources.

Microsoft Publisher 97 and 98

Microsoft Publisher is ideal for small documents such as fliers, brochures, newsletters, announcements, and stationery. Although Publisher 98 is now available, Publisher 97 is described since both programs operate similarly. Publisher 98 improvements include new wizards and document templates in addition to improved web site development resources.

When you start Publisher, you are invited to select PageWizard, Blank Page, or Existing Publication. Use PageWizard to create a new document from the selection list. You can also create a blank page and then place text, graphic, and table frames on the underlying page using Publisher's

toolbox. Finally, use Existing Publication to open a previously saved Publisher document. Passages of text and graphic objects can be imported from other documents using the Insert menu or by cutting and pasting or dragging and dropping content from other Windows programs. Following is an overview of each menu and its available selections.

File—The File menu is used to create a new publication, open an existing publication, and close the current publication, and also gives you access to the familiar Save, Save As, Print, Print Setup, and Exit entries. Other menu items are summarized in the following list.

File

Create New Publication...	Ctrl+N
Open Existing Publication...	Ctrl+O
Create Web Site from Current Publication	
Close Publication	
Save	Ctrl+S
Save As...	
Find File...	
Page Setup...	
Print Setup...	
Print...	Ctrl+P
Outside Print Setup...	
Print to Outside Printer...	
Print InfoSheet	
Send...	
1 C:\Program Files\Microsoft P...\Majors3	
2 C:\Program Files\Microsoft P...\Nbi9-97a	
3 C:\Program Files\Microsoft P...\Nbi9-97b	
4 C:\Program Files\Microsoft P...\Buy1get1	
Exit Publisher	Alt+F4

- *Create Web Site from Current Publication* creates a web site source document in HTML format from the current document.

- *Find File* displays a Find File dialog, which is used to locate one or more files on your system. You can choose the type of file you want to locate using the dialog settings.

- *Page Setup* is a special dialog that lets you choose the page layout, paper size, and orientation (portrait or landscape).

- *Outside Print Setup* helps you prepare your document for an outside printer. You can choose full four-color printing (the most expensive), spot color, or black-and-white and grayscale (the least expensive).

- *Print to Outside Printer* is used to print your document to a file which can be delivered to your commercial printer on magnetic media, i.e., diskettes, a high-capacity disk, or a CD.

- *Send* is used to send the current document to a customer or commercial printer using the Internet.

Edit

Undo Text Editing	Ctrl+Z
Cut Text Frame	Ctrl+X
Copy Text Frame	Ctrl+C
Paste Text	Ctrl+V
Paste Special...	
Delete Text	
Delete Text Frame	Ctrl+Del
Delete Page	
Highlight Entire Story	Ctrl+A
Select All	
Find...	
Replace...	
Links...	
Edit Story in Microsoft Word	

Edit—The Edit menu performs the same operations as many Windows application Edit menus. For example, Undo, Cut, Paste, Paste Special, and Delete operations all exist in Publisher's Edit menu. Publisher includes Cut and Paste commands for text frames in addition to a Delete Page command. The *Highlight Entire Story* command selects an entire story in one or more frames, while *Select All* selects all objects in the current document. The

selections change with the current selection. Notice that you can edit a selected story using Microsoft Word. This is a convenient feature, as it provides access to Word's full set of editing tools.

View—The View menu provides commands that change the way your document is displayed on the screen, provides two Go to commands, and provides access to toolbars and menus. A few of the more unique commands are described in the list that follows.

- *Go to Background/Foreground* is used to display the page background or redisplay the foreground objects.

- *Ignore Background* is used to hide background objects and colors to make it easier to work on objects and text in the foreground.

- *Picture Display* displays pictures at three different levels: Detailed Display, Fast Resize and Zoom, and Hide Pictures. If you are using a slow computer, you may want either Fast Resize and Zoom or Hide Pictures to speed up screen refreshing. Regardless of the way you set the Picture Display setting, the printed output provides detailed, accurate results.

- *Hide/Show Special Characters* is used to hide or display characters that represent such items as spaces, carriage returns (paragraph marks), and tabs.

- *Special Paper* is used to choose a paper type that matches a Paper Direct stock that is suitable for the current document.

Insert—This menu is used to insert text, picture files, clipart, and a variety of object types. Objects are typically spreadsheets, charts, and tables created by other applications. You can use *Scanner Image* to select a scanner and then acquire and insert a scanned image into your document. Use *Symbol* to insert special characters and symbols into your document. The *Date or Time* command inserts the current date or time based on your system's clock. Use *Page Numbers* to number the pages of your document. The *Page* command inserts a new page

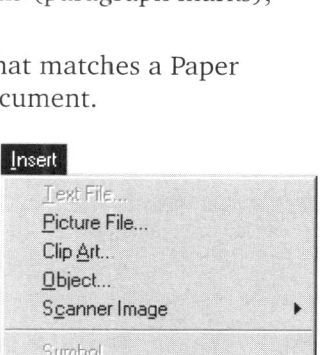

either before or after the current page. New pages can be blank or can contain all objects on the current page.

Format—The Format menu offers a rich array of commands that control the ultimate appearance of your document. Like so many menus, the Format menu items vary with the selection. The menu shown here corresponds to the selection of a text frame. Each of the commands on the Format menu is summarized in the following list.

Format
Text Style...
Character...
Spacing Between Characters...
Fancy First Letter...
Indents And Lists...
Line Spacing...
Tabs...
Border...
Fill Color...
Fill Patterns and Shading...
Shadow   Ctrl+D
Text Frame Properties...
Pick Up Formatting
Apply Formatting

■ *Text Style* is used to select, create, change, delete, or import paragraph styles. When a style is selected, it is applied to the selected text.

■ *Character* is used to select a font, style (regular, italic, bold, or bold italic), size, color, and effects (all caps, small caps, underline, double underline).

■ *Spacing Between Characters* kerns (adjusts the space) between selected text. Selections include Normal, Very Tight, Tight, Loose, and Very Loose.

■ *Fancy First Letter* provides access to a variety of drop cap and fancy first letter styles. This controls the appearance of the first letter of the selected paragraph.

■ *Indents and Lists* accesses the Indents and Lists dialog. Here, you can apply either a bulleted or numbered list to the selected paragraphs, or return one or more paragraphs to normal text. You can also set a variety of indent styles, including flush left, first line, hanging indent, quotation, and custom. This dialog also includes a Line Spacing button, which displays the Line Spacing dialog also accessed with the next menu command.

■ *Line Spacing* lets you set the space between lines, before paragraphs, and after paragraphs.

■ *Tabs* displays the Tabs dialog. This dialog is similar to Microsoft Word's dialog, which lets you place tabs on the text ruler and control tab alignment and leader styles (if used).

■ *Border* is used to apply a line border, color, and/or border art to the selected frame. A number of line and border art selections are available.

- *Fill Color* displays a Color palette from which you can choose a background fill color for the selected frame.

- *Fill Patterns and Shading* displays the Fill Patterns and Shading dialog. Use this dialog to apply tints/shades, patterns, gradients, and colors to the selected frame.

- *Shadow* applies a shadow effect to the selected frame.

- *Text Frame Properties* is used to set the margins, number of columns, and text wrapping, and to insert "Continued on/from page…" annotations when a text frame continues on a following page.

- *Pick Up Formatting* makes use of the Format Painter. Here, you pick up formatting from one paragraph so you can apply it to another.

Tools—The Tools menu contains several selections that are used to check the quality of your document, apply special effects, and to align objects using "*snaps*."

Tools	
Design Gallery…	
Add Selection to Design Gallery…	
Check Spelling…	F7
Hyphenate…	Ctrl+H
Design Checker…	
✔ Snap to Ruler Marks	
✔ Snap to Guides	Ctrl+W
Snap to Objects	
Options…	

- *Design Gallery* provides access to a number of design objects within various design categories. Categories include attention getters, headlines, ornaments, pull quotes, and more. Within each category you can select a number of different design elements.

- *Add Selection to Design Gallery* is used to add a new design selection set and then to insert frequently used items to the new set. For example, if you use a standard headline design for a newsletter or brochure, you can add the item and then apply it whenever you need it.

- *Check Spelling* launches Publisher's spelling checker to check for errors in the selected text.

- *Hyphenate* displays the Hyphenate dialog, which is used to turn automatic hyphenation on or off, to confirm each hyphenation point, or to change the width of the hyphenation zone. The hyphenation zone is typically 0.25 inches. You can modify this value to either increase or decrease the number of hyphenated words.

- *Design Checker* is used to determine the quality of your document. It checks for empty frames, covered (hidden) objects, text in overflow areas, objects located in nonprinting areas, disproportionate pictures, excessive special effects, spacing between sentences, too many fonts, and too many colors.

- *Snap to Ruler Marks* aligns text with ruler tick marks.

■ *Snap to Guides* aligns text with page guides.

■ *Snap to Objects* aligns one or more objects with other objects.

■ *Options* displays the Options dialog. Here, you can set your operational preferences. Included are controls that set measurement units, mouse clicks, mouse pointers, help levels, and more.

Arrange—The selections on the Arrange menu are used to control the position, alignment, and grouping of one or more selected objects on the displayed page. Each selection is summarized in the list that follows.

■ *Layout Guides* displays the Layout Guides dialog where you can set the position of margin, column, and grid guides. You can use this selection to create one or more symmetrical column guides on a new, blank document. Guides are displayed as blue lines on the underlying page to help you maintain a balanced document. Mirroring is also available to ensure layout symmetry of facing pages. Once the guides are in position, you can drag your text, picture, WordArt, and table frames onto the underlying page, using the guides to control their positions.

■ *Ruler Guides* are also displayed as alignment aids on the underlying page. You can add one or more horizontal or vertical ruler guides or clear all guides using this selection.

■ *Bring to Front* is used when you have two or more overlapping objects. If you want to select an overlaid object and bring it to the front of the stack, select it and click this command.

■ *Bring Closer* is used to bring a selected object one layer closer to the front when multiple objects are layered (or overlapping).

■ *Send Farther* is used to send a selected object one layer farther back when multiple objects are layered (or overlapping).

■ *Send to Back* is used to put a selected object at the back of the stack when multiple objects are layered.

■ *Group/Ungroup Objects* are used to merge and unmerge (group and ungroup) two or more objects so that they move and scale as one. To group objects, select two or more objects with Shift+Click so that their frame handles are displayed. Then click Group Objects. To break them apart, select the group and click Ungroup Objects. Note that the

Group/Ungroup Objects command changes to correspond to the current selection.

■ *Line Up Objects* is used to align two or more selected objects, such as picture objects, either top to bottom or right to left. A Line Up Objects dialog permits you to align either object edges or centers; you can also align to a margin.

■ *Nudge Objects* displays a Nudge Objects dialog that is used to move an object up, down, left, or right by a predetermined increment (you can set the nudge distance in this dialog). Nudging gives you fine control over the movement of one or more selected objects.

■ *Rotate/Flip* lets you rotate a selected object either left or right. A Custom Rotate dialog is available to perform angular rotation by entering a degree value. The Flip selections permit you to flip a picture object vertically or horizontally about the corresponding vertical or horizontal axis.

Table—Publisher provides table controls that are similar to those found in top-end word processing applications. Use the Table button on the toolbar to create a table. You can specify the initial number of rows and columns and pick a stored format using this dialog.

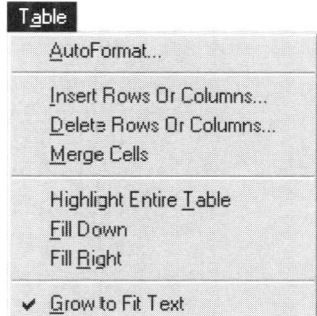

■ *AutoFormat* displays the same dialog that is displayed when you first create a table using the Table button. Here, you can pick a stored format from a wide selection of different table styles.

■ *Insert Rows Or Columns* permits you to position your cursor and then insert one or more new rows or columns either before or after the current row/column position.

■ *Delete Rows Or Columns* permits you to delete the current row or column. You can select multiple rows or columns by first selecting them and then performing the Delete operation.

■ *Merge Cells* is used to merge two or more selected cells into a single cell that spans adjoining cells. This selection is ideal for creating special row or column headings that span two or more subordinate rows or columns.

■ *Highlight Entire Table* is used to select the entire table. This might be done to perform an operation that applies to the entire table, such as changing the font size of all text entries.

■ *Fill Down* is used to repeat an entry in the top cell of a selected range of cells in the cells that follow. For example, to repeat the same date in the column of an expense statement, type the date in the topmost cell, highlight following cells, and click Fill Down to copy the date.

■ *Fill Right* operates in the same manner as Fill Down; this command fills a value across a row rather than down a column.

■ *Grow to Fit Text* is used to enlarge a cell automatically as text is entered. The cell simply expands vertically to accommodate the typed text. Other cells on the same row also expand to match the current cell. You can turn off automatic Grow to Fit Text as required.

MailMerge—You can use Publisher to distribute your documents based on a mailing list just as you can using the mail merge feature of most full-featured word processing pro-

grams. As with word processors, Publisher permits you to create a data source of names, addresses, etc. Next, you create a document and insert merge fields for names and addresses that are taken from the data source. Your data source can be a data list produced directly in Publisher or it can be an Access, dBASE, Paradox, or similar database file.

■ *Open Data Source* is used to open a stored data file that contains your distribution list, i.e., names, addresses, etc. If you don't have one, use the Create an address list Publisher (identical to *Create Publisher Address List* shown here) to enter the name and address information.

■ *Insert Field* opens an existing data source file or lets you create a new one. It then displays the field names in an Insert Fields dialog. Use the dialog to select field names and place them within the open document. For example, you can put title, name, and address fields in the appropriate spots of the open document. Be sure to add spaces and punctuation as you would if you were typing the content of the data source directly into your document. If you use a City and State field, enter the comma and space that separates them.

■ *Merge* places the source data into the document. A preview data dialog lets you step through the data records to see how each document looks before it is printed. It is a good way to check both the document and supporting source data to make sure that they are accurate and ready to print.

■ *Show Merge Results* shows the data from the current source data record on the displayed document. The data replaces the merge fields.

- *Show Field Codes* shows the merge fields, rather than the actual source data, on the displayed document.

- *Filter or Sort* displays the Filtering and Sorting dialog. Filtering permits you to establish rules that control which records are printed based on a field. For example, you can print all records for City "Is equal to" *city name*. Other filters include Is not equal to, Is less than, and Is greater than. You can use as many as three fields in your sort as well as Boolean Ands and Ors. Look at the following example:

  > City Is equal to *city name*, And/Or
  > ZIP Code is greater than *ZIP Code name*, And/Or
  > Age Is less than *age value*.

  Sorting permits you to reorder your document in either ascending or descending order based on the alphanumeric values contained in one to three fields. For example, you can sort by ZIP code, then last name, and finally first name if you wish.

- *Create Publisher Address List* is used to create an address list that can be used as a source data file for your merged documents.

- *Edit Publisher Address List* permits you to edit or add more records to your address list.

- *Cancel Merge* disconnects the link between your document and data source (or address list). This is done if you decide to use an alternative list for your mail merge work.

Help—Microsoft Publisher includes extensive help information. Perhaps this is because it is designed for entry-level users who may have a limited amount of experience using desktop publishing and frame-oriented applications. Included is an extensive index, demos, and an extremely useful list of keyboard shortcuts. A *Print Trouble-shooter* is available to walk you through printing problems. *Microsoft Office Compatible* shows you how to access the powerful resources of Micro-soft Office applications, which

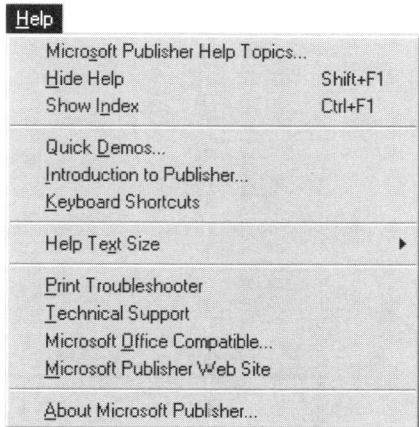

combines the power of both applications into a coordinated, powerful toolset. You can use *Microsoft Publisher Web Site* to browse Microsoft's repertoire of Publisher support resources via your Internet connection. New users can display help information in a window for quick reference. When they achieve competency, which is usually in a matter of an hour or two, the help information begins to get in the way. Just click the Hide Help button at the bottom of the Help window to gain more document workspace.

QuarkXPress

The QuarkXPress product was not reviewed in detail for several reasons. First, unlike all other software publishers who supplied their products in support of this book, Quark would only supply a demo edition of its product. I must apologize to the readers for my failure to convince Quark to take this project seriously. However, after examining the demo product, which only excludes the printing and saving functions, I concluded that it was not important enough to waste any more time in pursuit of Quark's commercial version. The evaluation of the demo version was sufficient to know that it could not be recommended to professional desktop publishers in light of the availability of superior professional products from Adobe and Corel Corporation.

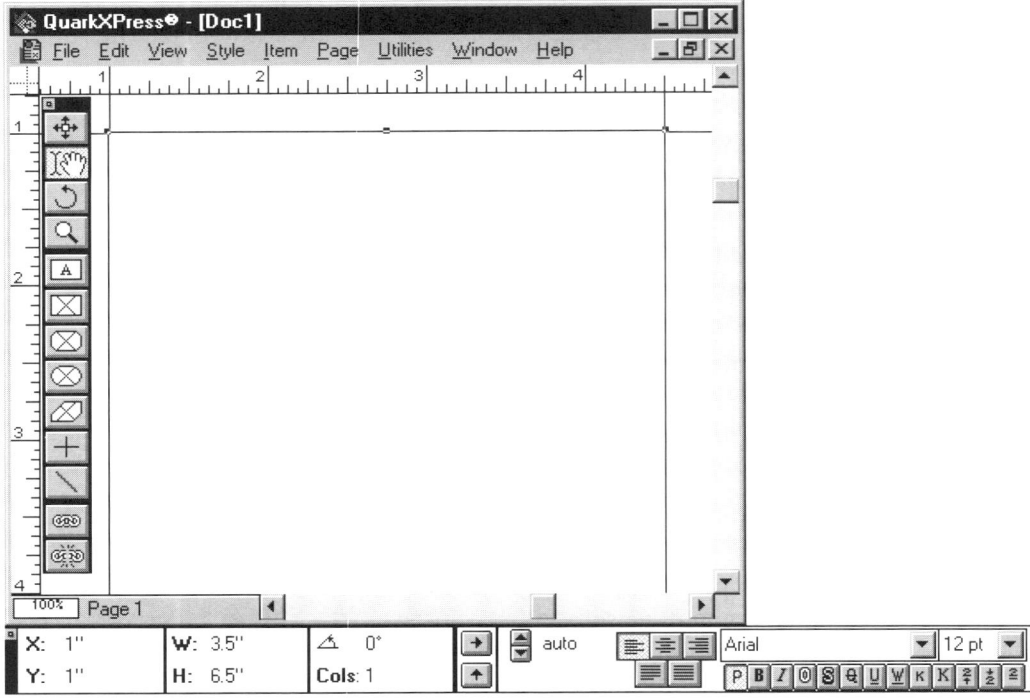

The QuarkXPress for Windows demo version was examined by Macintosh users who are fast to point out that the Windows version lacks many of the features found in Quark's Mac edition. Of course, some Mac users have an elitist attitude when comparing Mac stuff to Windows stuff. QuarkXPress for the Macintosh has been around a long time and over the years has

undergone a number of feature enhancements. Given time, Quark will probably develop an equally good product for the Windows platform—the company does have its roots in high-end desktop publishing software development.

A Quark representative revealed that the company is readying a beta release of the next Windows version of QuarkXPress. One would have to assume that Quark is adding improvements to the product. Perhaps after some of the products described in this book undergo significant revisions, a second edition of this book will be published. If Quark is still around, maybe they'll supply the real product so you can decide if it fits your requirements. It might.

DTP Checklist

Adobe PageMaker 6.5

Category—Intermediate

Uses—Brochures, fliers, newsletters, small catalogs, invitations, business cards, stationery, small books.

Disk Space—The typical installation occupies approximately 65 megabytes of hard disk space.

Learning Time—Most users should be able to produce simple documents during the first session. A few sessions should have you producing fairly complex documents.

Stability—Program operation was smooth and stable. Windows page faults were not encountered.

Windows Look and Feel—Excellent; complies with conventions typically found in Windows applications.

Ease of Use—Frequently used controls are available in palettes that can be displayed on the desktop for easy access. Moving between pages and frames, flowing text, inserting and editing frames, and creating and applying styles are all easy to accomplish with a little practice. Most users familiar with high-end word processors should master the most frequently used PageMaker features quickly and easily.

Number of Features—A relatively complete set of typographic features, including kerning and variable runarounds, exist. Minimal pagination features are included, but require more manual intervention than other top-end desktop publishing programs designed for multichapter book production.

Neat Stuff—Column and ruler guides, automatic text flow, the ability to change layouts and style settings on the fly, common Windows operating metaphors.

Things I Didn't Like—Although it's a short list, the creation and application of running headers and footers in large, multichapter documents is not intuitive. Many of the "plug-ins" might be better treated as standard features; to some, plug-ins seem like afterthoughts or patches. This comment excludes plug-in libraries from third-party developers.

Recommended—An emphatic yes. Adobe PageMaker 6.5 should work well for most desktop publishing applications. However, if you specialize in large, multichapter books, be sure to take a close look at Adobe Frame-Maker and Corel Ventura 7.

Adobe FrameMaker 5

Category—Advanced

Uses—Large, multichapter books, newspapers, newsletters, brochures, fliers, catalogs, directories; experienced users can also prepare invitations, business cards, stationery, and small books.

Disk Space—The typical installation occupies approximately 40 megabytes of hard disk space.

Learning Time—Most advanced application users experienced with typographic systems and terminology should be able to produce their first full-scale publication within a few days. Fairly complex documents can be tackled within a week or two.

Stability—Program operation was smooth and stable. A Windows page fault was only encountered once, when attempting to import an unrecognized text format.

Windows Look and Feel—Moderately good; complies with most conventions typically found in Windows applications. Escape codes and shortcut key sequences for special symbols were a bit awkward at first, but were soon mastered.

Ease of Use—Frequently used controls are available on the QuickAccess bar and Tools palette. Moving between the Master Pages and Body Pages was easy once I learned how. Flowing text, inserting and editing frames, and creating and applying styles are slightly more rigorous than simpler programs, but the control is precise. Most users who are familiar with high-end word processors and low-end desktop publishing programs should master the most frequently used FrameMaker features within a few days. Those who are new to desktop publishing will struggle.

Number of Features—The full set of typographic controls is available in FrameMaker. As mentioned, it is ideal for large, complex, multichapter books requiring precision control.

Neat Stuff—FrameMaker is loaded! Among the neat features are conditional text; markers; variables; frame control and rotation; automatic running headers, footers, and pagination; automatic table of contents and index; designer dialogs for paragraphs, tables, complex mathematical equations, and objects; cross-reference control; viewing and updating OLE objects; and the ability to quickly and easily change master pages, frames, and styles on the fly.

Things I Didn't Like—Although a minor complaint, I would like to see Adobe expand the content of the online help information in addition to improving the help structure to be more like that found in either Adobe PageMaker or Adobe Illustrator. Another improvement would be to supplement the shortcut keys for special symbols with a symbol dialog like that used by Microsoft Word's Insert > Symbol command.

Recommended—Both Adobe FrameMaker 5 and 5.5 can be used to produce the most complex publications. FrameMaker handles huge, multichapter publications with ease. It is a comprehensive, professional-quality desktop publishing program that is extremely rich in the features needed for any publishing task. I strongly recommend its use to serious publishing enthusiasts and professionals who have the time to master this full-featured Windows application.

Corel Ventura 7

Category—Advanced

Uses—Large, multichapter books, newspapers, newsletters, brochures, fliers, catalogs, directories; experienced users can also prepare invitations, business cards, stationery, and small books. Built-in templates help in the quick creation of several document types.

Disk Space—The typical installation occupies approximately 170 megabytes of hard disk space.

Learning Time—Most advanced application users experienced with typographic systems and terminology should be able to produce their first full-scale publication within a few days. Fairly complex documents can be tackled within a week or two.

Stability—Program operation was occasionally hindered by Windows page faults (not unlike Microsoft Word and other feature-laden Windows products). Of course, many users believe that this is a Windows 95 problem rather than a problem with the application. The author strongly recommends that users periodically save their publication to minimize the potential for lost work. This is particularly true before printing operations or before performing a global find and replace operation in a large, multi-chapter publication.

Windows Look and Feel—Exceptionally good; complies with the conventions typically found in Windows applications. The tool buttons display clarifying labels to help users make the right choices. Many of the toolbar buttons are identical to those found in popular word processing programs.

Ease of Use—Users of most Windows applications will feel right at home with the menus, toolbar buttons, and dialogs found in Ventura 7. Most experienced Windows application users should learn to perform basic operations in their first session. Mastering advanced typesetting features will take a few days, depending on the user's familiarity with typography. In particular, the user should explore the Ventura Navigator's selections and shortcut menu (right-click on a Navigator object). The Navigator lets you copy chapters, master pages, and style sheets from one open Ventura document to another.

Number of Features—The full set of typographic controls is available in Ventura 7. As mentioned, it is ideal for large, complex, multichapter books requiring precision control.

Neat Stuff—Corel Ventura 7 is full featured, interfaces directly with a number of text and graphic formats, and uses common Windows metaphors throughout, making it more intuitive than many other desktop publishing programs.

Things I Didn't Like—The primary complaint is the amount of disk space occupied by this program. It is fully twice as disk intensive as its closest rivals, Adobe FrameMaker 5 and 5.5.

Recommended—Corel Ventura 7 can be used to accomplish the most complex desktop publishing tasks. Ventura 7 is a comprehensive, professional-quality desktop publishing program that is extremely rich in the features needed for any publishing task. I strongly recommend its use to serious publishing enthusiasts and professionals who have the time to master this full-featured Windows application.

Microsoft Publisher 97 and 98

Category—Entry level

Uses—Ideal for newsletters, brochures, fliers, small catalogs, stationery, and web pages

Disk Space—The typical installation occupies approximately 65 megabytes of hard disk space. An additional 200 megabytes of clipart is available on the CD.

Learning Time—Most entry-level users should be able to produce their first finished document in less than an hour. Experienced users should finish in less than 30 minutes.

Stability—This program is as stable as most Microsoft Office applications running under Windows 95. Text flow from one frame to the next is sometimes unreliable and occasionally requires you to drag the frame's bottom edge up and then back to its original position to force interior text to display and print properly. Knowing this trick lets you fix this problem when it occurs. As with other feature-laden Windows 95 applications, you may experience an occasional page fault. (This may be a Windows 95 problem rather than an application problem.) However, they are rare and you may go for months without encountering an unwanted program termination. In any case, always save your documents after each major development step just to be on the safe side.

Windows Look and Feel—Exceptionally good; complies with the conventions typically found in Windows applications. Users of Microsoft Office applications will recognize many of the menu selections, toolbar buttons, and common print dialogs. Publisher's seamless integration with Microsoft Office applications and supporting resources makes it a natural for those who use such programs as Word, Excel, and PowerPoint.

Ease of Use—Users of most common Windows applications will feel right at home with the menus, toolbar buttons, and dialogs found in Publisher. It is by far the easiest program to use of all the desktop publishing programs described in this book.

Number of Features—Because Microsoft Publisher is aimed at small documents, it has a relatively small set of pagination tools and type control tools when comparing it to such programs as Ventura and FrameMaker. However, it has no equal in its rich set of built-in design aids including wizards, embedded designs, and the versatile Design Gallery. It also features a rich assortment of clipart and pictures; Publisher 98 even provides sound clips and animated clipart for producing multimedia web sites.

Things I Didn't Like—It would be neat if Publisher could support large, multichapter publications. However, the wizards to control automatic pagination, indexes, tables of contents, variable headers, footers, footnotes, endnotes, blank left-hand pages, etc. would require an extensive overhaul to the current product. These elements would require the addition of menus and dialogs that could bewilder entry-level Publisher users. Since the target market appears to be users who want to create simple documents, Microsoft probably figures it's a mistake to burden the current product with advanced features. The product is certainly successful as indicated by sales. However, one can always hope for a Microsoft Publisher Professional.

Recommended—I recommend Microsoft Publisher to those who want to create attractive newsletters and brochures quickly and easily. I have no less than three desktop publishing programs on my computer. One of them is Microsoft Publisher, which I use for product fliers, newsletters, and other small documents.

QuarkXPress

Quark was the only software publisher who wouldn't support this project with a real version of the software. They did send a limited demo version, but after spending a few hours with it, I concluded that without the commercial release, it was pointless to provide readers with sketchy information about what appears to be a product with limited features and an unfamiliar, Mac-like user interface. Perhaps the new version 4.0 is richer in features and has a more familiar look and feel for users of Windows applications.

Moving Ahead

The next chapter deals with book covers. If you are publishing a book for the consumer market, the cover design, title, and the "sell copy" contained on it mean the difference between success and commercial failure. Chapter 8 also describes how covers are prepared using the software tools described in this book.

Part 2

Publishing Secrets

Included In This Part:

- Chapter 8—Cover Design and Preparation
- Chapter 9—Understanding Publishers
- Chapter 10—Working with Commercial Printers
- Chapter 11—Self-Publishing
- Chapter 12—Administrative Requirements
- Chapter 13—Crossroad Decisions

Chapter 8

Cover Design and Preparation

Introduction

This chapter deals with books that are sold in retail bookstores. It discusses the three faces of a book: the front cover (or *lid*), the back cover, and the spine. It also presents the general approach to cover preparation using your PC, including a few essential tips. Millions of *trade paperbacks* or *mass-market paperbacks* line bookstore shelves. A few hundred thousand new titles hit the market every year. Is cover design important? You bet it is. It is one of the key elements that differentiate one book from another. Don't let the old adage, "You can't judge a book by its cover," lead you to underestimate the value of the title, color, and design elements found on the cover. Without a compelling cover, the pages of a book may never see the daylight. This chapter delves into book covers, their elements, and some design considerations.

Part
2

Cover Elements

Before exploring cover design, you should consider a number of packaging-related parameters. These include:

- Trim size
- Page count (thickness or spine width)
- Title
- Channels of distribution (trade bookstores, mass merchandisers, price clubs, etc.)

The **trim**, as you should know from previous chapters, is the width and height of a book. Common sizes, expressed in inches, include 5½ x 8½, 6 x 9, 7½ x 9¼, and 8 x 10. Unusual trim sizes should be avoided, particularly at either extreme of the size spectrum. Tiny trims are lost on the bookshelf, as they are obscured from view by surrounding books. Don't expect that a bookstore will make a special effort to display your product in a prominent location. They can't, as every publisher would want the identical treatment.

If you expect that bookstores will place your book in a special display rack or point-of-sale countertop display, think again. The store simply can't accommodate special handling for a number of good reasons. First, chain outlets often have rigid architectural policies that prohibit the introduction of extra stands, posters, and signs. The space at the cash register is usually so crowded, there's simply not any space for added point-of-purchase units. Finally, this is prime space and is frequently used to generate additional revenue by renting the space to suppliers or by restricting it to high turnover impulse items.

Large books, depending on their size, may not fit on standard bookshelves. Bookstore buyers frequently avoid unusual formats. Presenting an odd product gives buyers a ready reason to say "no" to your creation. Finally, oversize products do not nest well with adjoining books. Excessive exposure results in physical damage from normal stock handling. You can anticipate scuffing, bending, and tearing well in excess of those books that conform to standard trim sizes.

The **page count** is another factor that controls your final book package. You should aim for at least 150 or more finished pages if you want enough spine width to display the title and appealing design elements. Narrow spines, like small books, get lost in the shuffle. Therefore, be sure that your page count supports both a reasonable spine width and a price that is sufficient to achieve cost recovery and perhaps some profit, too. Pricing considerations are discussed in much more detail in the next chapter.

The **title** of your book is vital to its success. It must communicate the book's message and spark interest. If possible, use a title that can stimulate curiosity, create excitement, fulfill a need, or provide a service. "I want to read this book." "This book will teach me how to … ." "This book might help me make a fortune!" Whatever the "hook," find it and use it. If your title is not on target, or if you think there will be people who just won't understand it, use a clarifying subtitle. Although "cute" titles can stimulate people's interest, be sure that the words you choose clearly communicate the book's theme. And be sure that the book delivers the promise. Otherwise, you will get most of your books back from the bookstores, because book publishers are required to extend a 100 percent product return policy to their trade accounts. This, too, is covered in more detail in the following chapter.

The **channels of distribution** can also dictate your approach to book *packaging*. If you intend to sell your books in traditional bookstores, then a BOOKLAND EAN barcode and the printed price must be placed on the back cover. However, if you plan to sell it in mass merchandisers and price clubs within North America, publishing guidelines recommend that you put a UPC barcode on the back cover, and the BOOKLAND EAN (EAN 13) barcode on the inside of the front cover. The BOOKLAND EAN 13 barcode makes your book exportable. While the UPC code is fairly localized to the U.S. and Canada, both book trade and general retailing establishments in most industrialized countries use EAN. (See Barcodes later in this chapter.)

Failure to apply the barcodes and price may limit your distribution in bookstores, and will definitely keep you out of mass merchandise outlets, as the barcode is essential to their stock keeping systems. Although some publishers agree to apply adhesive barcode stickers, this is a time-consuming and costly step that you should avoid if at all possible.

Never attempt to place both barcode types on the same opening, as this confuses the scanning equipment and can create havoc with the connected system. Large distributors and chain stores can levy penalties against vendors who cause scanning problems. A scanning error can shut down a store's check-out and inventory system, resulting in thousands of dollars in lost sales and a lot of angry customers. Therefore, be sure that you know what you're doing when you apply a barcode to your books.

Part 2

Barcode scanners can't "see" red or yellow bars. Use black or process blue. A white background is recommended, although a red or yellow background is acceptable. Never use a screened black or blue background. The size of a barcode is critical for proper scanning. Print it at 100 percent and don't photo-reduce it.

Front Cover Design

The front cover should be as appealing as you can make it with your available resources. The design should compel the consumer to pick it up and study it, flip through the interior, and ultimately take it to the checkout counter. Thousands of attractive book covers are created every year; just go to your local bookstore and see. Most were given considerable care in design. When done right, the author and graphic designer collaborate. A good graphic designer either browses the book or spends time with the author so that he or she understands the book's purpose and content. Next, the designer then brainstorms ideas in an attempt to capture the theme of the book with pictures, colors, and type. A design should enhance the title to maximize its impact. Often, designers come up with several ideas and sketch them for the publisher's review. Once a design is picked, the final design process is put into motion.

Graphics

The high-end graphics software described in this book provide all the tools you need to create a stunning cover. Use these products with a wide selection of display fonts, a scanner, and/or a good assortment of photo and clipart CDs to achieve your design goals. You can project a season with a picture of autumn leaves, a snow-covered landscape, a palm-lined tropical inlet, or the arid dunes and cactus of the desert. Achieve a high-tech look and feel with a picture of a space shuttle against a black background, a lab full of technical apparatus, a montage of computer parts or integrated circuits, or use a group of white-coated lab workers calibrating their equipment. Many book covers are simple, but still impactual. For example, you can use a bright background color and contrasting type to set off the message. You can apply a drop shadow or texture to the type to give it pizzazz.

Use a program like Adobe Photoshop or Corel PHOTO-PAINT for pixel editing and retouching. Import the bitmap image into either Adobe Illustrator or Corel DRAW and then apply type and barcodes. Because Corel DRAW includes a barcode add-in utility, you might want to consider using it to prepare your cover artwork. Once the bitmapped images are imported into your vector graphics software, add the type and then scale it and place it in its final position. When finished, print a proof on a color printer to get an idea of what it will look like.

Using Color

When using a photo, drawing, or solid background, be sure to pick a color that contrasts your type. If the background is dark, use a white window for the back cover copy. Regardless of your content and selections, be sure to color balance your monitor, scanner, and printer using the built-in color balance features that are supplied with all high-end graphics and desktop publishing programs. The colors that you see on your monitor are projected (RGB); they are typically richer (more saturated) than printed colors, which are reflected (CMYK). Therefore, you can anticipate that the printed rendition of your colors will vary. However, color balancing will minimize the difference and if it's done carefully, you should obtain satisfactory results. Once you are satisfied with your output, print the cover to a Linotronics-compatible PostScript file (with the extension PRN). Then have a local service bureau or your commercial printer prepare the film.

It's a good idea to request a proof of your work before it goes to press to be sure the colors match your expectations.

Type

As mentioned in the preceding paragraph, your type should stand out. Use a contrasting color, a readable size, and special effects, such as black or white borders and/or drop shadows. There are literally thousands of type styles from which to choose. Be sure to pick a style that is clear; avoid Old English or cursive fonts that are hard to read. When using multiple type weights, keep them in the same font family. Mixing incompatible type styles, such as serif and sans serif, is a poor practice. This goes for the interior of your book, as well. One of the new features introduced in Corel DRAW 8 provides the ability to apply shadows to type. Prior to this feature, it was necessary to clone the type, change it to a contrasting color, and then slide it beneath and offset to the original type. This procedure yields a similar effect, but is a bit more trouble.

After studying the way that hundreds of people browse books, I've identified the most common patterns. This was done in the hope that I could derive a better understanding of what is important and what is not relative to how to design the most effective book cover. Most consumers see the spine first, because of the way books are stocked in most bookstores. A few books are positioned face-out, but this is an exception rather than a rule, because the face-out orientation simply occupies more valuable shelf space. Once a person sees a title of interest, they pull it from the shelf and examine the front cover. If the price is not on the front cover, many turn the book over to see the price marking on the back. This is where you want the price, as you can expect that most people, if at all interested in the book, will look for it. Next, people begin flipping pages. They read one or two random sentences from random pages, perhaps to check the author's style or to get a preview of the presentation. More often than not, they hold the book in their right hand and flip with their thumb from back to front. Left-handed people, who represent approximately one out of seven in the general population, flip books from front to back. Technical book browsers typically look for interior diagrams, read procedures and partial descriptions, and finally examine the table of contents and alphabetical index.

Part
2

The Spine

As mentioned in the introduction to this chapter, every book cover has three sides: a front cover, a back cover, and a spine. Although the spine is the smallest panel on the cover, it is certainly the surface that is seen the most. Consumers locate books by browsing spines. A spine with a readable title and attractive design and color may convince consumers to pull the book off the shelf. Now they can see the rest of your work, i.e., the front cover, back cover, and interior elements.

Back Cover

Publishers expend a major effort in writing back cover copy to provide prospective readers with a synopsis of a book's purpose, story line, or main features. Surprisingly, more than half the people who browse books never read the back cover copy. Nevertheless, for those who do, it's important to present good, succinct, and interesting information. With many, this is your only shot at a sales pitch.

Sales Copy

The copy put on most back covers attempts to highlight the most interesting features of the book. By presenting a series of "grabbers," you may be able to hook the browser into a purchase. If you are producing a technical book, identify the target audience by user category (who the book is for), level of expertise (beginner, intermediate, or advanced), and consider including a list of the key topics presented in the book. Information about author qualifications is also important. Readers should be confident that the author can deliver either an enjoyable tale or a useful, authoritative reference.

You may also wish to put sales copy elements on the front cover of your book. Remember, after the spine, this is the second most commonly examined cover element. If you have a list of features, consider adding them to the front cover as a bulleted or checkbox list. If the book contains companion items, such as a compact disk or valuable coupons, announce them with a starburst or round medallion. However, be careful not to clutter an appealing cover with excessive "noise." Your attempt to hook a reader may diminish the impact of your design elements and become ugly detractors rather than compelling enhancements.

Barcodes

The back cover of a trade paperback should include a BOOKLAND EAN 13 format barcode placed at the bottom of the back cover. If you use the Barcode Wizard bundled with Corel DRAW (versions 6, 7, or 8) or Corel Ventura 7, or any other barcode preparation software, you can select the barcode format from a list. Corel DRAW includes 18 industry standard barcode formats. Among them are UPC (A) (used by mass merchandisers), UPC (E), EAN-13 (used by the book trade), EAN-8, and Code 39. When running a barcode utility, you first select the desired barcode format, i.e.,

EAN-13, and then type the ISBN (International Standard Book Number) digits.

The EAN standard requires that the first three digits be the publisher's country code. U.S. publishers use 978 as the country code followed by the first nine digits of the book's ISBN number. The last (check) digit is omitted by the EAN-13 barcode standard. The UPC (A) barcode requires the check digit. EAN-13 is the European version of the UPC (A) Uniform Product Code. EAN-13 also permits you to add a 2- or 5-digit barcode supplemental, or "add on," which appears to the right of the main barcode. You can use the supplement to enter the price of the book, such as 51495 to represent U.S. $14.95. The number 50995 represents U.S. $9.95. Note that the first digit, 5, represents the currency U.S. dollars. You can look in any bookstore to see the local three-digit country code as well as the currency digit if they use the add-on block.

You can usually preview the resulting barcode on the screen before it is printed. In fact, when using either Corel DRAW or Ventura 7, the barcode is a graphic object within a frame. The barcode object is positioned and scaled using a pointing device, which is usually a mouse. If you wish, you can print a proof of the back cover to verify the barcode's readability. If you have a barcode scanner, read the barcode to be sure it produces the numbers that you typed.

Price

Price marking is important for a number of reasons. First, when the price is missing from a book, consumers have a tendency to put them back on the shelf and find another book that is price marked. It's simply too inconvenient to find a clerk and then wait while he or she looks up the book's price. A price mark also establishes product value. Even discount operations use the marked price as a basis for their discount.

Finally, most booksellers require price marking. When a price mark is absent, some distributors and booksellers apply adhesive price labels. This task can result in a publisher charge back, particularly from large, national book distributors. When bookstores return stickered books for credit, two problems can occur. First, someone must remove each price label when the books are restocked, and certainly before they are redistributed to the market. Second, many books are damaged during the label removal process. This results in scrap, or as a minimum the "hurt" book must either be sold to a "remainder house" or a paper recycler.

The approach to book pricing is presented in the next chapter. Setting an appropriate price is crucial to the commercial success of a book. You

Part
2

should make an effort to understand the dynamics between unit cost, price, and market conditions.

Design Tips

Cover designers most often combine bitmap pictures with vector text and barcodes. The general approach to creating a cover is outlined in the following steps.

1. Determine the trim size of your book and its spine width.

 **Tip:** You cannot complete your cover artwork until you know the spine width. The spine width is controlled by the book's page count and paper thickness, which is expressed in the *pages-per-inch* (PPI) rating of the paper used by your printer. For example, 351 ppi means that the thickness of 351 pages measures one inch.

2. Using your vector drawing program (such as Corel DRAW or Adobe Illustrator), set your page size to 100 percent of the cover size. This includes the back cover, spine, and front cover areas. If your book trim is 5½ x 8½ inches and you have a one-half-inch spine width, your page size should be set to 11½ inches wide by 8½ inches high.

3. Select one or more bitmap images to serve as a background for your front cover or front cover and spine. The image can be a photograph or picture in a common bitmap format such as BMP, TIF, or PCX. To assure good quality, your images should be large enough to fill the cover area without excessive scaling. Otherwise, your artwork may pixelate (look grainy).

4. Place vertical guidelines at the page edges; then place horizontal guidelines across the top and bottom page edges.

5. Turn on a 1/8-inch snap grid and place guidelines 1/8-inch outside the trim guidelines. This serves as a bleed boundary; your printer trims this area in the final manufacturing stage.

6. Type or import your back cover text and scale it to size. Also type the price and put it at the bottom right panel of the back cover.

7. Type your title, author name, and spine copy. Drag it into position. Your spine copy can be typed off the page, rotated, and then dragged and scaled into final position.

8. Add an author photograph to the back cover. If it is black and white, be sure it is 256 shades of gray (grayscale).

9. Use your barcode program (or wizard) to create your EAN 13 barcode. Drag it into position.

Tip: You must choose appropriate fonts, type sizes, and type colors. Back cover text should be black on white to make it readable. Title and spine text may be colored to contrast the colors found in the background artwork. Although some drawing programs let you apply drop shadows or extrusions, the best way to create an outline is to make a copy of your title and/or spine text and offset and superimpose the copies. Put the black (or whatever edge color you use) behind the main body text using the Arrange or Order command to move it back one layer. When the edges are adjusted to your liking, group the two superimposed text elements to keep them together. You can scale (stretch or shrink) the text elements as a single unit to adjust them to final size.

10. One at a time, click on the grayscale photo, barcode, and each of the back text elements on the back cover and make sure that they are CMYK. This will assure hard type and a photograph that doesn't get color separated with the cover's color elements. Separated grayscale photographs sometime pick up an unwanted color cast.

11. Turn on Snap to Guidelines (turn off Snap to Grid) and use a Bezier pick tool and the normal pick tool to crop and/or drag the edges of your artwork to the bleed guideline (1/8-inch outside the trim edges). The extra 1/8-inch ensures that your color *bleeds* off the cut page to assure 100 percent ink coverage. Draw vertical tick marks above and below the bleed guidelines to show the edges of the spine. Following is an example of a cover showing the guidelines and the spine tick marks.

Part
2

12. Save your artwork to a file for safekeeping. You can now print your color separations on paper or print to PostScript PRN files. (Use the Linotronics 330 print driver supplied with Windows 95.) Most fully equipped service bureaus have both Windows and Macintosh equipment. If you are using Adobe Illustrator or Corel DRAW, you can usually submit your files directly to your service bureau in their native graphic format. Or, you can print the separation files yourself (C, M, Y, and K) and submit these. The service bureau will supply you with a match print, which accurately reflects the way your colors will appear on the final printed cover. If you like the result, you're ready to submit the film to your commercial printer for final reproduction.

Moving Ahead

This chapter dealt with book covers, their design, barcodes, important features, and price marking. The next chapter enters a vital publishing element—working with legitimate book publishers. Once you understand your publisher's expectations, how publishing decisions are made, and why, you will be in a much better position to negotiate a favorable arrangement through your contacts within the publisher's acquisition and editorial organizations. You should also have an improved understanding of your role and responsibilities as an author.

Chapter 9

Understanding Publishers

Introduction

This chapter provides information about traditional book (or *trade*) publishers. As an author, you should know how to prepare an acceptable book proposal. You should understand what the terms of your publishing agreement mean. It's also important to know how to work with your publisher during the manuscript preparation process. Finally, you should know what you can expect your publisher to do during the life of your book. Once you know who does what and when, the entire process should be much smoother for everyone involved.

This chapter also provides information about several other frequently misunderstood topics. For example, the value and prudent application of copyrights, the author and publisher roles in book promotion, book pricing and finance, and the industry's long-standing practice of accepting returns from bookstores and book distributors are all covered.

With few exceptions, book projects begin with a close liaison between the author and an *acquisition editor* who is employed by the publisher. Acquisition editors (not to be confused with copy editors) are responsible for reviewing book proposals and influencing the decision to publish or reject a book project based on a number of factors that are discussed later in this chapter. Once the contract is signed, the acquisition editor establishes contacts between the author and key editorial, production, and graphics personnel who are assigned to the book project. Finally, the acquisition editor monitors the manuscript submission process and advance orders from the sales department, and sees that the manuscript meets established publication schedules.

If you work through an agent, your agent should assist you through the proposal and initial submission phases. However, once you are under contract and begin to deliver portions of your finished manuscript to the publisher, your agent will probably step out of the way to shorten the lines

Part
2

of communication between author and publisher. The agent does not want to be an impediment to communication by adding an unnecessary bottle-neck to the process.

Good acquisition editors are proactive. They determine which titles sell well. Their research includes examining their own sales statistics for top sellers, perusing trade journals for successful trends, browsing bookstore shelves to determine what types of books are stocked in multiple quantities, and talking to the booksellers themselves. Once the editor identifies potential "winners," he or she seeks out proven authors and/or subject-matter experts who can produce an authorita-tive or entertaining manuscript in the desired timeframe. This is typically done by contacting good, reliable authors either directly or through agents.

The Quest for a Publisher

It's a simple matter for an author to contact a publisher. You can go to any library and examine the *Literary Marketplace* or pick up a copy of *The Writer's Marketplace* in the writing and publishing section of your local bookstore. There, you'll find a rich list of publishers with names, addresses, and telephone numbers. However, be sure that you find a publisher that has an interest in the kind of book that you wish to propose. Probably the most common reason for rejecting the project is that it simply doesn't fit the book category produced by the publisher. For example, don't propose fiction to a scientific or medical publisher, or theology to a mass-market paperback house.

You can also go to the bookstore and find books that are in the same cate-gory as the one you want to publish. Check for the publisher's name and address. Many books include the publisher's telephone numbers, web site URL, and even an e-mail address. Once you find a few publishers that seem to fit your subject, give them a call or drop them a letter and discuss the project. See if there is interest. They may tell you that they are not interested; or they may tell you that they'd like to review your proposal. If you're a reasonably good promoter, you should be able to convince them to accept a proposal. By breaking ground early, the acquisition editor will not be surprised when he or she receives your book proposal. Because you've already talked to them by telephone or e-mail, there is some familiarity. It gives you the opportunity to deliver on your commitment, which is a first measure of performance. So don't blow it! Deliver a great proposal on time. Delivering the proposal gives you an opportunity to put your best foot forward; you now have the opportunity to show the editor your creativity and writing ability through written communication—the measuring stick of every writer.

The Book Proposal

From time to time, publishers receive finished manuscripts from prospective authors. As both an author and a publisher, I've never understood the logic of writing an entire book without a reason. If your reason is simply that writing is your hobby because you enjoy doing it, then by all means, enjoy. However, if you are writing for profit, then perhaps it would be better to start by creating some demand for your work. Having a finished book is depressing when all the hours one spends result in a useless stack of paper. It's certainly better to have a good outline, a few well-written chapters, and a clear understanding of what it will take in time and effort to finish the manuscript. The author should also understand the size of the target audience and be aware of competing titles. Depending on the book's category, people in the publisher's organization can make valuable contributions relative to the placement of vital material, organizational structure, graphics, and the ultimate layout. These inputs usually result in a better book. A better book is everyone's goal, as it equates to increased sales.

Here are the elements that every book proposal should include. There are a few others, but these are the important ones.

- A working title (The title may change, so don't fall in love with it.)
- A description of the target audience (who and how many)
- A list of competing books and any sales data you can obtain (You may be able to get sales information from bookstores, distributors, and even the publisher or author.)
- A comprehensive outline (two to three paragraph levels) with a paragraph-length synopsis of each chapter
- Two well-written, edited, and thoroughly spell-checked sample chapters (Choose chapters that make the reviewer want to read more.)
- An achievable final manuscript delivery date (Be realistic.)
- An author biography (Highlight your experience and education that qualifies you as an authority on the book's subject matter.)
- A description of the deliverable items including file formats and media (floppy diskettes, Zip drives, e-mail attachments, etc.)
- Complete contact information (telephone and fax numbers and your e-mail address)

Part **2**

■ A request for a copy of the publisher's standard author agreement if the proposal has merit (Ask for this only after a publisher responds with a favorable reply.)

It's difficult to overemphasize the importance of a clean proposal package. Be sure that it is on clean paper. Print your manuscript samples using double space. Number your pages. Be sure everything that is included in your package is well organized. It helps to include a friendly cover letter with an attachment that lists the contents of your proposal. Remember that a sloppy proposal is the perfect reason to reject your book. Even promising book proposals are discarded if a publisher anticipates manuscript problems. Publishers cannot afford to rewrite the author's manuscript. The excessive work created by sloppy authors is legendary in publishing circles. The acquisition editor and other reviewers, especially those in the editorial department, will do their utmost to kill the project before it becomes their problem. Bad manuscripts not only hurt the current book project, the rework causes other projects to fall behind schedule as well. Make the effort and do it right, but whatever you do, deliver your proposal on time.

The Author Agreement

Author agreements can range anywhere from two to a dozen pages. Two or three pages are usually sufficient to include all the important terms. You should know that your publisher's standard agreement has withstood the test of time. Hundreds of authors have subscribed to the same general terms. Although a few items are negotiable, such as author copies and royalty rates, most of the terms are fixed. If you decide to enlist an attorney to rewrite the agreement, you may lose the deal, as the logistics in using an unfamiliar agreement is simply too much trouble for most busy publishers. Therefore, review the terms. If you want legal advice, get your lawyer to review the agreement and point out any areas of concern. Then get clarification from your publisher. Whatever you do, don't give the agreement to your lawyer without clear instructions. If you simply send them an agreement for review, there is a good chance that your lawyer will begin to rewrite the agreement. The temptation to charge you for billable hours is always present. If you want to make a few minor adjustments in the language, discuss them with your acquisition editor. If they do not impact the economics of the deal or require special treatment by the publisher's accounting department, your changes may be acceptable.

Following are descriptions of the key terms found in many publishing agreements.

Names and Addresses

Every book publishing agreement includes the names and addresses of the author(s) and the publisher. The common names AUTHOR and PUBLISHER are typically established at the beginning of the agreement and used throughout. The date of the agreement is frequently established at its beginning.

The Title

More often than not, the title of the book is a *working title*—the best one that the publisher and author can think of at the time that the agreement is drafted. Depending on the development phase and the book's schedule, the title may undergo several changes before the book is actually published and cataloging and promotional activities begin. In the case of *fast-track* book projects, i.e., time-sensitive books that must be rushed into print to capture a perishable market or to beat the competition, the title must be known from the beginning. Book promotion and cataloging begins before the book is written. This kind of book project can happen whenever a big news story with book potential comes along. Computer books about common software programs have extremely short life cycles and therefore must be fast tracked. This means that the title must be known at the beginning, because the catalog that announces the book is often prepared and distributed within weeks of the agreement date. Normally, the agreement establishes the common name "Work," following the working title. The remainder of the agreement uses the term Work whenever the book is referenced.

Part **2**

The Copyright

When embarking on a new business venture, most attorneys advise us to limit our personal legal liabilities by forming a corporation. Those who listen, do just that by incorporating their business activity so that they can use the "corporate veil" to protect their personal assets. Why, then, would you ever want to put a copyright in your personal name? You increase your personal exposure. If your book has a value in a secondary market that is not serviced by your publisher, be sure that the contract includes an addendum that grants you distribution rights in this area. But don't think that the copyright will do this. It won't. As a practical matter, a copyright has little tangible value. The value resides in the distribution rights, discussed next.

Some agents and a few industry pundits advise authors to retain the copyright in their name. In reality, it is preferable to have the copyright in the name of the publisher. This permits the publisher to negotiate subsidiary rights opportunities and incidental permissions freely, without being hamstrung by the proverbial "fly in the ointment." For example, foreign language translation agreements are often stopped in their tracks when the copyright is not in the name of the promoting publisher. Why? Some translating publishers simply do not want the hassle that is involved in dealing with an unpredictable third party. In fact, some countries require formal documentation from the copyright holder before a book can be published and distributed in the local language. This complicates the administrative cycle and prevents the promoting publisher from finalizing a deal on the spot, because additional paperwork is required.

When a copyright is in the name of a publisher, unscrupulous people will think twice before attempting to plagiarize material without getting formal permission. However, if you think that the book has residual value once it is put out of print, be sure that the agreement specifies that the copyright will revert to you, the author. Most publishers include a clause to this effect in their author agreement. The subject of copyrights is covered in much more detail in chapter 12.

Distribution Rights

The value of a book is in its distribution rights. The author is required to grant the publisher unlimited distribution rights for the book. This typically includes all languages, all imprints, and all methods of reproduction. If you believe that your book has a realistic potential in another market, such as a motion picture or television story, then special terms for these markets may be in order. However, most publishers will want carte blanche distribution rights so that they are free to exploit every possible market. And as an author, the last thing you want to do is to prevent your publisher from selling your book into any potential market. If you press a publisher too hard for special terms, especially ones that limit their access to certain markets, publishers may abandon the book deal. They tend to believe that their book promotion effort provides the visibility that attracts secondary markets; the publisher expects a return on that investment from all sectors.

The Number of Pages

The author agreement typically includes a sentence that specifies the number of book pages that will be delivered by the author. Book pages are impossible to predict with precision until the manuscript is completed and the book is typeset. Therefore, the number of book pages is an approximate number. Think of the page count as a goal rather than an absolute. However, if achievable, you should be within 10 percent of that goal. Publishers price their books relative to the final size of the book and the corresponding manufacturing costs.

The Delivery Schedule

Every author agreement includes a final manuscript delivery date. This date is used to drive production, printing, and promotional activities, including the date shown for the book in the catalog and corresponding sales efforts. Advance orders from bookstores are solicited by the publisher's sales representatives based on the publication date, which is a derivative of the manuscript delivery date found in the agreement. Hence, the date serves as a basis for scheduling the book's production and manufacturing activities. The delivery date is something that every author should take seriously, because the publisher certainly does. Late delivery can set the entire project back and even jeopardize the publisher's ability to produce the book. The importance of schedules is presented in more detail later in this chapter.

Royalty Rates and Schedules

Royalty rates are expressed as a percentage of the net cash received from the publisher's customers. Although a few very small specialty publishers still pay a percentage of the list price, this practice is all but gone from the industry.

Part
2

Payment Basis

The term *net cash received* refers to the net cash that remains after customer return credits are subtracted from sales. Net cash received is different from net income; *net cash received* includes the dollars received from the publisher's customers; *net income* is calculated as the revenues received less direct project expenses. Net income deducts production, manufacturing, directly related sales and promotion expenses, and distribution expenses from the revenues. Calculations are complicated, and the way that accountants apply certain items as direct project expenses and others as overhead can vary greatly.

While many motion picture companies use net income to calculate the amounts due to their creative talent and investors, book publishers never use this royalty accounting method. Publishers tend to keep things very simple and, in contrast to motion picture studios, have a reputation for being ethical in their treatment of authors. Finally, there is legal precedent that permits an author's accounting firm to audit a publisher's records if the author has good cause. As a practical matter, many publishers will walk authors through their records if a discrepancy is suspected.

Flat and Stepped Royalty Rates

There are flat royalty rates, which typically range from 8 to 12 percent, and stepped (or incremental) royalty rates that frequently range from 10 to 15 percent. A flat rate requires the publisher to pay an author the stated percentage throughout the life of the book. Stepped royalty schedules typically begin at a nominal rate for the first 3,000 to 5,000 units sold and then escalate to higher rates based on established unit sales increments. For example, an author and publisher might use a schedule similar to the following one.

Units Sold	Royalty Percentage
1 to 5000	10
5001 to 10,000	12
More than 10,000	14

Deep Discounts

The royalty rates are most often adjusted to 5 percent of the net cash received from deep discount market channels. These channels include wholesalers, national and international book distributors, and price clubs. Deep discounts are typically 55 percent or more. The lower royalty rate provides an incentive to the publisher to aggressively market the book to these channels. Without the adjusted royalty rate, the publisher's residual income from these channels is miniscule. More information about the distribution of income is discussed in the pricing section of this chapter.

Royalty Payment Schedule

Although royalty payment schedules vary among publishers, royalties are typically paid once every six months. Some publishers pay royalties once each year for the prior twelve-month period; still fewer pay on a quarterly basis.

You can expect to be paid semiannually for the prior six-month period ending June 30th and December 31st of each year. It takes approximately three months for the author's account to settle due to return credits. In addition, publishers normally maintain a royalty reserve as a hedge against return credits. Liberal return policies are a reality of the publishing industry. Therefore, a reserve is necessary. It may be as little as 10 percent, or it can be much higher to reflect actual rates if your book experiences extraordinarily high return levels.

Flat Fee Agreements

Some publishers use *flat fee agreements*, which pay one or more authors fixed fees for developing a book manuscript or a portion thereof. This is essentially a work-for-hire arrangement. Fast-track book projects often employ the services of several writers who are assigned to write different chapters. If the book has a large sales potential, each member of the author team may receive between $1,000 and $2,000 for his or her work. Once paid, the authors have no claim to additional income, regardless of how many copies the book sells. One successful computer book publisher does extremely well using this technique. First, having multiple authors working in parallel results in fast manuscript turnaround. In addition, the publisher expects to sell at least 15,000 to 20,000 copies of the book. One flat-fee developed book sold more than one million copies. Obviously, the publisher does extremely well on these projects. And the members of the author team know the rules going in.

Royalty Advances

All earned royalties are ultimately paid to an author. Therefore, an advance against royalties draws funds from the author's account before royalties are earned from book sales. This means that the publisher must fund the project in its early stage, increasing the publisher's financial risk. An advance, therefore, doesn't mean that an author gets more money in the long term, it just means an early distribution. The author's early royalty statements will show earned royalties applied against the advance. Therefore, the author will not receive additional royalty income until the advance is earned through sales.

The royalty advance is rarely paid in a single lump sum. More often, publishers establish an advance schedule that ties several payments to project completion milestones. This approach provides an incentive to the author to meet each of the established milestones on schedule. If a submission is late, the distribution is normally withheld. For example, an author may receive installments based on the completion of three or four of the following milestones.

■ Upon signing of the author-publisher agreement

■ Submission of the first two chapters of the manuscript

■ Submission of the first half of the manuscript

■ Completion of the final manuscript

■ Return of the updated, edited manuscript (including the original, marked-up copy)

- Preparation and submission of the alphabetical index (based on publisher-supplied page proofs)
- Sale of the first 2,000 book units

Some authors are eligible for an advance against future royalties. If you watch the news or read the newspaper, you've heard or read about some of the advances received by famous authors—some of these book deals can be in the millions. However, the publisher knows that a book by a well-known author, like Clancy, Grisham, or King, is worth millions of dollars in income. You can count the authors in this league on your fingers and toes. Then there are the rest of us.

At any point in time there are hundreds of thousands of working authors in the U.S. alone. Because book publishing is basically a "penny business" that relies heavily on unit sales that exceed a few thousand units for each title, excessive advances can force your publisher to divert needed marketing funds into the author's pocket. Every reasonable author desires a good future for his or her book and wants to encourage the publisher to be generous with promotional activities. Therefore, be careful about what you ask for, or you may wind up with a good advance that cripples the promotional budget. The overall unit sales and ultimate royalty income may suffer.

The advance requires the publisher to pay the author anywhere from a few hundred dollars to several thousand dollars, depending on a number of factors that include:

- Author qualifications
- Book potential
- Author needs

Author Qualifications

If your publisher can't take your book deal to the bank, don't have unrealistic expectations about big advances. Remember, while you invest *sweat equity* in your book, the publisher invests thousands of dollars for production, manufacturing, marketing, and sales activities. If you are a known author with a successful track record, you may be able to negotiate a reasonable advance. However, the advance will always be based on the publisher's reliance on a successful financial outcome.

Book Potential

Even if you are unknown as an author, if you are a good writer, have excellent qualifications as a subject matter expert, and your book has high sales expectations, your publisher may consider an advance against royalties to provide an incentive for your prompt completion.

Author Needs

If your book has excellent sales potential, and you are a full-time author with a need for income or research funding, then you may be able to justify some up-front cash. In rare cases, it is possible to obtain a small nonrefundable grant when such funds are necessary to develop a book with high sales potential. However, you must justify your needs to the publisher.

Penalty Clauses

The agreements used by publishers who produce time-sensitive books that depreciate in value with each passing day often include a penalty clause. The royalty rate is reduced if the author fails to meet important submission dates. For example, on-time delivery may reward the author with a 12 percent royalty rate. A two-week delay may reduce the royalty to 10 percent. A one-month delay may reduce the rate to 8 percent. A longer delay may result in cancellation and the prompt return of any advances paid the author.

Full-Time Authors

A few more words about full-time authors is appropriate. Most of us have heard the expression, "Don't quit your day job." This is good advice when applied to inexperienced book authors. Many first-time authors have unrealistic expectations about their earning potential. Industry-wide averages indicate that most books sell fewer than two thousand copies; this includes a title mix from small specialty publishers; university presses; and the large, well-known trade publishers. This data tells us that the average author's royalty income will be well under two thousand dollars over the life of a book. In fact, thousands of authors only make a few hundred dollars per book. Of course, each book's royalty earnings rely on the list price, discounts, and the prevailing royalty rates.

There are a few strategies that can increase your income. First, consider writing and maintaining multiple titles, constantly updating your current titles (especially technology books, which typically have short shelf lives), and, if possible, specialize in writing large, expensive books. If you can keep several books in print at the same time, you can increase your income stream by receiving royalty checks for several titles. This is a tall order for many writers, but there are some full-time technology authors who make six figures in royalty income each year.

Deliverable Items

If the agreement does not specify the format of the deliverable manuscript and supporting illustrations directly, it may reference the publisher's submission guidelines. A few years ago it was common to require authors to deliver two printed, double-spaced copies of their manuscripts and all illustrations in final, camera-ready, reproducible format. Today, many publishers require authors to submit manuscript in both printed and digital format. The manuscript may be submitted on diskette, Zip drive media, or as an Internet e-mail attachment or an FTP transmission (if the publisher has an FTP site).

The copy editor uses the printed copy to conduct a grammatical edit. When editorial marks are minor, the publisher may decide to make corrections in house to save the time required to send the material back to the author for incorporating the editor's marks. This is particularly true when manuscripts are in digital format. Printed illustrations are also edited and then combined with the text. Note that most agreements require authors to deliver finished artwork. Publishers do not have a staff of artists and a typist to do author work. Most publishers will charge back the author's royalty account when they must perform this kind of work on behalf of the author.

Permissions

Every agreement requires that the author obtain permission from the owners of any copyrighted material included in the book. This includes excerpts from other books or periodicals, commercial artwork, maps, electronic media, photographs, etc. When photographs of people are used, you should obtain their signature on a release form that gives you permission to use their likeness in your book. Don't assume that they are cool. There are simply too many unprincipled people and hungry lawyers around to take unnecessary chances with property rights and unreleased photographs.

If your book has a companion diskette, CD, or audio-tape, get written permission from the software or music publisher to reproduce programs, data files, and/or music scores, even if it is shareware or you think it's public domain. Copies of these permissions must be sent to the publisher as soon as possible and certainly prior to the publication date. Failure to obtain written permissions can put the book project on hold. Your book project may be cancelled if you wait too long.

Indemnification

The author must indemnify the publisher against any lawsuits that may occur as a result of scandalous or libelous material or the use of copyrighted material from an unauthorized source. If you are the author of the book and the ideas in your book are your own, you should not be concerned with this clause. However, if you've lifted material from privately owned sources, you may be in trouble. Discuss it with your publisher; he will normally advise you on how to obtain the necessary permissions. If you can't get permission, then eliminate the offending material from your book.

Termination

Most agreements provide for publisher cancellation under the right circumstances. First, if the author fails to abide by the terms of the agreement or is generally uncooperative, the agreement can be terminated. Late manuscript submission and failure to respond to queries are the most common reasons for cancellation. The publisher can also cancel the agreement if market conditions for your book change. Examples that can lead to cancellation:

- Public interest in your book's subject matter diminishes.
- Your manuscript does not live up to your publisher's expectations in content or quality.
- Competing books on the identical subject are released prior to yours.
- Bookstore buyers refuse to stock your title for any of the above three reasons.

Part
2

Although publishers rarely cancel book agreements, it does happen. Therefore, be sure that you do everything you can to deliver a quality manuscript in accordance with the established schedule. A change in market conditions can be avoided by choosing a topic that is not vulnerable to a downturn in consumer interest.

Subsidiary Rights

Subsidiary rights refer to secondary rights that may be granted to third parties by your publisher. In every case, your agreement specifies the amount you can expect from these uses. Your royalty statement normally identifies and tabulates these revenue sources for you. Subsidiary rights include:

- Foreign language editions
- Alternate formats (audiocassette, videodisk and cassette, CD-ROM, Internet web pages, motion pictures, television adaptations, etc.)

- Excepts used in other books and periodicals
- Book clubs

Foreign Language Translations

Those publishers who produce books that appeal to a large number of people in other countries attend the Frankfurt Book Fair in October of each year. Thousands of foreign-language publishers attend the book fair to buy and sell translation and international distribution rights. If your book qualifies, your publisher will produce and distribute fliers to foreign-language publishers who may have an interest in your work. If there is sufficient demand, your book may be translated in several languages.

An agreement is executed between your publisher and the translating publisher. Translation agreements require the foreign-language publishers to pay a periodic royalty or a flat fee, depending on the location of the translating publisher. For example, flat-fee arrangements are typically executed with third-world developing countries or those with weak economies. This includes such countries as India, Pakistan, and Russia. The fee can range from $500 to several thousand, depending on the book's size, U.S. list price, and sales potential in the consuming country.

Royalty-based agreements are typically used with Western European, Asian, and South and Central American countries. Terms typically involve a nominal "good faith" royalty advance and a stepped, list-price-based royalty of 7, 8, and 9 percent for the first, second, and the third and subsequent printings, respectively. The agreements call for either one or two payments per year based on the preceding six or twelve months.

Alternate Formats

Each alternate format is accompanied by a corresponding agreement that details the terms. Like foreign-language translation agreements, advances, royalties, and payment schedules are specified. Motion picture deals may be large and complicated. They can include clauses that govern the author's role during movie production. Typically, the studio requires that the author grant them the full right to make all final decisions relative to content, talent, locations, etc. The author also indemnifies the studio against any actions, regardless of the nature. Authors typically receive 50 percent or more of the royalty income generated from alternate formats.

Excerpts

Periodical editors, organizations for the blind, and other authors may request permission to use excerpts from your book. If the excerpt benefits the visibility and sale of your book, your publisher will probably grant permission to the adopting organization or person at no charge. However, if an individual, another publisher, or company wants to reproduce and profit from your work, your publisher will require payment for such use.

Book Clubs

Book clubs buy copies of books from publishers at greatly reduced rates. They pay the publisher for manufacturing in addition to a small royalty for each book sold. The list price of the book and the number of copies purchased drive the financial terms. For example, the book club may pay the publisher $2.00 per copy to defray the manufacturing (paper, printing, binding, and freight) cost and an additional $1.50 royalty for each book sold. The royalties are typically paid twice each year based on the prior six-month sales. An advantage of a book club deal is that it permits the publisher to increase the print quantity by the number of books purchased by the club. This drives the publisher's unit cost down, which increases his profit margin (price minus cost). It also gives both the publisher and the author an incremental revenue stream, as the author receives a percentage of the royalty. The publisher, on the other hand, retains the manufacturing cost, as this is used to offset the publisher's out-of-pocket expense.

Many wonder if the books distributed by the club impact bookstore sales. Book club managers claim that their sales have no effect on bookstore sales. Some claim that it enhances a book's image, and that consumers sometimes buy the book at the store as a result of familiarity. I make no such claim and have no hard data to dispute or support these claims.

Part 2

Author Copies

The agreement typically stipulates that a half-dozen or more copies be supplied to the author at no charge. The author can normally purchase additional copies at a discount of 40 percent from the lowest list price. As a practical matter, your publisher will probably give you a reasonable number of additional copies at no charge for personal consumption or as promotional samples. However, if you plan to resell your book, the publisher will expect you to pay for them.

Subsequent Editions

The author agrees to produce a subsequent edition if, in the publisher's opinion, the market warrants one. If the author is unwilling or unable to update the book, the publisher may retain another party to do the work on the author's behalf. Any expense involved in employing a third party to update the book is deducted from the author's royalties. Also, the name of the person or persons performing the work may be credited in the book.

Competing Works

You must agree that you will not produce another book that would conflict with the sale of the book covered by the current agreement. This doesn't mean that you can't write a second book on the same subject, as long as it would not be purchased in place of the first one. For example, if you write an introductory tutorial for one publisher, you can still write an advanced professional reference for another. But get permission in advance, so that the first publisher understands the difference. If everyone is pleased with the author-publisher relationship, you will probably want to use the same publisher for both books. Also, this clause does not apply to articles in magazines or other periodicals. You are free, and even encouraged, to write articles that communicate your expertise in the subject area. In addition, a good byline should always mention the name and publisher of your book.

Final Disposition

When book sales fall below 500 units in a 12-month period, it is a candidate for what is referred to as "out-of-print" status, or OOP. To keep the book alive, the publisher must maintain stock in his warehouse and continue to promote it in the catalog. To defray the cost of maintaining a dying book that can no longer pay for its upkeep through sales, the author's royalty rate is typically reduced by 50 percent. This enables the publisher to keep the book alive while a few additional copies trickle out the door. Unfortunately, when a book nears OOP status, the returns are typically greater than the sales.

When a book is finally declared OOP, the publisher attempts to unload the remaining copies to remainder houses (half-price bookstores, discount book outlets, and distributors that specialize in supplying these outlets). Or, the books may be sold by the pound to a paper recycler. Most agreements stipulate that royalties are not paid when a book is sold at or below its manufacturing cost.

The publisher may offer the author copies of the books at manufacturing cost before they are destroyed, although he may not be required to do this. There was a time when publishers offered printing plates or film to the author. Printers no longer retain printing plates, and therefore it is no longer practical to make this offer. Some agreements offer to supply the author with the film, although this is also becoming impractical as printers now discard the film after about one year's retention.

Once a book is placed out of print, the copyright automatically reverts to the author. Upon a request from the author, the publisher will happily supply the author with a letter that confirms the copyright transfer. Once this is done, the author may attempt to find another publisher who might be interested in republishing his book with changes. As a publisher that has done this, my lesson was once a book goes OOP, don't try to bring it back to life. It was put out of print for a reason—because the sales turnover could not support the manufacturing and warehousing costs required to sustain the book. But good hunting, anyway. If you're persuasive and willing to invest the energy required to revamp your book, you might convince a publisher to reissue it.

Beneficiaries

Agreements always include a clause that provides for an author's death. This transfers the proceeds of the agreement to the author's heirs or "assigns." Therefore, when an active author dies, his beneficiaries continue to receive royalty payments and statements in the usual manner.

Governing Laws

The laws of the publisher's home state normally govern author agreements. Some agreements specify that arbitration be used as a vehicle to settle disputes. As a practical matter, as long as both the publisher and the author abide by the rules of the agreement, this clause never comes into play. Publishers do not relish lawsuits; they are bad for business in addition to being a drain on resources. Publishers typically go above and beyond the letter of the agreement to avoid problems. Their primary bargaining chip is not the court. It is the cancellation of your book project.

Part
2

The Manuscript

Having read the previous section, you are aware of the importance of a quality submission during the proposal phase. But quality doesn't end upon the acceptance of your proposal. Your continued focus on quality must continue. If your manuscript doesn't comply with your publisher's requirements, you may lose the project midstream. Here are some realities that can make the difference between a successful and satisfying publishing experience and one that leads to a disappointing conclusion for all of the involved parties—perhaps even a cancellation.

Accessibility

Once you begin working with your publisher, be sure that you are available. Answer telephone calls and e-mail promptly. If you don't, you are sending a familiar signal. Nonresponsiveness tells the publisher that you are behind schedule. It places your book project in extreme jeopardy. If you ever want to complete the project or do another in the future, talk to the publisher. Be forthright and explain your situation and what you can do to catch up. Then do it! If you don't, you will leave the publisher in the lurch. The publisher's investment in time and advance sales will be lost.

Schedule

The importance of on-time manuscript delivery has already been emphasized. Many important events are based on the manuscript delivery date found in your agreement. These include:

- Catalog preparation
- Promotional material preparation
- Advance marketing
- Samples and printed jackets
- Advance sales
- Editorial and production schedules
- Printing schedules
- Finance
- Promotional activities

Each of these items is discussed in detail in the Marketing and Distribution section that follows.

Responsiveness

When you receive feedback from your publisher, respond as soon as possible. You want to keep the copy editor and production people working on your book without interruption. If you receive questions or a request for additional files or artwork, let them know you're working on it and get it to them immediately. If you let it lay for several days without attention, your project must be put on hold in favor of another one that is ready to process. This means that your book may sit on the shelf for weeks while other, more complete manuscripts are processed. When your project is set aside, it is classified as a problem, and the other people on the project are notified. Publishers conduct production meetings in which schedules are set; problem books go to the back of the queue, while complete, process-ready manuscripts from other authors are assigned higher priority. You may miss several months of sales just because you didn't provide a prompt response.

Deliverable Items

Read the requirements in your agreement and your publisher's manuscript preparation guidelines to determine what you must deliver. Then follow these requirements to the letter. If you have any questions or wish to submit an alternate item, check first. Your publisher is probably reasonable and may make some exceptions as long as your request is reasonable. You both have the same goal: an on-time book that succeeds in the marketplace.

Grammar and Spelling

All publishers have people on staff who are responsible for guiding books through the editorial, production, and manufacturing processes. However, these folks are usually working at a breakneck pace just to keep up with all the projects that are already flowing through the system. Publishers do not have a staff of "fixer uppers" who are dedicated to cleaning up sloppy manuscripts or preparing your artwork. If your manuscript is poorly done, it will either be set aside in favor of one that is properly done or returned to you with general comments. This is a definite setback, as the unscheduled delay may jeopardize the book's schedule.

A common and unnecessary mistake that many authors make is the failure to run a spelling check on their manuscript. This problem shows up quickly, when the copy editor processes the first few pages of a manuscript. There is simply no excuse for a copy editor to spend hours marking misspelled words and typographical errors, when you could have caught these problems in a matter of minutes using your spell checker.

Part
2

Poor grammar is another common problem. If your manuscript is poorly written, the editor will know when you make your early submission. If you suspect that you need help with your manuscript, find someone in your area who can help you clean it up, so that it is good enough to give to your publisher's editorial department. Otherwise, your book may get bogged down in rework and excessive mailings.

Artwork

Unless you've specifically made prior arrangements to the contrary, never supply rough sketches of your artwork for your publisher to complete. Your publisher cannot convert your sketches to finished artwork without a major effort. If your agreement requires you to supply finished artwork, find a local illustrator to help you. Many colleges have art students who are willing to work for a few dollars per illustration. If you master your graphic programs, you may be able to produce your artwork on your PC. On the other hand, if your publisher agrees to prepare your artwork for you, be prepared to have the preparation cost deducted from your royalties.

Acquisition Editors

Acquisition editors most often specialize in a selected subject area. They may deal with travel, computers, pet care, or some other book category. The editors constantly search for new title ideas and promising authors. When a viable title idea is identified, the editor solicits a proposal from the author. A publishing committee, which may include representatives from sales and marketing, editorial, production, and manufacturing, meets periodically to review new book proposals. A number of factors are examined including the market size and sales potential, pricing issues, author qualifications, and the quality of the proposal document itself.

If your book makes the cut, the acquisition editor will typically contact you by telephone with the good news. Next, the agreement is sent to you in triplicate. It is usually accompanied by the publisher's manuscript submission and editorial guidelines. You are requested to sign all three copies of the agreement and return them to the acquisition editor for countersignature by an officer of the publishing company. Once signed, an original is returned to you for your records. If you haven't already started, it's time to begin preparing your final manuscript.

The acquisition editor must now assign an ISBN from a list of numbers obtained from the R.R. Bowker Company. Next, your acquisition editor will introduce you to other people within the publisher's organization. You will be given the names and numbers of people assigned to your project. This includes your copy editor, the production person responsible for your project, and a marketing person. Although the acquisition editor carefully monitors the progress of your book and stays in touch, much of your liaison shifts to the copy editor that is assigned to your project. As your book approaches completion, your interface with the marketing department increases. They want detailed information about you, the author, as well as your ideas as to what should be included in promotional copy in the catalog, fliers, and on the book's back cover. Marketing will also want your input relative to what you can do to assist with book promotions and sales. This may include your attendance at conventions, public speaking engagements, and book signings.

A major part of every acquisition editor's job is to maintain contact with good book authors. If your book is successful, your acquisition editor will stay in touch. You may be fed ideas for additional book projects and encouraged to begin work on a new proposal. However, the editor will not encourage you to consider a follow-on book project if your book is not successful. This is also true even when a book achieves moderate success but was problematic during the development phase.

Literary Agents

If you are a fiction writer, a good, well-connected literary agent can be extremely helpful. Many publishers rely on an agent's ability to screen book ideas and pick the ones with potential. The agents also know which publishers are receptive to different categories of books. They also assist authors during the development and proposal phase, act as a conduit between the author and an interested publisher, and then stay in touch, but not in the way, when the book enters the development phase.

Publishers appreciate the efforts made by agents. Some publishers require their authors to work through agents, simply because they do not have a large enough staff that can help every author with a book idea to develop an acceptable work.

Agreements

Agents require each author to sign an agency agreement. The agreement specifies that the author is willing to have the publisher send author royalties to the agent. The agent agrees to extract his commission, which is typically 15 percent of the amount due the author, and then passes on the balance to the author.

Part
2

Some agency agreements require authors to submit any future book proposals through the agent. Of course, all terms are negotiable. However, both agency and standard publishing agreements are highly structured, and changes are often discouraged. The logistics of keeping up with a large number of agreement nuances is difficult, if not impossible—especially for large companies that conduct hundreds of transactions each year.

Agents Offer Hope

Perhaps the most important product an agent has to offer an aspiring author is hope. Having an agent who believes in your work enough to invest hundreds of dollars in promoting it provides the kind of hope and confidence that you need to continue your writing efforts.

Publishers also have hope when dealing with agents. They hope that the agent has screened out 99 percent of the submissions that don't fit the publisher's market. They hope the agent has checked for bad plots, bad characters, duplicate scenes, and bad transitions. They hope the agent has smoothed out the grammar and helped with the marketing. Most of all, they hope the agent has integrity.

Agents on the Internet

The Tale Wins Agency is one of many that you can find on the Internet. If you are looking for an agent, you may wish to check their web site at http://www.talewins.com. They can be e-mailed at talewins@tale-wins.com. Following is information provided by the Tale Wins Agency:

Writers who hire the Tale Wins Literary Agency can expect an expert evaluation of their project. If light editing will bring it up to good enough (and we handle that type of project) the service is free. Our policies are spelled out for all to see. Our guidelines are clear and succinct. At least three writers have offered us THEIR contract, and we signed it. Writers can also expect professionally prepared sales literature for their projects, progress reports, and the chance to work directly with the publisher as far as content is concerned.

Publishers looking at proposals from Tale Wins can expect an honest evaluation of the projects. If one page is enough to describe the project they can know that is all they will receive. If thirty pages aren't enough to describe a unique work, we might well send fifty pages. Each project is different. We will not be bound to the rules set by someone who hasn't seen this project. The first book we sold used less than twenty words to describe it. Obviously, it needed no more.

Tale Wins believes the web will become the major marketing conduit for the literary field. One book was sold strictly over the web. The publisher never saw a scrap of paper from us from start to finish. Most older publishing houses are afraid of the success of the web though. An open E-me door for submissions generates so much traffic they are overwhelmed, and ask for hard copy to slow things down. Tale Wins very much favors those publishers who have an open E-me policy, or who send us their private E-mail address and say: "Don't pass this out, but if you have something we might want, send us a query." Those asking for hard copy submissions are getting material a week or so later than contemporaries with an open E-me policy.

The Tale Wins Literary Agency can't give personal help to everyone who picks up a pen or a laptop. So, we have created a web site that provides a free exchange of information between writers and publishers (and other agents). We pass on tips, requests for manuscripts, and warnings. Especially for our writers we have a whole page of search tools, another with the best literary links we have ever found, information on building their own home page, on marketing, and supplies. Others are free to use all the resources we provide.

Last of all, Tale Wins is driven by a sense of mission. Every good agent, whether that is Clint McCulloch or Jeff Herman, has a mission. Our mission is to help writers bring their G and PG rated material to the world at large. Good writers who share this vision are invited to submit their work to us, day or night. E-me, now. At talewins@talewins.com the door is always open.

Earl H. Roberts, Sales Director
Tale Wins Literary Agency
http://www.talewins.com   talewins@talewins.com

Other agency web sites can be found at the following URLs, which were found during a brief search.

http://www.writersnetwork.com
http://www.harrisonmiller.com
http://www.uslink.net/~reygen
http://www.concentric.net/~abbeyhse
http://www.oz.sunflower.org/~nordwolk
http://www.netcom.com/~cohiba
http://www.books.com/sinc/
http://www.authorlink.com
http://www.scripters.com
http://home.aol.com/AgentNB
http://www.hollywoodscriptwriter.com
http://www.spenceframe.com
http://www.skypoint.com/~brbotm19/otm/info.htm

Copy Editors

Copy editors usually have extensive experience in book editing, are familiar with proofing marks, and may have a degree in English. Regardless of their background and education, they are there to ensure that the text of your book meets grammatical and style standards.

Standards

Editors make extensive use of dictionaries and style guides. A commonly accepted style guide used extensively in the U.S. is *The Chicago Manual of Style*. Here, such issues as proper capitalization, hyphenation, punctuation, word forms, and much more is treated clearly and authoritatively. Clarifying examples are included to ensure that authors and editors alike understand the application of the guidelines.

Proofreading Marks

Copy editors typically use a red pen for marking your manuscript. If you plan to stay in the publishing industry, you should become familiar with these marks, as you may wish to use them yourself. Most good dictionaries include a table of proofreader marks. Check the current edition of *Webster's New Collegiate Dictionary* for a list of these. Some publishers provide authors with a list of proofreading marks, their meaning, and clarifying examples.

Consistency

In addition to checking the grammar of your work, the copy editor looks for consistency in terminology and proper nouns. They frequently encounter different terms for the same object, or the name of a person spelled in two or more ways. Which one is right? Most editors let the author choose. In the case of a misspelled last name, only the author can determine the correct spelling by referring to his or her sources.

Completeness

The editor also tracks down references to illustrations and tables. If one is missing, he or she will probably contact you and request that you send it. Without the illustration or table, the reference must be eliminated or, if critical to the book's message, the copy editor will go as far as possible and then set the manuscript aside until the missing element arrives.

Pride of Authorship

Most efficient editors are light handed. They rarely suggest changes without good reason. Therefore, when an editorial suggestion is made and you agree that it is reasonable, just do it. Don't let your pride get in the way of progress. It will only bog things down. If you consider yourself a professional writer, act like one. Your job is to produce a good book in the shortest possible timeframe. If you spend a lot of unproductive time haggling over issues that no one else will ever notice, you're wasting everyone's time. Your copy editor will probably label you as a problem author.

The Production and Manufacturing Cycle

People who specialize in book pagination and cover design staff the production department. Most prefer to work on a project from start to finish without interruption. Interruptions are inefficient and require extra time to stop, set aside, find, and then restart. If your manuscript and illustrations are production ready, the entire book can be desktop published in a matter of hours. For example, a 200-page, text-intensive book can go through the page makeup (*pagination*) process in a single day. If the book includes numerous illustrations, it will take a bit longer, as each graphic file must be located and inserted within a frame. If the artwork is submitted on paper, it must be scanned and saved as a graphic file before it is inserted. Things go faster and smoother when the author supplies artwork in digital format. When submitting artwork, be sure text labels and ruled lines are in vector format. Also attempt to scale your bitmap images to final size to optimize their quality.

Many people are under the impression that publishers own printing presses. They do not print books in house. A responsible manufacturing administrator within the publisher's organization typically faxes printing specifications to large, reputable printers. The printers respond by preparing cost estimates and committing to delivery dates. The printer's bids include the printing cost and the cost of the freight required to deliver the finished books to the publisher's warehouse. The successful bidder receives the paginated book from the publisher in either camera-ready reproducible format or in digital format with a printed reference copy.

Many publishers are moving away from camera-ready copy to digital format, as this saves time and improves the quality of the finished book. Once the printer produces film negatives for each page, a set of bluelines are generated and sent to the publisher for approval. The publisher's editing department examines the bluelines for cosmetic defects (caused by holes or scratches in the film emulsion) and errors that may have been missed during the editing process. Changed pages are marked and a new original is returned to the printer, who reproduces new negatives for each change. Next, the film is used to produce printing plates from which the book is printed. When bound, the books are packed in cartons, marked, stacked on shipping pallets, and shipped to the publisher's warehouse by truck. The manufacturing administrator checks the printed copies to make sure that they meet the specifications. If all is in order, the book count is entered into the publisher's inventory system and the advance orders are processed and shipped to the publisher's customers.

Marketing and Distribution

This section includes marketing and distribution issues. The promotional activities all rely on the delivery of your manuscript. None of these happen when a book is late and placed on hold. Pricing is a derivative marketing research and manufacturing cost.

Pricing

If the price of a book relied on cost alone, making a simple mathematical computation could dictate each book's final price point. However, market research also plays a role in book pricing. Here, you see how both market research and cost play an important role in the final price.

Before a book is adopted, it is important to understand the size of the final book package, i.e., the page count and trim size. Other elements that can impact the cost of a book include:

- Interior color work
- Companion media (audio cassettes, diskettes, CDs)
- Special binding (wire, plastic, etc.)
- Die cuts (perforations and tabs)
- Bleeds (Bleeds require ink to be applied past the trimmed edge of the page. When *bleed tabs* are used, paper consumption increases—the amount of paper that is trimmed from the books and discarded is lost.)

Once the final cost data is compiled, you can divide the total cost by the number of printed books. This provides a unit cost. Look at the following example.

Printing and freight	$5,680.00
Number of copies	3,000
Unit cost	$1.8933

Next, you will want to consider your cost-to-price multiplier. The multiplier varies with supporting expenses, overhead, and the number of books that can be sold from the first printing. Contributing factors include the book's estimated royalty rate, sales commissions, and the publisher's overhead, which are indirect expenses for such items as occupancy, utilities, company administration, shipping and receiving, and general marketing.

Following are some approximate factors. Remember, these are averages.

Item	Factor	Description
Unit sales	3,000	The entire first printing to sell in the first twelve months
Average discount	52%	The average discount granted all channels
Royalties	8%	An average resulting from retail and deep-discount sales
Sales commissions	7.5%	An average for sales to retailers and distributors
Overhead	55%	The applied amount for general and administrative expenses

Now you can calculate a price that will provide a reasonable profit.

Item	Calculation	Unit Amount
Trial price	$16.95	$16.95
Net income	0.48 x $16.95	8.136 (based on 52% discount)
Unit cost	$5,680 ÷ 3000	1.8933
Royalty	0.08 x $8.136	0.65088

Commissions	0.075 x $8.136	0.6102
Overhead	0.550 x $8.136	$ 4.4748
Total costs		$ 7.62918
Yield		$ 0.50682

The publisher must sell 698 books to recover the direct manufacturing cost ($5,680 ÷ $8.136). This figure excludes royalties, commissions, and overhead. As you can see from the calculations, the $16.95 price point is marginal. Dividing the price by the manufacturing cost derives what is called a *cost-to-price multiplier*. Dividing $16.95 by 1.8933 yields an 8.9526 multiplier. Raising the price to $17.95 produces a multiplier of 9.4. This is a much more attractive factor. But, can you sell as many books at the higher price? Unfortunately, price elasticity must be determined empirically. You may have to price a book and put it into the market before you understand the consequences.

Once a publisher understands his "multiplier," as it is commonly called, pricing estimates become much easier. Most manufacturing administrators maintain tables of cost data that are derived from actual printing charges. They must be updated regularly as the cost of paper and labor fluctuate over time. The people in the marketing department use the data to determine whether or not a price point is viable. If the royalty rate or a book's manufacturing cost is too high to support a reasonable price, the project will likely be rejected before an agreement is issued.

Part
2

The publisher's marketing and sales people typically discuss pricing with booksellers. They also spend a great deal of time examining bookstore shelves looking for similar books. They check price points, current designs, assortments, and stock levels. Armed with this information, a more rational publish/no-publish decision can be made.

Point of Interest:

Booksellers are not as concerned about high-priced books as some newcomers to the publishing industry may think. Smart bookstore buyers use mathematically driven revenue models to maximize the dollar turnover for each running centimeter (or inch) of shelf space in their stores or book category. This is true with every smart merchandiser. They want to pack the maximum value in the available shelf space. Smart booksellers understand that their stores can achieve higher revenues by stocking $39.95 to $59.95 books rather than a selection of $9.95 to $19.95 books. However, they also want the stock turns of the expensive books to be equal to that of the inexpensive ones.

The antithesis of this simple analysis is that the shelf space, time, and money invested in the expensive book is lost forever. When slow books are returned to publishers, the lost opportunity is gone. Another book takes its place; the replacement must turn off the shelf more quickly to recover. Therefore, the turnover velocity of each book is carefully monitored. Selling three $19.95 books in the same amount of time that it takes to sell one $39.95 book is definitely preferable. (Fast nickels are better than slow dimes.) Therefore, a good buyer balances price, stock turns, and selection. Price inelasticity hurts the sales of overpriced books; a space full of low-priced books reduces the revenue potential; a poor selection pushes customers to fully stocked competitors.

Promotion

A number of promotional activities occur once a book commitment is made. All of these activities are tied to the manuscript delivery date discussed earlier in this chapter.

- *Catalog Preparation*—As soon as your book is assigned a release date, it is put in a catalog. The catalog typically includes descriptive copy, an illustration of the book's front cover, the ISBN, price, and the delivery date. The publisher's sales representatives distribute catalogs to booksellers. Large publishers use direct sales personnel, while small to intermediate publishers use a mix of in-house salespeople and independent, multiline sales representatives. Catalogs are also mailed to key accounts.

- *Promotional Material Preparation*—Additional promotion pieces are prepared for distribution to bookstores, distributors, and the publisher's sales representatives. The pieces are also distributed at conventions, such as the Frankfurt Book Fair and the American Booksellers Association Convention. These pieces, which list the ISBN, price, and publication date for each title, typically highlight the features of a book in more detail. Also included is an expanded treatment of the author's qualifications. If your book fits into a series, a series brochure may be prepared and distributed. These are sometimes found in racks at bookstores or even distributed by direct mail. Finally, publishers offer examination copies to the press and broadcasting media for reviews. Depending on the book, examination copies may also be offered to colleges and universities to encourage adoption. This is accomplished by mailing self-addressed, postage paid response cards to the media and selected educators. Recipients can check a box next to each title to indicate which book(s) they want to review.

- *Advance Marketing*—The marketing department makes use of several pieces of the promotional material discussed above. Sales meetings are held to discuss each new book and available promotional materials. Sales meetings are conducted twice each year. In the U.S., the meetings are held in New York City in June and December. The publisher's representatives attend and are briefed on the upcoming list of titles in preparation for their selling activities using the publisher's new catalog. (Most publishers publish at least two catalogs a year. The first one covers the months of January through June; the second covers July through December.)

■ *Samples and Printed Jackets*—A sample of each book, or at least a printed book jacket, are two of the most important sales tools in the salesman's bag. First, having an actual copy of the book assures the book buyer that the book is ready for distribution. Second, if the buyer examines the book and finds it appealing, you can rely on an order.

■ *Advance Sales*—Armed with the promotional materials and an understanding of what's in each book, the sales team begins to call on their accounts. Independent sales representatives make presentations to independent bookstores, regional bookstore chains, and regional distributors. Publishers that are large enough to support an in-house sales staff designate the large bookstore chains and national distributors as *house accounts*. Rather than using independent sales representatives, they call on these accounts directly. This includes but is certainly not limited to such accounts as Barnes and Noble, Borders, Waldenbooks, and Ingram Book Distributors. When orders are collected from these accounts and fed into the publisher's order entry system, an advance order report can be prepared to show how many copies are on order. Advance orders are vital. They help the publisher plan the size of each book's print run. The order size provides an indicator of each book's long-term sales potential. Finally, when the advance order is large enough, the billings associated with the order fulfillment may earn enough to pay the printing bill. (Printer terms are typically 30 to 45 days; large bookstore chains and distributors take 60 to 90 days to pay.)

Part
2

The book trade was once populated by a mix of thousands of independently owned and operated bookstores (called *Class C* stores), regional bookstore chains (called *Class B* stores), and national bookstore chains (called *Class A* stores). Today, the large national chain stores dominate the landscape with approximately 80 percent of the bookseller market. This is similar to the *Wal-Mart Syndrome* that forced so many small, independent shops out of business in the 1990s. Consumers simply like the advantages offered by one-stop shopping, huge product selections, and bargain prices. Today, a number of attractive, well lighted, and fully stocked superstores, some with lounges and coffee shops, have captured the market. The independent booksellers are struggling for survival, as their store traffic has dwindled. The channels of distribution and the buying habits of consumers have shifted dramatically over the past ten years. Because independent sales representatives depend on the independent accounts (most publishers call on national chains and large distributors directly), the independent representative groups are suffering too. It is important to monitor the dynamics of this rapidly changing industry. Publishers must remain flexible and stay abreast of technological breakthroughs as the book trade rapidly gains sophistication in the way that it works to survive.

■ *Editorial and Production Schedules*—The manuscript date drives the publisher's internal schedule planning. If your publisher produces 120 books each year, they must schedule approximately 10 books per month. The books are placed in a queue like rail cars on a track. If a car gets derailed, it is pulled from the queue and may go to the end of the line. This means that the cars behind it fill the gap. When all the gaps are filled and the train is moving down the track, it can't be stopped until another car gets derailed. You don't want your car to be the one that is pulled from the train.

■ *Printing Schedules*—Printing schedules are also established in advance. Publishers often forecast books to their printers, who reserve a slot for each book. Printing is a fast turnaround, capital-intensive manufacturing operation that waits for no one. If your book misses its slot, its publication date may suffer several weeks delay.

■ *Finance*—The publisher lists every book planned for the current season (called the *front list*) on a spreadsheet. It includes the book's publication date, list price, net price, and unit sales forecast. The publisher can then forecast each month's revenue based on this analysis. In addition to the front list titles, the publisher can examine books published in previous seasons (called *back list*). The monthly income averages are calculated from actual back list sales data. The two amounts are added together to forecast the total monthly billings. Once expenses are examined and the billings are redistributed in time to show when the publisher's customers will pay their bills, the publisher can estimate cash flow.

■ *Promotional Activities*—Recall the self-addressed response card that was mentioned in the preceding Promotional Material Preparation section. Once the review copies are mailed, follow-up activities are conducted in an effort to produce orders. If your book has general appeal, radio and television appearances, bookstore autograph sessions, and author presentations to targeted special interest groups may be scheduled. These activities rely heavily on the book's availability and the author's willingness to participate. Some authors are highly promotable, which translates into improved sales and follow-on book assignments.

■ *Co-op Advertising*—Most publishers offer their customers co-op advertising funds in the form of a credit. Typically, the co-op funding allowance is 5 percent of the prior twelve-month sales. Customers can use the co-op funds to promote one or more of the publisher's books through local advertising, in-store posters, or special displays. The publisher's co-op policy requires the bookseller to send copies of the ads and directly related invoices to validate the expense and corresponding credit.

Distribution and Terms

Books are usually stored in your publisher's warehouse or at a distribution center that sells their distribution services to your publisher. In either case, customer orders are entered and fulfilled from the warehouse. Books are sent to bookstores, distributors, and individuals. Publishers strictly abide by standard discount schedules and established policies for each channel of distribution. These schedules are volume sensitive and based on the distribution cost experienced by the publisher. Special deals are avoided, as most large customer accounts require identical treatment relative to terms and premiums.

Part
2

■ *Bookstores*—Initial book orders are often written by the publisher's sales representative. These are submitted to the publisher's order entry department. Bookstores also submit orders to the publisher by mail, fax, and telephone. Most bookstores issue purchase orders and receive 30-day payment terms if they have an account with the publisher and are deemed credit worthy. Bookstores are granted reseller discounts, which range from 20 percent to 50 percent depending on the number of books ordered.

■ *Distributors*—Distributors, who resell to bookstores, send their purchase orders to publishers by mail, fax, telephone, or electronic data interchange (EDI). Distributors require a 55 percent discount and pay in 60 to 90 days. Distributors resell the books to resellers including bookstores, pet stores, and mass merchandisers. Distributors make their living by retaining the difference between the discount they receive from the publisher and the discount they give to their reseller customers.

■ *National Book Chains*—The discounts granted to these accounts vary with the way they receive their books. If books are ordered via EDI and sent to a central distribution center, the publisher's distribution costs are greatly reduced. The published discount for those accounts that use central distribution centers and EDI is typically 52 percent. If a book chain sends a paper purchase order or requires delivery to individual bookstores, the standard reseller schedule applies. Large national chains are typically granted 60- to 90-day payment terms.

▪ *International Distributors*—The terms granted international distributors can also vary with their region of the world. For example, books cannot carry the $U.S. list price in a country where the average worker earns $8 per day. Therefore, a local publisher may be given permission to reprint and distribute books at a highly reduced price. This is called a *cheap reprint edition* and falls into the subsidiary rights category. In industrialized, affluent countries, such as those in Western Europe, Australia, and Japan, publishers use book distributors that operate much like the ones in the U.S. and Canada. Typically, the discount schedules are similar to those used for similar domestic accounts. Terms may be extended to 90 or 120 days to accommodate the length of time that it takes for the books to reach the international distributor. First, it may take six to eight weeks for a book to go from the U.S. to Amsterdam by sea freight. The book must clear customs and be delivered to the distributor's warehouse. The distributor must then sell the book and invoice a local bookstore. After another 30 days, the distributor receives payment from the bookstore and can now pay the publisher. Obviously, the distributor doesn't pay for books one at a time. It requires the ability to know what to stock and sell, and the constant turnover of different titles from their warehouse.

▪ *Consignment*—Some publishers consign books to overseas distributors. These distributors attempt to maintain reasonable stock levels, which are sold using an in-house sales staff. Independent commissioned sales representatives sometimes supplement the internal sales organization. The discounts are similar to that of traditional distributors. These distributors issue a monthly sales report, which is used by the publisher for billing. Consignment sales are much more burdensome than firm sales arrangements, as the inventory levels are typically larger than necessary. Surplus books simply sit in the distributor's warehouse until they go out of print. Most publishers would rather avoid consignment deals, although some cannot be avoided.

Overseas consignment operators typically pay for either sea freight or airfreight from the U.S. port of embarkation to their warehouse. The publisher most often pays the freight to a designated consolidation point. Here, the distributor's orders from all U.S. and Canadian publishers are consolidated in one or more containers for shipping.

▪ *Direct Sales*—Publishers receive a few orders directly from individual customers who are unable to locate a specific title in their neighborhood bookstore. Others may place orders over the Internet, and still others will actually drop by the publisher's offices to buy a book. These books are sold at list price and are commonly paid by credit card or check. However, most publishers encourage people to purchase their titles from bookstores. A single-copy sale to an individual is not as important as multiple-copy sales to the publisher's trade accounts. Publishers should do everything possible to encourage turnover of their products from bookstore shelves. See the "Which Books are Returned" paragraph later in this chapter.

■ *STOP*—This is an acronym for Single Title Order Plan. This plan requires publishers to agree to grant a 40 percent discount to booksellers for single-title orders. Booksellers are required to send a check, money order, or credit card information with their order.

The discount schedules and payment terms are driven by the *cost to market*. The cost to market should comprehend every cost involved in promoting and delivering one or more related products to a specific market channel. Cost to market also requires a reasonable estimate of the unit sales volumes. Therefore, each discount schedule must be rationalized to yield acceptable profit levels. The payment terms are tied to the time it takes a book to pass through a channel to the end consumer. The example of the European distributor is similar to that of a major chain with a central distribution center. For example, it may take a week or more for the publisher to ship books over the road to a distribution center. Next, the books must be received, entered into the inventory center, and then wait for an order to ship it to a bookstore. Again, a week may pass before the book hits the back door of the bookstore. Another week may pass before a book is unpacked and placed on the bookshelf. It may take a few weeks for a customer to purchase the book. If the publisher delivers a book directly to a bookstore, the packing and handling cost applied to the book is much greater than that of shipping a carton full of books to a distribution center. In addition, the book appears on the bookstore's shelf in a matter of days. The entire cycle is shorter, and therefore the payment terms correspond to the cycle time.

Part
2

Returns

In 1937 accepting book returns became a requirement for all publishers in the book industry. Today, publishers must grant booksellers the right to return every book they purchase for full credit. Therefore, unsold books always make their way back to the publisher's warehouse. Although books are supposed to be returned to publishers in resalable condition, most publishers are liberal. However, damaged books add to the cost of doing business, as hurt books are either remaindered or sold to a paper recycler. Some booksellers are careless with returns, and a substantial percentage of the books in a return shipment are damaged as a result of poor packing. This adds to the publisher's unit cost, as the cost of each damaged book must be factored into the total cost and income of the project. When this happens, most publishers reserve the right to refuse damaged goods, which should be an incentive to booksellers and distributors to be more careful when they pack and ship books back to the publisher. Publishers who quietly "eat" damaged returns without a word of complaint effectively hurt their colleagues, who must work hard to meet their cost goals in what is an extremely competitive, low-margin industry.

How Many Books Are Returned?

The industry return rate fluctuates from year to year. A recent article in one of the leading industry trade journals claimed an average return rate of 22 percent. Some book categories experience higher return rates than others. For example, computer books that are tied to specific versions of software are highly perishable. When a new version of the software is released, sales of the publisher's remaining stock slow dramatically. Bookstore stock is returned to the publisher in favor of titles that cover the new release. The key to minimizing returns is sales turnover at the bookstore.

Even when books fall into a category that is not considered "perishable," they are often returned. If a book languishes on the shelf, the bookstore will return it to the publisher and put another book in its place. That's good business. If the book is a brisk seller, the bookseller will order more.

Which Books Are Returned?

Well-managed bookstores carefully track the sales of each book in the store. Today, most of them use computer systems that tie their cash register transactions to their inventory levels. When book sales cause stock levels to fall to an automatic reorder level, the system produces a purchase order. The book supplier, which is either the publisher or a distributor, receives the order and fills it in the usual manner. If a few copies of a book sit on the bookstore shelf for 60 to 90 days without selling, the system flags them for return. They are pulled from the shelf, packed, and sent back to the publisher for full credit. The credit is applied to the bookseller's account and deducted from the amount due. Negative balances are held and applied to future orders. Occasionally, small bookstores request a cash refund in place of a credit balance. The publisher must then decide whether to comply with the bookseller's request by either issuing a cash refund or maintaining a credit balance.

Dirty Return Tricks

Return policies are sometimes misused. A few unscrupulous distributors exploit the policy to delay the amounts due to publishers. Even when books are viable sellers, a distributor may return them for credit and then reorder the same titles. This is a "dating game" (not to be confused with the television show). The publisher's accounting department issues a credit, which offsets the balance due from the distributor. A reorder for the same titles resets the clock to another 60 to 90 days before the distributor must pay. The freight companies are the only ones that benefit from this despicable practice, as they collect the freight both ways. The distributor pays the freight bill, so their margins are reduced by the cost of the added freight. If the freight cost averages $0.15 per book (the unit freight cost varies with the number of books in a shipment), then the round trip will cost the distributor an additional $0.30 to extend the terms. Depending on the prevailing terms, a payment term of 60 days is extended to 120; 90 days is extended to 180, which amounts to six months.

Moving Ahead

This chapter reveals a substantial amount of information about the way that publishers operate. In the next chapter you learn more about commercial printers, who provide a vital service to the publishing industry. There, you find an expanded treatment of bid specifications, book submissions, and printing economies.

Part
2

Chapter 10

Working With Commercial Printers

Introduction

Commercial printers come in all sizes and shapes. Most specialize in a certain type of printing. You'll find small, offset duplicator shops that are equipped to do *short-run* copy jobs on 8½ x 11- or 11 x 18-inch paper stock. By short run, we mean less than 1,000 units. Some offset duplicator shops even have in-line collating and bindery equipment. Then there are intermediate sized printers that typically have one or two large format sheet-fed presses, collators, trimmers and an assortment of bindery equipment. These shops specialize in *intermediate-run* jobs that range from 1,000 to 10,000 copies. Finally, the big printing companies typically have several printing plants that specialize in different formats. They may have one or two intermediate-run plants and another equipped with *web-fed* presses that are geared for *long-run* jobs that exceed 20,000 copies. In fact, long-run print jobs are often in the hundreds of thousands.

Part
2

Obtaining Bids

Trade publishers typically send their work to printers that process intermediate- and long-run print jobs. These printers usually are equipped to print four-color covers, as well, although some printers farm out their color work to a specialty house. You really don't care if the printer subcontracts color and bindery work as long as they produce a good quality package in a reasonable amount of time. Regardless of the methods used, you should always prepare a clear print specification and obtain competitive bids for your job. In addition to obtaining bids, you may want to see examples of each printer's work to verify the quality. Some publishers who are preparing to send a number of large jobs to a new printer send their manu-facturing managers to the printing plant to establish a level of confidence before making a major financial investment.

Bid Specifications

Following is a typical bid specification. Each entry is explained following the bid example.

Quantity	2000, 3000, or 4000 plus additional 1000s
Trim Size	7½ x 9¼ inches
Text Pages	264 pages
Text Printing	1-color black throughout
Text Stock	50# White Vellum – 380 ppi or equivalent
Cover Stock	10-point C1S Cover White
Cover Print	4-color plus film lamination
Binding	Perfect bound
Samples	200 copies of cover

Quantity

This specification requests printing costs for three different quantities. This permits the publisher to compute the unit cost for different volumes to check the cost-to-price multiplier. Additional 1000s is the cost for each additional 1,000 units.

Trim Size

The 7½ x 9¼-inch trim tells the printer to cut the book to 7½ inches wide by 9¼ inches high. Printers recommend the most efficient trim format for their press size. The most efficient size is the one that minimizes waste.

Text Pages

This is the number of printed pages (or sides) that will be printed. Each page requires a film negative and corresponding position on the printing plate.

Today, film-free printing technology is rapidly displacing the older photo-lithography methods. The traditional method requires the printer to photograph camera-ready pages to produce high-contrast negative film. The film is used to expose metal printing plates on a "plate burner," which typically uses a high-intensity light source. The printing plates have a photosensitive emulsion that reacts to the light that passes through the negative film. The exposed areas harden and stay attached to the plate's metal substrate. The unexposed areas are wiped from the plate.

When the plate is clamped to the printing press's *master cylinder*, the residual emulsion picks up ink from an inked "blanket" cylinder (which acts much like a stamp pad). The ink on the plate is next *offset* to an *impression cylinder*, which finally applies the transferred image to the printed sheet of paper. Each rotation re-inks the plate and offsets the inked image to the paper. Hence, the term *offset press*.

Modern, film-free printing plants employ *electronic printing*. There are a few competing technologies, all of which are far superior to the traditional lithography techniques. One technology employs an argon-ion laser to expose a photopolymer plate with digitally controlled beams of ultraviolet light that paint the image on the plate material, much like exposing the traditional plate with high-intensity light. However, the control is significantly more accurate. For example, the problems encountered with misregistration or over/under exposure are omitted.

Another computer-to-plate (CTP) technology that is based on thermal exposure principles is also in use. Some printers believe that this system has the most promise. These plates have a temperature-sensitive coating. The areas on the plate that are exposed to heat retain the emulsion. While laser-exposed plates can be overexposed, the thermal plates cannot be overexposed. Once the emulsion reaches the proper heat threshold, it bonds to the base metal of the plate. Overheating doesn't change the properties of the emulsion.

Traditional printers supply a set of *blueline* prints to publishers as a proof copy. Blueline pages are made directly from the film negatives and therefore give the publisher a true replica of the final publication. Those printers that use electronic, film-free printing methods produce *digital bluelines*. Since there is no file, the digital blueline is a proof of the digital file, rather than of film. The identical file is used to expose plates, and therefore, the digital blueline represents a verbatim copy of the digital source that will ultimately expose the printing plate.

Color proofs are also produced from either film or a digital image source. A Kodak contract proof applies true, calibrated color to the paper or stock that will actually be used for the print job. This process is called a *contract proof* because once the customer approves it, the printer guarantees that the color of the final printed product will match the proof. Other proofing techniques, such as *iris* and *rainbow* proofs, do not use the dots to make up the colors, as does the contract proof. These are not color calibrated and therefore do not produce a contract proof; they essentially give the customer an idea of how the color will look. *Match prints* that are made from the separated film can also be obtained. Although match prints are not contract print quality, they are typically close enough to predict the color of the finished work.

Text Printing

The sample specification tells the printer to use black ink (one color). This item can also be used to specify two- or four-color interior printing.

Text Stock

This is the weight (50#), color (white), finish (vellum), and thickness (380 PPI) of the paper.

Weight—Printing papers are measured and identified by their *basis weight*. This is the weight of a ream (500 sheets) of paper. In the U.S., this is 500 25 x 38-inch sheets of paper. In the metric system, this is the weight of one square meter of paper measured in grams (g/m^2). In the U.S., the basic size of papers varies with the grade of paper. Following are some differences.

Basic Size (inches)	Paper Type
25 x 38	Book papers (offset, coated, text, opaque, etc.)
17 x 22	Writing papers (bond, ledger, mimeograph, duplicator)
20 x 26	Cover papers (coated and uncoated)
22½ x 28½	Index bristol
22½ x 35	Mill bristol and postcard
24 x 36	Tag and newsprint

The metric measurement system uses the A size as a basis. The A0 is a square meter in area; other A sizes are exact halves or multiples of two. The following table defines the various A sizes used by most countries of the world.

A Size	Dimensions		
	Metric	Inches	Square Meters
A0	841 x 1189	33.1 x 46.8	1.0
A1	594 x 841	23.4 x 33.1	0.5
A2	420 x 594	16.5 x 23.4	0.25
A3	297 x 420	11.7 x 16.5	0.125
A4	210 x 297	8.3 x 11.7	0.063
A5	148 x 210	5.8 x 8.3	0.031

The A4 is similar to the 8½ x 11-inch letter-size paper used in the U.S.

Paper bulk, sometimes referred to as *caliper*, is measured in thousandths of an inch, or mils. When a book is manufactured, the bulk of the book determines the thickness of the book. Rather than using caliper, book papers are measured in pages per inch (ppi) for the given weight. The bulking range for a 50-pound book paper can be 310 to 800 ppi. Each sheet of paper is two ppi.

There are many other paper qualities including color (whiteness), brightness, opacity, smoothness, and refractiveness. Vellum, used in the spec, has a smooth finish. Use higher opacity paper for lightweight papers, such as 40- to 45-pound offset, to prevent the print on the opposite side of the page from showing through. Refractiveness is light absorption in the surface of the paper that causes halftone illustrations to appear darker than they should. Check this property if you plan to include halftone pictures in your book.

Cover Stock

Coated and text papers are made in heavier weights for use as book covers. As a general rule, cover stock in the same basis weight as papers is twice as thick. Qualities that are common to good cover stocks are their dimensional stability; durability; uniform printing surface; and good scoring, folding, and die-cutting qualities. The C1S is a standard abbreviation for color on one side.

Cover Print

The four-color plus film lamination specifies that the printed side of the cover stock is CMYK four-color process. The specification also calls for film lamination. Laminations are applied on the press. Lamination material can be anything from clear varnish to an acrylic plastic coating. To minimize curl from humidity, plastic laminates are perforated. This is called *lay flat* laminate. The porosity from the perforations allows humidity to enter cover stock more uniformly from both the laminated and uncoated sides. This prevents the curling that occurs when nonporous lamination is used.

Part

2

Binding

Most trade paperbacks are perfect (or adhesive) bound. This gives the book a flat spine. Lay flat (breakaway) adhesive binding methods are also available. Called Otabind and Repkover (see "Covers" in chapter 6), these techniques add several cents to each printed copy. Some books are bound using plastic comb (GBC) fasteners or with wire. Hard back (or cloth bound) books are a variation of adhesive binding, except that paper- or cloth-wrapped chipboard is used in place of cover stock.

Samples

The subject printing specification calls for 200 samples. Many trade publishers use blank covers as sales samples. Book sales representatives can show the covers to prospective bookstore buyers. Because book salespeople cannot possibly carry every publisher's book in their bag, printed covers serve as excellent sales tools, especially when the front cover and spine are attractive and the back cover carries good features and benefits copy.

Cost Considerations

Consider all of the factors associated with cost and quality. But don't be penny wise and dollar foolish. Following are some additional considerations.

Number of Copies

The number of copies that you print is key to the unit cost of each book that you print and therefore the price that you must charge for your book. The *volume-cost curve* drops significantly as you exceed 2,000 copies. Your book may have a *landed cost* of $2.50 per unit for a print run of 2,000 copies, $2.20 per unit for 3,000 copies, and $1.92 each for 4,000 copies. The temptation is to go for the high number. The total printing bill associated with each of these volumes is $5,000, $6,600, and $7,680. The 4,000-unit print run is tempting for several reasons. You will only spend an extra $2,680 for the 2,000 additional copies (only $1.34 per copy). Your profit margin will be much better, and your cost-to-price multiplier will be much better.

However, before you spend an extra $2,680 (the difference between 2,000 and 4,000 copies), can you sell all 4,000 copies in twelve months? Do you need the extra cash to fund book promotion or perhaps another book project? Check your advance orders and the performance of other similar books, and then make a better decision relative to what you should do with the extra money. It's a little better than gambling, but not much.

Trim Sizes

Always use an economical trim size that minimizes waste. Your printer will tell you which formats are best for his operation.

Binding Methods

Unless there is some good reason to avoid perfect (adhesive) binding, use it. It's durable, provides a necessary spine, and is less expensive than other methods when doing the volumes indicated in the bid specification. Other binding methods, especially wire, can damage neighboring books when consumers drag them off the shelf and then jam them back into place. Most wire-bound books (not all) have no printed spines. Therefore, some bookstore buyers show reluctance to put wire books on their shelves.

Using Color

If you are printing a conventional trade paperback, plan on a four-color process cover rather than a cheap-looking two-color job. The difference in cost is insignificant, while the difference in appearance is major. The advances in software functionality now permit us to make color separations right on our PC. You should be able to achieve all your prepress work for less than $200. A few years ago separating a cover cost around $1,000. Before the PC and high-end graphics software such as CorelDRAW and Adobe Illustrator, color separation required expensive color scanners and precise registration of the film overlays.

Disposition of Film and Plates

When your print job is completed, if your printer does not use a plate-direct system, which eliminates film negatives entirely, the film negatives are stored for a period of time determined by the printer. A metal recycler almost always salvages the plates. The printer may store your film for a few years, in case you want to reprint a book. After that, you are usually notified that they will destroy the film unless you want to pay a nominal storage fee. Most publishers give the printer permission to destroy the film, because by the time the free storage period expires, the book is probably on its last leg. If a book is reprinted within the storage period, the film storage "clock" is normally reset to zero.

Part
2

Picking Your Printer

When you select a printer, you will usually begin by discussing your requirements with a printer's sales representative. You can obtain a list of the printer's equipment and determine the formats that best fit his operation. Once you believe that the printer is equipped to print your book, write a bid specification and fax it to several different printers so you can compare price and delivery. Be sure to include a quotation for freight, as this is also an important cost factor.

Check samples of their work, and look at the house papers to see if there is one that you like for the cost. It's usually less expensive to use the papers that the printer stocks as a standard item rather than buying a custom paper just for your job.

Some large publishing companies purchase large amounts of paper directly from a paper mill. The paper is typically shipped from the mill to their printer by rail. Of course, this requires a major investment in the paper and transportation, as well as total confidence in the printer. This is particularly true of printing plants equipped with large web-fed rotary presses, as web-fed presses use large rolls of paper that must be moved using specially equipped fork trucks.

If you have a long-run print job of 20,000 or more units, obtain bids from printers who are equipped with web-fed presses. These presses can process work at speeds in excess of 1,500 feet per minute. The paper is fed with automatic splicing from one roll to the next. Special fast-drying inks and dryers are used. The paper is sheeted and folded into signatures and then trimmed at the delivery end of the press. Book runs in the hundreds of thousands or millions of units require extremely fast, automated printing processes. Therefore, these kinds of runs are always processed by automated web-fed printing equipment.

Moving Ahead

In the next chapter you examine the prospect of self-publishing. There, you can determine whether self-publishing is for you. An attempt is made to introduce you to the risks and potential rewards by sharing some actual self-publishing ventures.

Chapter 11

Self-Publishing

Introduction

Before you decide to self-publish your book, read chapter 9 so you will be more familiar with how traditional trade publishers run their businesses. This information provides valuable insights into the many processes and important decisions involved in the publishing arena. Then read the balance of this chapter. After reading it, if you still want to go forward with a self-publishing venture, you probably should.

Why Self-Publish?

People choose to self-publish for a variety of reasons. Some are good; some are not. Let's examine some reasons to see if any of them apply to you.

You can't find a publisher that will publish your book.

If you still think you've got a winning book after being rejected from several legitimate trade publishers, then it's time to regroup and consider the alternative—self-publishing. Before you leap, be sure that you have several thousand dollars that you are willing to risk. Also, understand that it's easy to make books; anyone with a computer and a pocket full of money can do it. Remember that it's much more difficult to sell them.

Your publisher is not willing to incorporate your creative ideas.

Some authors become extremely discouraged, even despondent, when others do not recognize their brilliance. I wrote the book, I'm the expert, and the publishing people don't even understand what my book is about. Therefore, they can't appreciate my ideas. I've got a great cover design that incorporates flock (the white spray used on Christmas trees). My title is unpronounceable, which sets it apart from all the other titles and will definitely send sales through the roof. My idea for an interior design puts

Part
2

295

white print on a black background—this is definitely a stroke of genius. Think of the "flip appeal" as customers turn the beautiful pages of my book.

Some authors are simply nuts. In fact, maybe a poll would show that there are more author nuts per capita than most other categories. However, nuts or not, I've seen authors ask for contract cancellation based on such nonsense. That author decided to self-publish. That author's garage still houses a skid load of unsold books. Nuts? Yes. Brilliant? Hardly.

You want to start your own publishing company.

Although this is not a very practical idea unless you're ready to risk a small fortune, it makes more sense than the preceding reason. If you want to become a legitimate trade publisher, you need a list of titles (not just a book), a catalog, sales representation, and the financial ability to stand behind bookstore returns. A publishing company cannot survive with a single title unless you operate out of your home; have a ready-made captive market; and have the resources to process and fulfill orders.

You want all the money yourself.

Unless you have an expensive and essential reference and an established market, you may be self-delusional. You can sell a ten-dollar cookbook to gardening clubs, church groups, and a few local bookstores. But when you count your income and the time you spend hawking your book, you may be lucky if you make fifty cents an hour. You probably can find a better way to spend your time, like enrolling in a college course, learning to program in a new computer language, or even reading a good book.

You're publishing for pleasure and not for profit.

This is a reason that makes some sense. There are many people who write short stories, poetry, or family histories who have no desire to see their work published and distributed to the public. They may want fifty copies to give to friends and family members as gifts. If you fit into this category, then pursue your project and enjoy the experience. Consider using a small offset print shop to reproduce the copies of your work. Your reward will be the knowledge of having completed your book and the gratitude shown by those who appreciate your work.

Some of the reasons given to self-publish may seem flippant, but they actually happen. The example of "Your publisher is not willing to incorporate your creative ideas" is not as farfetched as it may seem.

Back in the early 1980s a friend of mine decided to self-publish his book because his publisher would not agree to use his title and some interior design elements he wanted. My friend convinced his publisher to abrogate the contract. When they agreed, he was ecstatic. He then spent $5,000 for production and printing and another $7,000 for an ad in *The Wall Street Journal*. He sold a few hundred copies over a period of several years. Most of these were sold to personal acquaintances. The *Journal* ad resulted in three inquiries and no sales.

Promotion

If you decide to go forward with your self-publishing venture, the key to success certainly involves your promotional abilities. Examine the promotional strategies employed by trade publishers in the Marketing and Distribution section of chapter 9. Present your book to independent bookstores in your area, go to your public library and check the names of book sales organizations listed in the *Literary Market Place*. If your book is industry specific, send cover letters and review copies to the editors of industry trade journals. If you are a public speaker or trainer, put your book in the back of the room and sell it following your presentation.

Internet Marketing

Marketing via the Internet is not nearly as effective as some would suggest. The companies that are successful with this vehicle are well established and advertise their web site address in advertising copy found in magazines, traditional mailings, and on television. This means that Internet sales are successful when consumers are driven to your site using other means. Most Internet users consider junk e-mail, called spamming, offensive. Most spams are deleted before they are read.

Part 2

There are Internet electronic commerce engines that use a number of methods to attract business. First, they buy advertising space on popular web sites. Popular pages include the home pages of AOL, Compuserve, MSN, and the Stock Exchange. Once a browser examines a web site, free shareware downloads are offered. A download adds your e-mail address to their prospect database. Once registered, you will begin to get e-mail offers advertising special pricing and other incentives designed to generate sales.

Another strategy is to add your web site to search engines (Yahoo, Magellan, etc.). This links searchers to your site when they search for the terms that you added as links. For example, if you added your site to "travel," the search engine will include a few sentences about your web site and a link to it. Unfortunately, there are so many inappropriate links and so much clutter that it is sometimes difficult to direct people to your site simply by adding your site to search engines.

Self-Publishing Partners

There is also a Self-Publishing Partners (SPP) web site that is dedicated to the sales of self-published books. Their Internet universal resource locator (URL) is http://www.electriciti.com/fmcnet/spp.htm. At this writing, SPP charges the following fees.

Six-month listing	$60 plus a one-time $50 setup fee
One-year listing	$100 plus the $50 setup fee
Order processing	$1.25 per order plus 10% of total sale

SPP processes Visa and MasterCard orders, provides a toll-free 1-800 order number, and includes a link to a page about your book from the SPP Book Mart page. Your page includes a cover photo, the ISBN, and a brief description.

SPP requests the following information:

- A sample of the book
- Pricing (retail, wholesale, shipping, and multiple-unit discounts)
- A 125-word description
- The URL of your web site
- Shipping instructions (your order fulfillment address)
- Your credit card number or a check or money order for SPP's service.

This is only one vehicle for selling your self-published book. A major advantage is a toll-free order number and credit card handling. You can do these things yourself for less money, but it is one less administrative hassle to deal with, and it's not a bad way to take care of a few of the administrative details at the beginning of your venture. However, if your sales begin to accelerate through a variety of market channels, you will want to move rapidly to consolidate your sales operations.

Direct Mail

Direct mail advertising is only effective when you have a sizeable list of books or a single title having a value of two or three hundred dollars. If you only have a $20 book to sell, your mailing expenses will exceed your potential revenue. If you don't believe this, invest $100 in a test mailing. Then you can measure the positive responses to develop a hit rate, i.e., the percentage of sales from each mailing. If you mail 120 pieces and receive three orders, your hit rate is 2.5 percent. This rate is high, as most direct mail campaigns realize less than 1 percent. If your $100 test campaign yields $60 or less, you now understand the dynamics of direct-mail marketing. If you have a $59.95 product, you may want to consider a direct mail program. However, you should be sure to test market before doing a

50,000-piece mailing. Chapter 5 discusses direct mail costs in more detail accompanied by examples that demonstrate the economics.

Warehousing and Distribution

There are a number of warehousing and fulfillment services from which to choose. These businesses typically charge a monthly fee for the space you use in addition to a charge for each order transaction. Transactions include order processing, invoicing, packing, and shipping. If you accept returns from booksellers (which you must), you will also be charged for restocking.

Order Processing

You can do your own order processing and fulfillment if you have the space, the appropriate order processing program for your computer, and the packing materials. (Wordware Publishing, Inc. markets an order processing program for small to medium size U.S. publishers.) You should also maintain your order records on your computer and in hard copy for accounting and tax purposes. Also consider maintaining customer contact information for future promotional activities.

A complete publisher management system, like the one that Wordware Publishing, Inc. uses and sells, includes many features. A list of these features follows.

Order processing—Enter customer orders and print invoices and packing slips. Maintain a record of each transaction.

Inventory control—Enter the number of books into an inventory database. As each order is processed, the quantity is deducted from the inventory database.

Reporting—Many reports are needed to effectively run a publishing business. Included are reports that show periodic sales; inventory levels; sales commissions; customer names, addresses, and purchases; marketing analysis information; and more.

Royalty processing—Calculate and print author royalty statements based on the terms of each author's agreement and the net revenues for each author's book.

EDI processing—Receive, acknowledge, process, and invoice electronic data interchange orders from major trading partners (national chains and distributors).

Part
2

Electronic Data Interchange (EDI) is used by all major bookstore chains and Ingram Book Distributors, the largest book distributor in the U.S., to order books. They transmit purchase orders to their publishers, who send an electronic acknowledgement to validate receipt. Next, the data is processed by the publisher's order processing system, which responds with an invoice for each book order filled. The invoice is transmitted back to the customer. Advance orders create backorder records, which are processed electronically when the book arrives from the printer and is entered into inventory. An EDI order can be processed and invoiced in a single day, as most systems automate the entire entry and invoicing process. Paper invoices and packing slips are also produced by the system. The packing slips are used by the warehouse to pick and pack the books; the paper invoices can be filed, as the electronic invoice suffices.

Prior to EDI, purchase orders were mailed to publishers. The national chains mailed hundreds of pages—one for each store. Publishers responded by keying in each purchase order manually, printing the invoice and packing slip, and finally addressing envelopes and mailing the invoices. The whole process, even when done quickly, typically took a few weeks. The advent of EDI has saved time, labor, and mailing expenses. EDI also minimizes human error, as the information is exchanged directly between the bookseller's and publisher's order processing systems.

Those publishers who use EDI typically subscribe to a network. They either access the network using an ISDN or T1 dataline or a modem and dialup networking. In either case, the network stores the order processing data for the booksellers and publishers until it is downloaded.

Vendor of Record

If you are a "tiny publisher," you may find it extremely difficult to establish a direct account relationship with a major bookstore chain. However, there are small to medium regional distributors that do have accounts with the major chains. If you convince a chain buyer to order your book, it will probably be ordered through a *vendor of record*. The vendor of record is the established distributor in your area that is selected by the chain. Establish a relationship with your vendor of record. Tell him about the upcoming order.

Your vendor of record assumes the financial risk for returns. If the chain returns your book to the distributor, he will return it to you. The distributor can issue credit; he typically stocks hundreds of viable titles. His credits are quickly reversed by new orders for other titles. If you only have one book, your credit has no value. Be sure that you maintain an adequate balance in your checking account so you can reimburse your vendor of record for the returns.

Risk Versus Reward

Every prudent businessperson makes investments based on the potential reward. Most people understand that high-risk investments result in high returns when they are successful. However, the investor should be willing to lose the entire amount of the investment. Hope and work for success; be fully prepared to fail.

There are examples of self-publishing ventures that achieved financial success. These instances typically found a fertile market; some even led to the formation of some of today's large trade publishing houses. However, for every success, there are probably a hundred failures. This success rate is not restricted to publishing ventures—it is typical of all start-up business ventures.

Conclusions

If, after reading this chapter, your self-publishing dream is not shattered, then you have a great deal of faith and enthusiasm in your book and your abilities as an entrepreneur. Therefore, if you have the financial and technical resources, reach for your dream. You just may achieve success that exceeds your wildest expectations.

Moving Ahead

As with every business, there are a number of administrative details that must be understood and processed. The next chapter presents everything you need to know about how to obtain a copyright, an International Standard Book Number (ISBN), and Cataloging-in-Publication (CIP) data from the Library of Congress.

Part
2

Chapter 12

Administrative Requirements

Introduction

This chapter presents information that is important to both publishers and self-publishers. It presents information you should know about copyrights, International Standard Book Numbers (ISBNs), and Cataloging-in-Publication (CIP) Data, and how to secure them from the authorized sources. Published books require all three of these.

There are service companies and attorneys who make their living charging naïve authors for obtaining an ISBN, copyright, and/or CIP data for their book. However, you can do these things yourself by reading the information supplied in this chapter.

Part
2

Copyright Basics

If you are publishing in the U.S., you can find everything you need to know about copyrights from the U.S. Copyright Office, which is a division of the Library of Congress. The U.S. Copyright Office maintains an extremely informative web site at www.lcweb.loc.gov/copyright/. Links to information about copyright basics, registration, copyright application forms, and much more are included on this site. Excerpts, summaries, and author commentaries are included here for your convenience.

What a Copyright Does

Copyright is provided by the laws of the United States (title 17, U.S. Code) as a form of protection to the authors of "original works of authorship." This includes literary, dramatic, musical, artistic, and certain other intellectual works. This protection applies to both published and unpublished works. Section 106 of the Copyright Act generally gives the owner of a copyright the exclusive right to do and to authorize others to:

■ Reproduce the copyrighted work in copies or phonorecords;

■ Prepare derivative works based upon the copyrighted work;

■ Distribute copies or phonorecords of the copyrighted work to the public by sale or other transfer of ownership, or by rental, lease, or lending;

■ Perform the copyrighted work publicly, in the case of literary, musical, dramatic, and choreographic works, pantomimes, and motion pictures and other audiovisual works;

■ Display the copyrighted work publicly, in the case of literary, musical, dramatic, and choreographic works, pantomimes, and pictorial, graphic, or sculptural works, including the individual images of a motion picture or other audiovisual work;

■ Perform the work publicly by means of a digital audio transmission, in the case of sound recordings.

In addition to these, certain authors of works of visual art have the rights of attribution and integrity as described in section 106A of the 1976 Copyright Act. For further information, you can request Circular 40 from the Copyright Office.

Violations of the rights provided by the copyright code are illegal. These rights do have limitations. Sections 107 through 120 of the 1976 Copyright Act establish these limitations. In some cases, these limitations are specified exemptions from copyright liability. One major limitation is the doctrine of "fair use." This doctrine is given a statutory basis in section 107 of the Act. In other instances, the limitation takes the form of a "compulsory license" under which certain limited uses of copyrighted works are permitted upon payment of specified royalties and compliance with statutory conditions. For further information about the limitations of any of these rights, consult the copyright code or write to the Copyright Office.

Who Can Claim Copyright

Copyright protection begins when the work is created in fixed form; that is, it is an incident of the process of authorship. The copyright in the work of authorship immediately becomes the property of the author who created it. Only the author or those deriving their rights through the author can rightfully claim copyright.

In the case of works made for hire, the employer and not the employee is considered to be the author. Section 101 of the copyright statute defines a "work made for hire" as either:

A work prepared by an employee within the scope of his or her employment; or

A work specially ordered or commissioned for use as a contribution to a collective work, as a part of a motion picture or other audiovisual work, as a translation, as a supplementary work, as a compilation, as an instructional text, as a test, as answer material for a test, or as an atlas, if the parties expressly agree in a written instrument signed by them that the work shall be considered a work made for hire....

The authors of a joint work are co-owners of the copyright in the work, unless there is an agreement to the contrary.

Copyright in each separate contribution to a periodical or other collective work is distinct from copyright in the collective work as a whole and vests initially with the author of the contribution.

Two General Principles

1. Mere ownership of a book, manuscript, painting, or any other copy or phonorecord does not give the possessor the copyright. The law provides that transfer of ownership of any material object that embodies a protected work does not of itself convey any rights in the copyright. (In other words, if you purchase a book or software, you are not entitled to reproduce it on the basis of ownership.)

2. Minors may claim copyright, but state laws may regulate the business dealings involving copyrights owned by minors. For information on relevant state laws, consult an attorney.

Copyright and National Origin of the Work

Copyright protection is available for all unpublished works, regardless of the nationality or domicile of the author. Published works are eligible for copyright protection in the United States if any one of the following conditions is met:

■ On the date of first publication, one or more of the authors is a national or domiciliary of the United States or is a national, domiciliary, or sovereign authority of a foreign nation that is a party to a copyright treaty to which the United States is also a party, or is a stateless person wherever that person may be domiciled; or

■ The work is first published in the United States or in a foreign nation that, on the date of first publication, is a party to the Universal Copyright Convention; or the work comes within the scope of a Presidential proclamation; or

■ The work is first published on or after March 1, 1989, in a foreign nation that on the date of first publication, is a party to the Berne

Part
2

Convention; or, if the work is not first published in a country party to the Berne Convention, it is published (on or after March 1, 1989) within 30 days of first publication in a country that is party to the Berne Convention; or the work, first published on or after March 1, 1989, is a pictorial, graphic, or sculptural work that is incorporated in a permanent structure located in the United States; or, if the work, first published on or after March 1, 1989, is a published audiovisual work, all the authors are legal entities with headquarters in the United States.

■ The work is a foreign work that was in the public domain in the United States prior to 1996 and its copyright was restored under the Uruguay Rounds Agreements Act (URAA). Request Circular 38b for further information.

What Works are Protected

Copyright protects "original works of authorship" that are fixed in a tangible form of expression. The fixation need not be directly perceptible, so long as it may be communicated with the aid of a machine or device. Copyrightable works include the following categories:

■ Literary works;

■ Musical works, including any accompanying words;

■ Dramatic works, including any accompanying music;

■ Pantomimes and choreographic works;

■ Pictorial, graphic, and sculptural works;

■ Motion pictures and other audiovisual works;

■ Sound recordings; and

■ Architectural works.

These categories should be viewed quite broadly: for example, computer programs and most "compilations" are registrable as "literary works;" maps and architectural plans are registrable as "pictorial, graphic, and sculptural works."

What is Not Protected by Copyright

Several categories of material are generally not eligible for federal copyright protection. These include among others:

■ Works that have not been fixed in a tangible form of expression. For example:

■ Choreographic works that have not been notated or recorded; or

- Improvisational speeches or performances that have not been written or recorded.

■ Titles, names, short phrases, and slogans; familiar symbols or designs; mere variations of typographic ornamentation, lettering, or coloring; mere listings of ingredients or contents.

■ Ideas, procedures, methods, systems, processes, concepts, principles, discoveries, or devices, as distinguished from a description, explanation, or illustration.

■ Works consisting entirely of information that is common property and containing no original authorship. For example: standard calendars, height and weight charts, tape measures and rulers, and lists or tables taken from public documents or other common sources.

How to Secure a Copyright

A copyright is secured automatically upon creation. The way in which copyright protection is secured under the present law is frequently misunderstood. No publication or registration or other action in the Copyright Office is required to secure copyright (see following Note). There are, however, certain definite advantages to registration.

Note: Before 1978, statutory copyright was generally secured by the act of publication with notice of copyright, assuming compliance with all other relevant statutory conditions. U.S. works in the public domain on January 1, 1978, (for example, works published without satisfying all conditions for securing statutory copyright under the Copyright Act of 1909) remain in the public domain under the current act.

Copyright is secured automatically when the work is created, and a work is "created" when it is fixed in a copy or phonorecord for the first time. "Copies" are material objects from which a work can be read or visually perceived either directly or with the aid of a machine or device, such as books, manuscripts, sheet music, film, videotape, or microfilm. "Phonorecords" are material objects embodying fixations of sounds (excluding, by statutory definition, motion picture soundtracks), such as cassette tapes, CDs, or LPs. Thus, for example, a song (the "work") can be fixed in sheet music ("copies") or in phonograph disks ("phonorecords"), or both.

If a work is prepared over a period of time, the part of the work that is fixed on a particular date constitutes the created work as of that date.

Publication

Publication is no longer the key to obtaining statutory copyright as it was under the Copyright Act of 1909. However, publication remains important to copyright owners. The Copyright Act defines publication as follows:

> *"Publication" is the distribution of copies or phonorecords of a work to the public by sale or other transfer of ownership or by rental, lease, or lending. The offering to distribute copies or phonorecords to a group of persons for purposes of further distribution, public performance, or public display constitutes publication. A public performance or display of a work does not of itself constitute publication.*

A further discussion of the definition of "publication" can be found in the legislative history of the Act. The legislative reports define "to the public" as distribution to persons under no explicit or implicit restrictions with respect to disclosure of the contents. The reports state that the definition makes it clear that the sale of phonorecords constitutes publication of the underlying work, for example, the musical, dramatic, or literary work embodied in a phonorecord. The reports also state that it is clear that any form of dissemination in which the material object does not change hands, for example, performances or displays on television, is not a publication no matter how many people are exposed to the work. However, when copies or phonorecords are offered for sale or lease to a group of wholesalers, broadcasters, or motion picture theaters, publication does take place if the purpose is further distribution, public performance, or public display.

Publication is an important concept in copyright law for several reasons:

- When a work is published, it may bear a notice of copyright to identify the year of publication and the name of the copyright owner and to inform the public that the work is protected by copyright. Works published before March 1, 1989, must bear the notice or risk loss of copyright protection. (See discussion "notice of copyright" below.)

- Works that are published in the United States are subject to mandatory deposit with the Library of Congress. (See discussion on "mandatory deposit," below.) Publication of a work can affect the limitations on the exclusive rights of the copyright owner that are set forth in sections 107 through 120 of the law.

- The year of publication may determine the duration of copyright protection for anonymous and pseudonymous works (when the author's identity is not revealed in the records of the Copyright Office) and for works made for hire.

Deposit requirements for registration of published works differ from those for registration of unpublished works. (See discussion on "registration procedures," below.)

Notice of Copyright

For works first published on and after March 1, 1989, use of the copyright notice is optional, though highly recommended. Before March 1, 1989, the use of the notice was mandatory on all published works, and any work first published before that date must bear a notice or risk loss of copyright protection. (The Copyright Office does not take a position on whether works first published with notice before March 1, 1989, and reprinted and distributed on and after March 1, 1989, must bear the copyright notice.) Use of the notice is recommended because it informs the public that the work is protected by copyright, identifies the copyright owner, and shows the year of first publication. Furthermore, in the event that a work is infringed, if the work carries a proper notice, the court will not allow a defendant to claim "innocent infringement"—that is, that he or she did not realize that the work is protected. (A successful innocent infringement claim may result in a reduction in damages that the copyright owner would otherwise receive.)

The use of the copyright notice is the responsibility of the copyright owner and does not require advance permission from, or registration with, the Copyright Office.

Form of the Copyright Notice (for Visually Perceptible Copies)

Part 2

The notice for visually perceptible copies should contain all of the following three elements:

- The symbol © (the letter C in a circle), or the word "Copyright" or the abbreviation "Copr."; and
- The year of first publication of the work; and
- The name of the owner of copyright in the work, or an abbreviation by which the name can be recognized, or a generally known alternative designation of the owner.

    Example:

    © 1995 John Doe

Notice that either the symbol or the word Copyright (or abbreviation Copr.) is used, but not both, as is the practice of many publishers. International copyright also provides for one or the other, but not both.

Variations

- In the case of compilations or derivative works incorporating previously published material, the year date of first publication of the compilation or derivative work is sufficient.

■ The year date may be omitted where a pictorial, graphic, or sculptural work, with accompanying textual matter, if any, is reproduced in or on greeting cards, postcards, stationery, jewelry, dolls, toys, or any useful article.

The copyright symbol (C in a circle) form is used only on "visually perceptible copies." Certain kinds of works—for example, musical, dramatic, and literary works—may be fixed not in "copies" but by means of sound in an audio recording. Since audio recordings such as audiotapes and phonograph disks are "phonorecords" and not "copies," the "C in a circle" notice is not used to indicate protection of the underlying musical, dramatic, or literary work that is recorded.

Form of Notice for Phonorecords of Sound Recordings

This is included here as a matter of interest rather than necessity. However, if you bundle audiocassettes or a CD with your book, you should understand the form described here.

The copyright notice for phonorecords of sound recordings* has somewhat different requirements. The notice appearing on phonorecords should contain the following three elements:

■ The symbol Ⓟ (the letter P in a circle); and

■ The year of first publication of the sound recording; and

■ The name of the owner of copyright in the sound recording, or an abbreviation by which the name can be recognized, or a generally known alternative designation of the owner. If the producer of the sound recording is named on the phonorecord labels or containers, and if no other name appears in conjunction with the notice, the producer's name shall be considered a part of the notice.

Note: Since questions may arise from the use of variant forms of the notice, any form of the notice other than those given here should not be used without first seeking legal advice.

---

* Sound recordings are defined as "works that result from the fixation of a series of musical, spoken, or other sounds, but not including the sounds accompanying a motion picture or other audiovisual work, regardless of the nature of the material objects, such as disks, tapes, or other phonorecords, in which they are embodied."

Position of Notice

The notice should be affixed to copies or phonorecords of the work (or CDs) in such a manner and location as to "give reasonable notice of the claim of copyright." The notice on phonorecords may appear on the surface of the phonorecord or on the phonorecord label or container, provided the manner of placement and location give reasonable notice of the claim. The three elements of the notice should ordinarily appear together on the copies or phonorecords. The Copyright Office has issued regulations concerning the form and position of the copyright notice in the Code of Federal Regulations (37 CFR Part 201). For more information, request Circular 3.

Publications Incorporating United States Government Works

Works by the U.S. Government, such as many of the passages in this section, are not eligible for copyright protection. For works published on and after March 1, 1989, the previous notice requirement for works consisting primarily of one or more U.S. Government works has been eliminated. However, use of the copyright notice for these works is still strongly recommended. Use of a notice on such a work will defeat a claim of innocent infringement as previously described provided the notice also includes a statement that identifies one of the following: those portions of the work in which copyright is claimed or those portions that constitute U.S. Government material.

Part
2

An example is:

> © 1994 Jane Brown. Copyright claimed in Chapters 7-10, exclusive of U.S. Government maps.

Works published before March 1, 1989, that consist primarily of one or more works of the U.S. Government must bear a notice and the identifying statement.

Unpublished Works

To avoid an inadvertent publication without notice, the author or other owner of copyright may wish to place a copyright notice on any copies or phonorecords that leave his or her control. An appropriate notice for an unpublished work is:

> Unpublished work © 1994 Jane Doe.

Effect of Omission of the Notice or of Error in the Name or Date

The Copyright Act, in sections 405 and 406, provides procedures for correcting errors and omissions of the copyright notice on works published on or after January 1, 1978, and before March 1, 1989. In general, if a notice was omitted or an error was made on copies distributed on or after January 1, 1978, and before March 1, 1989, the copyright was not automatically lost. Copyright protection may be maintained if registration for the work has been made before or is made within 5 years after the publication without notice, and a reasonable effort is made to add the notice to all copies or phonorecords that are distributed to the public in the United States after the omission has been discovered. For more information, request Circular 3.

How Long Copyright Protection Endures

Works Originally Created On or After January 1, 1978

A work that is created (fixed in tangible form for the first time) on or after January 1, 1978, is automatically protected from the moment of its creation, and is ordinarily given a term enduring for the author's life, plus an additional 50 years after the author's death. In the case of "a joint work prepared by two or more authors who did not work for hire," the term lasts for 50 years after the last surviving author's death. For works made for hire, and for anonymous and pseudonymous works (unless the author's identity is revealed in Copyright Office records), the duration of copyright will be 75 years from publication or 100 years from creation, whichever is shorter.

Works Originally Created Before January 1, 1978, But Not Published or Registered by That Date

Works that were created but not published or registered for copyright before January 1, 1978, have been automatically brought under the statute and are now given Federal copyright protection. The duration of copyright in these works will generally be computed in the same way as for works created on or after January 1, 1978: the life-plus-50 or 75/100-year terms will apply to them as well. The law provides that in no case will the term of copyright for works in this category expire before December 31, 2002, and for works published on or before December 31, 2002, the term of copyright will not expire before December 31, 2027.

Works Originally Created and Published or Registered Before January 1, 1978

Under the law in effect before 1978, copyright was secured either on the date a work was published or on the date of registration if the work was registered in unpublished form. In either case, the copyright endured for a first term of 28 years from the date it was secured. During the last (28th) year of the first term, the copyright was eligible for renewal. The current copyright law has extended the renewal term from 28 to 47 years for copyrights that were subsisting on January 1, 1978, making these works eligible for a total term of protection of 75 years. Public Law 102-307, enacted on June 26, 1992, amended the Copyright Act of 1976 to extend automatically the term of copyrights secured from January 1, 1964, through December 31, 1977, to the further term of 47 years and increased the filing fee from $12 to $20. This fee increase applies to all renewal applications filed on or after June 29, 1992.

Public Law 102-307 makes renewal registration optional. There is no need to make the renewal filing in order to extend the original 28-year copyright term to the full 75 years. However, some benefits accrue to making a renewal registration during the 28th year of the original term. For more detailed information on the copyright term, write to the Copyright Office and request Circulars 15, 15a, and 15t. For information on how to search the Copyright Office records concerning the copyright status of a work, request Circular 22.

Part
2

Transfer of Copyright

Any or all of the exclusive rights, or any subdivision of those rights, of the copyright owner may be transferred, but the transfer of exclusive rights is not valid unless that transfer is in writing and signed by the owner of the rights conveyed (or such owner's duly authorized agent). Transfer of a right on a nonexclusive basis does not require a written agreement. A copyright may also be conveyed by operation of law and may be bequeathed by will or pass as personal property by the applicable laws of intestate succession.

Copyright is a personal property right, and it is subject to the various state laws and regulations that govern the ownership, inheritance, or transfer of personal property as well as terms of contracts or conduct of business. For information about relevant state laws, consult an attorney.

Transfers of copyright are normally made by contract. The Copyright Office does not have or supply any forms for such transfers. However, the law does provide for the recordation in the Copyright Office of transfers of copyright ownership. Although recordation is not required to make a valid transfer between the parties, it does provide certain legal advantages and may be required to validate the transfer as against third parties. For information on recordation of transfers and other documents related to copyright, request Circular 12.

Termination of Transfers

Under the previous law, the copyright in a work reverted to the author, if living, or if the author was not living, to other specified beneficiaries, provided a renewal claim was registered in the 28th year of the original term. (The copyright in works eligible for renewal on or after June 26, 1992, will vest in the name of the renewal claimant on the effective date of any renewal registration made during the 28th year of the original term. Otherwise, the renewal copyright will vest in the party entitled to claim renewal as of December 31st of the 28th year.) The present law drops the renewal feature except for works already in the first term of statutory protection when the present law took effect. Instead, the present law permits termination of a grant of rights after 35 years under certain conditions by serving written notice on the transferee within specified time limits.

For works already under statutory copyright protection before 1978, the present law provides a similar right of termination covering the newly added years that extended the former maximum term of the copyright from 56 to 75 years. For further information, request Circulars 15a and 15t.

International Copyright Protection

There is no such thing as an "international copyright" that will automatically protect an author's writings throughout the entire world. Protection against unauthorized use in a particular country depends, basically, on the national laws of that country. However, most countries do offer protection to foreign works under certain conditions, and these conditions have been greatly simplified by international copyright treaties and conventions. For a list of countries which maintain copyright relations with the United States, request Circular 38a.

The United States belongs to both global, multilateral copyright treaties—the Universal Copyright Convention (UCC) and the Berne Convention for the Protection of Literary and Artistic Works. The United States was a founding member of the UCC, which came into force on September 16, 1955. Generally, a work by a national or domiciliary of a country that is a member of the UCC or a work first published in a UCC country may claim protection under the UCC. If the work bears the notice of copyright in the form and position specified by the UCC, this notice will satisfy and substitute for any other formalities a UCC member country would otherwise impose as a condition of copyright. A UCC notice should consist of the symbol accompanied by the name of the copyright proprietor and the year of first publication of the work.

By joining the Berne Convention on March 1, 1989, the United States gained protection for its authors in all member nations of the Berne Union with which the United States formerly had either no copyright relations or had bilateral treaty arrangements. Members of the Berne Union agree to a certain minimum level of copyright protection and agree to treat nationals of other member countries like their own nationals for purposes of copyright. A work first published in the United States or another Berne Union country (or first published in a non-Berne country, followed by publication within 30 days in a Berne Union country) is eligible for protection in all Berne member countries. There are no special requirements. For information on the legislation implementing the Berne Convention, request Circular 93 from the Copyright Office. An author who wishes protection for his or her work in a particular country should first find out the extent of protection of foreign works in that country. If possible, this should be done before the work is published anywhere, since protection may often depend on the facts existing at the time of first publication.

If the country in which protection is sought is a party to one of the international copyright conventions, the work may generally be protected by complying with the conditions of the convention. Even if the work cannot be brought under an international convention, protection under the specific provisions of the country's national laws may still be possible. Some countries, however, offer little or no copyright protection for foreign works.

Part
2

Copyright Registration

In general, copyright registration is a legal formality intended to make a public record of the basic facts of a particular copyright. However, except in one specific situation,* registration is not a condition of copyright protection.

Even though registration is not generally a requirement for protection, the copyright law provides several inducements or advantages to encourage copyright owners to make registration. Among these advantages are the following:

---

* Under sections 405 and 406 of the Copyright Act, copyright registration may be required to preserve a copyright on a work first published before March 1, 1989, that would otherwise be invalidated because the copyright notice was omitted from the published copies or phonorecords, or the name or year was omitted, or certain errors were made in the year date.

1. Registration establishes a public record of the copyright claim;

2. Before an infringement suit may be filed in court, registration is necessary for works of U.S. origin and for foreign works not originating in a Berne Union country. (For more information on when a work is of U.S. origin, request Circular 93.);

3. If made before or within 5 years of publication, registration will establish prima facie evidence in court of the validity of the copyright and of the facts stated in the certificate;

4. If registration is made within 3 months after publication of the work or prior to an infringement of the work, statutory damages and attorneys' fees will be available to the copyright owner in court actions. Otherwise, only an award of actual damages and profits is available to the copyright owner; and

5. Copyright registration allows the owner of the copyright to record the registration with the U.S. Customs Service for protection against the importation of infringing copies.

For additional information, request Publication No. 563 from:

Commissioner of Customs
ATTN: IPR Branch, Room 2104
U.S. Customs Service
1301 Constitution Avenue, N.W.
Washington, DC 20229

Registration may be made at any time within the life of the copyright. Unlike the law before 1978, when a work has been registered in unpublished form, it is not necessary to make another registration when the work becomes published (although the copyright owner may register the published edition, if desired).

Registration Procedures

To register a work, send the following three elements in the same envelope or package to the Register of Copyrights, Copyright Office, Library of Congress, Washington, D.C. 20559: (see "Incomplete Submissions," below, for what happens if the elements are sent separately).

1. A properly completed application form

2. A nonrefundable filing fee of $20* for each application

---

* For the fee structure for application Form SE/GROUP and Form G/DN, see the instructions for these forms.

3. A nonreturnable deposit of the work being registered. The deposit require-ments vary in particular situations. The general requirements follow. Also note the information under "Special Deposit Requirements" following this section.

   ■ If the work is unpublished, send one complete copy or phonorecord.

   ■ If the work was first published in the United States on or after January 1, 1978, send two complete copies or phonorecords of the best edition.

   ■ If the work was first published in the United States before January 1, 1978, send two complete copies or phonorecords of the work as first published.

   ■ If the work was first published outside the United States, send one complete copy or phonorecord of the work as first published.

To register a renewal, send:

1. A properly completed RE application form; and

2. A nonrefundable filing fee of $20 for each work.

Note: Complete the application form using <u>black ink pen</u> or <u>typewriter</u>. You may photocopy blank application forms; however, photocopied forms submitted to the Copyright Office must be clear, legible, on a good grade of 8½ x 11-inch white paper suit-able for automatic feeding through a photocopier. The forms should be printed, preferably in black ink, head-to-head (so that when you turn the sheet over, the top of page 2 is directly behind the top of page 1). Forms not meeting these requirements will be returned.

Part
2

Special Deposit Requirements

Special deposit requirements exist for many types of work. In some instances, only one copy is required for published works, in other instances only identifying material is required, and in still other instances, the deposit requirement may be unique. The following are prominent exam-ples of exceptions to the general deposit requirements:

■ If the work is a motion picture, the deposit requirement is one complete copy of the unpublished or published motion picture and a separate written description of its contents, such as a continuity, press book, or synopsis.

■ If the work is a literary, dramatic, or musical work published only on phonorecord, the deposit requirement is one complete copy of the phonorecord.

■ If the work is an unpublished or published computer program, the deposit requirement is one visually perceptible copy in source code of the first and last 25 pages of the program. For a program of fewer than 50 pages, the deposit is a copy of the entire program. (For more information on computer program registration, including deposits for revised programs and provisions for trade secrets, request Circular 61.)

■ If the work is in a CD-ROM format, the deposit requirement is one complete copy of the material, that is, the CD-ROM, the operating software, and any manual(s) accompanying it. If the identical work is also available in print or hard copy form, send one complete copy of the print version and one complete copy of the CD-ROM version.

For information about group registration of serials, request Circular 62. In the case of works reproduced in three-dimensional copies, identifying material such as photographs or drawings is ordinarily required. Other examples of special deposit requirements (but by no means an exhaustive list) include many works of the visual arts, such as greeting cards, toys, fabric, and oversized material (request Circular 40a); video games and other machine-readable audiovisual works (request Circular 61 and ML-387); automated databases (request Circular 65); and contributions to collective works.

If you are unsure of the deposit requirement for your work, write or call the Copyright Office and describe the work you wish to register.

Unpublished Collections

A work may be registered in unpublished form as a "collection," with one application and one fee, under the following conditions:

■ The elements of the collection are assembled in an orderly form;

■ The combined elements bear a single title identifying the collection as a whole;

■ The copyright claimant in all the elements and in the collection as a whole is the same; and all of the elements are by the same author, or, if they are by different authors, at least one of the authors has contributed copyrightable authorship to each element.

An unpublished collection is indexed in the Catalog of Copyright Entries only under the collection title.

Corrections and Amplifications of Existing Registrations

To correct an error in a copyright registration or to amplify the information given in a registration, file a supplementary registration form—Form CA—with the Copyright Office. The information in a supplementary registration augments but does not supersede that contained in the earlier registration. Note also that a supplementary registration is not a substitute for an original registration, for a renewal registration, or for recording a transfer of ownership. For further information about supplementary registration, request Circular 8.

Mandatory Deposit for Works Published in the United States

Although a copyright registration is not required, the Copyright Act establishes a mandatory deposit requirement for works published in the United States (see definition of "publication," above). In general, the owner of copyright or the owner of the exclusive right of publication in the work has a legal obligation to deposit in the Copyright Office, within 3 months of publication in the United States, 2 copies (or in the case of sound recordings, 2 phonorecords) for the use of the Library of Congress. Failure to make the deposit can result in fines and other penalties but does not affect copyright protection. Certain categories of works are exempt entirely from the mandatory deposit requirements, and the obligation is reduced for certain other categories. For further information about mandatory deposit, request Circular 7d.

Use of Mandatory Deposit to Satisfy Registration Requirements

For works published in the United States the Copyright Act contains a provision under which a single deposit can be made to satisfy both the deposit requirements for the Library and the registration requirements. In order to have this dual effect, the copies or phonorecords must be accompanied by the prescribed application and filing fee.

Who May File an Application Form

The following persons are legally entitled to submit an application form:

■ The author. This is either the person who actually created the work, or, if the work was made for hire, the employer or other person for whom the work was prepared.

■ The copyright claimant. The copyright claimant is defined in Copyright Office regulations as either the author of the work or a person or organization that has obtained ownership of all the rights under the copyright initially belonging to the author. This category includes a person or organization who has obtained by contract the right to claim legal title to the copyright in an application for copyright registration.

- ■ The owner of exclusive right(s). Under the law, any of the exclusive rights that go to make up a copyright and any subdivision of them can be transferred and owned separately, even though the transfer may be limited in time or place of effect. The term "copyright owner" with respect to any one of the exclusive rights contained in a copyright refers to the owner of that particular right. Any owner of an exclusive right may apply for registration of a claim in the work.

- ■ The duly authorized agent of such author, other copyright claimant, or owner of exclusive right(s). Any person authorized to act on behalf of the author, other copyright claimant, or owner of exclusive rights may apply for registration.

There is no requirement that applications be prepared or filed by an attorney. (As a practical matter, once you obtain the forms and register your first copyright, the entire process becomes a task that only takes a matter of minutes.)

Application Forms

The Copyright Office supplies free application forms. Requestors may order application forms and circulars at any time by telephoning (202) 707-9100, which is the Copyright Office Forms Hotline number. Orders are recorded automatically and filled as quickly as possible. You should specify the kind and number of forms you require. You can also download copyright registration forms from the Library of Congress web site. Once captured, you can print and copy the forms as required. To download and print the form, you will require Adobe Acrobat Reader. This software program is available as a free download from http://www.adobe.com. Following are descriptions of most of the forms used by authors and publishers.

For Original Registration:

Form TX: for published and unpublished nondramatic literary works (See the illustration of this form at the end of the list of forms.)

Form SE: for serials, works issued or intended to be issued in successive parts bearing numerical or chronological designations and intended to be continued indefinitely (periodicals, newspapers, magazines, newsletters, annuals, journals, etc.)

Short Form/SE and Form SE/GROUP: specialized SE forms for use when certain requirements are met

Form G/DN: a specialized form to register a complete month's issues of a daily newspaper when certain conditions are met

Form PA: for published and unpublished works of the performing arts (musical and dramatic works, pantomimes and choreographic works, motion pictures and other audiovisual works)

Form VA: for published and unpublished works of the visual arts (pictorial, graphic, and sculptural works, including architectural works)

Form SR: for published and unpublished sound recordings

Form TX, which is probably the one you will require to register your book's copyright with the U.S. Copyright Office. (Sheet 1 of 2)

FORM TX ■
For a Literary Work
UNITED STATES COPYRIGHT OFFICE

REGISTRATION NUMBER

TX   TXU

EFFECTIVE DATE OF REGISTRATION

Month   Day   Year

DO NOT WRITE ABOVE THIS LINE. IF YOU NEED MORE SPACE, USE A SEPARATE CONTINUATION SHEET.

1   TITLE OF THIS WORK ▼

PREVIOUS OR ALTERNATIVE TITLES ▼

PUBLICATION AS A CONTRIBUTION If this work was published as a contribution to a periodical, serial, or collection, give information about the collective work in which the contribution appeared.   **Title of Collective Work ▼**

If published in a periodical or serial give: Volume ▼   Number ▼   Issue Date ▼   On Pages ▼

2 a   NAME OF AUTHOR ▼

DATES OF BIRTH AND DEATH
Year Born ▼   Year Died ▼

Was this contribution to the work a "work made for hire"?
☐ Yes
☐ No

AUTHOR'S NATIONALITY OR DOMICILE
Name of Country
OR { Citizen of ▶
Domiciled in ▶

WAS THIS AUTHOR'S CONTRIBUTION TO THE WORK
Anonymous? ☐ Yes ☐ No
Pseudonymous? ☐ Yes ☐ No
If the answer to either of these questions is "Yes," see detailed instructions.

NATURE OF AUTHORSHIP Briefly describe nature of material created by this author in which copyright is claimed. ▼

NOTE

Under the law, the "author" of a "work made for hire" is generally the employer, not the employee (see instructions). For any part of this work that was "made for hire" check "Yes" in the space provided, give the employer (or other person for whom the work was prepared) as "Author" of that part, and leave the space for dates of birth and death blank.

b   NAME OF AUTHOR ▼

DATES OF BIRTH AND DEATH
Year Born ▼   Year Died ▼

Was this contribution to the work a "work made for hire"?
☐ Yes
☐ No

AUTHOR'S NATIONALITY OR DOMICILE
Name of Country
OR { Citizen of ▶
Domiciled in ▶

WAS THIS AUTHOR'S CONTRIBUTION TO THE WORK
Anonymous? ☐ Yes ☐ No
Pseudonymous? ☐ Yes ☐ No
If the answer to either of these questions is "Yes," see detailed instructions.

NATURE OF AUTHORSHIP Briefly describe nature of material created by this author in which copyright is claimed. ▼

c   NAME OF AUTHOR ▼

DATES OF BIRTH AND DEATH
Year Born ▼   Year Died ▼

Was this contribution to the work a "work made for hire"?
☐ Yes
☐ No

AUTHOR'S NATIONALITY OR DOMICILE
Name of Country
OR { Citizen of ▶
Domiciled in ▶

WAS THIS AUTHOR'S CONTRIBUTION TO THE WORK
Anonymous? ☐ Yes ☐ No
Pseudonymous? ☐ Yes ☐ No
If the answer to either of these questions is "Yes," see detailed instructions.

NATURE OF AUTHORSHIP Briefly describe nature of material created by this author in which copyright is claimed. ▼

3 a   YEAR IN WHICH CREATION OF THIS WORK WAS COMPLETED   This information must be given in all cases.   ◄ Year

b   DATE AND NATION OF FIRST PUBLICATION OF THIS PARTICULAR WORK   Complete this information ONLY if this work has been published.   Month ▶ _____ Day ▶ _____ Year ▶ _____ ◄ Nation

4   COPYRIGHT CLAIMANT(S) Name and address must be given even if the claimant is the same as the author given in space 2. ▼

See instructions before completing this space.

TRANSFER If the claimant(s) named here in space 4 is (are) different from the author(s) named in space 2, give a brief statement of how the claimant(s) obtained ownership of the copyright. ▼

APPLICATION RECEIVED

ONE DEPOSIT RECEIVED

TWO DEPOSITS RECEIVED

FUNDS RECEIVED

DO NOT WRITE HERE
OFFICE USE ONLY

MORE ON BACK ▶   • Complete all applicable spaces (numbers 5-11) on the reverse side of this page.
• See detailed instructions.   • Sign the form at line 10.

DO NOT WRITE HERE
Page 1 of _____ pages

*Form TX
(Sheet 2 of 2)*

EXAMINED BY

FORM TX

CHECKED BY

☐ CORRESPONDENCE
Yes

FOR
COPYRIGHT
OFFICE
USE
ONLY

DO NOT WRITE ABOVE THIS LINE. IF YOU NEED MORE SPACE, USE A SEPARATE CONTINUATION SHEET.

PREVIOUS REGISTRATION Has registration for this work, or for an earlier version of this work, already been made in the Copyright Office?
☐ Yes ☐ No If your answer is "Yes," why is another registration being sought? (Check appropriate box) ▼
a. ☐ This is the first published edition of a work previously registered in unpublished form.
b. ☐ This is the first application submitted by this author as copyright claimant.
c. ☐ This is a changed version of the work, as shown by space 6 on this application.
If your answer is "Yes," give: Previous Registration Number ▼   Year of Registration ▼

5

DERIVATIVE WORK OR COMPILATION Complete both space 6a and 6b for a derivative work; complete only 6b for a compilation.
a. Preexisting Material Identify any preexisting work or works that this work is based on or incorporates. ▼

b. Material Added to This Work Give a brief, general statement of the material that has been added to this work and in which copyright is claimed. ▼

6

See instructions
before completing
this space.

—space deleted—

7

REPRODUCTION FOR USE OF BLIND OR PHYSICALLY HANDICAPPED INDIVIDUALS A signature on this form at space 10 and a check in one of the boxes here in space 8 constitutes a non-exclusive grant of permission to the Library of Congress to reproduce and distribute solely for the blind and physically handicapped and under the conditions and limitations prescribed by the regulations of the Copyright Office: (1) copies of the work identified in space 1 of this application in Braille (or similar tactile symbols); or (2) phonorecords embodying a fixation of a reading of that work; or (3) both.

a ☐ Copies and Phonorecords   b ☐ Copies Only   c ☐ Phonorecords Only

8

See instructions.

DEPOSIT ACCOUNT If the registration fee is to be charged to a Deposit Account established in the Copyright Office, give name and number of Account.
Name ▼   Account Number ▼

9

CORRESPONDENCE Give name and address to which correspondence about this application should be sent.   Name/Address/Apt/City/State/ZIP ▼

Area Code and Telephone Number ▶

Be sure to
give your
daytime phone
◀ number

CERTIFICATION* I, the undersigned, hereby certify that I am the
Check only one ▶
☐ author
☐ other copyright claimant
☐ owner of exclusive right(s)
☐ authorized agent of _____
Name of author or other copyright claimant, or owner of exclusive right(s) ▲

of the work identified in this application and that the statements made
by me in this application are correct to the best of my knowledge.

Typed or printed name and date ▼ If this application gives a date of publication in space 3, do not sign and submit it before that date.

Date ▶ _____

☞ Handwritten signature (X) ▼

10

MAIL CERTIFI-CATE TO

Name ▼

Number/Street/Apt ▼

City/State/ZIP ▼

Certificate
will be
mailed in
window
envelope

YOU MUST
• Complete all necessary spaces
• Sign your application in space 10

SEND ALL 3 ELEMENTS
IN THE SAME PACKAGE
1. Application form
2. Nonrefundable $20 filing fee
in check or money order
payable to *Register of Copyrights*
3. Deposit material

MAIL TO
Register of Copyrights
Library of Congress
Washington, D.C. 20559-6000

11

For Renewal Registration

Form RE: for claims to renewal copyright in works copyrighted under the law in effect through December 31, 1977 (1909 Copyright Act)

For Corrections and Amplifications

Form CA: for supplementary registration to correct or amplify information given in the Copyright Office record of an earlier registration

For a Group of Contributions to Periodicals

Form GR/CP: an adjunct application to be used for registration of a group of contributions to periodicals in addition to an application Form TX, PA, or VA

Mailing Instructions

All applications and materials related to copyright registration should be addressed to the:

Register of Copyrights
Copyright Office
Library of Congress
Washington, DC 20559-6000

The application, nonreturnable deposit (copies, phonorecords, or identifying material), and nonrefundable filing fee should be mailed in the same package.

The Copyright Office suggests that you contact your local post office for information about mailing your materials at lower cost fourth-class postage rates.

Incomplete Submissions: What Happens if the Three Elements are Not Received Together

Applications and fees received without appropriate copies, phonorecords, or identifying material will not be processed and ordinarily will be returned. Unpublished deposits without applications or fees ordinarily will be returned, also. In most cases, published deposits received without applications and fees can be immediately transferred to the collections of the Library of Congress. This practice is in accordance with section 408 of the law, which provides that the published deposit required for the collections of the Library of Congress may be used for registration only if the deposit is "accompanied by the prescribed application and fee...." After the deposit is received and transferred to another service unit of the Library for its collections or other disposition, it is no longer available to the Copyright Office. If you wish to register the work, you must deposit additional copies or phonorecords with your application and fee.

Fees

All remittances should be in the form of drafts (that is, checks, money orders, or bank drafts) payable to: Register of Copyrights. Do not send cash. Drafts must be redeemable without service or exchange fee through a U.S. institution, must be payable in U.S. dollars, and must be imprinted

Part
2

with American Banking Association routing numbers. If a check received in payment of the filing fee is returned to the Copyright Office as uncollectible, the Copyright Office will cancel the registration and will notify the remitter. The fee for processing an original, supplementary, or renewal claim is nonrefundable, whether or not copyright registration is ultimately made. Do not send cash. The Copyright Office cannot assume any responsibility for the loss of currency sent in payment of copyright fees.

Effective Date of Registration

A copyright registration is effective on the date the Copyright Office receives all of the required elements in acceptable form, regardless of how long it then takes to process the application and mail the certificate of registration. The time the Copyright Office requires to process an application varies, depending on the amount of material the Office is receiving and the personnel available. Keep in mind that it may take a number of days for mailed material to reach the Copyright Office and for the certificate of registration to reach the recipient after being mailed by the Copyright Office.

If you are filing an application for copyright registration in the Copyright Office, you will not receive an acknowledgement that your application has been received, but you can expect:

A letter or telephone call from a Copyright Office staff member if further information is needed;
A certificate of registration to indicate the work has been registered; or
If registration cannot be made, a letter explaining why it has been refused.

Please allow 120 days to receive a letter or certificate of registration. If you want to know when the Copyright Office receives your material, you should send it by registered or certified mail and request a return receipt from the post office. Allow at least 3 weeks for the return of your receipt.

Search of Copyright Office Records

The records of the Copyright Office are open for inspection and searching by the public. Moreover, on request, the Copyright Office will search its records at the statutory rate of $20 for each hour or fraction of an hour. For information on searching the Office records concerning the copyright status or ownership of a work, request Circulars 22 and 23. Records from 1978 and after may be searched via the Internet. For access, see below.

Contacting the Copyright Office

The copyright information provided here attempts to answer some of the questions that are frequently asked about copyright. For a list of other material published by the Copyright Office, request Circular 2, "Publications on Copyright." Any requests for Copyright Office publications or special questions relating to copyright problems not mentioned in this circular should be addressed to:

Copyright Office
LM 455
Library of Congress
Washington, DC 20559-6000

Copyright information, including many of the other circulars mentioned in Circular 1, as well as the latest Copyright Office regulations and announcements, is available via the Internet. The site address is repeated here for your convenience: http://www.lcweb.loc.gov/copyright/.

To speak to a Copyright Information Specialist, call (202) 707-3000 between 8:30 A.M. and 5:00 P.M., Eastern Time, Monday through Friday, except Federal Holidays. If you are in the Washington, D.C. area, you can visit the office. The office is located in the Library of Congress, Madison Building, Room 401, at 101 Independence Ave., S.E., Washington, D.C., near the Capitol South Metro stop. Information Specialists are available to answer questions, provide circulars, and accept applications for registration. Access for disabled individuals is at the front door on Independence Avenue, S.E.

The Copyright Office is not permitted to give legal advice. If you need information or guidance on matters such as disputes over the ownership of a copyright, suits against possible infringers, the procedure for getting a work published, or the method of obtaining royalty payments, it may be necessary to consult an attorney.

Part
2

The International Standard Book Number (ISBN)

Each published book should include an International Standard Book Number on the copyright page (verso title page) and at the bottom of the back cover. Every country has an ISBN Agency. The United States ISBN Agency is operated by the R.R. Bowker Company. The Agency's address is:

U.S. ISBN Agency
121 Chanlon Road
New Providence, NJ 07974

You can contact the ISBN Agency by telephone at 908-665-6770 or by fax at 908-665-2895. You can also browse their web site at http://www.bowker.com, where both forms and telephone numbers are listed. The Agency will supply you with an application for an ISBN Publisher Prefix and an Advance Book Information form. Once completed, send both forms to the preceding New Jersey address. The ISBN Publisher Prefix application form accommodates information about the publisher; it is used to obtain both a publisher prefix number and a series of unique dash numbers to identify each book that you publish. You cannot apply the same number to more than one book, and you can never reuse a number. The forms are accompanied by a set of instructions that tell you how the numbers are used and where to apply them. The service charge for assigning ISBN numbers is $175, regardless of the size of the block a publisher is issued or the number of titles a publisher submits with his application. The normal processing time for an ISBN application is 15 business days. You can pay a $50 priority processing fee to get a 3-day turnaround. Your numbers are sent out on the second day following receipt of the application by UPS Next Day Air, for guaranteed 3 P.M. delivery on the next business day.

The application for an ISBN Publisher Prefix form requests the following information.

General:

- Company name
- Address
- Phone, fax, telex, e-mail, and web site numbers and names
- Name, title, and telephone number of Chief Operating Officer
- Name and title of rights and permissions contact
- Name and title of ISBN coordinator/contact
- If a division or subsidiary, the name of the parent company
- Imprint names
- Payment method

Publishing Information:

- The year you started publishing
- Available number of titles in print
- Number of titles published in the past 12 months
- Number of titles scheduled for publication during the next 12 months
- Indicate what type of products you produce (books/videos/talking books on audio cassette/software/mixed media)

Distribution Information:

- Are you distributed or represented by another company in the U.S. or abroad? (fields for yes/no, and name, address, phone number, etc. follow)

Processing Information:

The remainder of the form describes the need for complete information, describes priority processing procedures, and normal turnaround time. It also provides information on how to obtain a service charge waiver if you are a philanthropic organization and your publications are made available free of charge. This requires a copy of your bylaws that specify your charitable activities.

The *Advance Book Information* form is used to describe the book, its contributors, publisher information, and more. This form is used to place your book in the next edition of the *Subject Guide to Books in Print*. It is highly recommended that you also fill out and return this form as some bookstores will not place an order until your book is listed in the *Subject Guide to Books in Print*. You can mail both forms together. If you need to contact "Books in Print," their mailing address is:

R.R. Bowker Data Collection Center
P.O. Box 6000-0103
Oldsmar, FL 34677-0103

Cataloging-in-Publication (CIP) Data

Cataloging-in-Publication (CIP) Data is obtained from the Library of Congress. They supply a CIP Data Sheet For Books form, illustrated following, which comes with instructions, but oddly enough, omits the Cataloging in Publication Division's address. However, you can request a mailing label, which happens to be colored bright orange, with your form. Their address is:

The Library of Congress
Cataloging in Publication Division
Washington, DC 20540-4320

Processing time for CIP varies from a few weeks to a few months. Delivery time is erratic and some publishers complain that reasonable delivery is unreliable. Occasionally, publishers are forced to go to press without CIP Data in order to meet key order dates. However, if you intend to sell your book to libraries, it is necessary to put the CIP Data on the copyright page of your book. Librarians use the cataloging numbers to properly integrate each book into the DEWEY decimal cataloging system. The same number is used on the subject, title, and author cards, and of course, to place books within the proper section of the library. Without the cataloging data, referencing the book is difficult, if not impossible.

For questions about the CIP program, you can write:

John Celli
Chief, Cataloging in Publication Division
Library of Congress
Washington, DC 20540-4320
Email celli@mail.loc.gov

You can find the Library of Congress web site at www.lcweb.loc.gov. Unfortunately, they did not have a page dedicated to CIP data assistance when this book was written.

The CIP Data Sheet for Books includes roughly 21 fields, which request the following information (some are combined in the following list for brevity):

1. Name of publisher
2. Date form completed
3. First U.S. city named on title page as the place of publication
4. Projected publication date (month/year)
5. Author name(s) and birth date(s)
6. Title and subtitle
7. Number of volumes (if more than one)
8. Inclusion of bibliographical references and index
9. Titles of other English language edition(s) if different from the listed title
10. Language from which book was translated and original title (if applicable)
11. If part of a series, the series title (if applicable)
12. Distribution code (from supplied list of subjects)
13. Primary audience(s)
14. Book category (novel, fiction/literature/textbook/clinical medicine)
15. Audience age and grade if for children or young adults
16. ISBN
17. Summary of book's content
18. Name and address to which CIP data should be mailed (label supplied)

An illustration of the CIP Data Sheet for Books form is shown in the figure on the following page.

CIP Data Sheet for Books

Library of Congress
CIP DATA SHEET FOR BOOKS

AGENCY USE ONLY

1. Name of publisher exactly as it appears on title page

2. Date form completed

3. First U.S. city named on title page as a place of publication

4. Projected publication date

Month _____ Year _____

5. Contact person

Phone ( )   Ext.
Internet account number

6. In-house editor

Phone ( )   Ext.
Internet account number

7. Full names of authors appearing on title page (last, first, middle)

1. _____

2. _____

3. _____

Birth date

Month _____ / Day _____ / Year _____

Month _____ / Day _____ / Year _____

Month _____ / Day _____ / Year _____

8. Title and subtitle

9. If title in Block 8 consists of more than one physical volume, the number of volumes planned is

This application is for volume number

10. Check if book has

☐ Bibliographical references

☐ Index

11. Titles of other English language edition(s) if different from this title

12. If this is a translation from a foreign language, give original title

Language of original title

13. If the title belongs to a series having a comprehensive title, the series title exactly as it will appear in the book is

The series number is

14. If the series reflects a change in title, the earlier title of the series was

AGENCY USE ONLY

15. Distribution code

16. Primary audience

☐ General

☐ Other _____

17.

☐ Novel

☐ Fiction/Literature

☐ Textbook

☐ Clinical Medicine

18. If for children or young adults

☐ Age _____

☐ Grade _____

19. Indicate format for each ISBN listed. Check permanent paper (∞) box for each ISBN to which it applies

ISBN _____ ☐ ∞   ISBN _____ ☐ ∞

ISBN _____ ☐ ∞   ISBN _____ ☐ ∞

20. Summary of book's content

21. Name and address to which CIP data should be mailed

Type or print firmly in ink
NAME
ADDRESS
This label will be used to mail your CIP data to you.

Part
2

Note that the ISBN is one of the elements that must be entered on the CIP Data Sheet for Books. Therefore, if you are starting a new publishing operation, it may take as long as a few months to acquire both the required ISBN and CIP information.

Moving Ahead

The next section wraps up this book with several closing comments and a few encouraging words. There, you will also find some practical advice about writing and publishing, which hopefully, may help those who are preparing for a career in the writing and publishing field.

Chapter 13

Crossroad Decisions

Introduction

This, the final chapter, steps back and examines some of the philosophical issues involved in successful writing and publishing. Hopefully, it provides some insights gathered from a rewarding thirty-five-year writing and publishing career.

Decisions

Part
2

Every day you face numerous decision points. Many of these decisions are insignificant and have no long-term effect on your life. For example, what you decide to wear to a business meeting or whether to take soup or salad with a meal are normal maintenance issues that will not reshape your life. However, there are *crossroad decisions* that can reshape the rest of your life, or result in lost opportunities—and you'll never know what you missed, because you didn't choose to go for the ride.

We decide on the way we feel—happiness and sadness, contentment and anxiety, love and hate are in our heads. They are feelings—chemical secretions that invade the cells of our brains; the way we "feel" controls our emotional state, the way we relate to others, enjoy our work, and focus on the achievement of our goals. These are emotions that we choose; and they make our lives rich or full of despair. Unfortunately, neither wealth nor poverty changes the brain chemistry, so you've got to be in control. If you're normal (whatever that means), you can will your moods; if you're not normal, take your medication out of consideration for the rest of us.

Millionaires commit murder and suicide, while the poor people laugh and play in the park. Believe in yourself, but don't take yourself too seriously. Be gentle; feed on positive thoughts—remember that you are responsible for you. People who take charge of their lives like themselves. They know where they're going, they are happier, and they become a positive force in the lives of their families, friends, and co-workers.

Examine the lives of some of the people who have succeeded in their fields. See how they did it. They made every effort to understand what needed to be done. They studied. They worked and then they reworked. They never gave up. They bridged their relationships with others and established new relationships that helped them achieve their personal goals. The old saying "It took twenty years to become an overnight success" is right on target. Be prepared to take twenty years; start today or it will take longer. Or, just go to the park—you'll probably have a good time.

The Law of Intelligent Action

More than thirty years ago, when I worked in "Corporate America," my boss gave me a book to read. It was entitled *The Law of Intelligent Action* and was written by a fellow named William F. Reilly. I still remember Reilly's message. After years of research, Reilly concluded that there are only three general ingredients involved in the achievement of our goals:

- Desire
- Ability
- The Capacity for Human Relations

These three ingredients encompass every other personal attribute that you can name. Lack one of these, and you'll fail. What about bad hair, outlandish dress, or offensive hygiene? Try "capacity for human relations." Offensive behavior tells people that you don't care. A lot of people read meaning into things that aren't even there. Untraditional clothes, unkempt facial hair, and poor hygiene are all barriers to good human relations. If you're someone who says, "It's their problem, not mine," you're wrong—believe me, it is your problem.

Try to find other personal traits that reside outside the realm of Reilly's three ingredients to success. Think about them. You can always find a fit.

Desire

You must want to achieve your goal to succeed. If your goal is difficult, your desire must be strong. Without desire, you don't have what it takes to succeed. "He's a well-educated, friendly sort of chap. But he'll never amount to anything—he just doesn't seem to care about getting ahead." You probably know people like this. I do. They have extraordinary talent, even genius. But they either don't care or simply can't get along with the people who can help.

Ability

Ability includes education and experience (the necessary knowledge), tools, time, physical skills, and material resources. Knowledge is gained through formal and informal education, reading, observation, and practice. Different people acquire knowledge in different ways and have different capacities for retention. You must understand what knowledge is required to achieve your goals. With the knowledge, you can then determine what other resources are needed to achieve your goal. If you want to write a book about medicine, attend medical school, interview experts in the field, or commit a substantial amount of time doing research. Determine what you must know to achieve your goal.

The term *knowledge*, as used here, goes beyond the definition found in "Bloom's Taxonomy of Cognitive Thinking," which isolates knowledge as entry-level thought. Following levels in the hierarchy of thinking include understanding, application, teaching, and innovation, which requires one to be cognizant of every level of thought. In this text, the term knowledge applies to the entire realm—from knowledge to innovation.

The Capacity for Human Relations

Here's the ingredient that leads to the ruin of many intelligent, well-educated, hard-working people—even writers. Thousands of people undermine their goals through poor interpersonal skills. It doesn't matter if you're a genius with a burning desire to succeed; the hardest-working and most dedicated member of the workgroup; or even a brilliant, well-meaning manager. A few misplaced comments or offensive actions can destroy your effectiveness, as well as that of the other people involved in your project. If you're trying to publish a book and can't get along with your agent, acquisition editor, or copy editor, your project is in jeopardy. If you need to solicit information from subject-matter experts, be likeable or they'll limit your access. What can you do?

Put yourself in their shoes. Would you want to work with your clone? Would your clone be argumentative, stubborn, and perhaps belligerent? Or would your clone be friendly, a good listener, cooperative, and accept suggestions in a positive and courteous way? If not, you'd better change. And don't be cloned; one of us is plenty—maybe even more than enough.

Goal Setting

I started writing books for the Spectrum Division of Prentice-Hall, Inc. of Englewood Cliffs, N.Y. in 1978. I didn't quit my day job in "Corporate America." I got on splendidly with my acquisition editors, and we even became good friends (there's that capacity for human relations, thing). I wrote in the evenings and on weekends. My first book, *The Word Processing Handbook*, did quite well. My editor encouraged me to write more books. I bought a personal computer (TRS-80 Model II) and a daisywheel printer. I started with the CP/M operating system (the predecessor to MS-DOS) and WordStar. Everything worked well, so I agreed to write five more books for my friends at Prentice-Hall. My wife and I agreed that this would be a good way to supplement our income. And, if we could keep up the pace and hang onto our marriage, we might be able to get ten or even twelve books published in the next three years. My knowledge of writing and publishing grew rapidly as I continually asked questions, gained more and more experience, and began to understand the dynamics of the market. We (my acquisition editors and I) chose titles that the market needed—books about leading applications software, database programming, and operating systems.

The royalty income began to grow. It would soon be enough to allow me to quit my day job. But I knew that my day job would become that of a full-time author—I'd have to keep writing. We would have to maintain a reasonable level of royalty income.

But think of it. We could buy a beach house in a warm climate and live the good life. I could write like Hemmingway did—every day from 7:00 A.M. to 1:00 P.M. Uninterrupted. Dedicated. Grinding out reams of manuscript. Then, every afternoon beginning at 1:00 P.M., we could do anything we like—play tennis or golf, scuba dive, sail, or go fishing. Or, if we wished, we could follow in Earnest's footsteps. Fortunately, we don't like gin. Decisions. Desire. Ability. Good relationships. Lots of hard work.

On our way to the beach house, we hit a turn in the road. The people at Prentice-Hall liked my work—it was selling. I stayed in touch with my editors and made an effort to be reasonable and cooperative. In addition to using technology-based writing and editing tools, my wife and I were also using computers to typeset our books. We delivered final, camera-ready pages. This was desirable, because at that time, Prentice-Hall was publishing more than seventy computer titles per month (around 850 in a year). They were frantically trying to typeset and manufacture the books on schedule. The technology of the time was cumbersome. Phototypesetting equipment from companies like Linotronics, CompuGraphics, Addressograph-Multigraph, and Merganthaller were in use. These were expensive, slow, and required a substantial amount of manual intervention to cut and paste artwork, running headers and footers, and sidebars into position. Using personal computers to write, edit, and typeset impressed them; at that time, only a handful of people around the world were doing this.

"How'd you like to produce a series of computer books for us?" the editors asked. Decision. Desire. Ability. Human relations. After discussing project details, schedules, and economics, a governing specification accompanied by a proposal was prepared and submitted. The project was a reality within a matter of weeks. Wordware Publishing, Inc. was born on December 15, 1982. The company began as a "book packager" with firm contracts for 48 titles. Space was rented. Equipment and furniture was purchased. Writers were recruited. Copy editors, typesetting specialists, graphic arts specialists, and a bookkeeper were hired. I quit my day job.

A few months following operational startup, Wordware began its trade publishing division. The company began to market its own computer books to bookstores and book distributors. When the packaging contracts were finished, Simon & Schuster acquired Prentice-Hall, Inc. The computer book industry suffered huge returns; return rates reached 50 percent and higher. Several computer-book publishers filed for bankruptcy and liquidated their businesses. Even some of the large, old-line publishing companies fled the market by shutting down their computer book publishing operations. Wordware kept working, and survived.

We did buy that "house on the beach" in the form of a second home in Southwest Florida (Marco Island to be precise). It had 100 feet of seawall in the backyard, a boat dock, a solar-heated pool, and coconut palms and orange trees in the yard. You can achieve your goals, too. But don't quit your day job.

How About Your Goals

Before you dedicate your life to a career in writing and/or publishing, be sure that's what you want to do. Life is short, so none of us can afford very many false starts. Before you spend too much time writing, be sure that you can write. Get an objective person to read your work. Perhaps an agent or a professional editor can examine a few pages. Never count on an objective answer from a close friend or relative. Their objectivity can't be trusted, because they love you. They don't want to hurt your feelings. They want you to love them back.

Even if you're a good writer, if you don't have a strong knowledge base to help you tell your story, then you must be exceptionally intelligent, creative, and imaginative. Even fiction and fantasy writers must put factual information into their stories to hold reader interest. That's why some of today's best-selling authors are ex-policemen, doctors, and lawyers. (Joseph Wambaugh, Robin Cook, and John Grisham are some examples.) However, there are also successful authors who have no special professional training or experience from which to draw. Stephen King and Tom Clancy are two who come to mind. Clancy, an ex-insurance agent, is obviously bright and, more important, a master researcher. Stephen King is one of the most imaginative and creative writers of our time.

If you examine Clancy's work, you'll see that his writing has improved over time. Compare *The Hunt for Red October* to *Clear and Present Danger*. He's definitely improved. Your writing will also improve with work. If you don't like your first attempts, your next ones will be better. Keep working and you'll definitely improve.

Your Resources

Your creativity, writing talent, knowledge, time, finances, PC equipment, and software comprise your resources. You need them all. Assuming you have the first five (creativity through finances), you must master the rest through practice. Learn to use your word processor and all of its important tools (spelling checker, thesaurus, and grammar checker). Learn to use your graphics software and a good flatbed scanner. Understand the difference between bitmap and vector software and use both to produce quality artwork.

If you are reticent about making direct contact with a publisher, contact an agent. Your agent will evaluate your work. If it's good, he or she will help you find an appropriate publisher.

If you plan to self-publish, review the material on publishing and self-publishing. If you're still convinced that you can sell several thousand copies of your book, then choose and learn to use a high-end desktop publishing program. Learn the standard layout conventions presented in this book. Create and retain a good set of paragraph tags. Learn to create and adjust master pages and running headers and footers. Be able to import text and graphics, move chapters between publications, and automate your table of contents and alphabetical index with ease. Learn how to prepare a printing specification and obtain bids from several printers. Then produce a set of finished publication files for use by your commercial printer.

Obtain an ISBN and Cataloging-in-Publication Data. File the proper form with the Copyright Office. Use your graphics software to prepare a stunning cover. Put a barcode and the price on the back cover.

Study the information about marketing and sales. Decide how you will warehouse your stock, process orders, pack, ship, and invoice your customers.

Final Remarks

This book contains an extremely broad range of information about writing, illustrating, and publishing. It presents information about technology-based writing and editing tools. It also examines the key features and operating procedures used by the most popular graphics and desktop publishing software in use today. Finally, it presents many standard practices, business issues, and publishing economics. Much more is also included. Because you probably can't remember all of this in a single reading, keep this book close at hand. Use it for reference. Each time you have a writing, graphics, or publishing question, you may find some answers here.

Part
2

Appendix A

Writing Product Documentation

Document Types

Since writing and publishing for the book trade is the primary target of this book, the information contained in this appendix has been separated from the main part of the book and put here. You'll find information about the planning and development processes associated with the preparation of product documentation. In particular, the steps involved in preparing technical reports, business proposals, and technical manuals are described. If you wish to prepare greeting or business cards, invitations, announcements, small bulletins, and fliers, the information in this appendix is probably not very important to you. However, the same processes used to combine text and graphics into a pleasing product applies to all document types. Therefore, those chapters that provide information about the application of the software and hardware devices involved in publishing should still be of interest to those readers who are not involved in the product documentation process.

Although the information here is not specifically aimed at those who wish to write and publish a book for sale in a retail bookstore, there are a few areas that may be of interest. In particular, you should know how to prepare a suitable outline and how to estimate the time it will take you to prepare a deliverable manuscript. Therefore, read the information relating to outlines, cost estimating, and scheduling. This information should help you identify, rationalize, and measure each of the tasks involved in your writing effort.

Appendix

The Publication Plan

Before beginning the actual writing task, it's important to have a road map of where you're going. A thoughtful, well-designed publication plan, also known as a "publishing plan" to some, identifies the:

■ Need for a document

■ Target audience

■ Tasks to be performed

■ Organizational outline

■ Style conventions

■ Cost data

■ Developmental milestones (scheduling)

The publication plan is similar to a product specification. As such, it should reflect the style of the final document to set the tone for those who read and use the plan. Obviously, if you are writing a short story or article for a magazine, you can omit the preparation of a formal publication plan, as it would take longer to prepare than your article. Still, you should give serious thought to such elements as your target audience, style conventions, and developmental milestones, particularly if you are working against a deadline.

Needs Analysis

Before writing any document, a need must exist. Typically, an instruction manual is written because customers require information about how to competently operate a product. Without such a manual, the product may not provide its intended benefit, which can result in customer dissatisfaction. Repair and maintenance manuals are written for use by service technicians who need information about the proper care and maintenance of a product. Similarly, you should identify a clear need before you attempt to outline your document. In addition to a general need, such as product operation or maintenance, you should consider detailed needs. In the case of an operating instruction manual, you must carefully identify every operator control and indicator in addition to understanding the purpose and general operating procedures for each. The result of the needs analysis provides a compelling basis for the document and therefore often serves as an important element in selling decision makers on the need to provide the required resources to fund the documentation project.

Target Audience

Before you write a word, develop a profile of those who will read your document. Age, education, and any other experience or special training should be used in classifying your readers, or *target audience*. The readability level (most often expressed as a grade number) as well as special terminology, concept complexities, and the depth of technical narrative and diagrams should always take your audience into consideration. If you overwhelm or confuse the intended audience, you've missed the mark and diminished the usefulness of your document and the product it supports. Therefore, understand your reader's abilities so you can communicate in a useful and appropriate manner.

Task Analysis

The *task analysis* applies to documents that include instructional procedures. If you are writing such a document, it is critical to list every task and subtask that must be performed. Then organize the list of tasks in the order in which they must be performed. The task analysis should provide a skeleton of your document and drive the organizational outline. It's often helpful to include the tools, materials, and special skills required for the performance of each task. When you actually write the procedures required to perform each task, the skeleton takes on its flesh. Present each step in succinct, numbered entries. Keep them brief and to the point. Whenever possible, start each step with an action verb, i.e., remove, unscrew, replace, snap, connect, lock, turn, etc. Plan to include notes, tips, and clarifying examples and illustrations whenever necessary to convey information. Then move on to the document outline.

Outline

Once you understand the need for your book, the target audience, and the tasks to be undertaken, it's time to develop a finished outline. Your outline should be subdivided into chapters (or sections) and all major paragraphs. Most outlines include chapters and at least two paragraph levels, i.e., primary and secondary paragraph entries. Include a synopsis of each paragraph level that describes the information to be included. A good outline is crucial to a productive writing experience. The outline, combined with the needs and task analysis, comprises the blueprint for your document; careful development and then adherence assures a successful outcome. It keeps the writer on track and provides a checklist against which to measure progress.

Appendix

Style Guidelines and Specifications

In commercial publishing, *The Chicago Manual of Style* is the prominent style guide used by U.S. publishing companies. Other style guides also exist, so it's important to adopt one and stick with it. Because the English language is laden with regional and industry references, it is important to adopt and use a good style guide to take the guesswork out of such elements as hyphenation, punctuation, and capitalization. Without a good guide, writers can spend unproductive time fumbling for a suitable convention. Even worse, inconsistencies in style can contribute to reader confusion. Therefore, pick one and stick to it. Once you learn and incorporate an acceptable set of conventions into your personal style, it's easy to remember and apply them in a consistent manner.

Specifications are often referenced when preparing documents, such as reports or product specifications, for governmental agencies. These specifications often reference subordinate guidelines that govern style, abbreviations, drawing symbols, and more. Therefore, be sure to acquire and use these specifications to ensure that your document complies with your customer's requirements. You may have the best technical solution to your customer's problem but lose the business because of noncompliance in the structure or content of your document.

Cost Data

Cost data reflects an estimate of the time and material required to produce the document. This data serves as a basis for the financial and labor resources required for the project. The total time estimated for each labor category, usually recorded down to the tenth of an hour, serves as a basis for the schedule, which is reflected on the project's milestone chart. Both the cost estimating and scheduling processes are described in more detail in the paragraphs that follow.

Developmental Milestones (Scheduling)

Just as a ship charts its ocean journey with geographical waypoints, documentation projects also have established waypoints, or *milestones*, that are indicators of your progress. Therefore, be sure to establish realistic milestones that correspond to each of the required tasks. The time required to complete the documentation project is derived from the cost estimate. This time is subdivided incrementally across a chart that corresponds to calendar dates. Schedule charts may show days, weeks, or months, depending on the size and duration of the project. The Scheduling paragraph found later in this chapter expands on developmental milestones and provides an example of a milestone chart.

Cost Estimating

Cost estimating is an art that requires an understanding of every facet involved in the documentation project. The most qualified cost estimators are those with several years of experience in the "documentation trenches." Corporate publications (or publishing) departments normally assign the cost estimating tasks to senior-level writers, documentation project managers, and writing group supervisors.

The best way to estimate the costs that are required to fund a documentation project is to follow these steps:

1. Obtain the governing specifications.
2. Determine the content coverage based on:
    - The governing specifications
    - The product being documented
3. Determine the product delivery date.
4. Determine the deliverable items, i.e., manuscript and final illustrations, printed books, CD-ROMs, on-line help, etc.
5. Determine the time and labor resources available to perform each of the required documentation tasks.
6. Determine if subcontractor or outsourcing services are required and obtain a schedule of the prevailing rates.
7. Obtain the material costs associated with the development processes and deliverable items

Applying the Multipliers

Once you know this information, which also serves as a basis for your formal publication plan, you must develop an estimate of the pages and illustrations required for each chapter of the planned document. Pages and illustrations drive the labor that corresponds to each of the contributing labor categories. The best way to obtain page, table, and illustration multipliers for each labor category is from carefully collected historical data. If those involved in a project maintain time records, you can actually divide the labor hours expended by the number of pages, tables, and illustrations produced. The more data that you have, the better your cost estimate will be. However, be sure to weigh all involved factors that may make the job either easier or more difficult. There's no substitute for the application of a little common sense, or "windage," when you are aware of extenuating factors that can impact the time required to complete the job. For example, you may have access to an extremely productive writer with a reputation for bringing in projects under budget and ahead of schedule.

Appendix

You may also have access to a book on the same or a similar subject that can be used as both a model and a writing and artwork resource. On the other side, you may be working with a new, inexperienced product development team that can extend the time and associated costs required to complete the project. Whatever the case, be sure to change your multipliers or add a percentage based on your beliefs. Be sure to document your reasons and be ready to defend them.

The following three charts provide examples of how the page and illustration counts correspond to the contributing labor categories. Note that the writing category includes the research time required to competently write a page. Research time is typically spent collecting supporting technical information from product specifications, drawings, and product design personnel; installing, running, and examining the subject software or hardware; and building a comprehensive resource file to serve as a basis for writing. The ratio of research to writing time is typically 3:1, depending on the complexity of the product and technical background and experience of the involved writer(s).

Average Labor Multipliers (example)

Page Type	Write	Edit	Illustrate	DTP	Proofread
Text Page	4.0	0.25	0.0	0.2	0.1
Tabular Page	1.0	0.25	0.0	0.4	0.1
Run-In Tables	0.5	0.15	0.0	0.25	0.1
Line Drawing Pages	0.5	0.15	2.0	0.1	0.1
Run-In Line Drawing	0.4	0.15	1.0	0.1	0.1
Screened Illustrations	0.3	0.15	0.5	0.1	0.1

Document Page Count (example)

Description	Text Page	Tabular Page	Run-In Table	Line Dwg Page	Run-In Line Dwg	Screen Illus	Totals
Front Matter	3	4	0	1	0	0	8
1-Introduction	4	0	1	1	0	0	6
2-Installation	2	0	1	0	0	0	3
3-Getting Started	5	1	0	1	1	5	13
4-Operation	47	8	7	0	4	16	82
5-Reports	16	4	3	2	0	8	33
6-Troubleshooting	1	4	0	0	0	0	5
Appendixes	14	6	0	2	0	0	22
Totals	92	27	12	7	5	29	172

Hours by Labor Category (example)

Page Type	Units	Write	Edit	Illus.	DTP	Proof	Totals
Text Pages	92	368.0	23.0	0	18.4	9.2	510.6
Tabular Pages	27	27.0	6.21	0	10.8	2.7	73.71
Run-In Tables	12	6.0	1.8	0	3.0	1.2	24.0
Line Drawing Pages	7	3.5	1.05	14.0	0.7	0.7	26.95
Run-In Line Drawings	5	2.0	0.75	5.0	0.7	0.5	13.95
Screened Illustrations	29	8.7	4.35	14.5	0.7	2.9	60.15
Totals	172	415.2	37.16	33.5	34.3	17.2	709.36

Other Factors

In addition to the document elements and labor multipliers shown in the preceding tables, there are other factors that can influence the efforts required to complete the document. First, you should add time for supervision and project reviews. This can be a simple factor, such as adding ten percent to the writing and editing categories. Factor used should be based on experience with the project review practice normally applied by your company or workgroup. Another important factor is that of anticipated rework. If the product development team or customer has a reputation for indecision, extensive feature modifications, or turnover in personnel, add a percentage to all multipliers for rework time. Again, this can be a flat percentage that is applied to every labor category; application depends entirely on when the revisions normally occur. Typically, the writing and illustrating efforts suffer the most from product changes, which often take place before the document is submitted to the editorial and desktop publishing groups. Only last-minute changes substantially impact the editorial, desktop publishing, and proofreading staff.

In addition to adding time for administrative review and rework, you should consider all facets of the job. For example, be sure to include time for creating a four-color cover and adding barcode data. Other costs can include the acquisition and application of Library of Congress Cataloging-in-Publication (CIP) Data or an International Standard Book Number (ISBN), as applicable. Also consider the time and material charges for creating labels, producing companion CD-ROMs, diskettes, boxes, producing packaging material, and the time required to manage these activities.

The Historical Approach

The preceding cost estimating treatment reflects an estimate that is developed from scratch. If the project is nearly identical to others that have been completed in the recent past, you can use the historical data as a

Appendix

model for the pending documentation project. The product should be similar in size and complexity, the makeup of the project team should be substantially the same, and the allotted timeframe should be similar. Substantial differences in any of these items can invalidate your historical data. However, if you know which elements are different, you may be able to use the historical data and factor in the risk. For example, if the development schedule is compressed from three months to six weeks, you will need to assign at least two writers to the project. The output will be less efficient, and therefore your page multiplier may increase from 4.0 hours per text page to 5.0 hours per page. In addition, overtime may be required. Therefore, you can take the historical data and factor it up based on a loss in efficiency and overtime.

Scheduling

The first step in developing a good schedule is to get a copy of the cost estimate and examine every labor category associated with the project. Consider every task including research, writing, illustrating, editing, desktop publishing, proofreading, and printing or duplication (depending on the deliverable format). Once you've applied time estimates for every element of the document and the contributing labor categories, you can add the total hours and develop a reasonable schedule.

The Critical Path

From the preceding cost estimating tables, you can quickly determine that the *critical path* is in the writing category. The term critical path is a derivative of the Project Evaluation and Reporting Tool (PERT) chart process introduced in the 1960s to chart the progress of complex projects. A critical path is the major task timeline that has the most impact on the progress of a project.

The cost estimate indicates that 415.2 hours, or 2.4 person months, are required to research and write the manuscript. The illustrating time should occur during the final phase of the writing effort. Editing, desktop publishing, and proofreading must occur following the writing and illustrating efforts and are performed sequentially. Therefore, another two weeks of effort must be added to the end of the writing and illustrating tasks. Finally, three to four weeks may be required to print the book, depending on how fast the involved printer can produce final copies of your document. Therefore, the entire project can take between four and five months from start to finish. Anticipated rework factors can add time to the project in all categories.

The final schedule should show each task and the corresponding timelines for each spread across a calendar. A good scheduling program automates the scheduling process and provides an excellent array of reports. They can also be used and updated while the project is in process to provide feedback to everyone involved in the project, including management. If you don't have a scheduling program, you can use a spreadsheet or word-processed table to show the timelines. The schedule progress should be carefully monitored. Updates to your schedule document should be entered and distributed on a weekly basis.

The Milestone Chart

The established delivery date is at the right end of the chart. You can then spread the labor across the chart to determine when the project must begin to achieve on-time delivery. Knowing the calendar period and the labor hours involved quickly tells you how many people are required to meet the deadline. For example, if you have three months to complete the project and five person months of writing time, two writers must be assigned to the project; otherwise, one writer must work 80 hours per week. The chart quickly tells you if you can complete the job in a reasonable amount of time with the available resources. If a delivery date is impossible, the early warning gives all other involved groups time to readjust their expectations.

Always consider beginning, intermediate, and terminal (or ending) milestones, so you can more accurately measure the progress. Without intermediate milestones, such as the completion of one or more chapters or a group of illustrations, it's difficult to determine the percentage of work that has been completed. Because your milestones are spread across a calendar; the leftmost entry should reflect the project start date and the rightmost entry should represent the completion of the project. Be sure that every task is identified and scheduled. Finally, verify that the allotted times tie to the labor times estimated for each contributing labor category, i.e., writing, editing, illustrating, desktop publishing, etc.

Milestone Chart Example

Task	Jan	Feb	Mar	Apr	May
Writing	▲======	=======	===●		
Illustrating			▲==●		
Editing			▲=●	▲=●	
DTP				▲====●	
Proofreading				▲==●	
Printing				▲ ==	====●

Before finalizing your schedule, try to understand those outside forces that can influence it. For example, if you're documenting a completely new product that is in development, it's possible to suffer setbacks from redesign. Therefore, determine the reliance you have on a stable design. Increase the hours for rework and add that time to your schedule accordingly. If the project is essentially a new revision to an existing product, as is often the case in the software product industry, the rework effort should be light.

Minimizing Rework

To minimize rework, it's a good practice to wait until the product is approaching a stable state. In most companies, the responsible product manager knows that there is a need for a supporting user manual and often presses for an early commitment to the work. Starting the writing task too early often increases the documentation cost resulting from rework; it also extends the schedule. Therefore, try to avoid premature startup to ensure a more efficient, cost-effective documentation effort. However, never wait so long that shipment of the completed product is delayed because of the unavailability of the supporting documentation. Top management will definitely be unhappy for many reasons. Late delivery leads to a loss of:

■ Customers to competitive products

■ Credibility in the market

■ Orders

■ Revenues

Subject Matter

Uncharted waters are much more difficult to navigate than familiar channels. This principle certainly applies to the writing efficiency involved in writing about a subject with which you are quite familiar. Familiarity with your subject matter is a major contributor to every writer's efficiency. Familiarity is also important to the efficiency of the illustrating and editing tasks as well. The use of familiar terminology, acronyms, and operating principles eliminates the time required to understand and apply acceptable conventions. A reduction in research time lowers the per-page writing time; familiarity with the subject matter can also reduce the editing and illustrating labor multipliers. Conversely, if you are involved in a writing project that deals with a completely new technology, the *learning curve*, i.e., the time required to understand and effectively communicate the involved principles, can substantially expand the research-to-writing time ratio. Instead of a typical 3:1 research-to-writing ratio, it's possible to experience a 7:1 ratio. Needless to say, this expands the total writing time required to complete the project.

Complex Topics

In addition to familiarity with the subject matter, the type of book being written often expands or contracts the time required to write it. For example, if you are writing an overhaul manual for a complex mechanical or electronic device, the time it takes to gather all necessary illustrations and then write and validate detailed, step-by-step procedures can be extensive. The illustrating time associated with detailed manuals of this type can also be huge. For example, the exploded view of a complex mechanical assembly, such as an automotive transmission that shows every housing, shaft, gear, bearing, race, retainer, snap ring, nut, bolt, washer, spacer, and gasket, can take more than a week for an illustrator to draw. Think of the time required to write a detailed, accurate disassembly, repair, assembly, and test procedure.

Simple Topics

Extremely simple manuals are at the other end of the complexity spectrum. Consider what it requires to write an assembly instruction manual for a tricycle or an operating instruction manual for an electric toaster. The entire instruction manual can be written in one or two days—no prior knowledge required. In the case of the tricycle, more time will probably be required to prepare the artwork than to write the assembly instructions. This type of manual often requires the writer to provide detailed sketches to the illustrator as well as a first draft of the assembly instructions. If you are both the writer and illustrator, you can scan the artwork, import a CAD drawing into your graphic program, or draw one from scratch using one of the top-end illustrating programs discussed in chapter 3.

Both the writer and the illustrator should have access to the tricycle and all supporting engineering drawings. It is possible that engineering drawing excerpts will satisfy some of the illustration needs, further reducing the time required to prepare the assembly instruction manual.

Quality Control

Product support documents, such as operating, maintenance, or even programmer's references, should all undergo an established quality control program. The editorial department constitutes the first line of quality control. In addition to dealing with grammatical quality, project editors should be on the lookout for inconsistencies in terminology, missing steps in procedures, and misleading references to tables or other sections within the book. Beyond the editorial department, other quality control processes should also be implemented. First, a technical review of the supplied information should be conducted to ensure that the supplied information is accurate. Step-by-step procedures should be performed in house. The industry calls this in-house check *verification*. When a preliminary version of the book is sent to a customer for a procedural check, the process is called *validation*.

Validation and Verification

Many contracts call for a two-step quality control program. The first, referred to as "validation," involves a complete review of all information including the performance of all maintenance and operating procedures by quality control specialists within the contractor's organization. The writer records the changes and incorporates them into his manuscript. Once done, a preliminary copy of the manual is produced. The second step in the program involves what is called a "verification conference." This involves a complete review of all information and procedures in the field of operation by a joint team of contractor and customer personnel.

The feedback from the verification and validation processes is incorporated into the manuscript before the final document is published and distributed. The application of this quality control step also adds an element of quality control to the product itself. Verifying the procedures often helps uncover product deficiencies that might otherwise result in an expensive recall. When problems are found, these are remedied in both the product and the supporting documentation before they are delivered to the field.

Writers must ensure that procedural steps and program source code is thoroughly tested for accuracy. Source code should be compiled and executed. If a book is being written for the military, aviation, or automotive industries, it is entirely possible that a mistake in a procedure could lead to equipment damage or bodily injury. For example, an error in an aircraft's flight manual or the instruction or overhaul manual for heavy construction equipment could lead to a catastrophic event.

Conclusions

The required amount of document planning is directly proportional to the size and complexity of the project. Simple brochures, insruction booklets, and product fliers may not require much planning, while large publications that involve the contribution of many people should be carefully planned. This requires a publication plan that clearly defines the document and every involved person's role. Without a plan, you can expect chaos. However, with a good plan, your expectations can be positive.

Wordware Author Guidelines

Introduction

All materials must be prepared using a microcomputer-based word processing system that generates common document formats. Microsoft Word 7.0 and earlier, WordPerfect 6.0 and earlier, WordStar, and RTF files are all compatible with our system, as they can be imported into Corel Ventura for production. Authors must submit one double-spaced hard copy and acceptable document files on PC-compatible diskettes.

Early Reviews

Wordware requires all authors to submit a title page, table of contents, and a chapter or two of the final draft before continuing with the remaining manuscript, especially if this is the author's first book. Wordware requires that all authors submit at least two chapters within 30 days of contract signing as indicated in the contract. Always include the front matter of your book, which includes the preface, introduction, and table of contents, with the early review submission. A review of style, guidelines, and formatting, as well as organization on the first chapters will help to expedite your writing, editing, and publication timing tremendously. Always return edited manuscripts with the corrected (reworked) manuscript!

New Book Information Form

Enclosed along with the manuscript preparation guidelines is an annotated New Book Information Form. Please review this form and complete according to the specifications of your book and return to your editor at the time of contract signing. Wordware uses this form for a number of critical sales and marketing functions such as sales meeting, catalogues, and sales presentations to national accounts such as Borders and Barnes & Noble. If you have any questions about information on the form, please consult with your editor.

Manuscript Length

The number of pages noted in your contract is approximate, but you should follow that number as closely as possible. The number of words per page in the final book is obviously a reflection of the design, the number of illustrations, and the point size used. However, a good approximation is 300 words per page, although you should consult with the editor about sample chapters to determine appropriate manuscript length.

Text Preparation

To eliminate rework in the typesetting phase, please adhere to the following text conventions:

1. One double-spaced copy of all manuscripts are required upon submission. These should be printed with a black, like-new ribbon if you are using a dot matrix printer. Laser printed manuscripts are preferred.

2. When submitting the final manuscript be sure to include the appropriate updated front matter such as the title page, introduction, preface, and table of contents. The inclusion of front matter is necessary for processing our books.

3. Create an individual text file for each chapter, appendix, etc.

4. Include a header on every page specifying the chapter, section or module number, and book title.

5. Page numbers should be put on all manuscript pages. Use a continuous sequence of Arabic numbers (1 to n) throughout the book. Using a numbering system for each individual chapter is also acceptable.

6. Line lengths should not exceed 6.5 inches. Use 11- or 12-point type and be absolutely sure to double space all submissions for ease of editing. Also, be sure and use Times New Roman or another serif font.

7. Avoid formatting commands for bullets and numbered lists. Instead use a number, a period, and a space. Also avoid any special formatting or design elements since this is added in the production phase. Design preferences may be discussed with your editor.

8. Use automatic text wrap, single spaces at the ends of sentences, and align left.

9. Be consistent in any repetitious treatment or spelling of a particular word, term, or product name; e.g., commands are all caps throughout the manuscript; menu names are initial caps; a product name, when hyphenated, is always hyphenated; etc.

10. Boldface and italics must be clearly indicated on hard copy. (Also see section on Italicizing and Boldfacing.)

11. <u>Please proofread and spellcheck any manuscript submissions</u>. Look for incomplete sentences and missing words.

12. Screen text should be captured in graphic format. Program listings should be prepared using a monospace (Courier) font.

13. Screen illustrations should be captured as 256 color or grayscale, and must be supplied as separate files in PCX, TIF, or BMP formats at the time of final manuscript delivery. Please do not embed graphics.

14. Include screens/art/figures and their references or captions in the correct locations on the hard copy. The screen captures and illustrations must also be included as separate files (see the next section). Be sure to set screen preference appropriately before capturing screens for best appearance.

15. Listings, figures, examples, and tables should each be numbered as a separate category.

Screen Captures

All books about computer applications include screen illustrations. Good quality screen illustrations add to the "flip" appeal of a book, making their purchase more compelling.

■ Illustrations range from an entire screen to icons, command buttons, toolbars, menus, and dialogs. All screen illustrations should be easy to read, complete, and clear. Dialog, button, and menu frames should be complete; that is, the entire outline or frame should be captured along with the interior information. Moreover, background clutter around outlines or frames should be clipped away when captured, edited (with a graphic editor), and saved.

■ Examine the illustration and notice that the frame is attached and clean. This screen was captured using Windows 95 Paint.

■ Next, be sure your contrast is set so that it is readable. The following Display Properties dialog illustrates the Standard Windows Scheme.

■ Notice the contrast between the title bar text and the background color. This is ideal and eliminates the need to touch up illustrations for readability.

■ The Windows color scheme should be set to 640 x 480, 256-color resolution, and contrasting colors should be used to ensure text and

Appendix

screen elements are easily read. Set the Display Properties dialog (accessed from the Control Panel) as shown below.

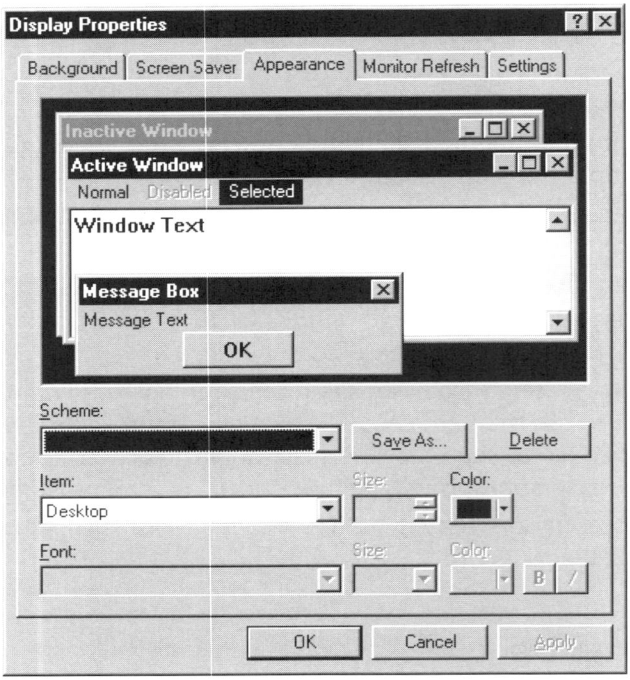

Capturing, Editing, and Saving Graphic Objects

Following are examples of additional screen elements and information about how they can be captured, edited, and saved. In our treatment of screen capture, the Windows 95 Paint utility is used because most authors have this utility. Other utilities that can be used include HiJaak, Corel PhotoPaint, and other graphics programs that process common bitmap or raster graphics. Acceptable formats include BMP, PCX, and TIF.

1. Display the screen element you wish to capture.

2. Press PrtScrn (which puts the displayed screen on the Clipboard).

3. Start Windows 95 Paint and press Ctrl+V to paste the screen into the Paint image area.

4. Press Esc or click the Select tool (the dashed box tool on the top row) and drag a frame around the desired dialog, menu, toolbar, or other graphic object. (Be careful to include the frame, but do not include unwanted clutter outside the frame.)

5. Press Ctrl+C to copy the framed object to the Windows Clipboard.

6. Use Edit|Select All (or press Ctrl+L) and then press Del to clear the unwanted background.

7. Press Ctrl+V to paste the clipped object back to the screen.

8. Perform any necessary cleanup; reframe the finished graphic object and use Edit|Copy To to save the clipped object to a file. Be sure to save it as a 256-color or grayscale BMP file. It should be put into a project folder used to maintain all of your screen illustrations.

   Look at the following examples of a window, menu, and toolbar. Be sure that your screen captures are as good.

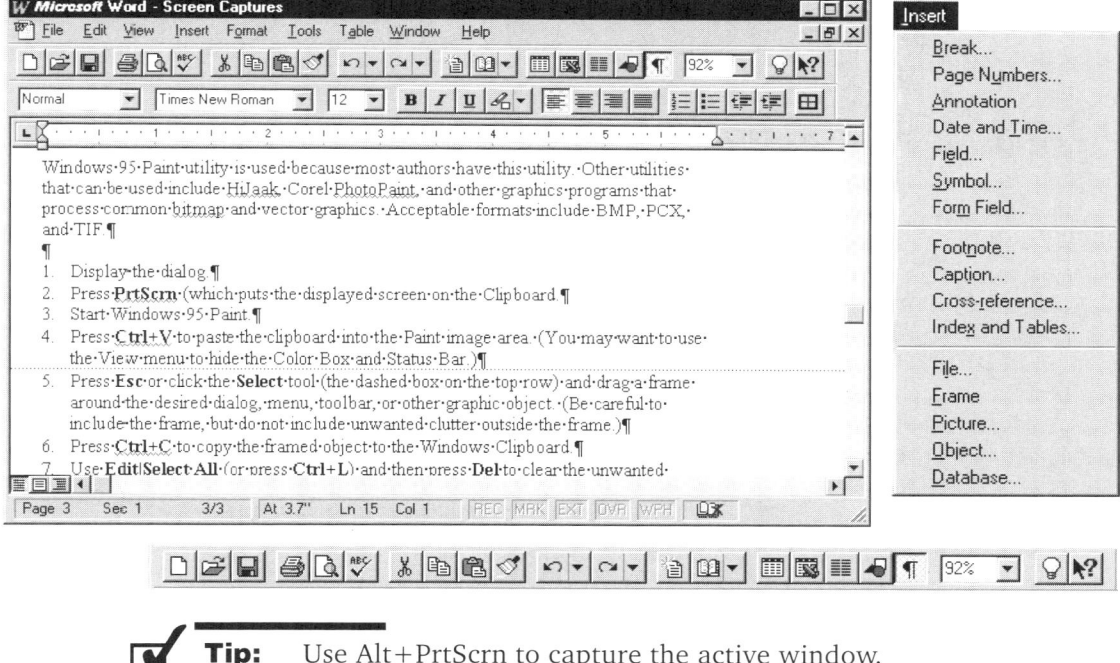

☑ **Tip:** Use Alt+PrtScrn to capture the active window.

Graphic Filenames

Be sure to give your screen captures filenames that correspond to their position in your manuscript. This is important if production personnel are to find and quickly insert your screens into the typeset document. Use a two-digit section or chapter number, a dash, and a two-digit sequential number within the section or chapter. Numbers from 1 to 9 should be saved as 01 through 09 so that these filenames sort properly (ahead of 10, 20, etc.). The third illustration in Chapter 5 should be given the filename 05-03.bmp (or pcx, tif, etc.). As mentioned previously, listings, figures, examples, and tables should each be numbered as a separate category.

Appendix

Annotations and Labels

Screen captures with annotations and illustrations should be in vector graphics format whenever possible. Use a program like CorelDRAW! to add annotations and create illustrations. The quality of your labels (if used) will be much better. With CorelDRAW, import the screen capture onto the blank drawing page, add the text, and export the finished illustration using the appropriate graphic format.

Style Preferences/Requirements

Wordware Publishing has developed the following conventions. We ask you to adhere to these.

Grammar, Punctuation

1. Use active verbs. Whenever possible, avoid sentences that trap you into using passive or future tense verbs like "will be" and "should be." In procedural steps, use the command form of the verb.

2. Avoid future tense:

Wrong:	You will see a character at the bottom of the screen.
Right:	Notice the character at the bottom of the screen.
Wrong:	This module will teach you...
Right:	This module teaches you...
Wrong:	Surfing will be described in Chapter 3.
Better:	See Chapter 3 for a description of surfing.

3. Use contractions sparingly, or not at all.

4. Pay particular attention to the placement of quotation marks around periods, commas, question marks, and semicolons. In a series, use a comma before the conjunction. For punctuation, see *The Chicago Manual of Style.*

    Examples of proper punctuation placement:

    Notice the word "Quit." Type SC, press Enter, notice the word "Welcome," and press the Spacebar. Look at the number "311"; type ENDTEXT and press Enter. Enter city, state, and Zip Code.

    Examples of improper punctuation placement:

    Notice the word "Quit". Type SC and press Enter. Notice the word "Welcome", and press the Spacebar. Look at the number "311;" then type ENDTEXT and press Enter. Enter city, state and Zip Code.

5. A sentence containing a parenthetical expression is punctuated outside the parentheses exactly as if the expression were absent. When a completely

detached sentence is parenthesized, the final punctuation comes within the parentheses.

> **Example:** Press Del (Delete), then press Enter to save your file. (If you do not press Enter, your file is lost forever.)

6. The first words in bulleted lists start with capitals. Indent subtopics of bulleted lists. Items in a bulleted list should either be all sentence fragments or all complete sentences. If using fragments, do not end with a period. Maintain parallel construction among the entries in a bulleted or numbered list. For example, start each item with a verb.

Numbers and Terms

1. Numbers from one to ten should be spelled out except when used as a dimension. Numbers greater than ten should be expressed in numeric form. Choose numerals in instances when their use makes the text clearer to the reader. Dimensions like 15 line spaces, 20 characters, and 3 inches are expressed just as in these examples.

> **Examples:** There are 11 more operations. Press Enter three times. Use 8½ x 11-inch paper.

2. Avoid seldom-used technical terms and jargon unless they are necessary to convey a concept or when there are no appropriate substitutes. Italicize and define a term when using it for the first time. Avoid the use of clichés.

> **Example:** A *block of text* is a string of words, characters, paragraphs, or pages.

3. Make your text match the on-screen style of the program you write about. For example, if your program has a "file menu," write it "File menu" if that is the way it appears on the display. Or, if your program requires certain entries to be made using capital letters, tell your reader about this and use capitalization consistently in your text. Do not arbitrarily capitalize words or expressions to emphasize them. As a general guide:

- Write system commands in all capital letters (SORT, EXIT, LIST).
- Write menu names in initial capitals (File menu).
- Write screens, modes, options, and windows in initial capitals (Help, Print).

Graphics, Illustrations

- Illustrations and tables or figures must follow and be close to their first reference. Avoid the words "above" or "below" when referring to them. Instead, use: "The following illustration...," "the following screen...," or "the following table."

■ When required, number illustrations and tables using the chapter, section, or module number followed by a dash and sequential Arabic number. For example, the first two figures in Chapter 3 should be numbered Figure 3-1 and Figure 3-2.

■ Avoid references to page numbers; use figure, table, and module numbers and paragraph titles where necessary.

Italicizing and Boldfacing

■ Be consistent in your use of italics.

■ Use italics to highlight words or phrases introduced for the first time and followed by a definition.

■ The use of boldface in any of the Wordware book series is reserved for headings or for words and key caps that are typed or pressed in procedural steps, such as hands-on activity sections of tutorial books.

Reserve boldface print for the following:

■ The exact characters typed in a procedural step

■ The name of a key (in initial caps) the reader is to press in a procedural step

■ Headings

Examples:

Type **WINSTALL** at the prompt.
Press **Esc** to return to the Main menu.

Headings such as DESCRIPTION, TYPICAL OPERATION, NOTE, CAUTION, and module titles.

■ Key caps are in boldface only when typed or pressed in a hands-on procedure. Use the word "key" only when the reference is in explanatory text, not a procedural step.

Example:

When you use the Del key, you erase unwanted characters. The Esc key always cancels the current menu.

Word Form Preference

In order to maintain consistency within the Wordware book series, please use Wordware's preferred form of the following words. If the preferred form differs from the one used on your software screens or diskette labels, then use the form presented on the screens or labels. Be sure to write us a memo listing these differences.

Keyboard Terms:		Others:	
Backspace	Num Lock	backslash	lowercase
Caps Lock	PgDn	back up (verb)	lower left, lower right
Ctrl	PgUp	backup (noun)	online
Del	Reset	backup file (adjective)	pop-up (adj.)
Down Arrow	Return or Enter	backward	printout
End	Right Arrow	database	right-hand
Esc	Scroll Lock	data file	rightmost
F1 through F12	Shift (the Shift key)	e-mail	set up (verb)
Home	Spacebar (the	field name	setup (noun)
Left Arrow	Spacebar)	filename	shortcut
	Tab	fine-tune	spreadsheet
	Up Arrow	forward	subdirectory
		hard copy	upper left, upper right
		keystroke	word processing
		left-hand (adjective)	word processor
		leftmost	word wrap
			Zip Code (or ZIP)

Notes, Cautions, Tips

Notes, Cautions, Tips or other stylistic "asides" that are appropriate for your book are an important sales and marketing features of Wordware computer books that enhance the value of the book. You may develop a set of these stylistic features that are appropriate for your specific book. Make a specific point of keeping these features concise. Also, it is important that they add value to the text by drawing the reader's attention to information of special significance not generally found in the text.

■ The headings NOTE, CAUTION, and TIP should be bold and flush left. The NOTE, CAUTION, and TIP text should begin below the heading.

■ Notes are used for information purposes and should usually precede corresponding text. A note should never contain a procedural step.

■ Cautions are used to warn of possible damage to equipment, software, or data. A caution must precede corresponding text.

■ Tips are used to give the reader extra suggestions.

■ Include the following note before the first use of key sequences connected by plus signs.

Examples:

NOTE

For key sequences connected by a plus (+) sign (such as Ctrl+C), hold the first key while typing the second key.

Appendix

CAUTION

Typing D at this time will delete all the worksheets called DATA.

TIP

The document is printed to disk and given a filename of "DOS.TXT." If you are doing this with more than one document, use the DOS Rename command to give the file another name.

Headings

Heading subordination is as follows:

Primary	Boldface and all capitals, stand alone with two blank line spaces above and one blank line space below.
Secondary	Boldface and initial caps, one blank line space above and one blank line space below.
Third order	Boldface and all capitals, run-in with text, followed by two character spaces; one blank line space above.
Fourth order	Capitals and lowercase, bold italics, run-in with text, followed by two character spaces; one blank line space above.

The following examples are representative of all heading levels:

FIRST LEVEL HEAD

This is a first level heading. It is all capital letters, boldface, and on a line by itself. It is preceded by two blank lines and followed by one blank line.

Second Level Head

The second level heading is initial caps, boldface, preceded by one blank line and followed by one blank line.

THIRD LEVEL HEAD The third level (tertiary) heading is all capitals and boldface, followed by two blank spaces (or an em space), and run-in with following text.

Fourth Level Head The fourth level heading is like the third-level heading except it is in bold italics and initial caps.

Procedural Steps

1. Procedural steps should start with an action verb, such as Press, Type, Notice, etc.

2. Keys with words and arrows are "pressed." This includes such keys as Alt, Ctrl, Shift, Esc, Del, Tab, Caps Lock, Reset, Arrow, and Enter. Alphabet, number, punctuation, and symbol keys are "typed." Use "type" key(s) or text, never "type in" key(s) or text. You may also use an abbreviated keypress form. A concatenated keypress, such as pressing Ctrl while typing C,

is written Ctrl+C. A series of separate keypresses, such as press Alt and then type F and P can be written "press Alt, F, P" for brevity. This convention should be introduced in narrative so that readers understand the difference between Alt+Esc and Alt, Esc.

Correct examples:

Press Del twice.

Press Spacebar; then press Esc to return to the document screen

Press Ctrl+S to save your document.

Press Alt and type FP to print the document.

Press Alt, F, P to print the document.

Select the Line tool; then pick coordinate 5.0, 6.5 and drag a line to 8.5, 9.0.

Select File, Quit, and OK to quit the program.

Use File|Quit and OK to quit the program.

Type W and pick a point beyond the upper left and lower right of the solid.

3. Learning activities, such as a Hands-On Activity section in a tutorial series, should be in numbered procedural steps to ensure concise, easy-to-follow instructions. Avoid putting instructions in narrative form when they can be put in procedural steps. The following example shows the same procedure in both narrative and procedural form.

Narrative Example — (Not recommended)

To mark a block of text, begin by moving the cursor to the first character of the passage. Then insert the beginning block marker by pressing Ctrl+KB. Next move the cursor to the space or character following the last character of the passage. Press Ctrl+KK. Notice that the marked block is highlighted.

Procedural Example — (Recommended)

Mark a block of text as follows:

1. Move the cursor to the first character of the passage and press **Ctrl+KB**.

2. Move the cursor to the space or character following the last character of the passage and press **Ctrl+KK**.

3. Notice that the marked block is highlighted.

4. Procedural subordination follows:

    1.

      a.

        (1)

          (a)

Appendix

Indexing Tips

A good index provides your readers with a roadmap to the information in your book. Good book indexes add quality to your books and to their use as a reference. Remember, your entries should be worthwhile. Take care not to send your readers on circular, wild goose chases. Try to cover all of the important subjects. Omit entries that are incidental or simply mentioned in passing.

Indexing Benefits

The indexing process accomplishes two important goals. First, it lets you examine each page for content accuracy, completeness, and presentation. Secondly, it gives you the opportunity to pick out important words, phrases, and/or concepts that the reader may want to find.

Indexing Procedure

A useful index is a valuable asset to your book, no matter how simple the subject matter may seem to you. Do not attempt to build an index while your book is in manuscript form. Build the index using final page proofs from the publisher.

- Use final page proofs to build your index.
- Examine every page and build the index word/phrase list using your word processor.
- Use an alphanumeric sort routine to arrange your index entries.
- Eliminate duplicate entries.

Using the following steps, your indexing task should take no more than three to six hours, depending on the size of your book. If you have any questions, contact Wordware's editorial department.

1. Turn to page 1 of your book's page proofs.

2. Scan the page for terms, expressions, short phrases, paragraph or section titles, or ideas that should be included in the index. Do not include a word or phrase if it is not treated adequately enough to be helpful to your reader. In other words, avoid sending readers to a passing mention of a word, title, or idea. The same word or short phrase may appear several times; enter it each time it is encountered with the current page number. Steps 8 and 9 below take care of identical or similar entries.

3. Using a word processor, type each term, phrase, etc., found on the page followed by a comma, space, and the page number. (Exclude generic titles like Introduction or General Information.) Capitalize the first letter of the first

word of each entry. Use all capital letters for commands. The following example shows typical entries.

About This Book, 1
Organization, book, 1
Conventions, style, 2   (Notice that entries may be entered
Style conventions, 2   in two or more ways to help readers
COPY, 23   find information more easily.)
FORMAT, 29
Formatting, low-level, 203
Low-level formatting, 203

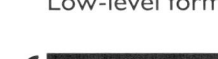

Tip: You may want to highlight index entries with a yellow marker on your first pass through the page proofs. Then go back through the pages and enter the highlighted information into your word processor. This lets you concentrate on one process at a time, i.e., indexing and then word processing.

4. Continue through the page proofs, examining each page carefully, and make your index entries. Entries may include reference tc important information contained in appendixes.

5. Spellcheck your index.

6. Save your index to disk.

7. If your word processor has a sort utility, sort the index alphabetically in ascending order. Otherwise, use the DOS SORT command:

    SORT index >index.srt

        where **index** is the name of the unsorted index file and **index.srt** is the name of the sorted index file.

8. Using your word processor, examine the sorted list for identical and/or similar entries, combine page numbers, and delete unnecessary entries as shown below.

    Before Combination: *After Combination:*

    Command Summary, 17   Command Summary, 17
    COPY, 105   COPY, 23, 68,105
    COPY, 23   Cost information, 46
    COPY, 68
    Cost information, 46

9. Check for entries that can be subordinated. These normally have the same basic word form with two or more modifiers. A before and after example is provided below.

Appendix

Before Subordination:	*After Subordination:*
Copying files, 15	Copying files, 15
Copying files to disk, 17	to disk, 17
Copying files to magnetic tape, 21	to magnetic tape, 21
Copying files to your printer, 19	to your printer, 19

10. Print your index file and edit it for appearance, accuracy, and completeness. As a rule of thumb, you should have an average of between one and one-half to three entries per narrative page. The index for a 224-page book should include from 336 to 650 entries, depending on type density, page dimensions, etc.

11. Return the page proofs with a copy of the printed index and the finished index file on a DOS disk to Wordware's production department.

Index

Other Books from Wordware Publishing, Inc.

For more information contact Wordware at 800 / 229-4949 or visit our web site at **www.wordware.com**

Bestsellers from Wordware Publishing, Inc.

The Tomes of Delphi 3: Win32 Core API

Ayres, Bowden, Diehl, Dorcas, Harrison, Mathes, Reza, and Tobin

A concise, detailed reference manual for using 32-bit Windows API functions in the Delphi 3 development environment.

816 pp. • 7½ x 9¼ • CD
1-55622-556-3 • $54.95 US
$104.95 AUS. • $82.95 CAN.

level: intermediate to advanced
category: Delphi 3/Win32 programming

The Tomes of Delphi 3: Win32 Graphical API

Ayres, Bowden, Diehl, Dorcas, Harrison, Mathes, Reza, and Tobin

This book describes the functions used to display graphics and user interface elements in addition to creating, managing, and printing graphical elements and text.

800 pp. • 7½ x 9¼ • CD
1-55622-610-1 • $54.95 US
$104.95 AUS. • $82.95 CAN.

level: intermediate to advanced
category: Delphi 3/Win32 programming

Digital Imaging in C and the World Wide Web

W. David Schwaderer

A unified quick-study of essential digital imaging concepts giving practical solutions to programming challenges on the WWW.

350 pp. • 7½ x 9¼ • CD
1-55622-602-0 • $39.95 US
$75.95 AUS. • $59.95 Can.

level: intermediate to advanced
category: Internet/digital imaging/C programming

Learn Visio 5.0

Ralph Grabowski

This tutorial describes the fundamentals and the new Internet features of Visio, Visio Technical, and Visio professional.

400 pp. • 7½ x 9¼
1-55622-568-7 • $29.95 US
$56.95 AUS. • $44.95 Can.

level: introductory to intermediate
category: CAD/drawing/business graphics

Learn AutoCAD LT 97 for Windows 95/NT

Ralph Grabowski

A step-by-step approach to learning AutoCAD LT quickly and easily by one of the industry's leading authorities on AutoCAD.

300 pp. • 7½ x 9¼ • CD
1-55622-597-0 • $24.95 US
$47.95 AUS. • $37.95 CAN.

level: introductory to intermediate
category: CAD/graphics

Learn Microsoft Exchange Server 5.5 Core Technologies

Ed Paulson

This book covers how to install and manage an Exchange 5.0 messaging network and prepares the administrator for the Microsoft Exchange 5.0 Certified Professional Exam.

350 pp. • 7½ x 9¼
1-55622-601-2 • $29.95 US
$56.95 AUS. • $44.95 CAN.

level: introductory to advanced
category: electronic mail

Visit our web site at **www.wordware.com**